DYEING FOR ENTERTAINMENT

Dyeing for Entertainment encompasses a wide range of methods of theatrical painting and dyeing to create beautiful artistic products for theatre, film, TV, opera, and themed entertainment.

Featuring examples and techniques from renowned international artisans in the field, this book provides a wealth of information on creating and changing colors, prints, and surface textures of fabric using traditional and nontraditional costume, scenic, fine-art, and metal-smithing techniques. It also includes new, safer materials and methods to minimize exposure to toxic materials and fumes. With more than 250 full-color images, this technical manual is designed to guide and inspire new artists in the collaborative art of painting, dyeing, ageing, and slinging blood and bling on costumes that is an essential part of creating characters for the entertainment industry.

Written for undergraduate and graduate students of costume design and technology, professional dyers and breakdown artists, and cosplayers, this book can be used as a reference and springboard to create your own magical processes, custom fabrics, and unforgettable costumes.

To access the online materials, including printable swatch sheets, a collection of relevant safety data sheets, and a source guide with links, visit www.routledge.com/9780815352327.

ERIN CARIGNAN is a costume designer, textile artist, and maker whose work spans regional theatre, opera, and entertainment. Her research centers around her most passionate subjects: textile surface design, costume design, and wearable art. She is most interested in the intersection of these subjects and in expanding her own knowledge of these areas as she continues to learn from and share information with those inside and outside the entertainment arena. As Assistant Professor of costume design and technology at Colorado State University, Fort Collins, her hope is to pass on her passion of these subjects to future generations, while instilling the wealth of information from the artists who make up our shared lineage as designer–artisans.

DYEING FOR ENTERTAINMENT
DYEING, PAINTING, BREAKDOWN, AND SPECIAL EFFECTS FOR COSTUMES

ERIN CARIGNAN

Routledge
Taylor & Francis Group
NEW YORK AND LONDON

Designed cover image: Jeff Fender Studio
Back cover image (apron): Erin Carignan

First published 2024
by Routledge
605 Third Avenue, New York, NY 10158

and by Routledge
4 Park Square, Milton Park, Abingdon, Oxon, OX14 4RN

Routledge is an imprint of the Taylor & Francis Group, an informa business

© 2024 Taylor & Francis

The right of Erin Carignan to be identified as author of this work has been asserted in accordance with sections 77 and 78 of the Copyright, Designs and Patents Act 1988.

All rights reserved. No part of this book may be reprinted or reproduced or utilised in any form or by any electronic, mechanical, or other means, now known or hereafter invented, including photocopying and recording, or in any information storage or retrieval system, without permission in writing from the publishers.

Trademark notice: Product or corporate names may be trademarks or registered trademarks, and are used only for identification and explanation without intent to infringe.

Library of Congress Cataloging-in-Publication Data
A catalog record for this book has been requested

ISBN: 978-0-8153-5231-0 (hbk)
ISBN: 978-0-8153-5232-7 (pbk)
ISBN: 978-1-351-13067-7 (ebk)

DOI: 10.4324/9781351130677

Typeset in Univers
by Apex CoVantage, LLC

Access the Support Material: www.routledge.com/9780815352327

CONTENTS

Acknowledgments vi
Foreword vii

	Introduction	1
1	**Dyeing in Vein** Safety Precautions and Dye Room Setup	3
2	**Who Can Make a Rainbow?** All About Color	24
3	**Ready, Set, Go!** Fibers, Additives, and Swatching	32
4	**The Law of Attraction** Fiber-specific Dyes	54
5	**All Together Now!** Union Dyes	78
6	**The Undo Button of Dye?** Color Removing	95
7	**Beauty Is Only Skin Deep** Changing the Color of Leather!	106
8	**The Three S's** Silkscreens, Stencils, and Stamps	126
9	**Stroke Couture** Printing and Painting With Dye	149
10	**Another Dimension** Paints, Coatings, and Other Embellishments	169
11	**Resist!!!** Making Marks With Resist Dyeing	205
12	**Burned Out?** Try Devore!	222
13	**It's Getting Real** Permanent and Removable Aging, Distressing, Breakdown, and Special Effects	233
14	**Arterial Motives** Permanent and Removable Blood for Costumes	266

Glossary	278
Appendix 1: Bibliographic Reference	283
Appendix 2: Cleaning Up: Stain Removal	286
Appendix 3: Swatch Sheets	288
Index	290

ACKNOWLEDGMENTS

I would like to thank my husband Chris for his continual support over the years – letting me yammer on about dye processes, workshops, successes and failures related to creating this book and for affording me the time and space to write by holding down the fort that is our kid–animal–home-improvement circus.

My mom for being an excellent accountability partner and proofreader, my dad for always supporting my wild ideas. My kids for their patience as I was glued to my keyboard and burned their dinners in creative distraction.

My mentors and teachers: Holly Poe Durbin, Teri Tevares, Stacy Sutton, Deb Dryden, and Elin Noble – your education is the backbone of this book. Deb, I'm still in disbelief that you wrote my forward; it is an honor to know you and to carry your legacy forth. Furthermore, to Elin, your proof of this book as an expert in textile modification and dye chemistry was invaluable.

My collaborator in the UK, Beth Herd, for her willingness to contribute to the breakdown chapter, give me many fantastic process photos, and to proofread the book through an international lens.

To the many designers and artisans that I had exciting conversations and "nerded out" with about dye processes and auxiliaries, and sources who gave me excellent tips, content, and photos, especially Chris Carpenter, Janet Cadmus, Bridget Kraft, Hallie Dufresne, Debi Jolly Holcomb, Hochi Asiatico, Gregg Barnes, and Jack Taggart. To Jeff Fender, in a very short time you shared so much of your talent and artistry with me that I feel proud to pass along a tiny part of your vast legacy. May your memory be a reminder to be generous with our time, to share our knowledge, and to laugh like we mean it.

The amazing technical staff at ProChemical and Dye and Dharma Trading – if they did not pick up the phone every time I called, much of these pages would not be as rich with information.

To my friends, especially Leslie Malitz Vukasovich, for helping me gather tons of imagery related to this book and then identifying it months later when asked "What film was this from?" To Jeannie Galioto for always being my personal academic crisis center. To Sedra Shapiro for giving me the push I needed to "get off the merry-go-round and just do the thing!"

To my co-workers who have encouraged and supported my drawn-out endeavor. To Elise Kulovany who always made space for me in the dye room for experiments and examples for the book. To Dr. Megan Lewis who let me pick her brain about publishing on a regular basis.

Last but certainly not least: the STUDENTS! From Weber State, to Purdue, and now to Colorado State University – you helped me understand what dye topics light you up, how to write dye instructions clearly, how important it is to teach how to fix mistakes, and how to take my lessons and create beauty beyond imagination. This book is for you.

FOREWORD

DEBORAH M. DRYDEN
AUTHOR, *FABRIC PAINTING AND DYEING FOR THE THEATRE*

Long ago, when I first published my books on dyeing and painting for the theatre (1981 and 1993), I was responding to a dearth of information on the subject of dyeing and painting of fabric specifically for the needs of the theatre practitioner. At that time there was no Google, there were no YouTube videos, no internet online discussion forums, and very little networking amongst other theatre dyers/painters.

Since then, the world has changed immeasurably. Access to shared information has increased exponentially. While there is now much information available publicly regarding the use of dyes and paints for textile artists, the specific needs of the dyer/painter for theatre and film remain scarce.

The need for a current, comprehensive theatrical dye paint resource is long overdue. Erin Carignan has met this need by writing this remarkable new book, *Dyeing for Entertainment*.

Drawing upon her many years as a professional dyer/painter and her extensive network of fellow theatre artists, Erin Carignan has created a wonderfully thorough and in-depth manual of all things dye/paint that meet the needs of the entertainment industry.

The theatrical ager/dyer/painter differs from artists in other textile fields primarily in the areas of specificity and time restraints. The theatre/film ADP (ager/dyer/painter) is required to have a wide variety of skills at their fingertips. The range of skills required for the theatre artist include the ability to match color, to age a garment in various ways, to print patterns or create texture, to work in single and multiple yardages, all of which occur often in less than ideal conditions. Time is most often the biggest factor differentiating the theatre/film artist from other textile artists. There are always time constraints, and one must be able to move swiftly and efficiently from one project to another, often involving multiple techniques.

Dyeing for Entertainment addresses these needs in a comprehensive and thoroughly researched way. Erin not only covers the "basics" (dyes, paints, safety, printing) but she also includes chapters on very specific theatre/film needs: how to ombré, dyeing leather, blood (!), recipes on how to "tech" a garment, how to dye shoes, elastic, buttons, and, especially, an excellent chapter on breakdown (aging, distressing) of costumes.

Dyeing for Entertainment is a wonderful resource for those at all levels of experience.

I am delighted to be able to recommend this invaluable resource to the next generation of agers, dyers, painters, and textile artists in the entertainment industry. I am convinced this book will be the "go-to" book for every student and professional interested in fabric dyeing and painting for years to come.

DEBORAH M. DRYDEN

INTRODUCTION

Understanding how to create custom fabrics, textures, and bling is a currency that is going farther than ever in the increasing fabric desert that is becoming the reality for all makers. My hopes for this book are that you, the maker, designer, artisan will use this text as a reference and springboard to create your own magical unicorn processes and costumes. I have added information that I have collected or created over the years in countless soggy notebooks and binders or jammed into my copy of Deb Dryden's *Painting and Dyeing for Theatre*. Please bear with me, my bad puns, and warped sense of humor as I attempt to be as authentic as possible in content delivery, but not so sterile that this text would be a snooze to the reader.

My hope in creating this book is to craft a technical manual that is also a narrative of the practical industry of storytelling and the artistic process. I would like to capture the concept that painting/dyeing/aging and distressing costumes is an art and that each artist brings their own perspective, experiences, and knowledge to each project they encounter. I hope to impress on new artisans that this subjective art requires a rich knowledge base in addition to practical experience that can only be gained from taking bold risks. I have compiled a resource that has contributions by the best in the industry of theatre, film, TV, opera, and themed entertainment. I hope, with help from this text, you continue the collaborative art of painting, dyeing, and slinging bling that is imperative in creating character for the entertainment industry.

I have added anything that will not fit in this book to my book's website on the Focal Press page. Please view the printable swatch sheets, an outline of amazing dyer–mentors and designers that are wild for surface modification, and a source guide with links. To keep the source guide up to date, I will host a live copy from my personal website www.erincarignan.com with your suggestions! Let's build a worldwide database!

Please see the following chapter synopses for a quick and dirty look at what each chapter holds.

- **Chapter 1: Dyeing in Vein: Safety Precautions and Dye Room Setup** discusses dye room setup and equipment, personal protective equipment, how to read an MSDS, and dye/paint storage.
- **Chapter 2: Who Can Make a Rainbow? All About Color** covers terms and misconceptions about color theory while briefly diving into the science of how we perceive color.
- **Chapter 3: Ready, Set, Go! Fibers, Additives, and Swatching** talks about fibers, additives, and swatching. There are examples of how different theaters swatch.
- **Chapter 4: The Law of Attraction: Fiber-specific Dyes** includes the major fiber-specific dye categories: acid, fiber-reactive, direct, vat, and disperse dyes. Each category includes how and when to use these products on specific fibers.
- **Chapter 5: All Together Now! Union Dyes** covers using union dyes on a variety of substrates and objects. Most of the discussion focuses on Dylon DyePro and Rit ProLine dyes.
- **Chapter 6: The Undo Button of Dye? Color Removing** contrasts several products used to remove color in fabric. There is a table contrasting health and safety of each product.
- **Chapter 7: Beauty Is Only Skin Deep: Changing the Color of Leather!** outlines changing the color of leather using many techniques: from vat dying skins, to painting finished leather, and everything in between. This chapter includes all you need to know about

DOI: 10.4324/9781351130677-1

dyeing several skins the same color in the vat, how to paint and finish leather so it doesn't bleed, and which paints and dyes I have used and prefer to alter the color of leather. I include leather dye sources, information about the pH, the fat requirement for suppleness, all of the leveling compounds, and stretching the leather afterward.

Chapter 8: The Three S's: Silkscreens, Stencils, and Stamps covers all you need to know about creating and using silkscreens, stencils, and stamps.

Chapter 9: Stroke Couture: Printing and Painting With Dye outlines custom print processes without relying on commercial mixtures to allow the dyer to customize fabric, garments, or any fabric substrate. Custom mixtures include print paste process using acid dyes, fiber-reactive dyes, and thiourea dioxide. Processes include painting with acid and fiber-reactive dyes, and ombré dyeing with dye and color remover.

Chapter 10: Another Dimension: Paints, Coatings, and Other Embellishments explores textile paints, coatings, and embellishing mediums and how to apply them. Much like mediums in the art world, textile mediums are available in a variety of colors and opacities and there are a wide array of binders and mediums available to the dyer. Paints specifically formulated for breakdown will not be covered in this chapter but are explored in Chapter 13. I will touch on textile mediums, UV fabric paint, using adhesives as coatings, how to use bronzing powders, hot fix crystals, textile embossing mediums, and texture mediums. Application techniques include dry brushing, sponging, airbrushing, spraying, syringing, squeeze bottling paint, and marbling.

Chapter 11: Resist!!! Making Marks With Resist Dyeing explores several types of resists, dyeing, and painting: from the Japanese art of shibori, to Indian batik, the French Serti technique, and many other physical resist techniques that come from experimenting with dye and fabric like low water immersion, ice dyeing, and more!!

Chapter 12: Burned Out? Try Devore! outlines the devore process on a variety of fabric types. This chapter lays out some history and the origin of the term devore, the basic process of etching fiber, techniques and tips on achieving fine lines and intricate motifs with etching, and tools and techniques for applying etching paste.

Chapter 13: It's Getting Real: Permanent and Removable Aging, Distressing, Breakdown, and Special Effects is set up in the following breakdown in categories: permanent breakdown, removable breakdown, specific garment breakdown techniques, specialty breakdown effects, blood, and breakdown dyeing. Related appendices include DIY recipes for breakdown mediums and blood, and sources used in aging and breakdown.

Chapter 14: Arterial Motives: Permanent and Removable Blood for Costumes covers permanent and removable blood effects. It also includes many tried and tested DIY blood recipes.

1

DYEING IN VEIN

SAFETY PRECAUTIONS AND DYE ROOM SETUP

To make textile magic, we must use dye, and not die from the array of products utilized in our craft! If we know how to protect ourselves when using powders, chemicals, and aerosols, the dye room will be set up in such a way that it supports our safety; this is why safety and dye room setup go hand in hand.

Safety is the most important knowledge base for a painter–dyer. Exposure to the chemicals we use is cumulative and eventually will have permanent effects (like premature death) if artisans do not take proper safety precautions. In the following chapter, you will find my recommendations for personal safety, how to decode SDS sheets, and how to apply the information therein. Additionally, I will discuss general dye room cleanliness, setup, and most wanted dye-room equipment.

Figure 1.1 A large light-filled film studio dye room.
Photo courtesy of Beth Herd.

KEEP IT CLEAN

Cleaning as you go in the dye room is much like putting away cooking ingredients as you use them – decluttering the workspace while preparing for your next steps. Having loads of old towels to dampen and wipe surfaces down while you are working is key in the dye room. This will minimize powders that can potentially be airborne and get inhaled by those using the space or that could

DOI: 10.4324/9781351130677-2

transfer to other damp projects in the room. Some dyers like to use a damp towel or newspaper on the powder mixing workspace for this very reason – the damp article attracts the dye particles so they don't go into the air, your lungs, or on the damp piece you just dyed that is hanging in the work room! Additionally, you will minimize exposure for the future you, as you will eventually be picking up this towel to launder it (or newspaper to throw away) and don't want particles flying everywhere when you do.

The "ProChem Studio Safety and Guidelines" leaflet sums up the basic and most important safety rules of a dye studio (Figure 1.2).

PRO™ CHEMICAL & DYE
STUDIO SAFETY GUIDELINES

The products listed on our web site are considered relatively non-toxic, but it is best to avoid unnecessary exposure. Keep in mind that they are industrial chemicals and not intended for inhalation or ingestion. We encourage teachers to advise students about safety precautions and proper use of safety equipment, clean work habits and responsible use of products.

ALL ARTISTS SHOULD USE THE FOLLOWING SAFEGUARDS

- Do not eat, drink, or smoke in areas where dyes and chemicals are used.
- Work in a well ventilated area.
- If you experience an adverse symptom to anything, move away from the area to fresh air. If the symptoms persist, stop using the product & consult your physician.
- Wear a disposable dust/mist respirator if you dye fabric occasionally. If you dye fabric on a regular basis wear a MSHA/NIOSH approved respirator with cartridges for dusts, mists, and fumes. Disposable dust/mist respirators don't help with fumes.
- Even though dyes are not absorbed by the skin you should wear rubber gloves, old clothes or protective clothing, and even old shoes.
- Wear goggles when working with corrosive chemicals such as acetic acid and lye (you only have one set of eyes).
- Contact lens wearers should be careful around powders to avoid eye irritation.
- Cover your work area with dampened newspaper. Weigh and mix dyes and other powders with local exhaust ventilation or use a mixing box. See Helpful Information at right.
- Do not mix powders near furnace or air conditioner intake pipes.
- Use appropriate utensils to stir solutions and dye baths. If you use food utensils as dyeing tools don't reuse them for food preparation.
- Avoid exposure to dye powders, auxiliary chemicals and vapors during pregnancy or lactation.
- Avoid prolonged or repeated contact with the skin.
- Vacuum floors and surfaces, do not sweep.
- Keep dye and auxiliary containers closed and in a cool dry place, away from food and out of the reach of children when not in use.
- Wipe up spills immediately. Liquid dye dried to a powder can be accidentally inhaled or ingested.
- Label dye container with purchase date to insure out of date dye is not used. See page 24 for shelf life information.
- Clearly label all solutions and containers of powder. Do not remove the supplier's name or hazard warning labels.
- Always add acid to water.
- Always add Lye to cold water.

Figure 1.2 ProChem's safety guidelines sum up the most important safety protocols when working with paint and dye.
Image courtesy of ProChemical and Dye.

DISPOSAL

Quantities of dyes and auxiliary chemicals used by home dyers rarely exceed limits set for disposal in municipal or even septic systems. Concentrated highly acidic or alkaline waste water can upset the balance of a septic system. The amount of rinse water used for a normal dye bath is sufficient to dilute your dye bath for disposal purposes. Therefore, waste water disposal should not be a problem. If you have questions about disposal contact your local board of health for guidelines specific to your area.

CLEAN UP

Clean up work area with damp sponge and towels. Remove dye stains with a household cleaner containing bleach. Do not use bleach to remove dye stains from hands. Instead use a specifically designed hand cleaner - ReduRan. While hands are dry, rub a small amount of hand cleaner on hands and work in well. Add a small amount of water and work until dye residue is loosened. Wash off thoroughly with soap and water and dry hands. Repeat as necessary.

Protect those who cannot protect themselves - children and pets. Clearly label dyes and auxiliary chemicals and keep in safe storage and out of the reach of children. Supervise children carefully.

HELPFUL INFORMATION

How to make a mixing box: Cut off the top and one side of a 10"x10" cardboard box. Cut a stack of newspapers the size of the inside dimensions and place them inside the box. Dampen the surface of the newspaper with a sponge or spray bottle filled with water. Measure dye or auxiliary powder and dissolve it with water. Once the powder is mixed with water, carefully roll up the top sheet of newspaper and discard. This way any excess powder that falls on the damp newspaper does not blow around.

WAX

Waxes pose a specific set of safety concerns. Read and follow the guidelines below before batiking with hot wax.

- Always use proper ventilation in your work area. Create a local exhaust system by putting a portable exhaust fan in a window, so it pulls air from the room to the outside.

- Heated wax releases irritating chemicals including acrolein and aldehydes. There is no approved MSHA/NIOSH filter for acrolein. A respirator is not a substitute for good ventilation

- Heat wax to the lowest temperature at which it remains liquid.

- Hot wax is a fire hazard. Do not leave it unattended.

- Wax forms potentially hazardous vapors at high temperatures and may ignite. Do not use open flames, such as a gas or propane burner, to heat wax. Instead use a crock pot or electric fry pan with a temperature control.

CALIFORNIA PROPOSITION 65

California Proposition 65 is a labeling act that requires a special label on products that contain (in any amount) any chemical on the Prop 65 list. Many household items including rubbing alcohol and some bug sprays are on the list, as well as car exhaust and cigarette smoke. You will find this label on many of our products because trace amounts of these listed chemicals such as copper, Ethyl Oxide and rubbing alcohol are on the Prop 65 list.

MATERIAL SAFETY DATA SHEETS (MSDS)

California Proposition 65 is a labeling act that requires a special label on products that contain (in any amount) any chemical on the Prop 65 list. Many household items including rubbing alcohol and some bug sprays are on the list, as well as car exhaust and cigarette smoke. You will find this label on many of our products because trace amounts of these listed chemicals such as copper, Ethyl Oxide and rubbing alcohol are on the Prop 65 list.

Figure 1.2 Continued

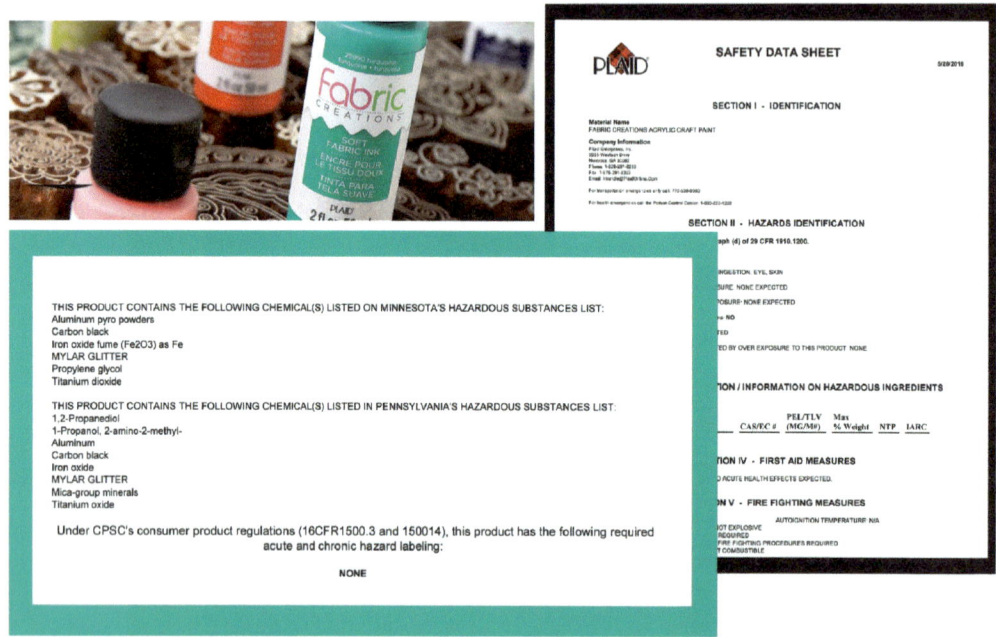

Figure 1.3 Notice on the SDS for a nontoxic and water-based fabric paint, these paints do contain chemicals considered to be toxic in some states!

LABELS

Reading product labels the first time you use a new product is a smart and worthwhile activity. You will encounter different types of labeling that may tempt you to use minimal safety precautions because the label states that the products are nontoxic or natural. These labels could not be more misleading. In her book *The Artists Complete Health and Safety Guide*,[1] Mona Rossol discusses these labels in detail. There are a few labeling terms I feel are important to mention including biodegradable, water-based, and nontoxic.

Rossol states,

> "Biodegradable" really means this: You won't get into trouble if you flush or trash the product, but there are no guarantees related to your health while you use it. And the product may not be safe for the environment in the long run either.

Regarding water-based products, Rossol adds,

> Many people assume that "water-based" products are "safe." But the material safety data sheets from the manufacturers reveal that many water-based products contain both water and solvents. "Water-based" really means this: Water is probably an ingredient, but the product may also contain solvents and other toxic substances. Consult the material safety data sheet for further information.

One of the most misleading and misunderstood labels includes the term "nontoxic." Rossol defines what this term really means: " 'Nontoxic' on a consumer product really means this: The ingredients don't kill half or more of the animals in short-term toxicity tests, but there are no long-term guarantees."

As you can see, these seemingly innocuous labeling verbiages do not mean the product is safe on your skin or near food. When you pull out that water-based paint and intend to use it through an airbrush, consult the SDS sheet to review safety precautions; you will be glad you did.

SDS: SAFETY DATA SHEETS

Being informed is your primary job as an artist, painter, and dyer. Learning how to read a *Safety Data Sheet* (SDS) (formerly known as MSDS or Material Safety Data Sheet) quickly and effectively is imperative in protecting yourself and others from the damaging effects of chemicals and solvents.

All states require employees to have access to a Safety Data Sheet (SDS), which contains information on health hazards, chemical ingredients, physical characteristics, control measures, and special handling procedures for all hazardous substances in the work area. The laws say that SDSs must be readily accessible to all employees and it is illegal to have any blanks on the sheet. If no information exists, "no information" must be written in the space. The laws also state that SDSs must contain complete, accurate, and up-to-date information. Nevertheless, many SDSs are inaccurate and incomplete; they may, however, still be very useful if you know how to read them and where to look for more information.

SDSs may differ slightly in organization, but they must all contain the same basic information on hazardous ingredients, health effects, legal and recommended exposure limits, physical properties, and control methods. Please see the following table (table 1.1) that breaks down each section of the SDS into digestible pieces.

Table 1.1 Decoding the Safety Data Sheet.

SECTION 1: **Identification**	**What is this product and who makes it??** The name of the product and trade name(s), recommended use, company address, and emergency telephone number of the manufacturer must be provided.
SECTION 2: **Hazards Identification**	**Am I dealing with any hazardous chemicals?** This section will identify hazardous products as applicable to law, including hazard classification (i.e., flammable liquid).
SECTION 3: **Identifies Ingredients**	**What is this product actually made of?** This section identifies chemical ingredients of the product, including impurities and stabilizing additives. Whether or not something is considered nontoxic by law will also be included in this section.

(Continued)

Table 1.1 (Continued)

SECTION 4: **First Aid Measures**	**What happens if I mess up and get this stuff on me...?** First aid instructions on how to mitigate exposure based on whether you inhaled the product, had skin or eye contact, or ingested it. This section also lists symptoms or effects of exposure. Unfortunately, a lot of MSDSs in circulation do not contain complete and accurate health hazard information.
SECTION 5: **Fire and Explosion Hazard Data**	**If this product lights on fire, how do I put it out??** This section should provide information on the fire hazards of a product and specific products used to extinguish a fire. **There are different types of fire extinguishers for different products!**
SECTION 6: **Accidental Release Measures**	**Whoops, I spilled it all over the place – how do I clean it up?** How to clean up and contain a spill of the product, methods and materials for containing the products, and what protective equipment is needed in cleaning up. Usually, we use such small amounts of products that this really isn't a huge concern.
SECTION 7: **Handling and Storage**	**When it's time to put it away, where's the best place?** This includes how to handle the product, what product or elements to NOT store it next to, and how to store the product properly.
SECTION 8: **Control Measures**	**HOW DO I PROTECT MYSELF??** The SDS must list control measures that can reduce or eliminate the hazard, including ventilation and other engineering controls, safe work practices, and personal protective equipment. For respirators, information on the type of respirator, degree of protection and the appropriate filter cartridge (such as acid gasses, dust or organic vapors) must be included. In addition, all gloves do not protect against all chemicals. The correct type of glove should be specified here on the SDS.
SECTION 9: **Physical and Chemical Properties**	**What does it look and smell like?** This section identified properties associated with the product including appearance, odor, pH, melting point, viscosity, flammability, solubility, flash point, etc.
SECTION 10: **Stability and Reactivity**	**Is it shelf stable?** Discusses chemical stability, any hazardous reactions during storage, and what are the hazards and the physical description of what may happen to the product as it decomposes.
SECTION 11: **Toxicological Information**	**In what way could this product kill me?** This section details routes of exposure (lungs, eyes, skin, etc.), a description of immediate, delayed, or chronic effect from exposure, measure of toxicity based on how many rats died in the lab, descriptions on symptoms of exposure, and a report on carcinogens.

SECTION 12: Ecological Information	**What if I spill this in a lake or river?** What happens if you release this product into the environment and how to mitigate.
SECTION 13: Disposal	**How do I throw this product away?** How to dispose of the product including containers to use, whether or not it should go to the landfill or down the drain.
SECTION 14: Transport Information	**How will this be shipped?** Guidance on transportation of the chemical by rail, road, air, or sea.
SECTION 15: Regulatory Information	**Even more info:** Safety, health, or environmental regulations that are not found anywhere else on the SDS.
SECTION 16: Other Information	**How old is this SDS? Is it the most current one available?** When the last SDS was prepared or when the last revision was made.

WHICH CHEMICALS ARE COVERED?

State laws differ about which chemicals are required to be listed on an SDS. Federal *OSHA* (Occupational Safety and Health Administration) hazard communication standards require evaluation of all chemicals and those found to be hazardous are covered by the law. Some state laws contain a list of thousands of chemicals that must be included, and a few require all ingredients to be listed, even those which are not hazardous. Companies can say that the blend of chemicals are a trade secret but still have to report hazards associated with chemicals used in the product. Assume that all of the chemicals that you work with should be included unless the manufacturer or employer can prove otherwise.

WHAT ARE THE NAMES OF THE CHEMICALS?

Chemicals are often known by different names: a *trade name*, such as Rit Color Remover, is the brand name of the product. It does not tell you what chemicals are in the product, or whether the product is a mixture of chemicals or a single chemical. A **generic name** describes a family or group of chemicals. For example, there are several different "isocyanates", and thousands of different "chlorinated hydrocarbons". Sometimes an SDS will try to get away with just listing the generic names. However, the law says that chemical names must also be listed. **The chemical name is the easiest name to use when doing research on the health effects of chemicals and how to protect yourself.** The SDS must list the chemical name of all hazardous ingredients that make up more than 1% of the mixture (or 0.1% for cancer-causing substances).

The CAS Number is a number given by the Chemical Abstract Service to each chemical. While different chemicals may have the same name, they will all have their own CAS number, which can be used to look up information. The Chemical Abstract Service publishes a book that contains a list of all CAS Numbers and the chemicals they represent.

PERSONAL SAFETY

Now that we have reviewed chemical designations and how to find information from a SDS, let's discuss personal safety in the dye room. Painter dyers use a variety of chemicals and powders on a daily basis. Exposure to these products create cumulative health impacts. So, while one or two exposures to the products will not kill you, the cumulative impact of using these products unsafely will.

WATER SOLUBILITY IS A BLESSING AND A CURSE
Some dye powder is **water-soluble**. This means powders want to find water and bond with it, dissolving in solution. Besides the dye pot or your rinse water container, what else nearby could be wet and attracts dye? Your eyes, nose, and mouth!!! Your eyes and mouth have glands that secrete moisture to keep those areas working properly, and the nose has mucus membranes that secrete moisture there to keep the body healthy. While these biological features help when taking a hike, they also attract dye powders with their moisture.

I had a student once who wouldn't wear a mask in dye class. We had been working on face casting and had a five-gallon bucket to wash the plaster off our hands. The craft room was a multipurpose room that also had a vent hood and dye vat. Another student dyed costumes that night, ten feet away from the plaster wash-off bucket. In the morning, the water in the bucket was a deep red color, matching the dye the other student had been using. I used this as an example, to the cavalier student, of how dye powder travels. For the same reason that wet white piece of silk hanging on the line 20 feet away from where you were mixing dye got speckled all over with dye, the bucket of water was dyed red. Both are full of water and attract substances that bond with that water the same way your eyes nose and mouth do! Have I beat this horse long enough?

Your drink or food will also attract dye powder from its moisture, therefore NEVER BRING FOOD OR DRINK INTO THE DYE ROOM!! Do not use any tools that you also use for preparing food or cook food in room used for dyeing. Seems like a no-brainer but you would be surprised how many theatres use the dye room sink to wash and dry their dishes. If your dye shop has a kitchen in it, do everything in your power to separate the two areas. If you cannot separate the areas, do not use the kitchen and advise your friends in the shop also to steer clear. Dye travels. Dye poisons. We like to use dye. Use it responsibly!

THE ACTUAL PRODUCTS – A PERSONAL CHOICE
Choosing safety products is an important and personal choice. I will discuss my experience with these products and give my favorite recommendations. Although these are my favorite products, you may have to try many types of gloves, masks, respirators, and so on, before you find your winning products.

APRON AND CLOSED-TOE SHOES

First thing I put on is my apron. It covers my chest, stomach, and the front of my legs, generally where dye and paint will splash. I always customize my apron to crisscross my back for comfort. Also, if you are going to be in the dye room long periods, sewing some ripstop/lightweight vinyl to the inside bottom half of the apron to repel dye and water transfer to clothes is a smart idea. My apron happens to be plastered with paint and glue, so it already has a waterproof barrier. I love having pockets in my apron where I can shove my mask and gloves if I have to run to a fitting! Don't forget about closed-toe shoes. You really don't want chemicals or paint splashing on your toes. Trust me.

Figure 1.4 I put on this crusty apron when gearing up to paint and dye. I have customized the straps to cross over my shoulders instead of hanging from my neck. Fifteen pieces of flair optional.

GLOVES

Gloves are the first line of defense against contact with dye in powder and solution. The skin, our beautiful protective organ that covers our bodies, actually absorbs chemicals and delivers them directly to our bloodstream. Gloves are available in several types of materials, lengths, and thicknesses that vary in price. I personally like my gloves to fit very tight so I don't accidentally transfer paint or dye with a baggy glove finger unknowingly to a place that I don't want it! Gloves have different resistances to a variety of chemicals – so check the box for the level (poor or good) resistance to the chemicals you are going to use.

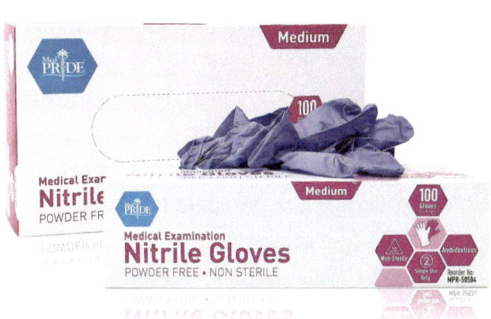

Figure 1.5 Nitrile gloves are great for a shared dye space to avoid allergens found in latex. Powder free eliminates the mess that happens when you handle your project after taking off powdered gloves!

DISPOSABLE GLOVES: LATEX VS. NITRILE

Many people have abandoned the traditional powdered latex glove due to latex allergies and the need to buy gloves in bulk. Also, powder can become a messy nuisance when an artist is taking gloves on and off all day and transfer to the piece you are working on, creating more work for you to remove the powder. Nitrile is a common choice of dye shops, but it does not stand up well to acetone, a substance often used in changing shoe color (see Chapter 6 for more information). Glove materials have a variety of degradation and breakthrough times from chemicals, depending on the glove material and chemicals used. For example, my favorite nitrile gloves only have a 4-minute breakthrough time with acetone. Will I finish removing the color from those shoes in 4 minutes? Nope. Therefore, I need to use another glove like latex (10-minute breakthrough time) or butyl gloves, when using acetone (which poisons your nervous system BTW). These gloves are given the designation of disposable but you can reuse them if you are careful. With lightly used gloves (used with water-based products and washed before removing), turn them outside in by blowing like a balloon into the wrist area. This should pop the fingers out and make the glove ready for a second go around. It's time to throw them out when there are holes and or they are covered in dye.

BUTYL GLOVES

These gloves are considered the go-to for using chemicals. They are black, and come in a variety of textures, lengths (up to 32"!), thicknesses, and sizes. It is always best to choose the correct size for your hands so you do not spill the chemicals you are handling, which can happen if your hands are swimming in the wrong-size glove. Order these from Grainger.com, who also happens to have store fronts in many cities that will allow you to try gloves on in person.

Figure 1.6 Cotton-lined full-sleeve gloves will keep you cool(ish) and covered when immersed in a hot dye bath.

THERMAL GLOVES

There are several brands of thermal gloves and many sources from whom purchase the gloves. Many people prefer the neoprene thermal gloves for vat dyeing so they can grab and manipulate the fabric by hand while withstanding the high heat of the vat. Others like the butyl gloves that are thicker than the disposable gloves but thinner than the neoprene ones, because they can feel the fabric through the gloves. Generally, the more thermal resistance the glove has, the higher the cost. They are sold in a range of glove sizes, some numbered and some small through extra-large. Fit is very personal, so make sure to try a few pairs to discover the size you prefer.

Masks

As we all know, there are a large number of masks on the market with have varying levels of protection against particulates, chemicals, and splashed chemicals. I will discuss two types used most frequently in the dye-craft area: dust particle masks and half-face cartridge respirators.

DISPOSABLE DUST PARTICLE MASKS

I know over the last few years we have all become experts on masks related to COVID particles. Masks used to filter dye particles are very similar to the best COVID masks. They feature a fantastic seal on the face and a bendy wire at the nose to create a custom fit. There are many brands and types of dust particle masks. They range from the surgeon-like over-the-ear kind to the charcoal filter ultra-seal $20-a-mask type. The cheap over-the-ear and around-the-head types are usually not adequate to filter out large amounts of particulate matter. The seals are terrible and usually the fit is strange at best. Masks of all types need a good seal and excellent airflow. For this reason, sampling many masks, I always choose N95 8511 by 3M (Figure 1.7) dust particle masks. There is a metal bar you can pinch above the nose and a foam rubber seal 360° around and it includes a generous valve on the front for ease of breathing. There are many other types of particulate masks on the market, some even charcoal lined for nuisance odors. In my opinion, you need two masks: an N95 dust particle mask as mentioned previously, and a half-face cartridge respirator.

Figure 1.7 3M N95 8511 dust particle masks. I feel like I can actually breathe in these!

Figure 1.8 A north half-face respirator and P100 cartridges – my personal favorite.

RESPIRATORS
When using products that contain volatile organic compounds (VOCs) or other chemicals for which the SDS requires use of a respirator, research which chemicals you are protecting yourself from, then order the cartridge accordingly. Every cartridge filters out different chemicals, vapors, or gases. This is indicated on the side of the cartridge by color and number. I have always preferred North respirators and the P100 cartridge has usually protected me from harm from any products in my dye room stock. If you work in a theatre or university, you should have to have the resident safety person come and do a fit test whenever you buy a new respirator or if this is your first time using one. A link to a DIY fit test can be found here: www.gemplers.com/tech/respfitcheck.htm.

GOGGLES
There are many types of goggles to choose from and you will choose the type that corresponds to what you are working on. While the safety-glasses style is usually the most comfortable, the goggles from your 10th grade biology class with a seal around the edge are the best protection against splashes and powder. If you are working with something very toxic and worried about splashing your face, there are face shields that will create a full barrier window in front of your face, although it will most likely fog up over a vat.

GETTING THAT DYE OFF OF YOUR HANDS!
For ages many dyers have used a dye reducer called Reduran; Kresto Kolor is the exact same thing (just a different name). It literally feels like sandy paste and smells like burning hair. It works better than hand soap but it is kind of expensive. A long-time dyer, teacher, author, and artist, Elin Noble, introduced me to using the orange scented mechanic soap – Gojo. It also feels like sand but doesn't smell like burning hair and REALLY washes that dye and paint off of your hands! It's also cheap because you can buy it in huge bottles. There are other brands of this type of soap that also work great. Try it out!

THE DYE ROOM SETUP

Dye room and paint space setup is really important to the artist's health and efficiency in the space. There must be a sink with water source, stove for heating dye, a ventilation system, surface for painting, washer and dryer, clothesline (which may be located outside), and storage for all paint dye products. There are many other important tools like a mixing box, computer for research, and spray booth to name a few, but these can be costly and there are workarounds for many of these tools. A fire extinguisher is always good to have around but check your SDS for fire extinguishing methods if you are using a unique product that requires a high level of safety protection; a normal fire extinguisher may not put out fires from certain chemicals.

DYE STORAGE

Most dye requires dark, cool storage. Many dyes are photosensitive and can be damaged by being exposed to light regularly, natural UV light being the worst. If you would like to store dye, like Rit that comes in a bag, in a wide-mouth container and your dye storage on a shelf is exposed to light every day, I like to use opaque containers (Figure 1.9) to store dye. These can be found at McMaster Carr and Grainger as well as other lab-equipment companies. I write the month and

Figure 1.9 Wide-mouth jars are perfect for storing powdered dyes and auxiliaries. I always add the date to the lid on a piece of tape when I add new products to the containers so I know how old the products are.

year on the top and side of the containers when I refill them with dye so I know how fresh the dye is. Always make sure to label dye color, color number, and dye company at the very least. This will make reordering so much easier.

Figure 1.10 The Oregon Shakespeare Festival dye room. From top left to bottom right: a large steam-jacketed dye vat with ramp to push dyed articles directly into sink, ventilated mixing box, bullet steamer, spray booth for airbrushing, computer setup for creating computer-printed fabric, and a small portion of their paint and dye storage.

VENTILATION

Proper ventilation will save brain cells! Noxious gasses and continual exposure to chemicals can and will affect your central nervous system! It is your responsibility to require appropriate ventilation for your workspace and to read the safety data sheets to understand what level of ventilation and protective personal equipment is needed.

ELIN NOBLE'S AT-HOME MIXING BOX!

Elin Noble, a seasoned dyer and textile artist, wrote a wonderful book on painting and dyeing called *Dyes and Paints: A Hands on Guide to Coloring Fabric*, that includes a description of a DIY powder mixing box. "Use a mixing box to limit airborne exposure to chemical powders. Cut off the top and one side of a 12" x 12" (30cm x 30cm) cardboard box, leaving a small 'room' for mixing. Set the mixing box on top of a drop cloth. Cut a small stack of newspaper to the inside dimension of the box. Place the newspapers on the bottom of the mixing box and spray them with water. If you spill any of the powder during the mixing process it will stick to the damp paper."[2]

Figure 1.11 Elin Noble's homemade mixing box.

Perhaps the most important tool you will have in your space is one that aids in room ventilation. I could really go down a rabbit hole describing the different levels and types of ventilation systems available but will focus on the 3 most commonly used in a dye room: mechanical hood, wall, and box systems. These systems and their uses can be somewhat interchangeable, but I will describe what I consider to be the safest setup.

Mechanical vents have a mechanism that actively processes the surrounding air through a changeable filter and discharges filtered air to the outside or back into the room. There are many levels of these – starting with vents that may be found above your kitchen stove, to those found in factories and laboratories. The ideal level of ventilation in a dye room will actively filter air particles resulting from mixing dye powder and spraying airbrush paint. Permanent vent hoods usually live above dye vats or mixing areas, venting off steam and any chemical vapor or gases from the products you are using. An example of when these are really helpful is when you are using color removers, as these products can be harmful to breathe in large quantities (think how huffing bleach over the sink can make you feel and triple that feeling! Yuck!). Wall vents may be adjacent to your dye powder mixing area, effectively pulling dye away from you. A **vent box** and its larger counterpart a **vent booth** (or spray booth) are the best line of defense when using toxic materials like leather paint, FEV, or anything with high VOC content.

DYE VATS

There are two major types of dye vats used in a dye shop: steam-jacketed dye vats and a large stove-top pot. Both are very useful for larger dye jobs that cannot be accomplished in the

PERMANENT VENT HOODS:
LEFT: LARGE VENT IN FILM DYE ROOM RIGHT: SMALL PERMANENT VENT AT PURDUE UNIVERSITY

PORTABLE VENT HOODS:
LEFT: STATIC PORTABLE VENT HOOD IN FILM SET UP RIGHT: VENT THAT ROLLS AROUND AT COLORADO STATE UNIVERSITY

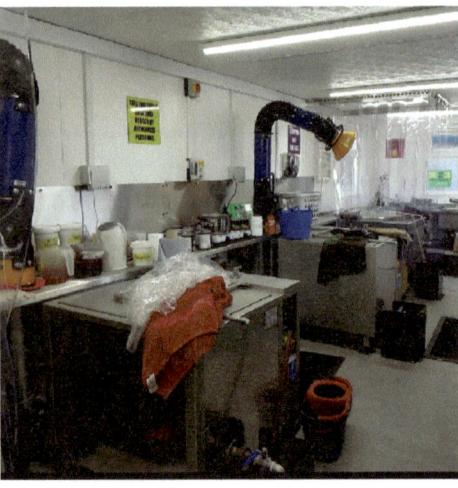
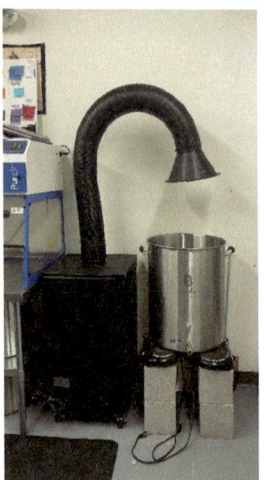

VENT BOXES AND BOOTHS:
LEFT: TABLE TOP VENT BOX AT COLORADO STATE UNIVERSITY RIGHT: VENT BOOTH AT OREGON SHAKESPEARE FESTIVAL

Figure 1.12 An example of a variety of ventilation systems ranging from large to small scale.
Photo credit: Beth Herd, Erin Carignan, Farrah Southam.

washing machine or in a smaller pot on the stove top. Both have pros and cons, and usually money and space dictate which type of vat you choose. Both types of vats require a water source above the vat as no one wants to lift that much liquid! Remember, water weighs 8.35 pounds per gallon (1 kilogram per liter) and to dye a large amount of material may take, at minimum, 10 gallons, which would be 83 pounds! If your spigot cannot swing directly over the vat, you can use a short detachable hose to lead the water to the vat. These can also be handy in spraying down the vat after use.

STEAM-JACKETED DYE VATS

Steam-jacketed vats are the ideal choice for dyeing large lots of material and can be purchased through commercial kitchen supply companies as soup kettles. There are two types of kettles: direct steam or self-contained and they are available in gas or electric models. Most models can be plugged in directly to the steam service if you happen to be in a large institution. Both generate steam inside a "jacket" that surrounds the kettle or vat to keep the contents in the vat at a consistent temperature. Capacity ranges from a few gallons to 200 gallons and are almost always bolted to the ground to avoid tipping. Some have agitators, others are mounted on a swivel that allows one to pour liquid out of the vat, but most used in theatre have a dedicated place, bolted to the floor and with a permanent drain set up. If the drain is near your vat but not under, which is very common, you can rig the drainage shunt to a longer pipe to expel spent dyebaths. Some universities and theatrical companies have an easier time justifying the purchase of a soup kettle to purchasing, rather than a dye vat, the latter, which can bring up chemical disposal concerns or a red flag hindering the ordering process. Steam-jacketed vats also require a special breaker box and steam pressure gauge; the vat company can help

Figure 1.13 A 40-gallon steam-jacketed dye vat. Depending on the scale of the work you do, size up or down accordingly.

you decide what you will need based on the size of the vat you are ordering, and your building superintendent can help you figure out what you need in terms of a breaker in your building.

These vats come with lids that can be easily removed for greater availability of space around the vat and constant access to goods in the vat. Since the dyer should be hovering over the vat and most likely constantly stirring, there is no need to close that vat and walk away like you would if you were cooking a pot of soup. The major manufacturers are Groen, Hubert, Hamilton, Dover, Vulcan, and Lee.

STOVE-TOP POTS AND KETTLES

Having a variety of small and large pots are a must in the dye shop. Pot material will depend on the type of burner your shop uses; for gas or electric burners, almost any material will do, but for

induction burners, you must use stainless, carbon steel, or cast iron. I like to buy old Revere Ware pots at thrift stores in 1/2 pint, pint, quart, and 2 quart sizes to set up a shop. 8-gallon and 10-gallon pots are handy when working with more yardage.

I have found that brew kettles (see Figure 1.16) are the most useful as a stand-in for a dye vat as they have an option to come with a spigot and a valve to drain water. These pots come in 8-, 10-, 15-, 20-, and 30-gallon sizes. If you have little space or have a modular set up that is on the move, this option is the best for you. There are optional pipe fittings you can buy that go from pipe thread to hose thread (did you know those thread systems were different from each other???) so you can attach a hose to the spigot to drain the vat. The best burners for these pots are large gas single burners like the ones marketed by kitchen supply stores as "backyard burners". They will support a pretty large brew pot as the burners are about 20" in diameter. In our shop at Colorado State, we do not have gas, so we have two double burners – that's 4 burners total, sitting under a 30-gallon brew pot. It works but if the kettle is halfway full, it takes over three hours to get the water to 180 degrees. Not ideal but it works.

Figure 1.14 A kettle used for brewing beer is a great makeshift dye vat. These kettles have a spout and valve that can be attached to a hose in order to drain the spent bath.

ACCESSORIES AND TOOLS FOR VAT AND KETTLE DYEING

You will want to invest in or create **a paddle** to stir your fabric or garments in the vat. Plastic will bend with the heat of the water so wood is a better choice. I recommend creating an oar-shaped paddle and shellack the heck out of that thing! That way, it won't become water logged or accept dye and transfer onto the next thing you dye. There are metal stirrers available specifically for vats but I find them heavy to use over a long period of time. If you find you have to screw two objects together to create the paddle shape, make sure there are no screw ends or pokey bits that will damage your fabric. Another useful tool for the vat, which can be found at restaurant supply stores, is a long-handled steel spoon or long-handled tongs. These can be useful when using large pots too (Figure 1.15).

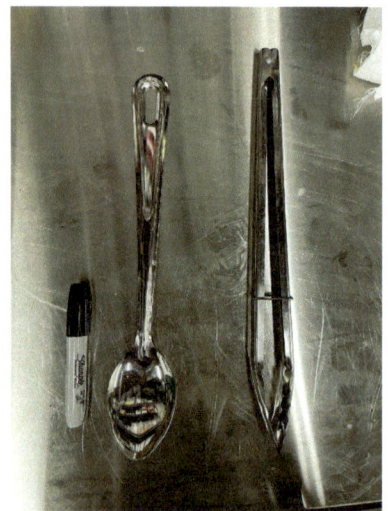

Figure 1.15 Long-handled spoon and long tongs! Sharpie for scale.

Another very cool item that a scene shop or metal fabricator can make for you is a little **metal ramp** that allows you to slide the fabric out of the vat and directly into the sink next to the vat. This is super helpful if you dye a large quantity of fabric like a Broadway shop or large Lort theatre.

THERMOMETERS

You can use old mercury thermometers or digital thermometers, just make sure the temperature range is high enough! I have fried a few temperature/pH monitors in my time from putting them in nearly boiling water. pH monitors do not generally rate high enough to stick directly into a vat or pot of hot water; you will want to remove water from the bath, let it cool, then test the pH. One of the best ways to quickly and safely measure temperature is with infrared thermometers – they are so easy to use – you just "aim and shoot" at the surface of the water to check your temperature!

Figure 1.16 Thermo Pro Infrared Thermometer, around $30 at Home Depot.

THE SINK!

This is one of the most important tools in your shop. A stainless steel kitchen sink with two deep basins and a work area is ideal. These can often be found at university surplus or on different marketplace apps. The idea is that the basins are deep enough to hold bussing tubs that you can soak fabric/garments in, or use to thoroughly wash out dyed fabric. A restaurant grade pre-rinse spray (Figure 1.19) valve is an ideal part of your sink setup. It will allow you to hose out silk screens and other stubbornly stuck products.

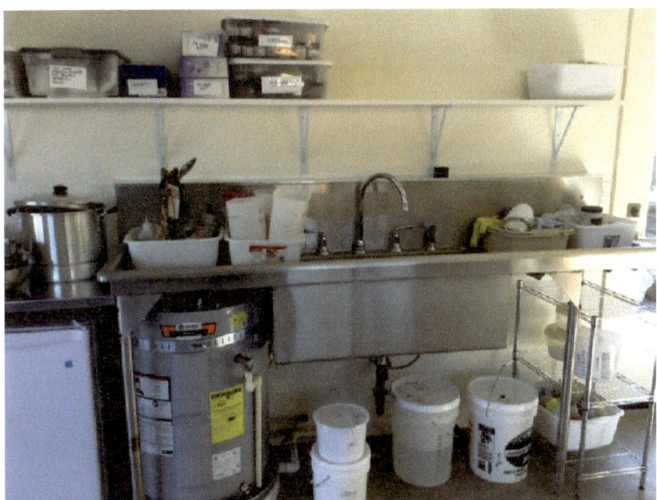

Figure 1.17 Deb Dryden's studio sink is a perfect dye sink because it has flat spots on both ends to dry bins and pots or store overnight baths!
Photo courtesy of Deborah Dryden.

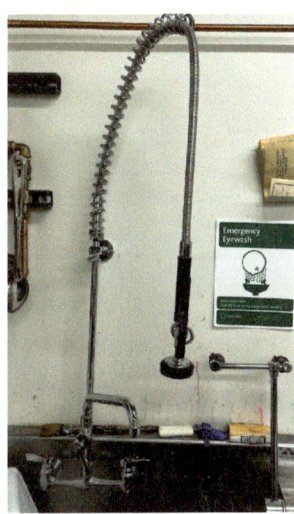

Figure 1.18 A restaurant pre-rinse sprayer and eyewash station on dye sink at Colorado State University.

LARGE BUSSING TUBS

The kind of bussing tubs used in restaurants work best. They are tough, cheap, and can be found at restaurant supply stores. They are larger than the ones used for a kitchen sink and can be bought in a variety of depths. My personal favorite size is around 15" x 21" x 5" deep. They accommodate more fabric and can be used to do low water immersion dyeing for larger pieces. They can also handle very hot water and don't bend or melt easily.

Figure 1.19 A variety of sizes of bussing tubs always come in handy in a dye room. Even cat boxes work great!

WASHERS AND DRYERS

Top-loading washers are the very best. Usually older-model washers work the best but you can disable the auto lock by putting magnets on specific areas of the washer. The old ones don't lock when you close the lid and they don't stop agitating when you want to open them to check your work. I often dye in the washer if I am toning something or just teching a bunch of white shirts, so the ideal washer is like a vat but with a spindle in the middle to agitate the fabric for you. Personally, I think one of those old-timey washers that have a ringer attached would be the coolest dye washer, ever.

Figure 1.20 Ideal washing machine properties and setup for dyeing!

INDUSTRIAL DRYER

An industrial dryer is huge and gets really hot! They have temperature controls but if you want to set Fiber Etch or fabric paint, you can set the temp on high and let it do the work for you – but only if the fiber etch or fabric paint is dry!

DRYING CABINET

A drying cabinet is one of my favorite tools for so many applications! This can quickly dry any fabric and it features 3–4 shelves that fold up to create a huge 6' drying space! Maximum temperature is 150° so it will not shrink or burn anything. These are great for wardrobe too – to dry corsets or bulky costumes more quickly. I use them to dry wigs, hat sizing, glue, sky's the limit!!! I have a Staber domestic drying cabinet. They retail around 2K and usually delivery is free. It is deeper than a traditional wig dryer so it can accommodate more items and of a larger scale.

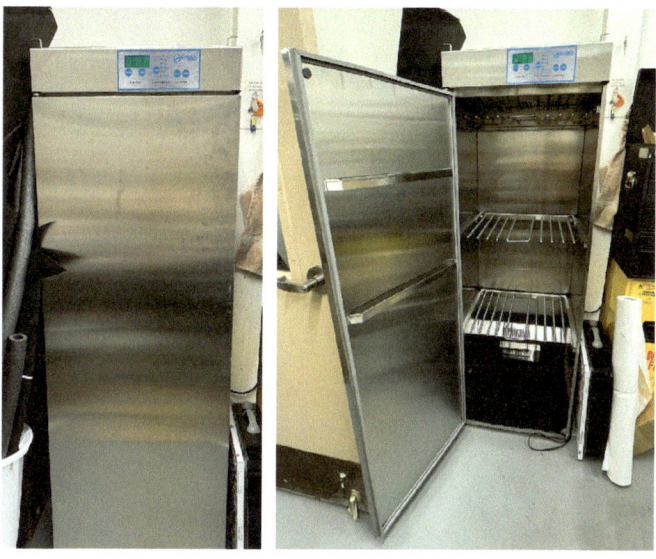

Figure 1.21 A Staber drying cabinet is an excellent addition to any costume shop! As you can see, the stainless collects finger prints; get white instead!

A FLAT SURFACE

You will require a large flat surface that can be covered in brown paper and/or plastic for painting and dyeing horizontally. So much breakdown is done this way, using the table for leverage when sanding or rubbing paint and dye into garments being distressed. A table that can become a vertical surface is also amazing as a vertical surface is fabulous for airbrushing or using gravity to paint or dye textiles.

MEASURING TOOLS

Certain dyes are mixed by weight and thus require a scale to measure them. A digital scale that weighs in ounces and grams is preferable. Other dyers, especially ones that use union dyes regularly, like to use measuring spoons. Either way, it is good to have a variety of measuring cups, spoons, and a digital scale. I love these tiny

 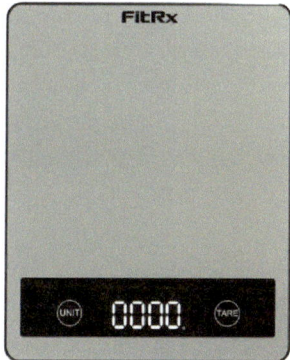

Figure 1.22 Tiny measuring spoons that measure 1/4, 1/8, 1/16, 1/32, and 1/64th teaspoon (left) and a digital scale (right).

spoons that measure down to 1/64th of a teaspoon and I've included a picture in Figure 1.22. These are also sold as pinch, smidge, and dash.

A CLOTHESLINE

So many options here. We have to have clotheslines. Those little drying racks that become a pile of sticks will not do. They pool dye where the cross bars touch the fabric, they are weak and have difficulty holding heavy fabric, and are very tricky to use to paint or spray with dye. I like to have clothes lines in a variety of places ranging from inside to outside. The dye room must have at least one line hung at least 6 feet from the floor. If space is an issue, a heavyweight retractable clothes line can be fantastic, you just have to realize it will have a stretching out period when you first use it, and you will need to tighten it a bunch. This stretching does stop, and when you want to use dress forms and mannequins in the dye shop and don't want to be encumbered by a line, you can stow it away!

Figure 1.23 Bodysuit painted on a mannequin specifically reserved for paint/dye projects. Bodysuit designed for *Mahagony*; costume design by Ann Hould-Ward for the LA Opera.

A MANNEQUIN IN A FULL LEOTARD (LONG SLEEVE FULL LEG IF POSSIBLE)

These are better than dress forms for many reasons. One being that they can stay in the dye room and you don't have to worry about distressing them like you would about a shop dress form. Also, they have legs so you don't have to feel like you're hogging one of the two hanging forms from the costume shop! I like to cover my mannequin in a full body leotard, preferably knit or something somewhat absorbent, so the paint or dye does not pool on the plastic/plaster of the mannequin. Also, the leotard is a handy way to keep the mannequin clean, and can be thrown in the wash. A rayon or cotton Zenti suit would be the ultimate!!!

BULLET STEAMER

Bullet steamers are long metal tubes mounted to a heating element that create steam in an enclosed space. These are used for setting painted or printed dyes on fiber. Please see Chapter 9 on making your own steamer and steaming instructions; commercial steamers are almost totally unavailable for purchase. To see a commercially made bullet steamer see the images of Oregon Shakespeare Festival's dye shop (Figure 1.10). Check out Chapter 9 for detailed steaming instructions.

A FIRST AID KIT AND EYEWASH STATION

This is self-explanatory but if you are the head/master dyer you should make sure your first aid kit is stocked with burn salve, Band-Aids, and a quick-break ice pack.

THE BOTTOM LINE

In the same way Smokey the Bear says that "Only YOU can prevent forest fires", only YOU can allow yourself to be exposed to dangerous fumes and chemicals. Please make sure to protect yourself and **demand** appropriate protective equipment, spaces, tools, and ventilation in your workspaces!

NOTES

1. Rossol, Mona. *The Artist's Complete Guide to Health and Safety Guide*. New York, NY: Allworth Press, 2001.
2. Noble, Elin. *A Hands-on Guide to Coloring Fabric*. East Freetown, MA: Elin Noble, 1998.

2

WHO CAN MAKE A RAINBOW?

ALL ABOUT COLOR

Color, pattern, and texture are the very soul of fabric. When combined with a garment silhouette, it is the essence of character creation, evokes emotion, and captures our attention on stage and screen. As you can see in the image of Derek Weeden in Figure 2.1, all three of these elements are evident in creating Prospero's image in Oregon Shakespeare Festival's *The Tempest*. In correspondence with the costume designer, Deborah Dryden, she notes:

> The initial impulse to ombré the red came from more pragmatic design choices. I was looking for a color that would accent/contrast with the golden tones of the "aged parchment" quality used for the rest of the robe. The dramatic vibrancy of the red seemed to bring the rest of the robe into focus. . . . Those elements of color tension and movement (ombré vs rectilinear shapes) felt more dynamic to me.

Figure 2.1 Derrick Lee Weeden as Prospero. Note the drama the ombré from red to cream creates in his costume.
PHOTO CREDIT: Jenny Graham.

DOI: 10.4324/9781351130677-3

If this were purely a cream garment, even with the printed and drawn motifs, it would lack the incredible drama created by Dryden's design and Chris Carpenter's artistry.

The resident costume designer of the Old Globe Theater, Charlotte Devaux, used to enter my dye room waving a piece of fabric, singing "Who can make a rainbow . . . ?" Yes folx, we are responsible for the rainbow. With this responsibility it is important to understand how we as human beings process color, how to communicate using appropriate color terminology, and what colors are best used for toning, skin tones, creating greys, greiges, and blacks.

THE NUTS AND BOLTS OF COLOR

HOW DO WE PERCEIVE COLOR?

Many of us have been taught that by mixing the primaries – red, yellow, and blue – we can mix every color of the rainbow when in fact this is incorrect. To describe why this is incorrect let's jump into a quick lesson on color perception and additive and subtractive color mixing. Dr. Scot Westland, color scientist and professor at University of Leeds in Art and Design, described this really well so, I will paraphrase in the following sections what I learned from his webinar,[1] videos,[2] and correspondence on color theory.

**Warning: this gets a bit "science-y". Expect to learn a few new terms and get a little confused before you reach clarity . . .

First to discuss color, we have to talk about how we perceive color. Color perception is the basic physical process of the cones in our eyes and the perception of how lights and colorant mix where the three-color perceiving cones in the eye (red, blue, and green perceiving cones) process these colors with different spectral sensitivities. Where light and color land on the color spectrum creates a visual perception of color – and colors can land all over the color spectrum but the eye can perceive several different color mixtures (landing in different places on the color spectrum) as the same color. This similar perception is called **metamerism**. What the what?? Let's break this down!

Color primaries are a set of lights or colorants that, when mixed together, create a useful gamut of color. We use color primaries in color mixing but the best primaries for color mixing (as we have been taught for generations) are not red, yellow, and blue. Rather, these "primaries" vary between additive and subtractive color mixing. Additive and subtractive colors are almost mirror images of each other as one is adding light and the other is subtracting light (Figure 2.2).

Why do we care about additive and subtractive color mixing? Understanding the processes that happen in the eye can help a dyer choose which colors to mix to create a wide color gamut, to match or tone a specific color, or to understand how to dye pure colors with different dye classes. Not to create confusion but this blew my mind – additive color is used to predict how the eye will perceive color when mixing dyes and colorants, while subtractive color is what is actually happening when light reflects on the fabric–dye–pigment combination. Let's dive deeper . . .

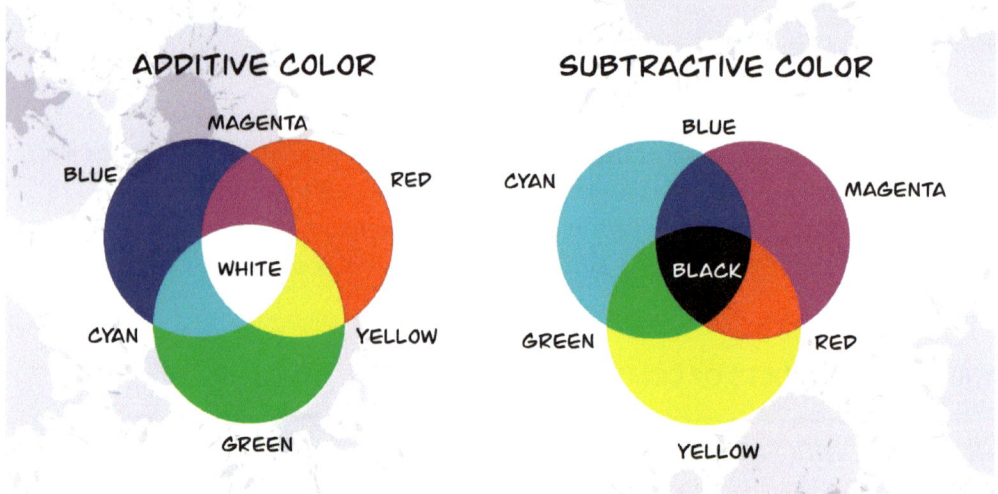

Figure 2.2 Additive and subtractive color mixing diagrams. Note how they are mirror images of each other.

ADDITIVE COLOR

The primary color system used in additive color is RGB (red-green-blue) and is the system that best describes human color perception but is also the basis for displaying colors in most digital screens. To describe **additive color**, I will use the projector analogy. When blue, red, and green are projected on a white screen, the overlapped areas of **incident light**, or the light that falls on a subject, create magenta, cyan, and yellow with white in the center. The white in the center of the projected light is the reflection of most of the incident light as most light sources are close to white, and if all the light is reflected, then all of the color cones in the eye are activated: thus, we perceive the color as white. So, why do we get yellow when we mix red and green wavelengths? We get yellow because the eye responds to this mixture in the same way it would respond to a single wavelength of yellow light: thus, perceiving yellow. Additive color mixing occurs when an object reflects more than one wavelength; the eyes' perception is of the wavelength of the mixed color. Optimal color primaries in this system that create the best gamut of colors are red, green, and blue.

SUBTRACTIVE COLOR

The application of dyes and pigments creates a rainbow of colors in fabric. When light reflects from a surface (like fabric for example) the subtractive color mix is perceived by the eye. The colors that appear on the fabric is the light that is not absorbed in the substrate. Most dyes absorb all wavelengths to some extent but they absorb most efficiently at different wavelengths.

Emerging color theory can best be described from my correspondence with Dr. Westland.[3] He explains with an example:

> To understand this idea let's consider the spectrum split into thirds: blue, green, and red. . . . When we apply yellow dye to cotton . . . the graph [Figure 2.3] shows the light that is reflected. The yellow dye absorbs mainly in the blue third of the spectrum, meaning that the light in the other two thirds is reflected. The color of the yellow-dyed

fabric is determined not by the color of the light that the dye absorbs (blue) but rather by the light that the fabric reflects (which is the green third and the red third). What happens when we mix together red and green light? Well, this is additive color mixing. Red and green makes yellow. It is in this sense that additive mixing (or mixing of light) explains the colors that we see when we look at dyed fabric.

Figure 2.3 Dr. Westland's spectral graph (upper right) depicting how yellow light falls on the spectrum when reflected from fabric dyed yellow.

Figure 2.4 Top: An actual color wheel made from red, yellow, blue primaries. Note the muddy purples and greens. Bottom: A color wheel made from cyan, magenta, and yellow. Notice how the purples and greens are clearer, brighter, and less muddy than the wheel on the left. Wheels by Victoria Toth.

The CMY system of color mixing is used in subtractive color mixing where cyan, magenta, and yellow are the subtractive primaries and create a larger gamut of colors when mixed. Printers use this system but add black to get more saturated dark colors. This is called the CMYK system. These subtractive primary colors are the ones we use when dyeing. An example of this in dyes would be the Dharma brand fiber-reactive dye equivalents of these primaries: turquoise, fuchsia, and lemon yellow.

So, what's the bottom line on primaries and why we are moving on from the traditional RYB system? Many distributors of fabric paint still recommend using the traditional RYB (red–yellow–blue) color system when using their paints. This is the primary system we were all taught as children. Why do I insist in switching it all up now? Well, in my experience, red and blue do not make purple. It makes some dreary version of purple. How many times have you just used purple paint instead of mixing purple?? A color gamut using this system yields a muddy and limited palette (Figure 2.4). This is why we now turn to the CMY and RGB color systems and use modern color theory to think about mixing color!

In his webinar "Color Mixing," Dr. Westland discusses how primary colors can be defined in a few ways. One definition is the principal hues used to mix colors in a variety of color systems. Another definition is the specific colorants used to create the largest gamut for a specific industry. Modern dye houses and entertainment dye shops use around 20 colors of dyes to mix a large gamut of colors. This would be called a 20-primary system. This doesn't mean we use all 20 colors at one time – usually 3 or 4 maximum colors are mixed – but experienced dyers find that it takes a variety of colors to create the optimal gamut. My friend Beth Herd, a film breakdown artist and assistant master dyer for the Royal Shakespeare, says "One of my mentors taught me that you only need three colors in breakdown: Red, Yellow, and Black. You can make almost any color from those three".[4] This would be the breakdown primary system – who knew!? For more info on being broken down and bloodied, see Chapter 13 on breakdown and distressing for more from Beth.

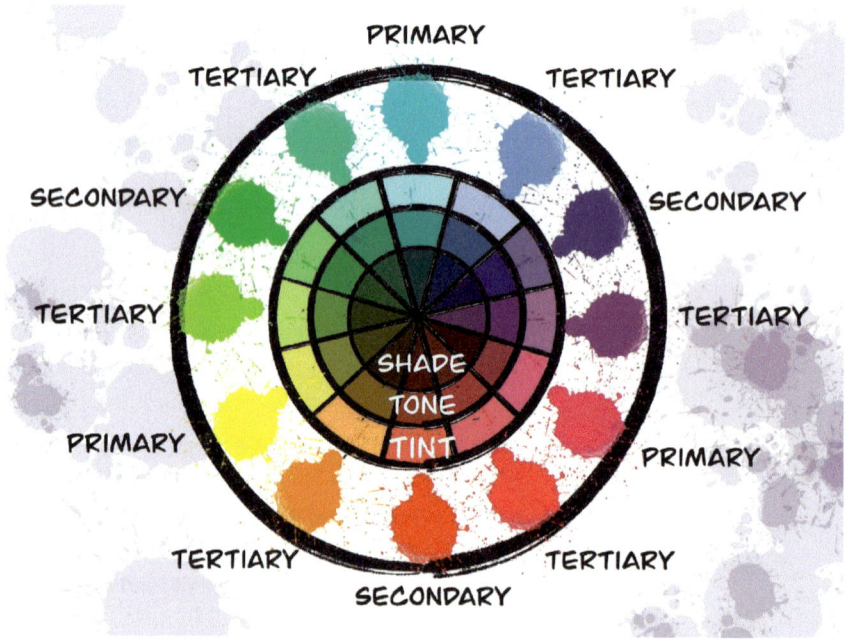

Figure 2.5 Visual diagram of primary, secondary, tertiary, tint, tone, and shade CMY wheel.

Using the first definition of **primary colors** – the principal hues used to mix colors in a variety of color – let's discuss the names for different types of colors created from mixing these primaries. **Secondary colors** are achieved by mixing two primary hues. **Tertiary colors** are a mixture of all three primary hues. The colors in break-down (or distressing) are usually a version of tints or shades of tertiary colors – those that look like dirt, mud, blood, excrement, sweat, or any color a garment may turn after being dragged by a car or making it through a zombie apocalypse.

Complementary colors are those opposite from each other on the color wheel. These are the major players in toning color. For example, when your fabric is too yellow, you can tone it with a teensy bit of purple, yellow's complement. **Split complements** are a hue plus two hues on either side of the complimentary color, which can be used to tone more subtly than using the direct complement if you want to push a color one way or the other. The difference between being an ok dyer and being a great dyer is that the great dyer understands how to fix, save, tone, and remove color using all of the tools in the toolbox. Understanding compliments and how to use them is one of these very important tools!

LET'S TALK ABOUT COLOR: COLOR NAMES AND TERMINOLOGY

Figure 2.6 The red military jacket section of the Old Globe Theater stock. Note how many different versions of red there are!

First, let me say, using color names outside of the primary/secondary spectrum always drove me insane as a dyer. When you look through any costume stock you will notice how many variations of simple colors there are like cream, red, navy, and black (see Figure 2.6 for red variations). Aside from using wacky color names like coquelicot (a red–orange) to describe color, no two humans can conjure the same exact color in their minds from a color name. Also, those names just create confusion! Maybe the dyer's chartreuse is more yellow than the designer's chartreuse? This is why I insist, as a designer and a technician, on having color conversations in clear primary–secondary–tertiary hue-based vocabulary, accompanied by a fabric swatch or Pantone, rather than using color names. Dye company color names like "Scarlet" made by both Rit and Aljo, for example, can yield very different colors! Another reason I find it's best to keep the language basic. In addition to using confusing color names, many artisans and designers alike confuse basic vocabulary that we use to describe color. To dispel any confusion related to these terms – let's review these descriptors.

COLOR AND HUE

A **color** can be described as any color visible to the human eye. This can include primary, secondary, tertiary colors, black, and white. **Hue**, on the other hand, can only be used to describe the pure state of color or as Ingamells[5] describes it: "colors perceived by the human eye that can only be created by red, yellow, and blue lights with appropriate intensities". Hue can be described as cool or warm to describe color in terms of temperature. Warm colors are considered the colors of heat like red, yellow, and orange. Cool colors evoke colors of the cold and are blues, greens, and purples. This is clearly represented in the character creations of Heatmiser and Snowmiser in the Rankin/Bass Production *The Year Without A Santa Claus* and can be seen in Figure 2.7.

Figure 2.7 The cool colors of a glacier with northern lights juxtaposed above the warm colors of fire. Photo courtesy of Pixabay.com.

VALUE AND SATURATION

There are varying **values (or lightness)** of color – meaning darkness or lightness of color. You can also have varying **saturation (or chroma)** meaning the intensity or colorfulness is bright (most intense) or dull (less intense). Less intense colors are less saturated (and often have some complementary colors in them). Just because colors are less intense does not mean the value is lighter. You can have a color that has darker value but has dull or low saturation. Black, white, and grey have zero saturation and an indeterminate hue.

TINTS, TONES, AND SHADES

If that wasn't confusing enough, there are more ways to describe color: tints, tones, and shades. **Tint** refers to any hue that white is added to. Unfortunately, white pigment cannot be added to dye because white is always opaque where dye is transparent. You can use the term tint when working on dye projects to describe how you will be creating a very light "pastel" version of a color on light fabric that would look as if white was added to the color. **Tones** are what I call "designer colors" and include all hues that are greyed. These are usually achieved by adding the complement to the hue. These are most interesting on stage as they play nicely with lights and are generally more unique colors than those straight off the shelves of the fabric store. **Shades** are hues that have black added to them. For an example of each of these, please see Figure 2.8.

MONOCHROMATIC AND ANALOGOUS COLOR

A few other color descriptors you may come across is analogous and monochromatic color. Analogous colors are those next to each other on the color wheel like red, red–orange, and orange or, as in Figure 2.8, yellow–green, green, and blue–green. Monochromatic colors are in the same hue family but in varying values and intensities. There is a fantastic blog on munsell.com where they discuss how color and musical composition are similar. They discuss how, like musical cords, there are common guidelines on "color cords" that create harmonious compositions. They further discuss how using analogous and complementary colors help us compose the most harmonious color arrangements.

Figure 2.8 A visual description of value, chroma/saturation, and analogous and monochromatic color.

WHAT IS A PANTONE??

Pantones are color chips, swatches, and color swatch strips used by designers across all disciplines from entertainment design to interior, graphic, and apparel design. Anyone in the world can buy and reference Pantone products on-site. Every color, tint, tone, and shade can be found in Pantone books and other formats. Some books feature swatches that are coated with a gloss and others that are matte. If a designer in Canada wants a dress dyed chartreuse she can tell the dyer in France that she wants Pantone 15–0343 and the dyer can pull out their Pantones and see 15–0343 in their own studio. Likewise a designer in the same theater or film set can pull a Pantone chip from the book and hand it directly to the dye shop. Using Pantone chips eliminates color-name confusion, the time required to mail a swatch, or color distortion between different computer screens. Pantone books are on average around $300–$500 or more, new. Older gently used Pantone books can be purchased on EBay for significantly less. Go down the rabbit hole that is pantone.com for color education and to view all things Pantone.

Figure 2.9 Pantone books can be bought used for a fraction of the price!

THE BOTTOM LINE

Hopefully, by now, you have a strong foundation and understanding of color theory, what it takes to make useful color gamuts for whatever type of shop you work, an understanding of color terms, and some basics to get you started mixing color. If you still feel uncertain about color and all of these science terms I've thrown at you – don't worry! With time and experience you will "see" color and, after a while, will be able to tint and tone it any way you like! If you would like some instruction with mixing colors in the dye room, there are starting points for color mixing with union dyes in Chapter 5. If you are super-duper interested in color and color theory, there is a great website by the folks at Munsell[6] (of the Munsell color wheel): Munsell.com.

NOTES

1. Westland, Steven. "Contemporary Colour Theory-Color Primaries." Webinar from Society of Dyers and Colourists, England, May 19th, 2020. https://colour.network/.
2. "Color Theory in Under Two Minutes Videos 1–11." Colour Chat, Last modified July 9th, 2018, https://colourware.org/.
3. Dr Steven Westland, Email to author, October 29th, 2020.
4. Beth Herd, Facebook Message to author, July 2nd, 2020.
5. Igamells, Wilfred. *Colour for Textiles: A User's Handbook*. West Yorkshire, England: Society of Dyers and Colourists, 1993, 147.
6. Munsell Color. "Visual Analytics with Complementary & Analogous Color Harmony." https://munsell.com.

3

READY, SET, GO!
FIBERS, ADDITIVES, AND SWATCHING

Dyeing fabric can be tricky business! Although dyeing becomes easier the longer you practice, it continues to provide challenges to even the most experienced dyer. In this chapter I attempt to lay out the major players that lay the foundation for dyeing: fiber identification, how to prepare your fabric for dyeing, descriptions of additives and auxillaries, and swatching colors.

Figure 3.1 Fabric warehouses like LZ's fabrics (pictured) in Chicago have a multitude of fabric choices – it's up to you to identify if the fabric is dyeable and then which dye to use; this is based on fiber content.
Photo courtesy of August Mayer.

DOI: 10.4324/9781351130677-4

FIBERS

Let's talk about the WHAT first. What are we dyeing? Knowing how to identify fiber is the only way to choose the most appropriate dye. There are multitudes of fabrics to choose from and each have their own unique properties and chemistry. The main categories I will discuss will be based on dyes used to color these fibers: cellulose, protein, nylon, and polyester.

CELLULOSE FIBERS

Fibers that fall into this category are derived from plants or trees. They include cotton, hemp, linen, jute, bamboo, ramie, sisal, rayon, lyocell, and so on. Some of these, like cotton, are considered natural fiber because they are minimally processed and still retain properties close to the original form of the plant. Other cellulose fibers are considered synthetic like rayon for example; the cellulose fibers are made into a pulp and then go through further processing to create rayon fabric. Whether the fabric is natural or man-made, all cellulosic fibers have a similar molecular structure, and therefore the dye made for cellulose, fiber-reactive dye, works to color all cellulose fibers. It is worth noting properties of a few of these fibers in their relation to the dye process.

Figure 3.2 Cellulose fibers: where they begin and end!
Photos courtesy of pixabay.com.

Cotton dyes well, can handle high temps, and takes ages to dry. Mercerized cotton has round fibers resulting in high reflectivity rate and therefore results in bright hues. Permanent press fibers have been smashed permanently and thus have low reflectivity and result in dull colors.

Linen, the oldest fiber in the lot, is actually stronger when wet and dries much quicker than cotton but has very little resilience[1] and therefore wrinkles quicker.

Rayon swells to twice the size when immersed in water and the fibers also become very weak and rip easily so, be gentle with rayon in the dyebath!

PROTEIN FIBERS

You are a protein fiber! All fibers that are derived from animals and insects contain molecules that are similar enough that all can be dyed with a similar dye process. Acid dyes are the go-to dye for these fibers but fiber reactive and vat dyes work as well when paired with an acid additive. Protein fibers include wool, cashmere (goat), angora (rabbit), camel, alpaca, silk, leather, hair, and so on.

Wool has an outer layer of scales that overlap like roof tiles that swell and open with heat, moisture, and agitation. These scales close in cool water so when the rinse water temperature is lowered drastically, these scales can lock on each other: felting and shrinkage being the result. This is a one-way street, once you shrink or felt wool, it will live in that state to the end of its days.

Silk comes in a variety of colors and textures and each variety comes from different types of caterpillars! Here's the deal – the caterpillar creates a cocoon of one continuous filament that can be up to 3,000 feet long that is held together with a gum called sericin. Silk organza contains a lot of sericin, which gives organza its stiff hand. The finest and smoothest silks are made from using the continuous filament of one cocoon spun together with other continuous filaments. The moth eats its way through the cocoon fibers when it emerges so, to prevent this, the cocoons are boiled, steamed, or set in the sun to kill the moths before they emerge to preserve the continuous filament. There are nonviolent silks (see wanderingsilk.org) that are made by allowing the moth to hatch then spinning the shorter filaments of silk together, but the price is about double that of regular silk. A big PSA about silk and wool: both are damaged by the sun and by *chlorine bleach*.

Figure 3.3 Protein fibers come from a variety of sources; here are the most common.
Photos courtesy of pixabay.com.

COOL FACT ABOUT SILK FOR COSTUME DESIGNERS!

Not all silk is made by killing moths. Actually, all non-filament silks, known as spun silk, allow the moth to hatch cocoons, then the shortened filaments are spun together. This creates a rougher texture and luster; it is favored by Buddhist monks[2] because of the nonviolent nature of the fabric's origin.

Figure 3.4 Spun silk (left), Buddhist Monk wearing raw silk robe (right).
Photos courtesy of pixabay.com.

Leather has an entire chapter devoted to it, Chapter 7, so I will not review the qualities of leather here. I will note that leather dries out after being exposed to water, acid, and dye, and therefore requires fat liquor and stretching in addition to an extremely detailed dye process. Acid dyes are also used on this protein fiber.

Figure 3.5 Synthetic fibers like polyester are often derived from petroleum sources.
Photos courtesy of pixabay.com.

SYNTHETIC FIBERS

These are fibers made from materials that require maximum processing. The most commonly used are polyester, nylon, and acrylic. Each synthetic fiber bonds with specific dyes and carriers made just for that fiber.

Nylon is a synthetic fiber made in a very similar fashion to polyester. It has a molecular structure similar to that of protein fibers and can therefore be dyed with acid dyes! It can also be colored with disperse and vat dyes.

Polyester is a wide category that covers TONS of different fabric names. It is inexpensive to create and textile scientists have become very good at creating synthetic fibers that look and feel like natural fibers, at a fraction of the price. These fibers must be dyed with disperse dyes. Polyester and nylon can be permanently creased, pleated, or manipulated with heat.

FIBER IDENTIFICATION

You must get as get as close as possible to identifying the fiber type of your material; then and only then can you start making choices as to which type of dye and method to use. It is very important to not skip this step! The correct choice in dye will result in the best **color fastness** and chemical bond.

There are tips and tricks I have learned and shamelessly stolen from textile scientists to identify mystery fibers. The main point of identifying fabrics is to find out if the fiber is cellulose, protein, nylon, acetate, or polyester. There are a few things you can do to learn the fiber content of fabric: the hand of fabric and to light the fabric on fire! The hand of fabric is the surface feel of the fabric and how it acts when you squeeze it in your hand. Real silk will have a tooth to it while synthetic poly-silk will not have the same tooth. Real silk will wrinkle while the poly-silk will not wrinkle as quickly. That said, textile manufacturers are getting very good at creating synthetic fabrics that look and feel like the real thing. The best way in my opinion to figure out fiber content is the **burn test.** I swear I'm not a pyro, but I have been known to sneakily light swatches on fire in the back room of fabric shops with loads of mystery fabric to discern whether or not it is dyeable. I have created my own burn chart that I share with my students (Figure 3.6) that has the essential qualities of burning fibers that an entertainment dyer must know. There are many other techniques that textile chemists employ to identify fibers – for example to observe if a fiber melts in acetone or formaldehyde. Since we as dyers are exposed to so many other toxins, and the burn test is so straightforward in identifying fibers to the level we require in entertainment, I have left these techniques to the chemists and out of the dye room.

FABRIC PREPARATION AND RINSING

SCOURING FABRIC AND TEXTILE DETERGENTS

When do we need to scour fabrics before dyeing? Unless the fabric or garment is from a reputable dye supplier and labeled that it has been prepared for dyeing, it must be scoured. Make sure, if a garment is marked "prepared for dyeing", it is made with cotton or polyester thread; this way you will know if the threads will dye or not (if that's important to your project).

Commercial garments and fabrics are always sized with some sort of substance and have been handled and packaged by humans and therefore contain sizing, starch, waxes, oils, fingerprints, silk gum, or other substances that can inhibit the bonding of dyes. To prepare fabric for dyeing, these substances must be **scoured** or washed out using an industrial textile detergent. The two most popular are Synthrapol (Metapex in the UK) or Dharma Textile Detergent.

These detergents can be used as a pre-wash or an after wash for dyed and painted fabrics. They also work as wetting agents or **surfactants** to break the surface tension of water, which makes the water molecules "slippery" to create less resistance to dye particles: especially those that have poor water solubility. These detergents have another wonderful aspect – they are pH

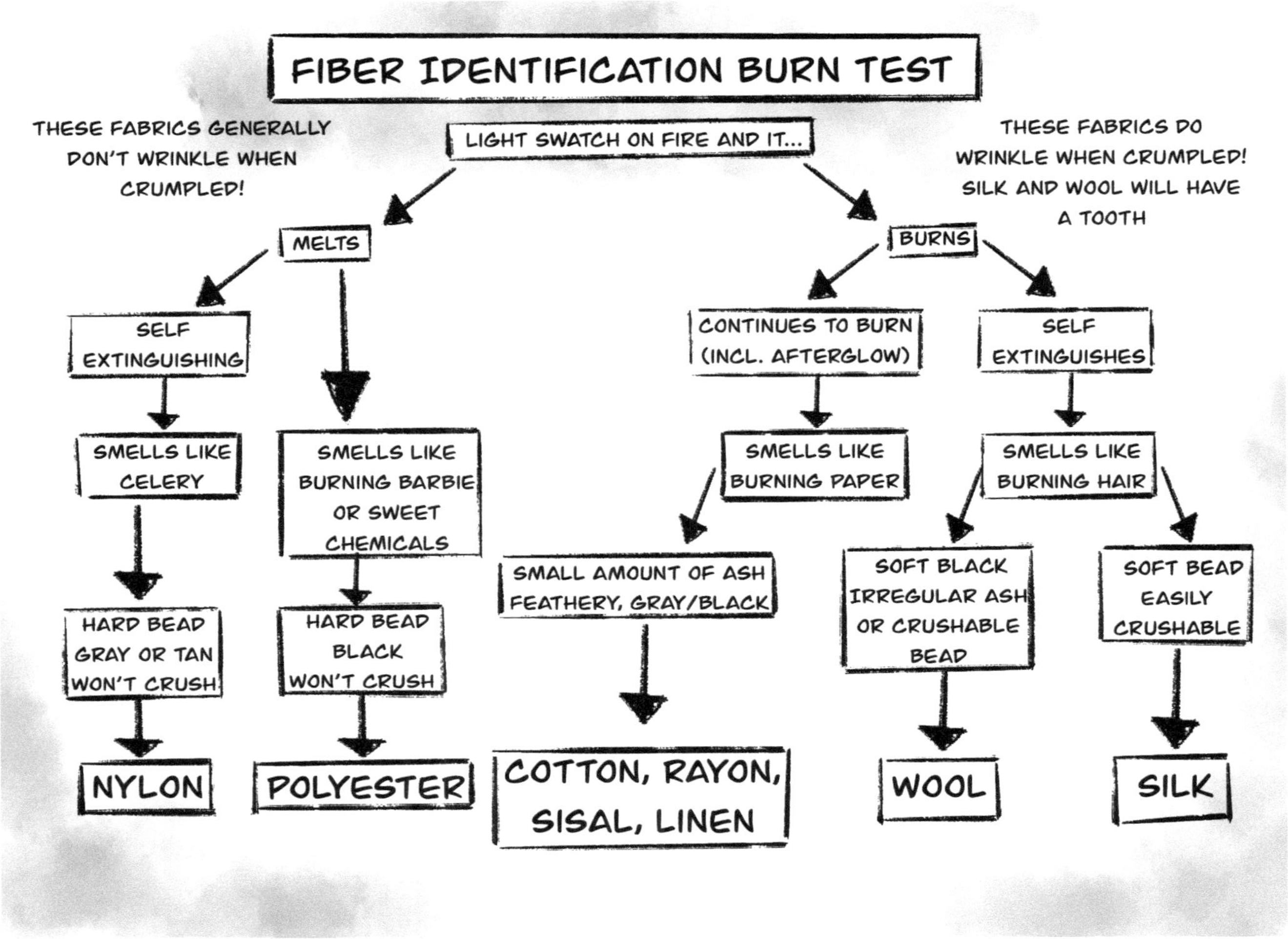

Figure 3.6 Use this to guide you through the identification process. Have a cup of water to extinguish flame under your burn area.

neutral and keep fugitive dye suspended during washing, thus preventing back-staining. Follow the manufacturer's directions for detergent quantity and required water temperatures based on fiber content; as a general rule of thumb halve the amount of detergent you would use in the top loading washing machine if you are using a front loader or washing silk. So, if using 1/4th cup in a top loader, use 1/8th cup in front loader or when washing silk.

Scouring Silk and Wool

This process is different from scouring cellulose and some dyers even use different detergent specifically formulated for silk and wool. If you are dyeing yarn all the time, this may be a great option for you. Otherwise, use Synthrapol or Metapex to scour all fabrics.

Supplies:
- Scale to weigh fabric
- Industrial Detergent like Synthrapol or Metapex, or detergent specifically for protein fibers: Orvus paste soap
- Vessel for hot water scour, large enough to contain fabric and allow it to move freely in water

HOW TO SCOUR SILK AND WOOL

1. **Gear up:** Gloves, apron.
2. **Set up:** Weigh your fabric. Finding your WOG (weight of goods) will help to calculate quantities of detergent needed.
3. In a tub, vat, or pot, measure enough hot water (140°F/60°C) to cover the fabric and allow it to move freely.
4. Add a 1 tsp synthrapol or Orvus paste soap per pound of fabric.
5. Using a long-handled spoon, gently swish fabric for at least 30 minutes to an hour.
6. Let bath cool and rinse fabric in warm water. If in a time crunch: rinse fabric in same-temperature water then successively cooler baths as not to felt wool or shock silk.

Scouring Cellulose

This can be in a stove top pot, vat, or **washing machine.** I prefer to throw it in the washer because it saves my arms for other processes!

Supplies:
- Scale to weigh fabric
- Soda ash
- Industrial detergent like Synthrapol or Metapex
- Vessel for hot water scour, large enough to contain fabric and allow it to move freely in water

HOW TO SCOUR CELLULOSE

1. **Gear up:** Gloves, apron.
2. **Set up:** Weigh your fabric. Finding your WOG (weight of goods) will help to calculate quantities of detergent needed.
3. In a tub, vat, or pot, measure enough hot water (180°F/82°C) to cover the fabric and allow it to move freely.

4. Add 2 tsp of Synthrapol and 3 tbl soda ash for 1 lb of fabric OR 1 tsp Synthrapol per gallon (4L) of water.
5. Simmer for 30 minutes to an hour, swishing with a long-handled spoon.
6. Make sure to rinse thoroughly in hot water (10–15 minutes); rinse until the "slimy" feeling is gone.
7. **If using a washing machine to scour:** add 2 Tbl industrial detergent to a hot (140°F/60°C) and 2 tbl soda ash, wash and let agitate for about 15 minutes. In a front-loading machine, use 1 tbl textile detergent and wash for 15 minutes.

THE FINAL RINSE – SILK AND WOOL
This is the final rinse to ensure dye does not transfer to your performer! It will break any weak bonds and allow fugitive dyes to leave the fabric, thus coloring the water.

Supplies:
- Industrial detergent like Synthrapol or Metapex
- Vessel/tub for room temp–cool water rinse, large enough to contain fabric and allow it to move freely in water

HOW TO DO FINAL RINSE CELLULOSE AFTER DYEING
1. **Gear up:** gloves, apron.
2. Fill vessel with *room temperature* water to cold water because hot water will actually break the bonds of acid dye to fiber.
3. Add 1/4th tsp industrial detergent per pound of fabric.
4. Gently swish and wash fabric for at least 5 minutes – don't be too vigorous with silk and wool, that can felt wool and remove the luster or shine of silk! You will notice the water taking on dye color – this is a good thing! You are actually breaking the weak dye bonds in this rinse instead of on your actor!
5. Follow this rinse with a few rinses in cold water until the water runs clear.

The Final Rinse – Cellulose
This is the final rinse to ensure dye does not transfer to your performer! It will break any weak bonds and allow fugitive dyes to leave the fabric, thus coloring the water. This rinse is performed following cold-water rinses to remove soda ash. Once the "slimy" feel is gone, your soda ash has been washed out and you are ready for the final rinse.

Supplies:
- Industrial detergent like Synthrapol or Metapex
- Vessel for hot water scour, large enough to contain fabric and allow it to move freely in water

HOW TO DO FINAL RINSE CELLULOSE AFTER DYEING
1. **Gear up:** gloves, apron.
2. Fill vessel with hot water (180°F) add 1/4th tsp Synthrapol or Metapex per 1 lb fabric.
3. Vigorously swish fabric with a long-handled spoon for at least 5–10 minutes. You will notice the water taking on dye color – this is a good thing! You are actually breaking the weak dye bonds in this rinse instead of on your actor!

4. Follow this rinse with a few rinses in cold water until the water runs clear.
5. If dyeing cellulose, add 2 tablespoons of soda ash.
6. Make sure to rinse thoroughly (10–15 minutes); if using soda ash, rinse until the "slimy" feeling is gone.

DHARMA TEXTILE DETERGENT VS. JAQUARD SYNTHRAPOL

Because of supply chain issues in 2020 and 2021 there was some difficulty purchasing the textile detergent Synthrapol. In response, Dharma Trading came out with their own detergent: Dharma Textile Detergent. From Dharma's website they say that their product is more eco-friendly (although they do not describe why . . .) and in comparing the SDSs of both products (the most recent Synthrapol SDS is from 2016 in the ProChem SDS Database) the Dharma Detergent requires less protective equipment, but both products cause skin and eye irritation, so wear gloves and goggles.

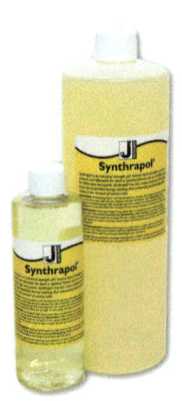

Figure 3.7 Jacquard Synthrapol (left) and Dharma Textile Detergent (right). Many brands offer Synthrapol.

WETTING OUT FABRIC

Wetting out your fabric is not the same as a prewash but it can be all done at the same time. This literally means getting your fabric wet – but doing it *evenly* to ensure your dye reaches the entirety of the fabric. You can scour then soak fabric in water until you are ready to dye or keep fabric covered by a towel or add it directly to your dye bath. If you have scoured your fabric and dried it, it is best to wet out fabric in a few gallons of hot water and a half teaspoon (for 2.5 lbs of fabric) of synthrapol (water and detergent amounts depend on amount of fabric you're using). Make sure to wring out excess water before adding fabric to your dye bath.

To wet out felt, it is helpful to add a cap of calsoline oil to your water before wetting felt. This will help to further break the surface tension and deliver water deeper into the felt.

DRYING FABRIC

Drying fabric can be done in many ways including drying on a clothes line, in the dryer, and in a towel. There are considerations when choosing which way to go. I would choose a drying line if I had a large amount of fabric, I was drying wool, or delicate garments. I would chose the dryer if I was drying silk (dry on medium–high for industrial dryers), cotton, rayon, or synthetic fibers. For extremely delicate fibers or garments I use the squeezy towel technique where I lay the item flat on a towel and roll the towel up, slowly squeezing with every fill roll (Figure 3.8). In my sample, I was drying two rayon-silk swatches.

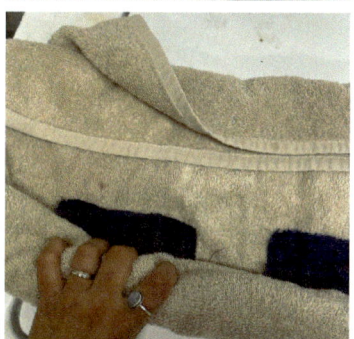

Figure 3.8 Wringing out delicate fabric with a towel. From top to bottom.

TECHNIQUES

Figure 3.9 Mixed up dye concentrate ready to be directly applied or used to create a bath!

DYE CONCENTRATES

This is a concentrate made with dye powder (and often urea water) that can be diluted for immersion dyeing or used as is for direct application. It is fabulous for using a variety of colors in a classroom environment because you don't have students mixing dye powder continually, which limits exposure to dye particles! Concentrates are also beneficial because once they are mixed up, you can work and mix colors very quickly and easily; many film/TV dyers use this method because of the speedy results. See individual sections on creating dye concentrates for specific dye classes.

MIXING DYE CLASSES

Many experienced dyers actually mix dye classes together when faced with manufactured garments and mystery blended fibers. It takes knowledge and experience to know how much soda ash, acid, or other auxiliaries you may need when mixing dye classes. Union dyes (Chapter 5) are commercial dyes that premix dye classes taking their best guesstimate at which ratios of different classes need to be included to dye most fabric.

PASTING OUT DYE

Paste out dye by using a small glass or metal container, adding dye and a SMALL amount of water at a time, smashing the dye into the water to create a paste. When your mixture has absorbed all of the water, if there is powder remaining, add a few more drops of water. If you added too much water and you have chunks of powder floating in your bowl, add a little more dye (better than wasting the original dye) or mix in the powder as best you can. Do this until all dye is dissolved. For acid, disperse, or vat dyes, boil a quart of water then add it to your dye paste slowly until it all dissolved in the boiling water. For MX fiber-reactive dyes, bring the water temperature to no higher than 105°F; higher temps will destroy dye and produce less than desirable results. Strain this through a strainer covered in pantyhose. This will be your dye concentrate and will have a shelf life of a few weeks or longer if you keep it refrigerated.

ADDITIVES

Dyes, in and of themselves, are not always the hazardous part of the dyeing process, but some additives like **carriers** and **auxillary chemicals,** that help the dye bond to the fibers, can be extremely harmful to the user so please read carefully how to handle these products, and, when in doubt, consult the SDS!

Figure 3.10 Pasting out dye. Take the time to do this and you will be happy you did! Mix water in gradually to make sure you don't add too much and mess up your measured amounts of dye.

ACIDS

We add acid to the dyebath when dyeing protein fibers. Acids come in many forms and choosing which one depends on what you are dyeing and how much solution (size of the dyebath) you want to end up with. You CAN use these acids in conjunction with each other, especially ammonium sulfate and other acids.

- **56% Acetic Acid** is one of the strongest acids used in dyeing textiles, aside from glacial acetic acid. This can help by adding very little liquid to the dyebath to lower pH, thus keeping the ratio of dyebath solution to dye low.
- **Ammonium Sulfate –** This product is used mainly as an additive to acid dye baths to slow the strike time of dye. This is useful when using super milling acid dyes as the wash fastness is fantastic but the strike is quick, often leading to uneven color. You can use ammonium sulfate in combination with citric acid – see the following box for Dharma's experiment using citric acid and ammonium sulfate together and separate with the same dharma acid dye. Comes in powdered form. Use 1 tbl for 1 lb of fabric.
- **Citric acid crystals** are my favorite. This is a powdered substance that looks like sugar or salt. It stores well and you don't need much to acidify your dye bath. A dust mask and eye protection is required for use. Get this from any large dye supplier. Comes in powdered form. Use 1 tbl for 1 lb of fabric.
- **Glacial acetic acid (food grade)** is the big dog of the acids used in leather dyeing. This is a very concentrated acetic acid with very little liquid (especially compared to vinegar) at a whopping 99.7% acetic acid. It gets the name glacial because it becomes ice when cooled to 61.7°F/16.5°C. **It is caustic, ignites with flame, and can cause severe burns – so take care!** One tablespoon of glacial acetic acid is the equivalent of around 12.5 table spoons of vinegar. I know, you're thinking to yourself "that's not so much more liquid to add to a solution . . . it won't increase my bath that much! I'd rather use something I can eat over something caustic!" While vinegar is much safer to use, there are instances where you must use a stronger acid. Some acid dye processes, like leather for example, require a very low pH in a very small solution to fully use the dye and achieve good color. If you are dyeing 10 lbs of leather, you would probably need around 16 oz (or 2 cups) of glacial acetic acid for the entire process. To get 16 oz/2 cups of acetic acid from using vinegar, you would need to use about 50 cups of vinegar. That is a lot of liquid! Comes in liquid form.

- **Vinegar** – yes, just plain old household white vinegar can help to create an acidic bath. It is the least toxic, as it is edible (but not in large quantities of course) but compared to the other acids, there is very little acid at 4–10%, and there is a lot of water in vinegar, thus creating a very large dyebath if you want to have a very acidic bath. Buy from the grocery store as a liquid!

DHARMA TRADING EXPERIMENTED WITH ACID![3]

We did five tests to demonstrate the effect Ammonium Sulfate can have on your results. Because of our sample sizes we used solutions of Citric Acid and Ammonium Sulfate created with 1 tbls dry powder to 16 oz of water.

1st Test: Control – Used 2 tsp Citric Acid solution – mottled
2nd Test: Just Ammonium Sulfate – 2 tsp of solution – did not exhaust, all color did not strike
3rd Test: 4 tsp of Ammonium Sulfate solution – some did, not all
4th Test: 2 tsp each Citric Acid and Ammonium Sulfate solutions added at the same time – mottled, struck too fast as with 1st Test.
5th Test: 2 tsp Ammonium Sulfate solution used at start of bath, 2 tsp citric acid solution added at the end of the bath – perfect! Even. Exhausted.

Figure 3.11 Dharma's test results: from left to right, 1st test to final test.
Photo courtesy of Photo for Dharma Trading Co. by Elizabeth Holdmann.

CALSOLENE OIL

This product can be added to a dye bath or be used to presoak to break the surface tension of water even more than an industrial detergent. It is great for tightly woven fabrics and felt, where the dye may have a hard time penetrating fiber. It also makes the dye take more evenly and is recommended in fiber-reactive immersion dyeing.

LUDIGOL

This additive can be helpful in direct painting, printing, and dyeing. Ludigol keeps the dyes from reducing as they normally do when mixed with water, hence creating more vibrant colors. It is generally not used for immersion dyeing. Some people swear by it, especially silk artists.

METAPHOS

Hard Water? Use Metaphos!
Hard water can present challenges to a dyer because hardness fills the molecular space in water and prevents dye or additives from filling this space. You can often tell if you have hard water when adding soda ash to water and it **flocculates** or forms clumps. To counter this water hardness, we add metaphos 1/4th teaspoon per 8 oz. dye solution (dharma.com). Some use Calgon to soften water, but it is scented, which often discourages dyers from using it.

MILSOFT
This product is an industrial fabric softener that can help if your dye process has left your fabric rough or stiff. Use this product AFTER you have completed your dye process as Milsoft can inhibit additional dye from bonding with fabric. To use add 1 teaspoon per gallon in a hot bath and agitate for 10 minutes. Rinse with warm water.

RETAYNE
If you're dyeing a mystery blend fabric and are afraid your dye is going to bleed because you're not exactly sure which dye to use AND you can make sure your finished garment is never washed in hot water, Retayne is a great product to help in prevention of color bleed. This product helps to positively charge dye molecules[4] to improve adherence to fabric. This product can be used before or after dyeing. Quilters often use it before dyeing and direct dyers use it after dyeing to set dyes.

HOW TO USE RETAYNE
1. Fill a container with enough hot water ~140°F (60°C) to cover your fabric.
2. Add 1 teaspoon of Retayne per 1 yard of fabric.
3. Add dry fabric and swish and soak in the bath for 20–30 minutes allowing the water to fully penetrate the fabric.
4. Wash with cold water and let dry. Never wash in hot water – it may release the Retayne and your dye.

SALT
- **Non-iodized salt** is used as an exhausting agent in dyeing. It has an electrostatic charge that pushes dye through the water on to the fabric. I buy salt in 50 lb bags and store it in 5 gallon buckets with gamma lids (see Figure 3.12: bucket with gamma lid).
- **Glauber's salt** is a type of salt that some like to use when dyeing silk, nylon, or wool and using fiber-reactive turquoise; the claim is that it can yield brighter colors! Honestly, I only ever used non-iodized because the dye shops I worked in bought it in bulk!

Figure 3.12 Five-gallon bucket with gamma lid that can easily be screwed on to store salt and solutions.

SODA ASH

A chemical that causes a molecular reaction to take place between fabric and dye. Also known as sodium bicarbonate. Also used to scour fabric before dyeing. Some breakdown artists use it to lightly age commercial garments. This chemical raises the pH of a dyebath creating an alkaline bath, a perfect environment for bonding fiber-reactive dyes to cellulose fabric!

2% SODA ASH SOLUTION (SODA ASH SOAK RECIPE)

This is the solution you can use to presoak garments for direct application.

Supplies

2/3rd cup (100 g) soda ash
1 quart (1 liter) warm water
Container to hold and/or store solution
Long spoon to mix and dissolve powder

How to Make a Soda Ash Solution

1. **Gear up!** Gloves, apron, dust filter mask.
2. **Fill** your container with warm water.
3. **Dissolve** soda ash into water by adding gradually, mixing with a spoon.
4. **Store** solution for up to 3–6 months. Water will start to evaporate at this point. Stir before reusing.

SODIUM HYDROSULPHITE (A.K.A. HYDRO)

This additive is used to reduce vat dyes, removes color from fabric, and helps whiten antique textiles as it is not as aggressive as bleach. It is the main reducing agent for indigo dye, a type of vat dye. Dharma claims it works especially great on wool and silk when using indigo or other vat dyes. Hydro starts to work at 90°F and at higher temps (140°F) works faster. This product has a long shelf life and provides a quicker reaction than thiourea dioxide. To use as a discharge agent, it must be used in equal parts with soda ash at a rolling boil. Highly flammable! **Use acid vapor cartridges in half-face respirator with this product.**

Thiourea Dioxide (a.k.a.Thiox): a reducing agent that lifts specific types of dye – also used in reducing vat dyes. Must be used hot. Releases an acid gas as it decomposes – **use acid vapor cartridges in half-face respirator with this product.**

UREA

A synthetic nitrogen compound that increases the solubility of dye. It makes dye think it is in more water than it really is, so this is great for mixing up concentrated solutions. Some say it makes water wetter!

10% UREA WATER SOLUTION

This is the solution you will use as the water for your *fiber-reactive* dye concentrates and powder pasting!

Supplies

- 1 quart (1 liter) hot water (95° F/35°C)
- 2/3rd cup (100 g) urea
- Container to hold and/or store solution
- Long spoon to mix and dissolve powder

How to Make a Urea Water Solution

1. **Gear up!** Gloves, apron, dust filter mask.
2. **Set up!** Spread out a towel misted with water under the vent hood or mixing box. This is where you will mix your urea.
3. **Measure urea:** with a level measure of 2/3rd c urea, add to an empty 1 quart container.
4. **Add water:** measure 1 quart of hot water into the container continually stirring until all urea is dissolved.
5. **Store:** cap container – this can be stored for up to 6 months. If it starts to smell like ammonia, it has gone bad and needs to be tossed.

SWATCHING

Swatching is a very important step in the dye process, especially when matching color. There are many reasons swatching is important: to conserve dye and additives, to save fabric that you may ruin just sending into a vat of the wrong color, to know what colors will look like **on the actual fabric or garment** (this can be very different from the dye companies' color swatch), and to know what different colors will look like together on a specific fabric.

CAPTAIN'S LOG: DYE CONDITIONS ON THIS PLANET ARE FAVORABLE FOR SWATCHING!

Get ready to log your variables when swatching! This is the place you will track all of the conditions like: how much water, the temperature, quantity of dye and additives were used in each swatch process. This will enable you to show a designer or assistant your swatches, let them hmmm and haw over them for a while, then for you to be able to repeat your swatch result on the real-deal fabric or garment. Please see the appendices and web content for this book for a variety of swatch sheets from Broadway to Lort dye shops. Not all variables and conditions need to be tracked for every swatching session but following is a list of things you might consider tracking.

CONDITIONS AND VARIABLES TO TRACK
- Original fabric swatch and desired color; pantone or color swatch design team gave you
- Denote what side of fabric to be dyed (isn't always the one you think!)
- Water temperature: initial and end temps
- Time in and time out
- Quantity of dye(s) used
- Quantity of additives used and time lapsed in using them, e.g., "soda ash added 15 minutes after adding fabric to bath"

- pH of dye bath
- Percentage of concentrates used (if using concentrates)
- Additional dye/mordants/time/etc., for following swatches (see OSF swatchbook)

READY, SET, SWATCH! SWATCHING WITH POWDERED DYE

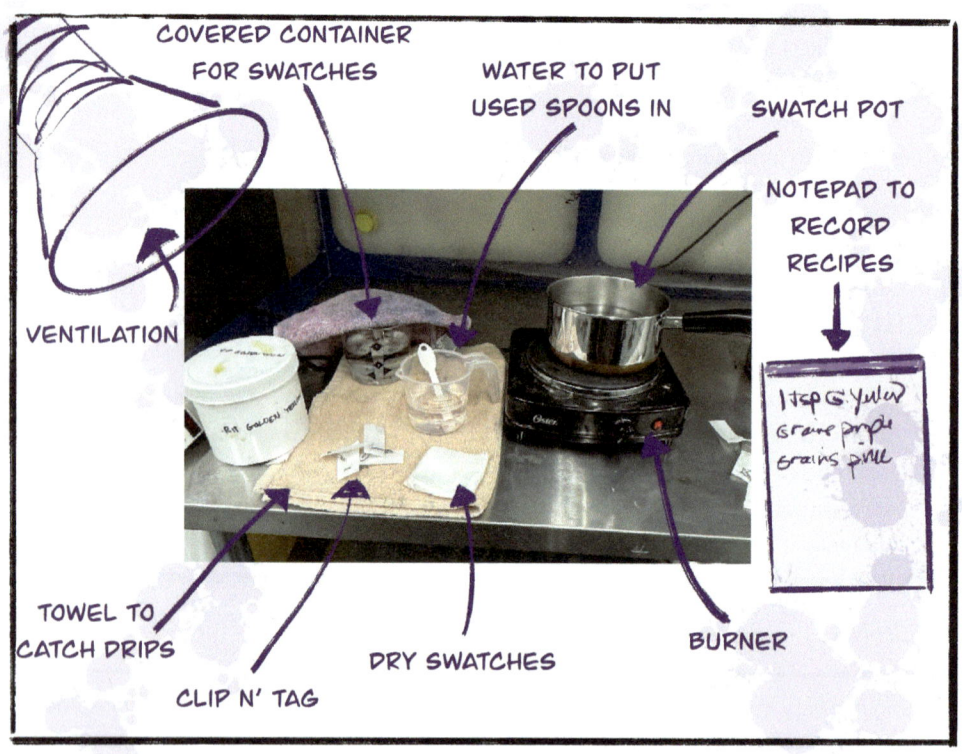

Figure 3.13 The ideal swatch setup. A water-filled covered container for wet swatches, a wet cup with water to minimize releasing dye powder into the air, and many other useful elements to keep things neat.

CUSTOM NOTATIONS

Over the years I have met many a dyer who use custom notations on dye quantities that I think are useful. They come from the need for just a tiny bit of another color dye to tone the current swatch bath color. The wet dip is where the measuring spoon is wet (not dripping) and then dipped in dye powder. Wet tip is similar but only the tip is dipped in dye powder. Grains are the smallest amount you can use, and I have used grains, in toning color. I created this drawing (Figure 3.14) of different notations shared by dyers I've worked with through the years.

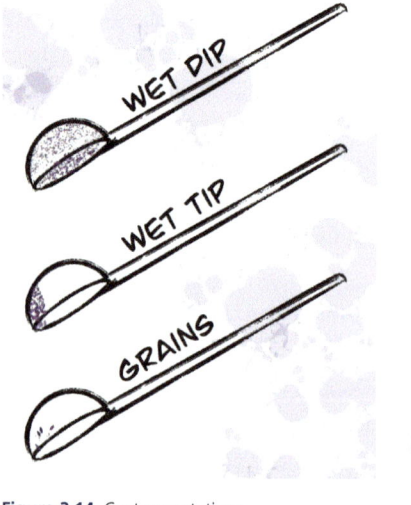

Figure 3.14 Custom notations.

Supplies:

- Extra scoured fabric cut into 3" x 3" pieces (or about that size). Yes, you will need to sacrifice some of your fabric to the dye gods to determine the correct color mixtures!
- 2 cup container to keep undyed swatches wet
- Container to rinse powder off spoons
- Measuring spoons (I like the ones that go down to 1/32nd") or digital scale
- 2–4 quart steel pan
- Burner
- Towel to lay wet spoons on
- Swatch book/notes and sharpie (or other pen that will work on any paper)
- Stopwatch/clock/timer to track time

HOW TO CREATE DYE SWATCHES

1. **Gear up!** Gloves, apron, dust particle mask.
2. **Set up!** Get out your swatching notes and a sharpie. Note how much water, the temperature, quantity of dye and additives used. Add your pile of cut swatches to the water container and cover to keep fugitive dye from landing on swatches. Heat 2–4 cups of water depending on dye concentration desired.
3. Once dye is pasted, add it to the pot. Note: START SMALL . . . do not use more than 1/2 teaspoon or 6 grams of dye TOTAL in swatching. Using more will give a quantity ratio of dye that is wasteful when moving to a vat. At this point, depending on the dye class you are using, perform the entire dye process exactly as you would for the real process on your final fabric. This includes additives and rinsing!
4. Dry your swatch with a hairdryer (see Chapter 1 for Oregon Shakespeares' cool drying rig for a swatch hair dryer!) and iron it. It is difficult to tell what your color looks like on a wrinkled piece of fabric.
5. Add amount of time in bath, amount before adding additives, after adding additives, etc.

SWATCHING TIPS . . .

1. **Wet your swatch:** when you find the perfect recipe for a beautiful color as evidenced in your swatch and now it's time to create a big vat of dye, I recommend wetting your swatch with *water* and hanging it over the edge of the vat. As you dye your yardage, you can compare if the wet yardage is the same color as the wet swatch on the side of the vat! Remember, your swatch is already dyed so, don't dip it into the dye to wet it – that will make the swatch darker!
2. **Use dry-cleaning tags:** use clip 'n' tag waterproof tags and a sharpie to label swatches so you can keep track when swatching multiple pots at once (Figure 3.15).
3. **Dry swatches** with an iron using a paper towel on top and a towel underneath so as not to transfer dye to the ironing boards (Figure 3.16). Switch out paper towels often so you do not transfer dye to another swatch!

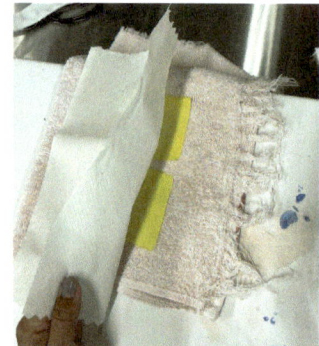

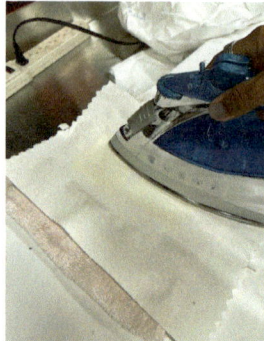

Figure 3.16 Drying a swatch with an iron.

Figure 3.15 Dry-cleaning tags.

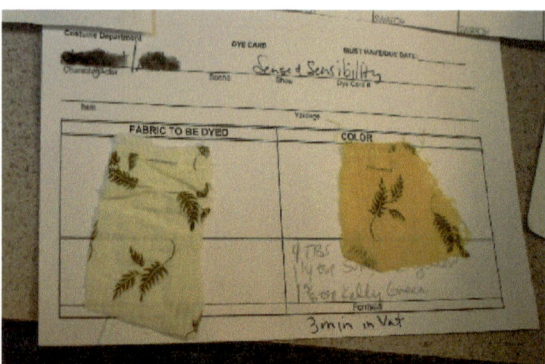

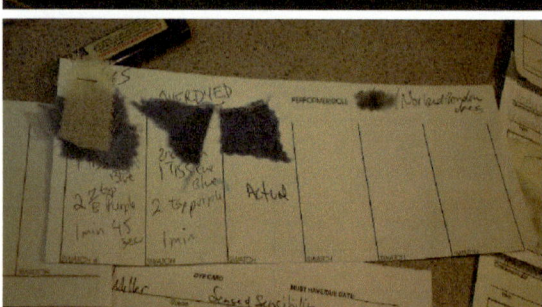

Figure 3.17 As you can see, there are different types of swatch cards – one for the process and ones that track where the dyer started and ended.

SO, NOW WHAT? HOW TO GO FROM A SWATCH TO THE VAT!

A ratio is a mathematical expression that represents the relationship between two numbers, showing the number of times one value contains or is contained within the other. When using acid dyes or fiber-reactive dyes, weighing powders to create ratios is best. When using union dyes, because of the varying salt content in each scoop, I never use a scale and instead use measuring spoons.

How to Find the Ratio When Using Volumetric Measurements

To increase the amount of dye needed for vat dying: find your ratio.

If we used **1/8th teaspoon** (tsp) blue dye and **1/4th tsp** orange dye for our dye sample, the ratio of dye would be **(1:2).** I found this by finding the smallest increment in the ratio (1/8th tsp) and using this number to divide the quantities.

Figure 3.18 An example of a less formal route to track swatch recipes – the back of an old script! Swatch book on right is for 12th Night (C.Des David Reynoso); on the left for the original production of Bright Star (C.Des Jane Greenwood). Bright Star swatches were on vintage 1920s fabric, so the swatches had to be tiny!! Once we built a cadre of swatches Jane liked, she put them all together to make sure they worked well (photo on left).

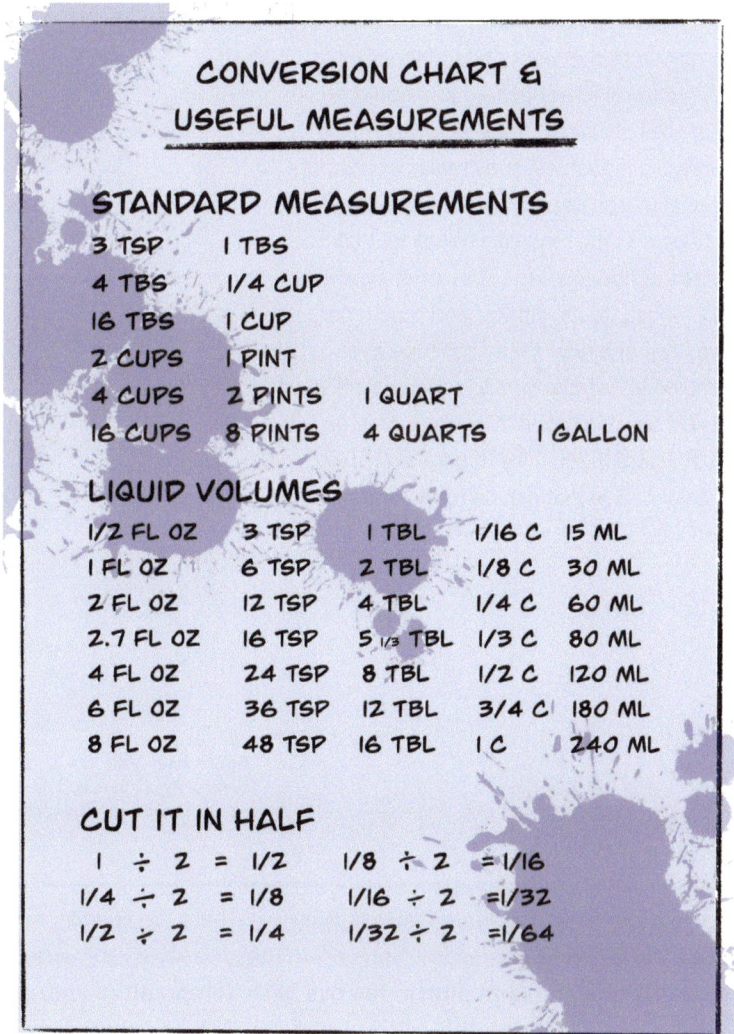

Figure 3.19 Helpful measurements and conversions.

For example
- Blue Dye: 1/8th tsp ÷ 1/8th tsp = 1
- Orange Dye: 1/4th tsp ÷ 1/8th tsp = 2
- Our ratio is 1 portion of blue dye to 2 portions of orange dye, or 1:2

It can be helpful to create a concentrate of this ratio, in a larger amount, that can be used to create a dyebath; just make sure to swatch once more from your to make sure it is a match. You can also just increase powder by ratios again, swatching your increased amount straight from the vat.

Whether you use teaspoons or a digital scale, these measurements will be a place to start when sizing up to a larger vat. It is not foolproof and your fabric may end up being slightly different in color; therefore, once I get my dye mixed up in the vat, I swatch from the vat in a pan, going through the process again to make sure it is an accurate match.

TEST FABRIC SWATCHES

I would be very remiss to not mention Testfabrics.com. They are an amazing family owned and operated company that supplies products to the entertainment and commercial textile industries. They make wonderful swatching products: materials that feature a variety of combinations of fibers in the form of a roll of test fabric in 8 or more stripes of fiber content. They offer synthetic, natural, a blend of these, tools, fabrics, and much more. In Figure 3.20 you can see how each fiber type dyes differently depending on which dye and additives are used. These swatches can be purchased in yardage or large 50 meter rolls (top of Figure 3.20). I like to do a swatch for every type and color of dye that can be found in the dye shop I am working in.

Figure 3.20 Testfabrics 50 meter roll (top), fiber blend undyed (right) and dyed (left) swatch, and natural fiber swatch dyes and undyed.

VARIABLES

Variables are perhaps the most important element in dyeing. There are specific variables that can be altered to achieve whatever outcome you desire. These variables are: **amount and type of dye used, quantity of water, and time in the dye bath, temperature and/or hardness/softness of water, amount of carriers/additives, and pH of the dye bath.** Let's say you are dyeing silk and your silk is not getting the saturation in color you desire. Consider your variables:

is the dye to water ratio high enough? Is the pH low enough there enough acid in my bath (I may not need more dye)? Does the water need to be hotter (may not need more dye)? Does the piece need more time in the bath (this may be the only variable needed to increase)? Is all of the dye dissolving in solution (add additives like urea)? As these variables are adjusted, you will notice that other variables will not need to be adjusted because each variable affects the other. See the graphics on troubleshooting after acid dyes and fiber-reactive dyes in the next chapter.

THE BOTTOM LINE

The ability to identify fiber and quickly recall the corresponding dyes and additives is extremely important knowledge for the dyer. As you will see in the chapter about union dyes (Chapter 5) this knowledge doesn't pertain to fiber-specific dyes as much as they pertain to the pH, specific fiber, and dye conditions. The skill to do dye swatches/samples quickly, in which the conditions can be recreated to dye large amounts of yardage, comes with practice. Choose the logging technique that suits your practice best as you practice and find the best techniques that suit you.

NOTES

1 Brackman, Holly. *The Surface Designer's Handbook: Dyeing, Printing, Painting, and Creating Resists on Fabric.* Loveland, CO: Interweave Press, 2006.
2 Wanderingsilk.org. "Ahima Peace Silk: The Story." www.wanderingsilk.org/ahimsa-silk-the-story.
3 www.dharmatrading.com/home/did-you-know-how-to-take-it-to-the-next-level-with-acid-dyes-using-ammonium-sulfate.html.
4 www.dharmatrading.com.

4

THE LAW OF ATTRACTION

FIBER-SPECIFIC DYES

When we are faced with dyeing a fabric or a garment of known or unknown fiber content, dye choice will be the most important part of your process. The wide variety of fibers in the world require specific dyes and this is why we separate dyes into groups, called **classes**, based on what fiber specific dyes will bond with and/or how the dyes are applied. Because this book is intended for entertainment dyers and artists, I will cover the most commonly used dyes that are applicable to dyeing smaller lots of fabric in a studio or dye shop, and not in a factory setting. The main dye classes I will discuss in this chapter are: **fiber reactive, acid, disperse, direct, and vat dyes**. There are pros and cons to all dye classes and these range from the finished appearance, i.e., color brilliance, to the exposure levels of toxic additives that must be used with certain products.

Figure 4.1 Bob Ross quote on happy accidents. Listen to Bob.
Photo Courtesy of Bob Ross Incorporated.

In this chapter, I have split up dyeing processes by class; however, many dyers prefer to use a mixture of these dyes and additives because it serves the artist dyeing mystery fibers and

DOI: 10.4324/9781351130677-5

unknown blends in manufactured garments. I recommend if you are just embarking on the road to Dyeville, try these processes with the recommended amounts first, then start to play. To become a knowledgeable dyer, experimentation is key! Many times, the dyer learns more from accidents and experiments than performing the perfect process. So, be like Bob Ross and experiment and have happy little accidents.

IT'S A BONDING EXPERIENCE

In order to dye fabric, we apply colorant to the surface of fabric to create a uniform color by creating an aqueous solution, or dyebath, using dye, water, sometimes a heating source, and additives/auxiliaries. Dye diffuses into the fabric as it is absorbed from the dye bath in an attraction process where chemical bonds form between fiber and dye. If you have chosen the appropriate dye and additives for your fabric the result will most likely be that your fabric is very **colorfast** (color does not fade or run easily) and that you have chosen a dye with good **substantivity** (the attraction between dye and fiber). So, in other words, if you choose the correct dye class for your fabric, your dye will not bleed all over your actor! Art dyer and prior PRO Chem Lab Manager Elin Noble talks about creating and breaking these fiber-specific bonds:

> When you apply fiber-reactive dyes to fabric, a chemical reaction occurs and the dye molecules bond with the fabric molecules. The chemical bond cannot be broken or reversed, so the fabric is washfast. To remove color . . . you must destroy the color part of the molecule.

The way to break this bond is with heat and chemicals. Information about this can be found in the chapter on color removing, Chapter 6.

Why is all of this talk about molecules important to the dyer?? In Elin Noble's workshop, "Subtractions and Additions", she notes molecule sizes of the different dyes in relationship to how far the molecules will travel into a fabric that have a mechanical resist like folded and clamped pieces or shibori. Paraphrasing, she says "acid dyes are small particles . . . let's call them mouse sized, while MX fiber reactive dyes are a bit larger, the dog particle; vat dyes are the largest . . . the elephant!" This really helped me visualize the molecules: mouse, dog, and elephant, trying to work their way into the fabric that is folded or stitched and helped me to anticipate how much of the inside parts of my folds would be reached by which types of dyes. She continued, "[This will help you] how to think like a dye – instead of what you want to do . . . what will it [the dye] let you do?"

THE DYES!

It's important to know your dyes. Know them in the way that you understand where to source them, how to use them, what mordants and additives work best with each product, the idiosyncrasies and nuances of each class and brand, and how permanent your bond of dye and fiber will be. Knowing these things comes with experience and trial and error (remember happy accidents!) and will help you anticipate results clearly (or at least clearer) and become quite fast at dyeing. I have created Table 4.1 as a quick reference that includes the major dye suppliers, pros

56 FIBER-SPECIFIC DYES

Table 4.1 Dye Group Characteristics.

Dye Group	Fiber Type	Brand Names	Advantages	Disadvantages	Wash-fastness
Fiber Reactive	Cellulose (cotton, linen, rayon, hemp, etc.) and protein (silk, wool, feathers, fur, hair, leather, etc.)	Dharma, Jaquard, Greatful Dyes, PROChem, Kemtex (UK)	Bright saturated colors; excellent for use in shibori/resist techniques; can use in room temperature water	Process is not quick in a fast-paced environment; difficult to match colors with process time	Very good if final rinse is done well
Acid Dyes	Protein and nylon	PROChem, Aljo, Kemtex (UK), Dharma, Jaquard	Bright saturated colors, dyes nylon well	Must steam directly applied (stamped or printed) dye, must have hot process	Very good
Disperse Dyes	Polyester, acetate, nylon, acrylic	Aljo, PROChem, Rit (DyeMore), Jaquard (iDye Poly)	Dyes polyester well (not Rit or Jaquard)	Dyes acrylic a pale hue, carrier is toxic and smells bad	Very good if you used a carrier and got to the appropriate temperatures in the dye process
Direct Dyes	Cellulose	Aljo, PROChem	A more straightforward dye process compared to fiber reactive	Poor lightfastness and washfastness; availability is low	Poor if not washed in cold water
Union Dyes	All fibers	Rit, Dylon, Jaquard (iDye)	Ubiquitous in entertainment dye shops; easy to use; premixed with salt; used regularly so can predict color outcome	Poor lightfastness and wash fastness; often transfers dye that doesn't bond to fiber (as it has a mix of dye classes)	Good to poor depending on fiber blend and dye process; often a re-dye occurs in a long run of a show
Vat Dyes	Cellulose and protein	Maiwa, PROChem, Aljo	Permanent bright colors even on top of dark colors; beautiful "halo" when using in resist dyeing	End of the road – you cannot discharge this dye; have to use lye and thiox in the process	Very washfast – the highest of all
Natural Dyes	Cellulose and protein	Maiwa	Beautiful "earthy" tones; dye powders mostly sustainably sourced	Limited color gamut; process is long and impractical for fast-paced dye shop (1–2 day process)	Good on cotton; excellent on wool and nylon

and cons of each class of dyes, and how wash fast these dyes are. Another important aspect of dyeing is pH. Understanding what the pH of your dye bath should be can make or break your washout process by either retaining most of the dye (appropriate pH used in bath) or washing out much of your dye (pH of bath too high or low). Please see table 4.2 for pH info for different fibers.

> ## SO, WHAT'S WITH pH AND DYEING? WHY SHOULD I CARE?
>
> As discussed throughout this chapter, the most effective way to color fabric is to choose the correct dye that corresponds to the fabric you are dyeing. Then your job is to create ideal conditions to ensure the dye and fiber are going to bond. These conditions or variables in dyeing include: amount of water and dye used, heat of the dye bath, amount of time fabric is in the bath, and pH! The pH scale is 1–14 ranging from an acidic bath to an alkaline bath (remember high school chemistry?!). See pH ranges for specific dye purposes in Table 4.2.
>
> **Table 4.2** Ideal pH for Dyes and Fabrics.
>
> | | **Very Acidic** | **Acidic** | **Neutral** | **Basic/ Alkaline** | **Very Basic/Highly Alkaline** |
> |---|---|---|---|---|---|
> | **pH value** | 1–3.9 pH | 4–6.9 pH | 7.0–7.9 pH | 9–11.9 pH | 12–14 pH |
> | **Idea Use for Fiber and Dye Types** | Silk, wool, leather, especially leveling acid dyes or when using fiber-reactive dyes to dye protein | Silk, wool, leather, especially Super-milling/ milling and lanaset acid dye | Best for washing silk and wool and to neutralize an acidic or alkaline bath. | Best for using fiber-reactive dyes on cellulosic fibers like cotton, rayon, and bamboo | Vat dyes require a pH 12–14! Only use to scour cotton or other soda ash based products. This can damage wool, silk, and other protein fibers |
>
> **How to measure pH?** There are test strips and pH meters. I prefer to use a meter for two reasons: it gives you an accurate number to the first decimal point and the result is not clouded by dye! Test strips also become dyed and the result is often obscured. Take it from someone who has destroyed a few pH meters in their time . . . when considering which pH meter to purchase, make sure yours comes with calibration fluid and is in the higher temperature threshold (so it doesn't melt in hot water). Remove a cup of the bath water, allow to cool, then using your meter, test the pH. I like Hanna meters which cost around $30.

ACID DYES

Acid dyes are not dyes that people took in the 60s. The name comes from the acidic bath that is required to dye protein fibers (polyamide fibers) including wool, silk, feathers, all animal hair fibers, leather, and even nylon whose chemical composition is similar to silk. In a dye bath, acid dye molecules are negatively charged or **anionic**, so we add acid to the bath, like vinegar or citric acid crystals, to lower the pH of the dye bath and this is where it gets really cool – when the wool or silk in the bath absorb the acid, they become positively charged or **cationic**. It is a strong bond and gives great wash fastness properties to fabric dyed with acid dyes but can be reversed in an ammonia bath which changes the ionic charge.

In industry, we use vinegar, citric acid crystals, and sometimes when dyeing leather, food-grade glacial acetic acid to lower the pH of the dyebath (see Chapter 3 for descriptions of each type of acid). The higher the acid content of your additive, the more rapidly it will lower the pH, and the faster the dye will **strike** or fix itself to the fabric. Please see the additive section of this chapter for descriptions of acid types. Even though these acids seem like "safe acids" to use, take precautions with these additives just as you would with all other dyes! There are many brands of acid dyes; they can be made into concentrates, used directly in a dye bath, and in direct application. They can be used very successfully in direct application like painting or stamping but require steaming or microwaving to fix the dyes. There are a few different types of acid dyes and each type requires a slightly different process. I will list a few of the most frequently used acid dyes and processes.

Figure 4.2 Textile artist Chris Carpenter created soft undulation of color using acid dyes, dyeing 120 yards china silk. Oregon Shakespeare Festival's *Head Over Heels* costume designed by Loren Shaw for the Oracle, played by Michele Mais.
Photo courtesy of Jenny Graham.

CLASSES OF ACID DYES

If you want to get nerdy about it, acid dyes are divided into 3 groups: leveling acid dyes, super-milling/milling acid dyes, and premetallized (or fast acid dyes). The acid dyes we use in entertainment are sold as proprietary names like Dharma Acid Dye, PRO WashFast Acid Dye, Sabraset Acid Dye, etc., and contain a mixture of types of acid dye that are often combined with fiber-reactive dyes so dye companies can provide a large range of colors. In the technical data sheets for each product, the ratio of each dye class and type is often listed.

- **Leveling Acid Dyes** are small molecules and can migrate easily into the fibers creating even and bright colors. The downside is that the wash fastness is poor and the fabric has to be washed in cold water or dry-cleaned. Ideal pH 2.5–3.5.

- **Super-milling/milling Acid Dyes** are large molecules and migration into the fabric is a little more difficult than leveling acid dyes BUT the wash fastness is good! This slow migration means your fabric may not dye as evenly and will require some different additives and constant agitation. Instead of adding acid, add **ammonium sulfate** to the dye bath to "slow" the reaction process, as it starts at a neutral PH, then becomes acidic as the dye bath heats, allowing the larger molecules time to penetrate the fiber more evenly. Ideal pH 5.5–7.0.
- **Lanaset Dyes/Premetalized Acid Dyes** are an even larger molecule that as Dharma Trading[1] notes, bond to the fabric quickly so you have to be careful to apply these dyes evenly and agitate properly. Dharma recommends adding ammonium sulfate to help with this problem just like milling and super-milling dyes. These dyes work especially well on dyeable Nylons and other synthetic polyamide fibers. Ideal pH 4.5–5.0.

*****Safety measures for all acid dye procedures: nitrile or latex gloves, dust filter mask, apron, close-toed shoes, and a well-ventilated space.**

ACID DYE CONCENTRATES!
These are concentrates that last about 6 months at room temperature but there is a possibility colors will become less vibrant after storing for 1 month or more. Some say to store these in the refrigerator but when cold, dyes can push out of solution and become colloidal. They can be used to create a dye bath, directly dye or be added to a thickener to paint on fabric. They are a great way to limit repetitive exposure to dye powder.

Supplies: (to create a cup jar of concentrate)
- 1 tsp dye (2.7 gm)
- 1 quart of almost boiling water
- Small mixing container and spoon for pasting dye
- A GLASS jar with matching lid that can hold 1 liter of concentrate
- Measuring spoons
- Pan to heat water in
- **Optional:** hot Urea waterWhat is a 1% solution?

> **WHAT IS A 1% SOLUTION?**
>
> The solution you are creating will be using liquids in measurements or cups or milliliters (ml). The powdered dye that you add to these solutions will be in teaspoons, tablespoons, or grams (gm). The easiest way to calculate what strength percentage your concentrate will be is to use the metric system. For example, a 1% solution contains 2.5 gm (1 tsp) powdered dye and 250 ml water (1 cup). 2.5 gm/250 ml = 0.01 or 1% gm dye per ml of water. We abbreviate this by just using the percentage when referring to strength of solution.

HOW TO MAKE ACID DYE CONCENTRATES (1% STOCK SOLUTION): SHELF LIFE IS ABOUT 6 MONTHS IF STORED IN THE REFRIGERATOR
1. **Gear up!** Gloves, apron, dust filter mask.
2. **Set up!**
   - Heat 1 liter of water (around 4 cups/1 quart). You can add hotter water if you are having problem with dye dissolving.
   - **Measure:** 10 gm dye powder (2 1/2 tsp should work for any brand but for Jacquard acid dyes, use a bit more)

3. **Dissolve dye** in boiling water by stirring. Once dye is dissolved, add the rest of the 3 cups of hot water.
4. **Decant** concentrate into glass jar. Don't forget to write the date and color/color number on the lid of the jar!
5. **Speckles!** If there are speckles of dye on the lid the next time you open your concentrate, dump the whole jar into a pot and reheat the dye. This should dissolve the dye powder.

TIPS ON USING ACID DYES:

1. To dissolve powder: use hot water and stir.
2. To get powder to dissolve further (if you get spotting) add hotter water.
3. Try concentrates! You can use acid dye in powder form straight from the container – you don't have to mix concentrates to use acid dye, but they are much easier to use and the exposure to dye powder is limited. The results are very repeatable with concentrates too.
4. Don't throw wetted wool into a boiling bath. The bath much match the temperature of the wetting/soaking bath and then raised gradually. Put wool into a hot bath and bring it up to ALMOST a simmer then cool the wool, gradually. This way you will not felt or shock the wool.
5. Acid dye can color 1 LB fabric with 1/4th–1/3rd oz dye (or 2 1/4ths to 3 level teaspoons).
6. Hold off adding salt or acid to the bath until you see an even strike, usually at about 15 minutes, then add salt and acid.
7. Use twice the amount of dye from #5 and double the time in the vat for *black and navy*. After bringing your bath to a boil stir an additional 30 minutes to achieve dark colors.
8. If dye is speckling fabric or not dissolving, use metaphos before dissolving dye in water. Additionally, use a strainer, covered in the foot of an old panty hose, to pour your mixed dye/water combo through to create your concentrate or bath.
9. Thoroughly wet all fabric or yarn before adding it to the dyebath so your colors are even.
10. Neutralize citric acid in protein fibers by using 1 tsp ammonium acetate/quart in 70°F water for 10 minutes.

IMMERSION DYEING WITH ACID DYE FROM CONCENTRATE (FOR 1 LB OF FABRIC)
This process uses acid dye in concentrate form to create a dye bath in which fabric can be dyed a solid color, ombréd, or resist dyed. Also known as "dip dyeing".

Supplies: (using a 1% concentrate or stock solution)

- 1/4th c dye concentrate (or more for darker colors)
- 1 tablespoon non-iodized salt or Glauber's salt
- 1 tablespoon citric acid crystals or 11 tablespoons vinegar
- 1 quart water
- 1 teaspoon
- Synthrapol
- Pot to heat water

HOW TO IMMERSION DYE WITH ACID DYE CONCENTRATES (1 GALLON OF WATER)

1. **Gear up!** Gloves and apron.
2. **Set up!** Wet out your fabric in Synthrapol for at least 30 minutes. Have a clean basin ready to collect the newly dyed fabric, then make sure your jar of concentrate doesn't have dye separation; if dye has separated, heat the concentrate up in a pan or a microwave only used for dyeing.
3. Add a gallon of water to your pan and the 1/2 cup of concentrate. If you need more water for your fabric to move, calculate how many times you must multiply this recipe. Add your concentrate to the solution by pouring it through a strainer covered with nylon pantyhose. This will strain any undissolved dye and keep your piece from freckling. You will eventually adjust how much concentrate you are using based on the desired color.
4. Add wetted fabric to the bath and begin to heat. When the bath is close to boiling (for silk no greater than 180°F!!) push aside the fabric and add acid. Let this solution simmer (for silk simmer around 175°) for around 10 minutes.
5. If the color is to your liking, take your fabric out of the bath and rinse fabric in a tub Synthrapol (small capful) hot water, then warm, then cold water.
6. If your fabric is not dark enough, it can be put back in the bath. Add more acid: about 1 tablespoon of citric acid, or 11 tablespoons of vinegar. Observe if the bath is beginning to become clearer; this means your dye is being absorbed by the fabric. Repeat rinse when satisfied with color.
7. Toss dye bath down the drain.

> **How many yards of silk is in 1 lb of silk??** Momme, a Japanese word (pronounced "mommy" and abbreviated "mm"), is the weight in pounds of a piece of silk material that is 45 inches by 100 yards. So, for example, a 100 yd bolt of 8 mm Habotai Silk (on the lightweight side) would weigh 8 lbs. So, 1 lb of 8 mm silk = 12.5 yards.

IMMERSION DYEING WITH ACID DYE FROM POWDER (FOR 1 LB OF FABRIC)

Simular to immersion dyeing with concentrate, this skips the making the concentrate step and goes straight into making a dye bath with powder. This technique is often used when the dyer is swatching.

Supplies:
- Acid Dye (see Table 4.3)
- Non-iodized salt or Glauber's salt
- Citric Acid Crystals or Vinegar
- Synthrapol
- Pot filled with enough water for fabric to move freely

Table 4.3 Acid Dye Quantity for Immersion Dyeing (1lb Fabric).

	Pale	Medium	Dark	Black
ProChem WashFast Acid Dyes and Sabraset Dyes	1/2 tsp (1.2 gm)	1 3/4th tsp (4.5 gm)	3 1/2 tsp. (9 gm)	10 tsp (25 gm)

	Pale	Medium	Dark	Black
Dharma Acid Dyes (website uses % of fabric wt. and varies by color – see dharmatrading.com)	3/4 tsp (3gm)	2 1/4 tsp (7 gm)	3 tsp (9 gm)	6 tsp (18g)
Aljo Acid Dyes	1% dye to fabric weight	2% dye to fabric weight	3%–5% dye to fabric weight	6%+ dye to fabric weight
Jaquard Acid Dyes (varies with each color –see website dharmatrading.com)	1 3/4 tsp (7gm)	3 1/2 tsp (14gm)	10 tsp (42 gms)	Up to 20 tsp (85gm)

HOW TO IMMERSION DYE USING POWDERED ACID DYE (1 LB OF FABRIC)

1. **Gear up!** Gloves, apron, dust particle mask.
2. **Set up!** Wet out your fabric in Synthrapol for at least 30 minutes. Fill a vessel or vat with enough water to cover your fabric, so the fabric can move freely. Heat to room temperature.
3. **Choose intensity** of dye form table 4.3, depending of which brand of acid dye you have.
4. **Measure and paste out dye** – this can be by the teaspoon or measured by weight. I recommend doing swatches first then converting your ratio of water to dye to your larger vessel. Acid dye can dye 1 lb fabric with 1/4th–1/3rd oz dye (or 2 1/4 to 3 level teaspoons). 1 lb of 8 mm habotai silk is 12.5 yards.
5. **Add dye and salt to your pot.** Add the dye and water mixture to the vat by pouring it through a strainer covered with nylon pantyhose. This will strain any undissolved dye. *Add 1 tablespoon* of non-iodized salt or Glauber's salt. Stir the solution well to make sure all the dye is dissolved.
6. Add your pre-wetted fabric to the vat and begin to stir every 3 minutes, gradually raising the temperature to boiling (about 40 minutes). **If dyeing silk** – silk will lose its luster over 185 degrees and become very crunchy, so bring temps to around 175° for silk.
7. Once the bath is at boiling (or 180° for silk), push aside the fabric and add acid. Let this solution simmer (for silk simmer heat to around 175° – this is not a simmer) for around 10 minutes. **For Sabraset Dyes, heat for 60 minutes, especially to achieve dark shades.
8. Check the color; if it is too light, let the yardage cook a bit longer (up to an hour for really dark colors). Make sure you continue stirring the fabric! Observe if the bath is beginning to become clearer; this means your dye is being absorbed by the fabric. Repeat rinse when satisfied with color.

For information on direct dyeing and painting/printing with acid dye, see Chapter 9 on painting and printing with dye.

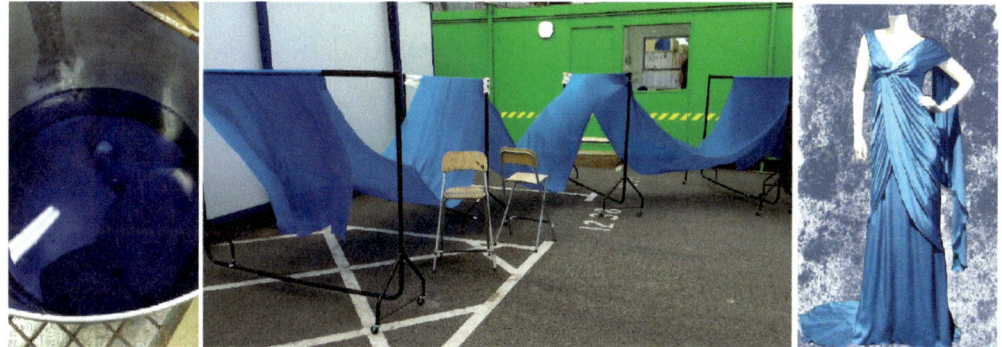

Figure 4.3 This is a perfect example of immersion dyeing for film. In this example, enough silk was dyed to create more than 5 replicas of the blue dress worn by Gal Gadot.

Photo courtesy of Beth Herd.

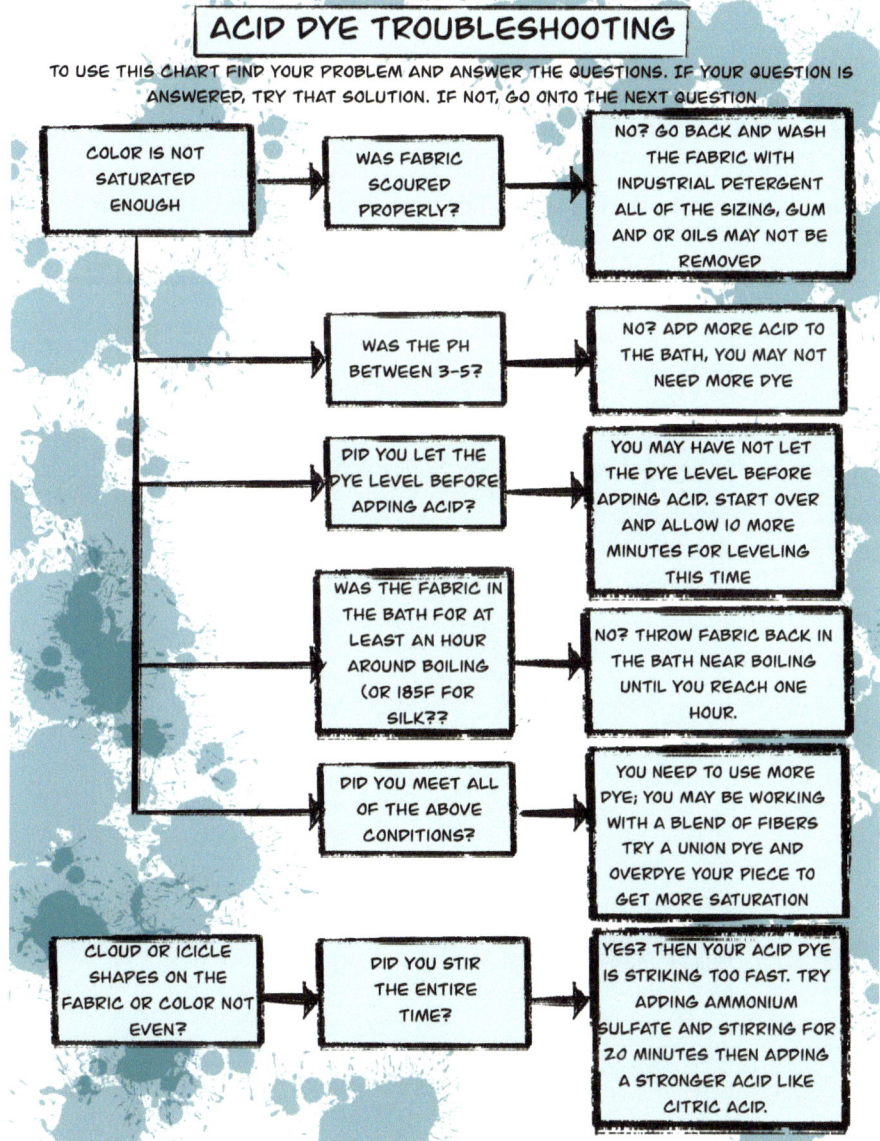

Figure 4.4 If you are having problems with acid dye, please see the following Q&A chart. Really, it's just a process of elimination!

MR. TURQUOISE, MS. FUCHSIA, AND SIR YELLOW.

Turquoise and yellow are the most difficult dyes to remove from fabric. It is best, if you are on the fence about using these colors to wait and use these colors last, because of the brightness and permanence of dyes. Also, red dyes strike first but they also leave first. This means if you have mixed a purple using red and blue dyes, because the blue dye particles are larger, have less substantivity than red, are slower to move, and often have metal components and red is smaller and moves faster into fabric, the blue will get further into the fabric because it dyes slower (when doing resist folding) and the red will not go as far (because of high substantivity) BUT the whole fabric will be more red because of red striking first and taking the dye reception sites. If you need to use red in a mixed bath, consider adding this dye into the process later to give the blue dye a chance to strike. Miss Fuchsia is the first to strike and the first to leave, so expect fuchsia to lighten a bit and bleed if not rinsed properly.

If you decide you would like to do a color removal or overdye process with fabric that begins turquoise, know that there will always be residual turquoise, even if you boil that fabric in color remover. Yellow is very similar and you will find that after using almost any color removing product, yellow will be the last color standing. Yellow can be used to our advantage though – yellow can be used to brighten other colors that may have missed the mark with vibrancy.

Figure 4.5 You can create a really cool color mixing grid with these dyes with results in the corresponding intersection of both swatches you are mixing in the grid. In this example (top two grids), yellow is mixed with the solid colors at the bottom to result in this beautiful array by textile artist, Doshi. These can be simple grids or very complex! One could make these for the rest of their lives! For information on Doshi's work see https://doshifiberart.com.

FIBER-REACTIVE DYES

These are the most brilliantly beautiful dyes often used for tie-dye. They can be difficult to predict outcome in mixing color if you are in a hurry and trying to match another color; the process is somewhat long. In my opinion fiber-reactive dyes are best used when there is some wiggle room in color preference and an exact match isn't required – unless it's a primary color that can be achieved by one color of dye. See Figure 4.6 where I matched color by choosing the exact color from Dharma Trading.

It is worth mentioning that there are a few types of dyers that often overlap: entertainment dyers that are in a hurry, dyeing mystery fabric or garments and art dyers who have a more controlled environment and aren't at the will of someone else's fabric choices. There is a brilliant art-dyer named Carol Soderland who can color match all day long with fiber-reactive dyes – and she does this through careful weighing of dye and fiber, using dyes and fabrics she knows will dye and can predict accurate color outcomes. For the entertainment industry, namely theatre, this process is rather long and the time it takes to match fabric that could be made up of any number of cellulose blends is not really worthwhile. However, to add a brilliant and vibrant base color of turquoise to white jeans, tees, or other cellulose fabric, it is totally useful. Some popular brands are ProChem Pro MX Fiber Reactive Dye, Grateful Dyes, Dharma Fiber Reactive Procion dyes, and Jacquard Procion MX Fiber Reactive dye.

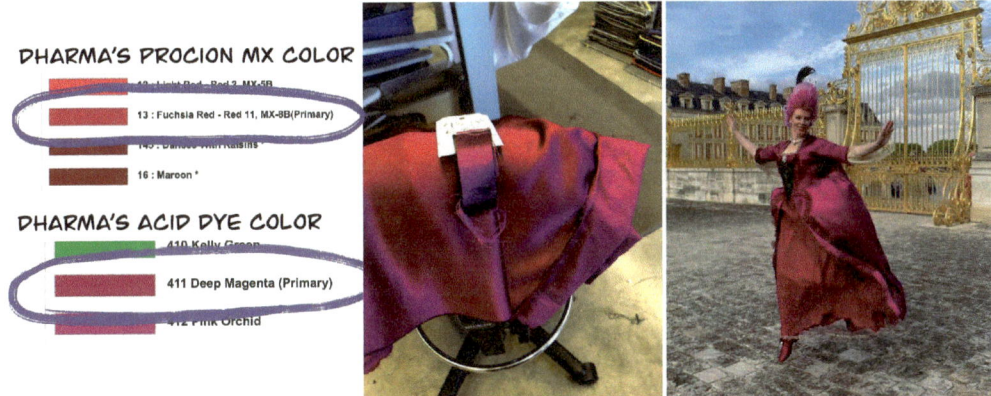

Figure 4.6 A good friend, Leslie Malitz-Vukasovich, wanted to make a gown to wear to the ball at Versailles. She had a swatch of fabric that she was going to use for part of the gown and needed two separate pieces of silk charmeuse and a cotton sheet dyed to match the swatch. Choosing the midtone of the changeable swatch (thanks a lot Leslie!!!) I decided to choose the color that was closest in a fiber-reactive dye for the cotton sheet, and a close acid dye for the charmeuse. Thankfully, neither required much toning.
Photo courtesy of Leslie Malitz-Vukasovich.

These dyes are sold in over 100 colors but are mixed from fewer than 20 dye powders called chemical or manufactured colors. You can tell which colors are chemical colors in Dharma Trading's catalog by looking for the *asterisk next to the color name/number. Most companies have dyes designated as primaries which they use to mix their colors. If you are limited on funds, it is worthwhile to buy these mixing colors to create the largest color gamut. The dye processes for fiber-reactive dyes that I will cover will be the cold processes. There are fiber-reactive dyes that work when hot (Sabracon F Reactive dyes for example) but they are not nearly used as much as the cold process dyes because, often, entertainment dyers are using these dyes on cotton or linen and trying not to shrink a garment that already fits an actor and therefore need to utilize a cold process. If that same dyer could use a hot process, the garment would most likely go into a union dye because that is what we all seem to have on hand!

Reactive dyes are unique because they attach to the fiber with covalent bonds. This bond forms from a chemical reaction between dye and fiber, creating a very strong bond that is impossible to break. The color component can be removed from fiber but the dye site will remain occupied by the reactive dye. With a bond strength like this it means we have excellent wash fastness properties (which means the dye does not wash out of the fabric easily) and excellent **light fastness** properties (which means the dye is very resistant to fading when the fabric is exposed to light). These dyes can be applied at a range of temperatures depending on the fiber you are dyeing namely, cotton and wool. They require **soda ash** as a **fixative** and **salt** as an **exhausting agent**, namely non-iodized salt, which both contribute to a basic pH (pH of 7 or above) dye bath (the opposite of acid dyes).

FIBER-REACTIVE DYES: MIXING DYE CONCENTRATES

Safety measures for all fiber reactive dye procedures: nitrile or latex gloves, dust filter mask, apron, close-toed shoes, well-ventilated space.

Fiber-reactive dyes are most readily used by mixing up solid-color concentrates that can then be mixed with each other to provide an array of colors. Dye concentrates are excellent for direct application like painting fabric. They are also fantastic for immersion dyeing when diluted with water. I will illustrate how to mix a 5% solution (a medium shade) for direct application and immersion dyeing.

The following recipe will make 1 cup of dye concentrate. If you want to prepare more concentrate, like a gallon perhaps, you will have to multiply this recipe to the desired amount. Note: one cup of concentrate will color roughly 1 1/2–2 yards of muslin.

The following measurements for varying intensities come from Elin Noble's book *Dyes & Paints*.[2]

Supplies:
- Dye in the amount that created the intensity of your choosing
- Non-iodized Salt or Glauber's Salt
- 10% Urea Water Solution

Table 4.4 Quantity of Dye to Make 1 Cup of 5% Dye Concentrate.

Value	Light	Medium	Dark
	1/2 tsp (1.25 g)	2 tsp (5 g)	4 to 6 tsp (10 to 15 g)

HOW TO MAKE DYE CONCENTRATES – 5% SOLUTION

1. **Gear up!** Put on apron, gloves, and a dust filter mask. A respirator works too.
2. **Set up!** Spread out a towel misted with water under the vent hood. This is where you will mix your dyes. To do this without a vent hood Elin Noble recommends mixing concentrates in a cardboard box lined with newspaper misted with water (see photo in Chapter 1). The wet towel will attract dye particles instead of your mucous membranes!
3. **Measure:** For this concentrate we are making a medium shade or 5% solution.
    - 1 tsp dye
    - 1 c urea water
4. **Mix dye:** create a paste by slowly adding two tablespoons of urea water to your powder. Once dye is pasted, add the rest of the urea water and stir until dye is dissolved.
5. **Strain dye:** pour dye through a strainer with nylon stockings spread over it. This will ensure there are no chunks of dye in your concentrate.

Voila! Your concentrate is finished! It will last about 2 weeks. Some concentrates will last longer, but test first!

IMMERSION DYEING: CREATE A FIBER-REACTIVE DYE BATH

This is the immersion technique if you would like to dye your fabric a solid color. If you use very little water, you will create a mottled low-water immersion look; see Chapter 10 for more details.

FIBER-REACTIVE BATH USING DYE CONCENTRATES

To dye fabric in a dye bath, you will need a few more chemical solutions: a urea solution and a soda ash solution (see previous section on additives). See chart table 4.5 for amounts of concentrate needed to create an immersion bath.

Supplies:
- 5% Dye Concentrate(s) in the color of your choosing
- Non-iodized Salt or Glauber's Salt
- 10% Soda Ash Solution

Table 4.5 Immersion Dyeing Color Intensities Using 5% Concentrates (Adapted From Elin Nobles *Additions and Subtractions* and PRO Chem).

	Pale	Medium	Dark
5% Dye Solution	20 ml	50 ml	100 ml
Soda Ash	5 Tbl (45 gm)	5 Tbl (45 gm)	7 Tbl (65 gm)

Supplies:
- 5% Dye Concentrate in the color of your choosing
- Non-iodized Salt or Glauber's Salt
- 10% Soda Ash Solution

HOW TO MAKE A 1 GALLON FIBER-REACTIVE DYE BATH FROM CONCENTRATE

1. **Gear up:** gloves, particle mask, apron
2. **Set up:**
    a. **Choose intensity:** decide what intensity of color you would like and measure out that amount of concentrate.
    b. **Choose a container:** the container that will hold your bath should be large enough that your piece is fully immersed (if going for all over color) in the bath.
3. **Add water:** add 3.5 quarts of 95° F water into your container. We use 3.5 quarts because we will be adding about another half quart of liquid with the liquid dye concentrate. You can also use soda ash concentrate but make sure to use less water, as soda ash concentrate will add to solution total volume.
4. **Add dye and salt:** add measured dye and salt to your bath.
5. **Add fabric:** add wetted fabric to bath, agitate and fondle your fabric (if folded or in shibori form) for 15 minutes!
6. **Add soda ash:** pushing fabric aside, add the amount of soda ash needed. Mix solution around in container with fabric. Let this sit in the bath for at least 60 minutes. If dyeing black, let it sit for 90 minutes.
7. **Rinse:** rinse in cold water until the sliminess of the soda ash goes away. The water does not have to run clear at this point.
8. **Wash:** wash in hot water above 140° F (60° C) and 1/2 teaspoon synthrapol for at least 15 minutes. Rinse well. If the water does not run clear, wash it in hot water again. Dark colors frequently need another wash.

FIBER-REACTIVE BATH USING POWDERED DYE

This is the immersion technique if you would like to dye your fabric a solid color without having to mix concentrates first. Use amounts in table 4.6 based on desired color intensity!

Supplies:
- Fiber-reactive Dye MX Type
- Non-iodized Salt or Glauber's Salt
- Soda Ash
- Dye tub

Table 4.6 Fiber-reactive Dye and Additive Quantities for Immersion Dyeing (1 lb Fabric)

	Pale	**Medium**	**Dark**	**Black**
Dye Powder	1 tsp (2.5 gm)	3 tsp (7.5 gm)	6 tsp (15 gm)	15 tsp (45 gm)
Salt	1 lb (454 gm)	1.2 lb (680 gm)	2 lb (900 gm)	2 lb (900 gm)
Soda Ash	5 Tbl (45 gm)	5 Tbl (45 gm)	7 Tbl (65 gm)	7 Tbl (65 gm)
Calsolene Oil (optional)	2 tsp	2 tsp	2 tsp	2 tsp

HOW TO MAKE A FIBER-REACTIVE DYEBATH WITH POWDERED DYE (1 GALLON)

1. **Gear up!** Apron, gloves, dust particle mask.
2. **Set up:**
   - **Prep fabric by scouring, as usual.**
   - **Choose intensity:** decide what intensity of color you would like and measure out that amount from the table. Dissolve in two cups of water.
3. **Measure water:** Measure about 2 1/2–3 gallons of 95°F water per 1 lb of fabric. **Choose a container** that will hold your bath should be large enough that your piece is fully immersed (if going for all over color) in the bath. If you want even color, make sure the vessel is large enough to swish your fabric easily and remain covered in the solution.

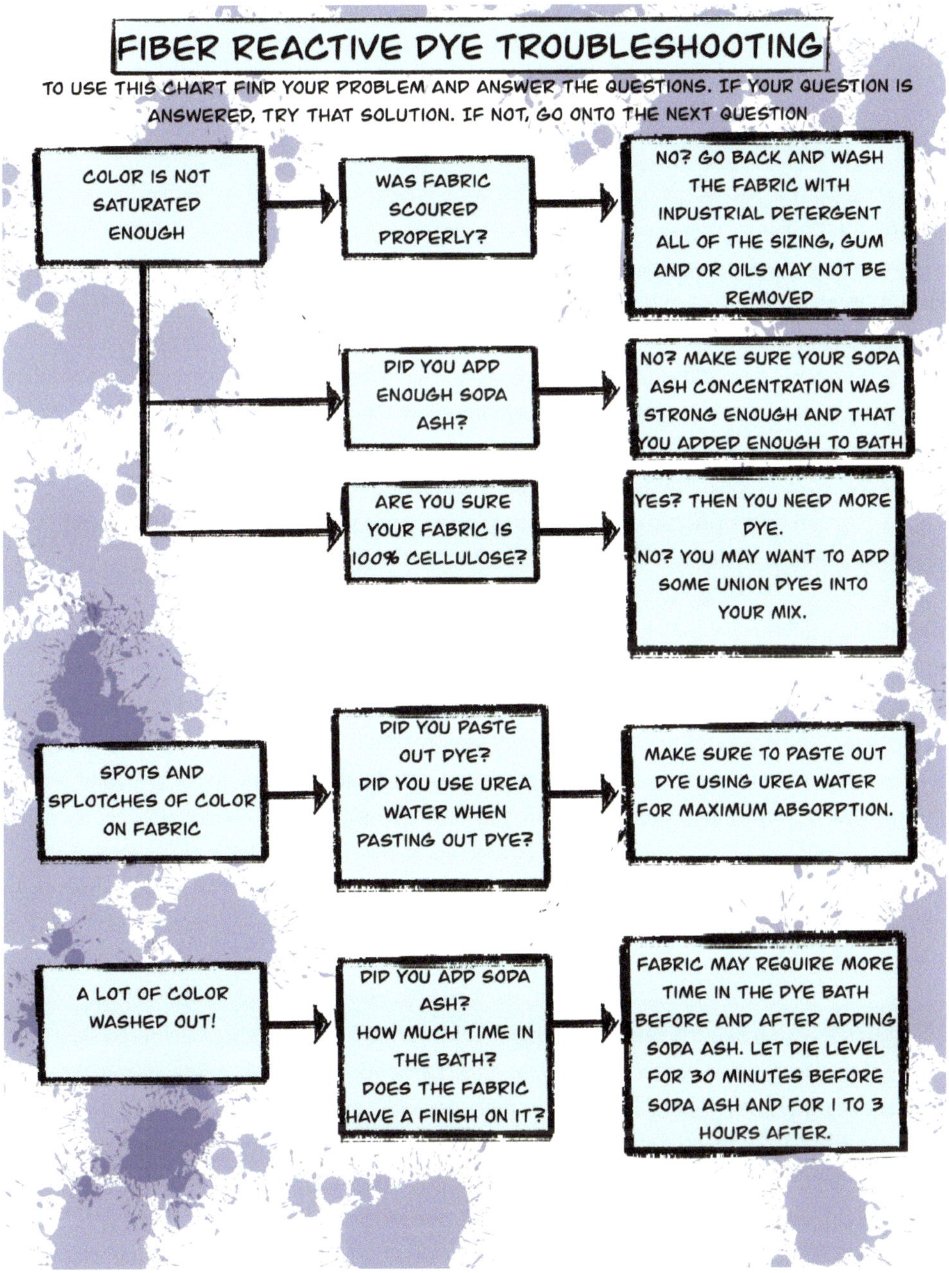

FIBER REACTIVE DYE TROUBLESHOOTING

TO USE THIS CHART FIND YOUR PROBLEM AND ANSWER THE QUESTIONS. IF YOUR QUESTION IS ANSWERED, TRY THAT SOLUTION. IF NOT, GO ONTO THE NEXT QUESTION

- **COLOR IS NOT SATURATED ENOUGH**
  - WAS FABRIC SCOURED PROPERLY? → NO? GO BACK AND WASH THE FABRIC WITH INDUSTRIAL DETERGENT ALL OF THE SIZING, GUM AND OR OILS MAY NOT BE REMOVED
  - DID YOU ADD ENOUGH SODA ASH? → NO? MAKE SURE YOUR SODA ASH CONCENTRATION WAS STRONG ENOUGH AND THAT YOU ADDED ENOUGH TO BATH
  - ARE YOU SURE YOUR FABRIC IS 100% CELLULOSE? → YES? THEN YOU NEED MORE DYE. NO? YOU MAY WANT TO ADD SOME UNION DYES INTO YOUR MIX.

- **SPOTS AND SPLOTCHES OF COLOR ON FABRIC**
  - DID YOU PASTE OUT DYE? DID YOU USE UREA WATER WHEN PASTING OUT DYE? → MAKE SURE TO PASTE OUT DYE USING UREA WATER FOR MAXIMUM ABSORPTION.

- **A LOT OF COLOR WASHED OUT!**
  - DID YOU ADD SODA ASH? HOW MUCH TIME IN THE BATH? DOES THE FABRIC HAVE A FINISH ON IT? → FABRIC MAY REQUIRE MORE TIME IN THE DYE BATH BEFORE AND AFTER ADDING SODA ASH. LET DIE LEVEL FOR 30 MINUTES BEFORE SODA ASH AND FOR I TO 3 HOURS AFTER.

Figure 4.7 If you are having problems with fiber-reactive dye, please see the following Q&A chart. Really, it's just a process of elimination.

4. **If water is hard,** add metaphos, before dye and salt!!!
5. **Add dye and salt:** add measured dye and salt to your bath.
6. **Add fabric:** add wetted fabric to bath, agitate and fondle your fabric (if folded or in shibori form) for 10–15 minutes!
7. **Add soda ash*:** dissolve amount of soda ash needed from table above into 2 cups 120°F water, making sure it is fully dissolved. Pushing fabric aside, add the amount of soda ash needed. Mix solution around in container with fabric. Let this sit in the bath for at least 60 minutes agitating, especially for the first 15 minutes. If dyeing black, let it sit for 90 minutes. ***Once soda ash is added to a dye bath, the bath has been activated and cannot be stored and used again.**
8. **Rinse:** rinse in cold water until the sliminess of the soda ash goes away. The water does not have to run clear at this point.
9. **Wash:** wash in hot water above 140° F (60° C) and 1/2 teaspoon Synthrapol per pound of fabric for at least 15 minutes. Rinse well. If the water does not run clear, wash it in hot water again. Dark colors frequently need another wash.

DISPERSE DYES

Disperse dyes are a dye class that color all synthetic fibers like polyester, acrylic, and nylon. This dye is mostly **water insoluble**, meaning it doesn't dissolve in water well. High temperatures and other additives or dispersion agents for fiber-specific dyeing, e.g., a swelling agent for polyester, are required to diffuse dye into fiber. The type of bond are hydrogen bonds and van der Waals forces, which are secondary bonds, are not as strong as covalent bonds of fiber-reactive dyes or ionic bonds of acid dyes. They do, however, have good wash fastness because they are **hydrophobic** or water-hating, and do not want to bond with water in the washing machine or in the lake when you wear that bathing suit you dyed!

Rit and Jaquard both make a version of this dye: Rit DyeMore and Jaquard iDye Poly. The jacquard dye includes a small carrier packet in the package but I have never completely been successful with these products. Rit says the DyeMore is nontoxic but if you get it in your eyes you must wash for 15 minutes and seek medical attention. With these products it is important to bring the bath to a boil for 30 minutes to achieve any sort of coverage on synthetic fabric. Not all synthetic fabric will dye, and some, with synthetic–natural blends, you can actually add a union dye or other fiber-specific dye to the bath in order to dye both fibers in the blend. I have had mixed results with these dyes however, they can be easier and yield quicker results if you just need a bump or tech of color (see Figure 4.8 for use of RIT on polyester garments).

PROChem and Aljo make the real deal Prosperse (ProChem) and Polyester Disperse Dye (Aljo), selling a disperse dye and separate carrier, and the carrier is considered mildly hazardous. However hazardous, it will actually dye your fabrics evenly and to a shade you desire – those hours over a 212°F vat could potentially pay off. Note: carrier is only required for dyeing polyester. There are varying temperatures, powder quantities, and amount of acids used with acetate, nylon, and acrylic; consult manufacturer's directions. While you can also use this dye for nylon, acid dyes have better wash fastness and are simpler to use in my opinion. None of these require NSC carrier but acrylic requires a rapid cool after dyeing while polyester requires high temperatures for dyeing and washing out the NSC carrier.

These dyes can be used to print (direct application) on polyester but frankly, for the little time entertainment dyers have, the process is lengthy, requires 4–24 hours of cure time, and Dye-na-flow that is already mixed up will work just as well.

As a side note – I found it amusing that when looking for a product from Dylon to dye polyester, their website states that blends with no more than 50% poly or synthetic fiber can be dyed domestically; greater than 50% synthetic cannot be dyed (in the UK). They mean it cannot be dyed with Dypro or Dylon products but people do dye synthetics in the UK! When I asked a friend in the UK what they use to dye synthetics, she said "We try to say no, we won't and can't dye that fabric!" I love this response – put it back on the buyers.

DISPERSE DYEING

Disperse dyeing is used mainly to dye polyester fibers with help from a dye carrier. Use these dyes if you would like to dye polyester well. The reason these dyes are called disperse dye is because the dyes are ground down or "dispersed"[3] into smaller particles in order to find a way into tight synthetic fibers. The reason a **carrier** is used in dyeing polyester is because even though the disperse dye particles are small, polyester fibers are tighter and therefore a chemical is needed to carry the dye into the fibers.

The following recipe uses materials from ProChemical and Dye and therefore includes ProChem brand chemicals. You can use Rit DyeMore or Jaquard iDye, but for consistent results that you can count on, I would stick to ProChem or Aljo's disperse dye products. This is an involved process that requires three separate baths, one for dyeing and two at different temps for rinsing, so make sure you have the space and pots available. These directions can be followed using Jaquard iDye because they include a small packet of NSC carrier with their product. Rit, on the other hand, does not and therefore does not work as well but will definitely work to knock color around a bit. I would love to hear any results from dyers out there who may have used Rit DyeMore and a NSC Carrier on polyester, though!

Figure 4.8 These were pre-made western-wear garments that started in a tan color, were recut, and dyed using Rit DyeMore. Luckily, this was for *Come and Go* by Samuel Beckett and required muted tones for the three women. This was as deep as the color would go after over an hour of boiling and several bottles of dye. Lx designer Price Johnston, actors left to right: Alexandra Ruth, Maggie Albanese, and Nicole Gardner.

Photo credit: Photo courtesy of Colorado State University School of Music Theatre and Dance. *Four Times Four*, directed by Eric Prince. December 2019.

Dharma sells polyester dye and NSC carrier that can be thrown right into the washing machine. They have a disclaimer that the colors will not be bright but I suppose there are some people out there who want to tint all their prison uniforms pink; in that application it could be useful.

Safety measures for all disperse dye procedures: nitrile or latex gloves, NIOSH approved half-face respirator with P100 cartiges, apron, close-toed shoes, *extremely well-ventilated space.*

Supplies:
- PROsperse Disperse Dye or Also Disperse Dye
- PRO Dye Carrier NSC **(for dyeing polyester only)**
- Metaphos (optional, but use if you have hard water)
- Citric Acid Crystals or White Distilled Vinegar
- Synthrapol
- Soda Ash
- Large pot for dye process with 2 1/2 gallons (10 liters) of water
- Large pot to boil water for rinse process
- Burner or vat large enough to boil large quantity of water
- 2 cup heat-safe container to dissolve dye
- 2 cup heat-safe container to dilute carrier

Table 4.7 Disperse Dye Quantity of Dye Based on 1lb Fabric.

	Pale	**Medium**	**Dark**	**Black**
PROChem and Dye PROseprse Dye	2 tsp (1.3 gm)	12 tsp (3.8 gm)	3 tsp (7.5 gm)	6 tsp (15 gm)
Rit DyeMore	1/4th bottle	1/2 bottle	1 bottle	2 bottles
Jaquard iDye Poly	1/4th oz	1/2 oz	3/4ths oz	2 oz

HOW TO DISPERSE DYE (1 LB OF FABRIC) USING PRO CHEM OR ALJO DISPERSE DYES (ADAPTED FROM PRO CHEMICAL AND DYE)

1. **Gear up:** gloves, respirator, good ventilation, apron
2. **Set up:**
    - **Scour the fabric** by machine washing in hot 140° F (60°C) water or by hand in a pot on the stove with Soda Ash and 2 tsp (2.5 ml) Synthrapol per pound of fabric. Rinse until the soda ash slimy feel is gone.
    - From Table 4.7 *choose how much dye* based on the depth of color you would like to achieve. Dissolve the dye in 1 cup of boiling water. Let mixture cool to room temperature and stir well again. Before adding to dye bath, strain it through pantyhose.
    - **Dilute the dye carrier** NSC by mixing 2 tablespoons (30 mL) of carrier into one cup (250 mL) of boiling water. **(SKIP THIS STEP IF DYEING NYLON OR ACETATE RAYON).**
3. Prepare the dye bath in a stainless steel or enamel pot. Add ingredients in the order listed: Two 2 1/2 gallons (10 L) of 120°F (49°C) water add:
    - 1/2 tsp (3.5 gm) metaphos (if you have hard water)
    - 1/2 tsp (2.5ml) Synthrapol

- 1 tsp (5ml) citric acid crystals or 11 teaspoons (55 mL) white distilled vinegar
- Diluted dye carrier NSC from "Set Up"
- Dissolved and strained ProSperse Dispersed dye

4. Stir well and add the scoured damp fabric.
5. Bring the dye bath rapidly to a boil (212°F/100°C), stirring constantly. Simmer 30 minutes for pale shades and up to 45 minutes for black, stirring intermittently and gently to prevent the fabric from creasing or distorting. While dye bath is going, bring another pot of water to a minimum temperature of 180°F (82°C).
6. Rinse the fabric. Remove the fabric for that pot and immediately plunge it into a pot of 180° (82°C) water. Water below that temperature leaves residual dye carrier NSC crystals and an unpleasant odor in the fabric, which is very difficult to remove.
7. Wash the fabric. Dispose of the fabric down the drain and refill the pot with 160°F (71°C) water. Add half a teaspoon (2.5 mL) Synthrapol. Transfer fabric from the first rinse spot to this washpot. Stir intermittently for 5 to 10 minutes.

Rinse in hot water and wring out. Smell the fabric. If you detect the odor of the carrier in the fabric, repeat steps seven and eight. If you don't smell carrier, finish by drying the fabric.

VAT DYES

Vat dyes are the magical unicorn of the dye world. They are also the "elephant" particle of dyes, and therefore if you are dyeing a resist piece with these dyes, the dye particles will only get into your fiber so far, leaving a reduction halo around the original color of fabric. They cannot be removed easily; as a matter of fact, they are known for their permanence.

The vat dye process removes and deposits color simultaneously, using thiourea dioxide in a reduction oxidation process; removing the oxygen to make the vat dye color soluble, then adding oxygen back in the bonding process. According to Elin Noble in her *Additions and Subtractions* workshop[4] "as new color (vat dye) is laid down, the old dye (reactive dye usually) is stripped out." In this workshop we learned how to use a variety of dyes to discharge color and

Figure 4.9 A pre-made dress that was vat dyed turquoise. I love the halo around the turquoise.

redeposit in layers. Using vat dyes, we created magnificent halos around inner-folded fabric and dark saturated color on the areas that were not inside the resisted area. You can see this halo in Figure 4.9 where I used a store-bought dress that started a solid fuchsia color, wrapped and tied it around a huge rope where the fuchsia area was tucked inside the resist (arashi style – see chapter on resists), and immersed it in a turquoise vat dye bath. The light part between the fuchsia and the turquoise is the halo. If a larger halo is desired, Elin suggests using sodium hydrosulphite as the reducing agent.

Vat dyes can be directly applied and thickened using gum tragacanth, guar-gum, or locust bean gum.

SAFETY

Sulfur dioxide gas is released in this process so make sure to have a half-face respirator with acid/gas cartridges. This process also uses lye, so double up on gloves with your usual nitrile and some longer elbow-length gloves in case you splash in the bath. Goggles always complete the look and will protect your eyes as well.

Supplies:
- Lye
- Thiourea Dioxide (thix) (preferred) or Sodium Hydrosulphate (hydro)
- Vat dye
- Respirator
- Gloves
- Apron
- Large heat-safe (steel) pot or vat for dye
- Large pot (to fit project) of boiling water
- Bar of Ivory soap
- Spoons
- Wash basin
- Stove top or burner
- Cup to paste out dye

Table 4.8 Vat Dye and Additives Quantities (for 1 Pound of Fabric) From PROChemical and Dye.

	Dark	**Black**
Dye Powder	3 Tbl (22.7 gm)	6 Tbl (45 gm)
LYE	All colors except black 2 Tbl (27 gm)	4 Tbl (54 gm)
Thiourea Dioxide	All colors except black 2 1/2 tsp (9 gm)	5 tsp (18 gm)

HOW TO USE VAT DYES

These recipes are general recipes and can be applicable to AljoZymo-fast vat dyes and Maiwa vat dyes; please reference manufacturers instructions for amounts to use for their products.

1. **Gear up!** Gloves, acid/gas half-face respirator, excellent ventilation, close-toed shoes.
2. **Set up:**
    - Using a 2 cup container, always add lye to cold water while stirring. **Take care that you don't splash.**
    - Measure at least 3 1/2 gallons (14 L) of water and heat to 120°F–160°F; the reduction temperature varies between specific dyes (see the technical data sheet (TDS) for specific reduction temperatures on manufacturer's site).
3. Paste out dye powder in warm water and add to bath.
4. Sprinkle Hydro thiox (thiourea dioxide) or (sodium hydrosulphate) into the bath and stir to dissolve.

5. Add dissolved lye to the bath.
6. This is where the magic begins: observe the color change in the bath. This means the dye is reduced and ready to use. Maintain the temperature of the bath for the color you are using; avoid boiling the bath.
7. Add soured and wetted fabric to bath for 1 and up to 30 minutes. The longer the fabric is in the bath, the darker the color.
8. Remove fabric and squeeze excess liquid back into bath. Throw it into a bucket of cold water. If using vat dye for shibori or folding, unfold your piece and let it dry on the line for 10 minutes to oxidize, then rinse one more time.
9. Boil a pot of water large enough to contain your piece with a bar of ivory soap to remove excess dye. When water boils, remove soap, add fabric and let sit for 30 minutes.
10. Rinse in cold water and hang to dry or throw in dryer.
    A vat dye bath can be revived by reheating and adding more reducing agent (amount required in original recipe). Allow bath to reduce and change color. If bath is not reducing and looks somewhat opaque, you may need a little lye. Begin by adding 1/4th of the lye required in the original recipe.

TIPS ON USING VAT DYES

1. There are two ways to control the depth of shade: time in the bath and amount of dye.
2. **Always add lye TO cold water, not the other way around.** Lye can make cold water boil.
3. This dye is the last stop on the train line. **You will not be able to remove or discharge this dye!** Yes, you can make black fabric purple in one step but the purple will never be able to be removed, no matter what you do.
4. **Silk . . .** create a darker bath so you can get the depth of color desired in a shorter amount of time. Use a vinegar rinse instead of soaping to neutralize. Lower the dyeing temperature; once bath is reduced allow bath to cool (150° or lower) before adding silk.

DIRECT DYES

These dyes for dying cotton, linen, rayon, and other cellulose fibers. I do not personally have a lot of experience with this class of dyes but have some friends that love them, especially when used in combination with other classes of dyes. The process is much like fiber-reactive dye in which you add soda ash to activate the dye. However, dye, soda ash, Synthrapol, metaphos, and the fabric are all added in the same step and salt is added in increments, following. PRO Chem mentions that these fabrics are not very wash fast and recommend using Retayne at the end of the dye process.

Supplies
- Direct Dye Powder Synthrapol
- Soda Ash
- Common Salt
- Metaphos (use if you have hard water) Retayne (optional)

Table 4.9 Direct Dye and Additives Quantities (for 1 Pound of Fabric) From ProChemical and Dye.

Dye Powder	Pale	Medium	Dark	Black
Soda Ash	1/4th tsp (0.5 gm)	1 tsp (2.25 gm)	3 1/2 tsp (9 gm)	5 1/2 tsp (13.5 gm)
Synthrapol	2 1/2 Tbl (22.7 gm)	2 1/2 Tbl (22.7 gm)	2 1/2 Tbl (22.7 gm)	2 1/2 Tbl (22.7 gm)
Metaphos (optional)	1 1/4th tsp (9 gm)	1 1/4th tsp (9 gm)	1 1/4th tsp (9 gm)	1 1/4th tsp (9 gm)
Common Salt	1 1/2 Tbl (22.7 gm)	2 Tbl (31.8 gm)	3 Tbl (445.4 gm)	6 Tbl (90.8 gm)

HOW TO USE DIRECT DYES

1. **Gear up!** Gloves, apron, and dust mask.
2. **Set up!** Scour and wet your fabric. Locate the vessel you will be dyeing in and make sure it is large enough for your fabric to move freely. Measure 2 1/2 gallons per pound of fabric you will be dyeing of 75°F–95°F (24°C–35°C) water.
3. **Measure dye** powder from table 4.9 and dissolve in 2 cups (500 ml) room temperature 75°F–95°F (24°C–35°C) water and set aside.
4. **Add Metaphos** (optional, use if you have hard water)**, Soda Ash, Synthrapol** to the dye bath and stir until dissolved. Add **dissolved dye** and stir. **Add washed and damp fabric**. Stir continuously for even results for 3 to 5 minutes. Raise the temperature to a boil over a 30 minute period while stirring occasionally.
5. **Dissolve the salt** (from table above) in warm water. Slowly add the salt in 3 equal parts with 5 minutes between additions. Dye for an additional 20 minutes at a boil. Turn off heat and let the fabric continue to dye for an additional 15 minutes. Carefully pour the dye bath down the drain and rinse the dyed fabric in cool water.
6. **Set the dye.** Refill your dye pot with 7 1/2 gallons (30 liters) of 140°F (60°C) water. Add 1 Tablespoon (15 ml) of Retayne for each pound of fabric. Add the fabric. Swish your fabric around in the hot Retayne bath for 20 minutes with a spoon or wooden dowel. After 20 minutes, rinse with cold water and dry at once, in your dryer.

OTHER DYE CLASSES WORTH MENTIONING: BASIC DYES AND NATURAL DYES

These are two classes of dyes that I will not be covering in depth for this book. They are not often used (with exceptions of course!) in entertainment dyeing. I will, however, give you a short overview of my perspective on these dyes, resources on how to use them, and where they may be applicable in your life.

BASIC DYES

Basic dyes are used to dye reed, wood, jute, leather, beads, shells, and more. Some people like this dye for hand-painting silk. It is not very light fast so it cannot be used in applications that will be exposed to sunlight (say goodbye to outdoor shots or theatre . . .). This dye also uses methyl or denatured alcohol to reduce spread of color and to permit fast drying. Overall I would say since many of you cannot get your hands on methyl or denatured alcohol, this product may not be as useful to the entertainment dye world.

NATURAL DYES

Natural dyes are taking off in a big way yet, the question remains: when is it appropriate to buy a whole stock of natural dyes and mordants in order to dye a single show or cast of characters? Leslie Stamoolis at the University of Gonzaga in Spokane Washington gave a wonderful lecture on using natural dyes in theatre at the 2022 KCACTF Region 7 conference. She used natural dyes in the show *The Burns* to portray the use of locally derived dyes in the post-apocalyptic Simpson play. The beautiful array of colors really lends themselves to create a naturalistic and cohesive world. While I was enamored with the array of toned, natural color I thought to myself: when else would this be applicable? When doing a show like *Not on this Island* or the island-bound cast in *The Tempest*? It is my opinion that a full complement of natural dyes would be very costly especially considering the amount it would be used compared to fiber-reactive, acid, or union dyes in dyeing the majority of films, TV, and theatre. These dyes take longer to process but the wash fastneses and light fastness are poor in comparison to other dye classes.

Now, I don't want to start an argument here but there have been several questions raised about how natural dyes, when not derived from the region the dyer is working, can be just as caustic to the environment if the dyes are not derived from natural elements found in that ecosystem. There is also the question of toxicity. Many people think, because natural dyes are made of many edible plants and insects that the dye powder will naturally be safe to inhale or handle. This is not true! Inhalation of any powder over a prolonged amount of time can cause damage to the lungs. Workers in spice factories often develop allergies, contact dermatitis, and anaphylaxis from inhaling edible spices. The same thing can happen with natural dyes. Also, mordants used in natural dyeing should not be taken lightly. Some of these include metals including aluminum and chromium, calcium hydroxide, and other additives that can prove as or more harmful to the environment than the dyes we use in entertainment dyeing.

THE BOTTOM LINE

When using fiber-specific dyes, creating concentrates can be a real game changer, especially if you find yourself dyeing large lots of fabric or teaching a class in fiber-reactive or acid dyes. Make sure to read how to rinse each type of fabric as not all fabrics get washed in hot or cold water with industrial detergent!

NOTES
1. Dharmatrading.com. "Did You Know . . . How Acid Dyes Work?" www.dharmatrading.com/home/did-you-know-how-acid-dye-works.html.
2. Noble, Elin. *Dyes and Paints: A Hands on Guide to Coloring Fabric*. East Freetown, MA: Independently Published, 1988.
3. Joshi, Rashmi M., Vignesh Dhanabalan and S. K. Laga. "Carrier Dyeing: Pros and Cons." *Textile Today*, 2013, Bangladesh, India.
4. Noble, Elin. "Subtractions and Additions Workshop." Pacific Northwest School of the Arts, 2021.

5

ALL TOGETHER NOW!

UNION DYES

Figure 5.1 Dypro and Rit and the most commonly used union dye brands.
Photo courtesy of Kim Lennox.

Union dyes have several classes of dye unified into one product that target different fiber types. This is where we get the name "union" dye. These dyes are the "broad brush" dyes, containing disperse, direct, fiber-reactive, and acid dyes in hopes of bonding with whatever fiber or blend of fibers you happen to be dyeing. These dyes do the job most of the time and are fantastic for dyeing mystery fibers (garments or fabrics where it is difficult to discern fiber type). This is

DOI: 10.4324/9781351130677-6

the reason this particular dye is ubiquitous in entertainment dye houses where **overdyeing** commercial garments is a daily task.

Understanding the processes used to dye specific fibers, as outlined in Chapter 4, is crucial in order to push a union dye in one direction or another if you can identify some of the fiber content in the fabric. For example, if you know there is some cotton in your fiber blend, but you aren't sure of the other fibers, you may choose union dyes so if the other fibers are synthetic, the heat will drive some of the disperse dye into those fibers followed up by a soda ash soak as the bath cools, before rinsing. You may get lucky and dye a really saturated color with these dyes but, more often than not, these dyes yield less vibrant color results than fiber specific dyes. That is the reason these are very commonly used in aging and breakdown! Dull, murky colors are exactly what a breakdown artist needs to overdye, **tech**, and **tone** new clothing fresh from the store.

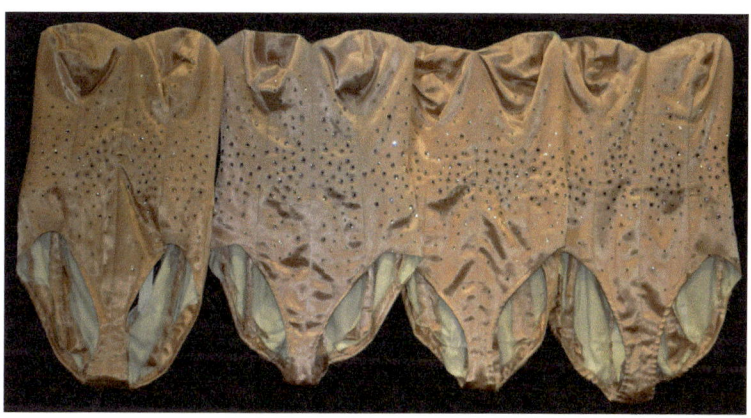

Figure 5.2 Nylon blend bodysuits color matched to skin tones using Rit union dye. Old Globe Theatre, *Sammy*, Costume Designer Fabio Toblini.

For smaller dye shops, sometimes union dyes are the entire stock and there may be a little cash to buy some additives to use with these dyes in fiber-specific processes. I have totally used union dyes to dye silk, cotton, and nylon pushing each bath into a low or high pH depending on the fiber. Generally, these less vibrant colors work for stage because of the bright stage lights and desire for character, not a bright block of color, to be of highest priority to the stage picture. They also work because dyers who use them all of the time understand how colors will mix and which colors to use to tone other colors, quickly and beautifully. Many dyers use union dyes to dye flesh tones, tech white shirts, dye black blacks, and everything in between. This chapter will dive into several professionals' recipes and techniques to achieve these colors as well as address the stranger things we dye like buttons and feathers.

Figure 5.3 Patches of shibori resist dyed with union dyes for a specific black-and-white-haired villain's fashion show (2021). Costume designer Jenny Beavan, dyer Beth Herd.

Photos courtesy of Beth Herd.

I will be using three brands of union dyes in my process instructions and discussions: Rit Powdered Dye, Jacquard iDye, and Dypro (used to be Dylon's professional line but is now owned by a different company). I am using specifically powdered versions of these dyes because they are waaaaaay more cost effective and have a longer shelf life than the liquefied version (Rit specifically). Rit has salt mixed in already, which means larger amounts of dye required (it's really salt). See table 5.1 for weight and measurement differences for the same intensities.

TIPS ON USING UNION DYES!

1. Swatch in a pot with no more than 2–4 cups of water and a 1/2 tsp of dye. To reproduce more than that quantity of dye in a 30 gallon vat could use great amounts of dye or your whole stock!
2. Weighing and measuring the union dye brand Rit can be complicated because they premix salt into their dye and therefore each time you use it you may be getting different amounts of salt in your mixture. Some people like to shake the dye containers before measuring dye to keep the salt distributed – this is not a good idea unless you are using a sealed mixing box as shaking it will create a cloud of dye powder for you to inhale when you open the container.
3. **Transfer** bags of dye to plastic containers (Figure 5.4)! I like these from ULINE because you can see how much dye you have without opening the container.
4. When swatching make sure to **note all conditions** even if they weren't ideal. For example: pot came to boil by mistake or forgot to rinse measuring spoon and stirred pot accidentally. These notes will help you troubleshoot and choose which way to go next.
5. USE A STRAINER even if the dye looks dissolved. With union dyes, different dyes have different rates of diffusion into the solution. There will always be SOME dye that didn't dissolve. That will be the dye to freckle on the center front of your garment.

Figure 5.4 Containers that fit a 5 lb bag of Rit perfectly!

Check the color of the fabric when dyeing – take fabric out of dye bath and rinse. Squeeze out water and cover bin with a towel so dye powder does not attach to wet fabric and create speckles. Pull one corner or cut one corner off the fabric and dry with a blow dryer. Compare to original swatch or desired color. If fabric is too light, re-wet fabric and put it back in the dye bath. If your fabric was in the bath for an hour, <u>you need more dye.</u>

CREATE CONCENTRATES WITH UNION DYES

Similar to creating concentrates with acid and fiber-reactive dyes, these concentrates can be handy for creating quick color mixtures and can be easily converted for a larger solution using fluid measurements. I recommend using a beaker to measure in milliliters. Usually, academic surplus stores have tons at great prices!

A note on containers for concentrates! I prefer glass; dye may be hot when you pour it in. Some people mix these up in bowls because they are easy to take liquid out of but you would only do this if dyeing in large volumes, otherwise water will evaporate.

Figure 5.5 Mixing concentrates in bowls that work on induction burners can be fantastic, especially if your shop is processing a lot of dye work.

Photo courtesy of Beth Herd.

Supplies:
- Container to rinse powder off spoons
- Measuring spoons (I like the ones that go down to 1/32nd tsp) or digital scale
- 2 quart steel pan
- Burner
- Towel to lay wet spoons on
- Union dye
- Container with lid to hold 1 qt

 ### *HOW TO* CREATE CONCENTRATES USING UNION DYES*

*Increase or decrease concentrations as needed. This is a place to start.

1. **Gear up!** Gloves, apron, dust particle mask.
2. **Set up!** Have towel, container to rinse spoons, measuring spoons, and 1 qt container nearby.
3. Heat 1 quart of water.
4. Measure 2 tsp of Dypro **or** iDye; measure 3 1/2 tsp Rit. No need to paste dye.
5. Dissolve dye directly into water and bring it to almost a boil.
6. You will see a foam form for Rit. Cook dye until foam disappears, stirring to dissolve.
7. Let mixture cool and strain through pantyhose into your concentrate container.

Figure 5.6 When adding Rit to dye bath it forms a foam of dissolving materials on the surface. Wait for this foam to mostly clear before swatching or adding to a larger dye bath so you are insured that all dyes and salts have been dissolved.

IMMERSION DYEING WITH UNION DYES

These are instructions for 1 lb of fabric dyed immersion dyed on a burner or in a vat. Play with the amounts of dye you use; the amounts in the following table aren't hard and fast rules, rather they are a jumping off point.

Supplies:
- Scoured and wetted fabric
- Container to rinse powder off spoons
- Measuring spoons (I like the ones that go down to 1/32nd") or digital scale
- 1 quart steel pan if using powder
- Steel pot or vat
- Burner
- Towel to lay wet spoons on
- Union dye
- Long steel mixing spoon (I like restaurant supply ones!)
- Non-iodized salt

Table 5.1 Amount of Union Dye by Brand; Dyes 1 lb. of Fabric.

	Pale	Medium	Dark	Black
Rit	3 tsp (16 gm)	6 3/4ths tsp (32 gm)	10 tsp (48 gm)	13 1/4th tsp (63 gm)
Dyepro	1 1/4th tsp (6 gm)	2–2 1/2 tsp (10–12 gm depending on color)	3 tsp (15gm)	4 1/4th tsp (20 gm)
Jaquard iDye	1 1/4th tsp (6 gm)	2 3/4ths tsp (14 gm)	3 1/4th tsp (16 gm)	5 1/2 tsp (27.5 gm)

HOW TO IMMERSION DYE WITH UNION DYES

1. **Gear up!** Gloves, apron, dust particle mask (if using powder).
2. **Set up!** Have towel, container to rinse spoons, measuring spoons, and 1 qt container nearby. Set up your dyebath by filling pot or dye vat with enough water so your piece can swish freely. Make sure to wet your fabric and keep it covered with a towel so airborne dye powder doesn't attach to wet fabric.
3. Begin to heat dyebath to a temperature appropriate for your fabric. Around 140°–180° F for cellulose, 175° F for silk, 180° F for wool if adding wool directly to the bath – otherwise, the batch should be brought up to the temperature of the wetting/soaking bath of wool (probably your hottest tap water temperature).
4. Measure out dye using table 5.1. Your results may vary – these are starting points. If using concentrates, 1/4th c will be a pale hue. Increase amounts for darker shades. Swatch first!!!
5. Fill 1 quart pot with water and heat. Add dye directly to pot and stir until it begins to simmer. For Rit, add dye to pot, simmer and wait for foam to clear. The dye should be dissolved at this point.
6. Strain dye into main dye bath through pantyhose.
7. Stir bath with long steel spoon until dye is fully mixed with the water.
8. **Dypro and iDye:** Add 2 TBS salt directly to the dye bath for every pound of fabric you intend to dye. **Rit:** add 1/2 cup of salt for every pound of fabric you intend to dye. Stir until dissolved. **IF DYEING CELLULOSE: add 1 cup of salt to the bath.**
9. Add wetted fabric to bath and leave fabric in the bath from 10 to 60 minutes. **Make sure to always keep swishing fabric if you want even color!** When desired shade is reached, remove fabric from bath, rinse and dry. See the box on "Tips on Using Union Dyes!" for checking if your color is at the saturation you want.
10. Remove fabric and wash in cold water. Ring out fabric or **spin in a washing machine. Throw in dryer or hang dry.**

DYEING WOOL AND SILK WITH UNION DYES

The process is identical to dyeing mystery fabric or cellulose from step 1–8.

Supplies:
- Scoured and wetted fabric
- Container to rinse powder off spoons
- Measuring spoons (I like the ones that go down to 1/32nd") or digital scale
- 1 quart steel pan if using powder
- Steel pot or vat
- Burner
- Towel to lay wet spoons on
- Union dye
- Long steel mixing spoon (I like restaurant supply ones!)
- Non-iodized salt
- Vinegar or citric acid crystals

HOW TO DYE WOOL AND SILK WITH UNION DYES STOVE TOP OR VAT IMMERSION

1. **Gear up!** Gloves, apron, dust particle mask (if using powder).
2. **Set up!** Have towel, container to rinse spoons, measuring spoons, and 1 qt container nearby. Fill pot or vat with enough water so your piece can swish freely. Make sure to wet your fabric and keep it covered with a towel so airborne dye powder doesn't attach to wet fabric.
3. Begin to heat water for main bath: **for silk heat to no more than 180º; wool can get to boiling but must go in dry or if prewetted the dyebath must match the temperature of the wetting bath.**
4. Measure out dye using table 5.1. Your results may vary – these are starting points. If using concentrates, 1/4th c will be a pale hue. Increase amounts for darker shades. Swatch first!!!
5. Fill 1 quart pot with water and heat. Add dye directly to pot and stir until it begins to simmer. For Rit, add dye to pot, simmer and wait for foam to clear. The dye should be dissolved at this point.
6. Strain dye into main dyebath through pantyhose.
7. Stir bath with long steel spoon until dye is fully mixed with the water.
8. **Dypro and iDye:** Add 2 TBS salt directly to the dye bath for every pound of fabric you intend to dye. **Rit:** add 1/2 cup of salt for every pound of fabric you intend to dye. Stir until dissolved.
9. Add wetted* fabric to bath and leave fabric in the bath for 15 minutes.
10. Pushing fabric aside, add one cup of vinegar or 2 tbl citric acid and stir. Simmer and swish fabric for anywhere from 15–45 minutes until the depth of shade is reached.
11. Remove fabric from bath and rinse in warm, cooler, then cold water. Gently wring in a towel and hang dry.

Figure 5.7 Two samples of rayon-faced silk dyed in same pot of Rit royal blue dye. On left, sample was dyed using acid; on right no acid used. You can see how the saturation is greater in the sample using acid. Rayon material absorbed same amount of dye in both samples.

DYEING NYLON

This process is the same as dyeing silk and wool except that nylon takes on color very quickly! Therefore, you may want to do a less concentrated bath when dyeing nylon. This goes for acid dyes as well. Elin noble has a great trick for slowing the strike of acid dyes. She waits to add salt to the dyebath, 10 minutes before the acid is added, because salt acts as an exhausting agent and will push the dye on quickly. She emphasizes that without the salt, the dyer has more control.

DYE FABRICS IN THE WASHING MACHINE* USING UNION DYES

Dyeing and teching items in the washing machine is an excellent way to spare your back, shoulders, and hands when letting the machine do the work! As literally illustrated in Chapter 1 – top-loading machines, preferably ones that don't lock when you're filling them, are the best for this. You MUST be able to unlock the machine during dyeing to check the progress and depth of shade. It is also ideal to use a washing machine that you can do a spin cycle on command. The most ideal situation is to have two washing machines next to each other, one used as your dye vessel, and the other to spin out fabric so you can check the color without dumping your dye bath. You can use a front loader but you will be at the mercy of the result, not having the ability to stop the cycle and check the color of the item you're dyeing.

*You can dye in a front loader but the color is difficult to control as you are at the mercy of the wash cycle to complete or you may have to switch to your spin cycle, which will dump your bath. If you need to make color darker, another bath must be made. Professionals who dye constantly use washers to tech white, add a base color to fabrics, or to knock back color; they understand the quantities of dye needed and that those particular tasks are not color matching – rather they are processes whose results have wiggle room in color. The BIG difference in the dye process using a front loader is that your dye, salts, or vinegar must go through the detergent drawer and the drawer must have loads of hot water pushed through it after adding your dyes and additives.

Supplies:

- Container to rinse powder off spoons
- Measuring spoons (I like the ones that go down to 1/32nd") or digital scale
- 2 quart steel pan
- Burner
- Towel to lay wet spoons on
- Union dye
- Non-iodized salt
- Optional: vinegar if dyeing nylon or silk. This technique is not recommended for wool.

Figure 5.8 Let the washer do the work! As you can see, dye gets everywhere so it's important to do a load of bleach and towels and wipe the washing machine down after dyeing in it. As you can see the washer on the right is happy with the dye job!

HOW TO DYE USING A WASHING MACHINE AND UNION DYES

1. **Gear up!** Gloves, apron, dust particle mask.
2. **Set up!** Have towel, rinse container for spoons, measuring spoons, and 1 qt container nearby.
3. Dissolve dye in boiling water using the techniques from the stove top/vat immersion process.

4. Fill washing machine with hot water. Some people actually turn up their thermostats so their water is really hot. A tankless water heater is the best because with the push of a button, you can raise the temperature of the water and have immediate results!
5. Add dissolved dye through pantyhose on strainer.
6. Dissolve salt in hot water. Add to the washer bath.
7. I like to turn on the washer for a minute to mix the solution (let the washer do the work!).
8. Add pre-wetted and scoured fabric to the bath. Make sure it is completely submerged.
9. Turn the washer on. I prefer to leave the lid open so I can easily monitor what I'm dyeing.
10. When you feel the appropriate color is reached, remove fabric and rinse in cool water then in hot water with a little synthrapol. If your color isn't dark enough, throw fabric back in the bath.
11. I like to do a bleach load of towels at the end of the day to clean out the machine of residual dyes. If you don't want to go this route, you can do a bleach wash without towels and wipe down the inside of the lid, spindle, and underside of the top of the basket.

WHAT *IS* A PALETTE DYER?? BY DEBI JOLLY HOLCOMB

There are two primary approaches to dyeing. One is empirical, a measure and testing approach to achieving a desired color. The other is intuitive, using concentrates and adjusting in real time. Many dyers refer to this as "palette dyeing". Both methods are very useful, and experienced dyers will choose an approach for their project based on several factors particular to their needs.

Empirical dye method: For general color application, where the color advertised on the product is close enough to what is desired and the anticipated results are flexible, then following the manufacturer's directions and measurements is ideal. Samples of the fabric to be dyed are tested and a recipe is developed by measuring time, temperatures, using OWG to convert dye powder and auxiliary amounts. The dyer may need to experiment with adding an additional color or two, but essentially a recipe is developed in a sampler batch and scaled up to dye the yardage.

Palette dye method: For precise color matching, where there needs to be many minute adjustments within a bath to create an imperceptible continuation of color. This method eliminates the sampler testing phase and relies on the dyer to have a strong sense of what colors are produced from the dyes being used. For more active dye shops, every dye that comes into the space has a test fabrics (testfabrics.com) swatch done to establish what that particular dye lot looks like. Taking that knowledge, a palette dyer will choose base colors that make up the goal color and create a palette of dye concentrates. This intuitive knowledge will take time to develop. It is learning to see color and understand what hues are making up the whole color. A concentrate may be one teaspoon of dyestuff to one cup of water, strained, and added slowly to the bath in small increments after checking the fabric. Checking the fabric is done by removing the fabric from the bath, keeping it moist in a vessel, and drying a corner to check the color. Then an appropriate color concentrate is added to the bath to adjust the overall color and the fabric re-submerged. It is also common to adjust auxiliaries, water level, and temperature when the fabric is being checked. The benefit to this

> method is that it is exceptionally faster than attempting precise color matching by the empirical method.
>
> It is also common to combine the two. The dyer may achieve a large portion of a color by following a developed recipe and layering adjusting colors on top to make it closer match a standard.
>
> It is also worth noting that tried and true dye recipes do not always work. In entertainment, we rarely work with calibrated, high-end, maintained equipment and facilities. Dye results can vary widely from: daily water quality, pipe materials, ambient temperature and humidity, quality of auxiliary chemicals. Relying solely on someone else's, even the manufacturer's, instructions can give undesired results. However, being flexible on methods of color development can help you overcome many issues that may arise.

TONING, TECHING, AND MIXING COLOR WITH UNION DYES

Mixing color quickly and effectively comes from years of trial and error as well as using the same products over a length of time. There are dyers that use ratio recipes and stick to one class of dyes; there are others that use all classes of dyes mixed together – others that use concentrates of one or all classes combined – others that do all of the above. There are recipe dyers and palette dyers; see the following box to understand the difference.

The process of toning and teching fabric is the same as general dyeing with union dyes except that you use much less dye; sometimes even less than what the "pale" amounts require in the measurement chart. Generally toning means to dip the entire garment or fabric that is already a color and over dye it with a very pale wash of another color. Let's say a fabric is too purple, then you would want to tone it with perhaps a little yellow to knock back the vibrancy. Toning in skin tones has a slightly different approach than using direct compliments – see section in the skin tone section. Teching a garment can happen on colored or white fabrics and usually it consists of a very weak dye bath to tone down brightness or dirty up or tea dye something to make it look worn or used. For more on breakdown, see Chapter 13.

I had a great Facebook group chat[1] about mixing color, toning, and teching with four professional dyers who range in geographic locales from the West to East coast of the US to Europe: Bridget Kraft (Oregon Shakespeare Festival), Becky Hanson (St. Louis Opera Festival), Hallie Dufresne (previously Los Angeles Opera, currently director of design/manufacturing at Rethreaded), Beth Herd (EU film breakdown and formerly the Royal Opera). I've included their comments on favorite recipes. This is NOT and exhaustive list, but hopefully it will give you a head start!*

*A note about the following mixtures: I've included general recipes for union dyes to achieve tech colors, get good blacks and greys, and to provide jumping-off points for flesh tones.

CREAM

RIT

One of the best recipes for cream I learned from Hallie Dufresne at the Los Angeles Opera. When creating and recording your swatch recipe, those tiny measuring spoons from Chapter 1 are super helpful. These parts will be in very small amounts as the value of cream is a very pale color. If your fabric is too yellow, tone with purple (yellow's complement).

> Golden Yellow
> Pink
> Dash (grains) of Purple to tone

DYPRO

From Beth Herd: Dypro Gold can make a nice off-white cream color. It has a touch of pink to the yellow we used it for lightly teching shirt colors in a bucket.

BLACK

RIT

To get a really great black on another color fabric (not-white) use the complement to knock out that color first.

Then, use Bridget Kraft's Recipe For Black:

> Black Dye
> Lemon Yellow or Kelly green (to tone the purple–red out)

Bridget uses the same recipe for charcoal but doesn't use as much dye and time to make the color go as far as black.

GREY

RIT

Hallie Dufresne has two great recipes for grey.

According to Hallie: A decent warm grey is black/golden yellow and a wonderful blue–grey start is denim blue/tangerine.

DYPRO

Beth Herd shares: I had a lovely accident finding windsor purple and emerald green made a really nice grey.

TECH

RIT

A great warm tech, a.k.a. tea dye, is shared by Bridget Kraft: I use gold yellow, cocoa brown, and royal blue or a tiny bit of navy to make that tea color.

DYPRO

Beth Shares: this is a tech recipe I learned from Jo Weaving: 1 part olive green, 2 parts desert dust. This will give you a warm tech base to then tweak if need be. For a Cool tech – part ebony black, part Windsor purple, and part golden glow.

FLESH TONES

Matching and dyeing flesh tones make up a significant amount of a dyers' workload. Many dyers create their own swatch rings to match skin tones. The fabrics used to create these swatch rings can depend on what industry you are in but most contain basic dye ratios on the back. Many theatre companies use habotai silk because the luminescence of silk is similar to that of skin. In dance or lingerie companies, swatch rings are made of spandex, viscose, or a stretch net. For wig folx, their rings are made up of wig lace so the swatch can be placed directly on the forehead (or body part being wigged) and matched accordingly.

If you decide you do not have enough time to create a skin tone swatch ring or "wheel of flesh" as I like to call it (very *Silence of the Lambs*, I know . . .), there are other options. There is a brilliant company called TA-OSH Nhudes (www.taoshnhudes.com) whose primary interest is to provide fabric colors that meet the needs of a diverse world by providing 37 base colors and over 360 skin tone swatches. They also sell many types of stretch fabrics in colors that correspond with the swatch rings! You could easily order a swatch ring from them to use to color match and come up with your own recipes and ratios. See Figure 5.9 for an example of one of their swatch rings and Figure 5.10 for an example of how dyers in the UK utilize these swatches! For those who do not dye loads of mesh or wig lace, you may want to try DyeNamix but you have to have a resale number to purchase services or swatches from them. Pantone, the maker of THE go-to swatch books for industry, has created a skin tone swatch book with holes in the center of the swatch to match skin tone. The price is similar to the TA-OSH.

Figure 5.9 One of the many TA-OSH swatch rings.
Photo courtesy of Beth Herd.

Figure 5.10 Dyers in the UK utilize TA-OSH swatches to match skin tone then create their own recipes depending on fiber type they're dyeing. This lot of fabric was for an ensemble of over 100 dancers. Photo courtesy of Beth Herd.

THE LM RING IN THE DAYS BEFORE TA-OSH

There is a well-known swatch ring of flesh colors that live in almost every New York costume studio: The LM ring.

When *The Little Mermaid* went to Broadway, it was such a huge show that several shops were building the show at the same time. There were so many characters with stretch net incorporated into their costumes that the shops were calling each other seeking skin tone matches. One shop finally created huge swatches (a few yards each) then cut them up and sent them out to the different costume studios. Unless a shop already had a skin-tone ring, the LM ring has been the standby ring in costume shops in NY since 2007! I think Ta-Osh will replace these rings eventually, but if you ever work somewhere with an LM ring, now you know a little history!

Figure 5.11 The LM ring at Eric Winterling's studio, New York.

FLESH

Debi Jolly Holcomb, an entertainment and fashion industry dyer, had a great comment about matching skin tone:

> I teach people to match skin tone around the shoulder for a general shade and then see how that related to faces and arms since those areas can shift so quickly with sun and makeup. . . . A tip I have for novice dyers or those short on time is to find a fabric that has half of your color instead of white. When I worked in a shop that did Rockette's costumes, I was always matching skin tone panels. We kept a few of our go-to base colors in 3–4 commercial shades and I could quickly adjust them for a particular dancer.

Debi also has notes about toning skin tones:

> One big thing about skin tones is not to adjust with direct complements. Aim for a color that is mid-way. Skin is layers of pigment, fluid, blood, and tissue. It absorbs light and refracts under the surface – similar to reflective paints. Therefore it has a highly deceptive chroma. Chroma is killed when you play with complements too much. So, let's say you have something that is too yellow, you want to dull [knock it back] a little. A little purple may be what is first thought of, but a tan many be a better choice to maintain the inherent brightness but mellow it out a bit.

RIT
Hallie Dufresne: For darker skin tones I usually start with Tan, Cocoa or Dark brown with additions of golden yellow, rose pink, peach, or whatever was needed [to tone the color].

Becky Hanson: Caucasian flesh maybe tangerine and teal. But of course, it also depends on which lot of tangerine and teal you have as they [Rit] change formulas from time to time.

DYPRO
Beth Herd shares: For skin tones at Royal Opera House they use blue, red, and yellow.

For a quick "I need 50 pairs of shiny white underwear to go Caucasian to go under kilts", we would just dump those in some desert dust. It's not a match for anyone but for something that is most likely never going to been seen – it's a quick fix.

When trying to match African/Caribbean skin tones I might start off with coffee or havana but those two colors are not clean colors so end up going with red black and yellow. To keep the richness of color in the fabric I will add windsor purple.

STRANGER THINGS: DYEING ODD ITEMS USING UNION DYES

Of course, the wide world of dyeing doesn't begin and end with dyeing fabric. We are often asked to dye all sorts of other things like buttons, feathers, felt hoods, flowers, zippers, wig lace, hair, lace, and elastic.

BUTTONS

Buttons are usually acrylic or some version of plastic, which can be dyed at high temperatures. Mix up a 2-liter bath of dye and bring it to a boil. Remember you have to retrieve your buttons from the dye pot so you may want to use a mesh strainer inside of your pot or add a loose string though a hole in the buttons so you have a way of pulling them out. Don't allow the buttons to sit on each other, they will resist color.

ELASTIC

Elastic is covered in polyester, nylon, cotton, or a blend of these fibers so it can be attached to fabric. Union dye is a fantastic way to dye these fibers at high heat just in case one of the main players happens to be polyester. This is definitely a good use of Rit DyeMore or Jacquard iDye or even regular powdered union dyes. Elastic should be dyed at temperatures near boiling. Some elastic reacts poorly to prolonged high temps in the dye pot – so best to keep this dye bath under the boiling point. Because elastic is often covered in nylon, you can use union dyes with an addition of vinegar to target the nylon. Silicone-backed elastics can often turn a few different colors: the silicone taking on one color and the elastic taking

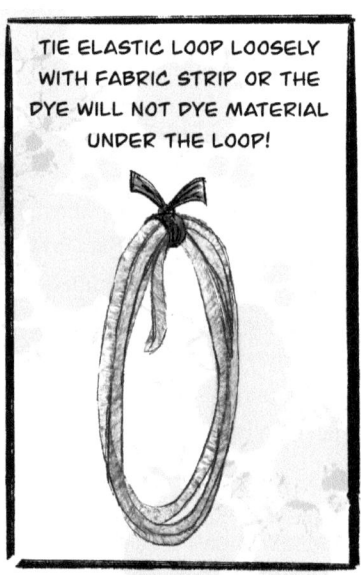

Figure 5.12 When dyeing elastic or any length of bias or trim, tie loosely at the top so it does not resist on itself.

on another. Do swatches first! Make sure to loosely tie looped elastic (or any yardage of trim, bias, etc.) loosely at the top and leave tails that you can grab to remove the material from the dye bath.

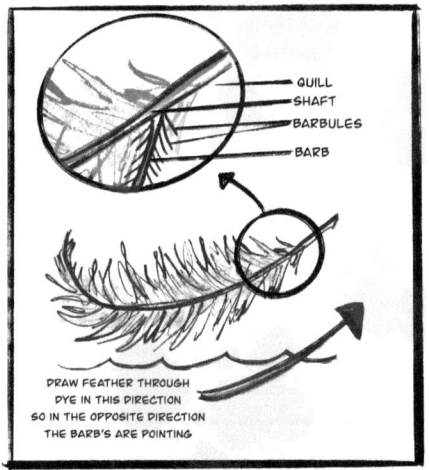

Figure 5.13 Feathers must be dyed in one direction so the barbs do not get broken!

FEATHERS

Feathers are a protein fiber; follow the instructions for dyeing wool and silk, but remember feathers have a direction and pulling them through the water and drying them should be done carefully. They should be pre-washed with Synthrapol before dyeing. They can be dyed in a stovetop pot, just make sure it is large enough so you don't break the quill. Remember to pull them through the water so the barbs are pointing away from you in the washing, dyeing, and rinse process. They can be blow-dried or hung to dry and powdered with cornstarch when dried to fluff. For ostrich feathers, I have had success on a low temp dry in the dryer. See Figure 5.12 for directional dyeing.

FELT HOODS

Felt hoods are special animals (literally) that require a long pre-wetting period before dyeing. Because we stretch, shape, and cut felt, we want it dye to really saturate the fabric. I like to add synthrapol and calsoline oil (a wetting agent) to a tub of water large enough to immerse the hood. If you do not want a soapy environment, use a tablespoon of rubbing alcohol in the tub of water as a wetting agent. Squish and squeeze the hood, forcing it to take up the solution. Leave the hood in the tub for several hours – I recommend overnight. The next day, while gently wringing it in a towel, prepare your dye bath and follow the instructions for dyeing wool. Depending on what your dye stock consists of, acid dyes or union dyes will both do the job – just make sure to get the pH lowered using acid like you would for wool, and you can add an additional tablespoon of alcohol to the dyebath as well to make sure the wool takes the dye completely.

ARTIFICIAL FLOWERS

Flowers are similar to buttons because they are usually made of some sort of synthetic material. Even though they are made of synthetics, you may not want to dye flowers at high temperatures because the shaping of petals and leaves are done with plastic spines and heat. Remember that poly and nylon can be permanently shaped with heat and therefore can lose their shaping and melt the plastic spines off the petal and leaf backs. Some flowers are silk and therefore can be dyed with union or acid dyes at the proper pH. Flowers can also be painted by Dye-Na-Flow, a premixed dye (see Chapter 14 for more info on Dye-Na-Flow).

HAIR

Human or yak hair can be dyed just like silk and wool. A hot dye bath and the later addition of acid will create brilliant colors. These can be achieved using union or acid dyes. Like feathers, hair has follicles that are stacked in one direction and therefore must be pulled through wash, dye, and rinse water in the direction of the follicle, not AGAINST it. You will be creating a big-hair-band-sized rat if you dye hair in the wrong direction! Synthetic hair can be dyed with union dyes, also at high temps. If your hair is curly, there is a chance you may have to re-curl after dyeing, but most likely not.

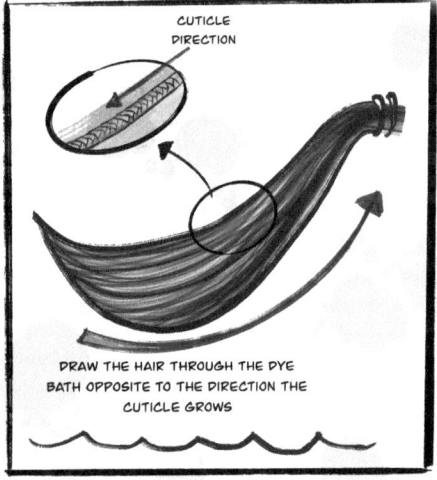

Figure 5.14 Dyeing hair is another directional process. If you do not take care with hair, your dyed piece will be ratted more than a big-hair band!

LACE TRIM

This should be like dyeing fabric, right? Well, because lace is created in tighter or looser weaves than fabric and often finished with stiffeners and sizing, they can be very difficult to get into saturated colors. I recommend getting hard-to-dye laces into a base color using union dyes and the appropriate pH modifier (soda ash or salt for cotton, acid for silk/nylon) and then hitting them with transparent fabric paint or inks like Dye-Na-Flow.

LACE YARDAGE

This process is the same as dyeing any fabric with union dyes or fiber specific dyes except it is mostly see-through, so make sure lace is dried completely before assessing if the color is correct. Much of the lace yardage these days is made of nylon and can be dyed beautifully by adding acid to the bath.

SHOES

Although I cover painting shoes in the leather chapter, it is worth noting that shoes can be dyed! We all know that silk "dyeables" can be colored using a premixed silk dye specifically for dyeable shoes. But did you also know that you can use union dye and actually spray or **dobber** on hot dye? Another product called Dye-Na-Flow (covered extensively in Chapter 8) can be applied to most materials, but make sure to wet your area to be painted first – then paint. You can also dip dye shoes that will not be damaged by being fully submerged in dye – those that do not have leather soles or uppers (the leather can and probably will shrink and do horrible things when exposed to warm/hot water). Just make sure, when dyeing shoes, to pre-wet and wash the shoes just like you would fabric you are prepping to dye. If you do not want the rubber on tennis shoes to dye, then this technique will not be suitable for you; use Dye-Na-Flow instead. You can fully submerge shoes in a dye pot and rinse them in the wash or in a tub of water. This works great for teching Chuck Taylors or Keds.

WIG LACE

Wig lace is often made of silk or nylon. Nylon takes dye very quickly and therefore a less saturated bath or the use of some ammonium sulfite could be helpful to slow down the strike of the dye. Remember that reds take first so if you need to tone into the reds add that last. It is hard to tell if wig lace is fully dry. Use a blow-dryer to fully dry before checking color.

ZIPPERS

Zippers. Oh zippers! They can be a complete pain because the fabric, teeth, and pull can all take dye differently. Ideally, I shoot for the teeth and pull to match the fabric (if possible) using union dyes and then use Dye-Na-Flow to tone the fabric part last. It all depends how well the zipper has to match your fabric.

THE BOTTOM LINE

Whatever fabric you choose to dye with union dyes, make sure to understand which additives to use for best results!

NOTE

1. Beth Herd, Janet Cadmus, Hallie DuFresne, Bridget Kraft Facebook group chat with author, July 1st, 2020.

6

THE UNDO BUTTON OF DYE?

COLOR REMOVING

Is color remover really the undo button of dye? The answer is: yes, no, maybe? Color remover can strip color from fabric but it is very common to see remnants of whatever color dyed the fabric previously; often the usual suspects hang around: yellow and turquoise. This is why color remover doesn't always work to age garments, because when removing color from garments that have been dyed, the result isn't necessarily reflective of the color they would turn as they age. A great example of this is trying to remove color from a black garment. It could turn red, yellow, blue; it's anyone's guess! This result is not what a black shirt would look like if it aged; it would be a faded gray color most likely, no bright yellow!

Figure 6.1 Resist discharge using two different color removers in a two resist-pattern sequence: thiox and bleach on black rayon. Note the yellow color left in the background. Created by Kayleigh Owen, Colorado State University student.

Breakdown artists use bleach regularly because it can break down color in the most stubborn fabrics. Color remover does not lift vinyl prints or heat transfers on clothing in any circumstance; chlorine bleach may do some strange cool color changing, but paint and physical breakdown will be your best option to deconstruct prints and transfers. For more on aging and breakdown see Chapter 13.

Color removing (or **discharging** color) can be so much fun! Removing color in patterns by pairing color removal with shibori and clamp resists, discharge paste, and other cool dye techniques can create such unique textures and colors. This chapter will focus on three

DOI: 10.4324/9781351130677-7

common color removers: thiourea dioxide, sodium hydrosulfite (Rit Color Remover), and bleach (sodium hypochlorite). I will also discuss buying a commercial color removing paste (discharge paste) and making your own discharge paste with a color remover of your choice.

THE PRODUCTS

All color removers are also known as bleach: a substance that removes color. There are three main types of bleach including chlorine, hydrogen peroxide, and sulfur-based bleaches. In the case of fiber-reactive dyes, each one causes the **chromophore**, or color part of a molecule (Elin Noble calls these the "color heads" attached to pincers that bond with the fiber), to gain or lose electrons, causing the chromophore to change into a different substance or to lose visible color. Either way, you are decapitating the color head of the molecule! These bleaches work on other dyes by removing fabric, which weakens the fibers and degrades the cloth. Check out table 6.2 on brands, notes, and health data on color-removing products.

Figure 6.2 Three samples of the same black rayon fabric resist tied and immersed in (left to right) Rit color remover, Clorox bleach, and Thiox. Check out how the color lifts differently with each product. Samples made by Kayleigh Owen, Colorado State University student.

SAFETY PATROL!!! A note on using all of these products: this process requires strong chemicals and results in harmful gas. Proper ventilation, a well-fit acid gas respirator, apron, gloves, and goggles are a must.

CHLORINE BLEACH, A.K.A. SODIUM HYPOCHLORITE

Chlorine bleach, a.k.a. the bleach that's in your laundry room, contains chlorine as its major player. This is what creates the reaction that removes color but also destroys fabric. **Bleach never stops bleaching!** This chemical reaction continues and it actually dissolves and destroys many types of fibers. Bleach is especially nasty when used on silk and wool. Remember when I talked about textile scientists using chemicals to identify fibers? Well, if a fiber is put in bleach and it dissolves completely, it is wool. Silk has a similar reaction as wool but takes longer to dissolve. Cotton can take bleach but the process has to be stopped by using anti-chlor (sodium bisulfite). Funny enough, Clorox[1] recommends using a hydrogen peroxide bath to neutralize bleach. Using hydrogen peroxide or vinegar to neutralize bleach must be done if peroxide or vinegar is the only material you have, as these combinations push the bleach out of the solution and volatize it, creating chlorine gas. The only substances that couple up the bleach to stop it and hence do not create chlorine gas is sodium bisulfite (or and metabisulfite). Bleach can create some interesting colors when used as a color remover but the fumes are really toxic and, in great quantities and close quarters, incur major nausea and vomiting if using bleach without a respirator and proper ventilation.

Chlorine bleach comes in liquid, gel and powdered form. The powdered form is much more potent and contains more chlorine, so color is removed quickly (but at what cost to your health?). Please see table 6.1 on neutralizing agents for chlorine bleach.

Table 6.1 Ratios and Amounts Needed to Neutralize Bleach.

	Ratio/Amount Needed
Anti-chlor	1 tsp anti-chlor to 2.5 gallons water
Hydrogen Peroxide	1 part hydrogen peroxide to 10 parts water (1 c HP to 2 1/2 quarts water)

HYDROGEN PEROXIDE-BASED BLEACH

This category houses the color safe bleaches, oxygen cleaners, and one of our favorites: sodium carbonate or soda ash. Yes, soda ash can move color off cloth, but it is very mild; it is more effective at scouring fabric and creating an alkaline solution. Elin Noble says to think of it as the amount of energy in the environment: a high pH + hot water = increased energy and removal of color. Hydrogen peroxide itself is fab for removing stains made by organic substances like blood or berry stains. OxiClean is another mild yet effective brightener but will not lift any real amount of color. Peroxide is also added as a hair lightener in many hair dyes. Most of these come in liquid form.

SULFUR-BASED BLEACH – A.K.A. THIOUREA DIOXIDE (THIOX) AND RIT COLOR REMOVER (HYDRO)

Sulfur-based bleaches are the most effective in removing color but also some of the worst for the environment and human use.[2] These materials began use as burning sulfur in the presence of fibers. Since then we have found safer ways to use this material as a color remover!

Sodium hydrosulfite, a.k.a. Hydro, Rit Color Remover, Tintex Color Remover, Jacquard Color Remover, Dylon Run Away for Whites, Carbona Color Run Remover decomposes in water to release sulfur dioxide, sodium sulfite, sodium thiosulfite, sodium oxide[3] into waste water posing an environmental threat. Thiox, conversely, is biodegradable. Both substances release hydrogen sulfide (rotten-egg smell), which is irritating to the nose, throat, and lungs, and sulfur dioxide, which is a neurotoxin and is considered damaging to the brain. Hydro decomposes quicker than thiox and therefore, more is required to discharge color.[4] Hydro is very flammable and has issues with instability regarding heat. It is affordable and readily available as Rit color remover at drug and craft stores. This product tends to be unstable overtime, limiting the shelf life. I would NOT use this product if you are on a septic system and are not sending waste through a treatment plant. These come in powdered form.

Thiox, a.k.a. Spectralite, and Dharma Dyehouse Color Remover is wonderful for removing color from wool, which takes time to fully saturate fibers. The affluent is fully biodegradable and it does not release the same qualities of sulfuric acid gas that hydro releases. It is excellent for removing a range of dyes and has a long and stable shelf life. All of these come in powdered form.

OTHER BLEACHES
SODIUM HYDROXYMETHANESULFINATE

This product is the main ingredient in deColourant. deColorant is a pre-made paste (Dharma, ProChem, Jacquard calls it Rongolit ST) that removes color when exposed to direct heat, namely, an iron. I have had some cool results with this product but after reading the SDS, I have a new understanding of the care that needs to be taken with this product and may just make my own paste with Thiox! Both techniques using these products will be covered in this chapter.

USING COLOR REMOVERS

Now that I've scared you half to death with health, safety, and environmental information on color removers, you are prepared to use these products safely! So, it's time to get on to the fun stuff: using them!

CHLORINE BLEACH

Chlorine bleach is a ubiquitous, toxic, and aggressive-to-fibers substance used in many homes. As we know, bleach comes in liquid form and must be neutralized with hydrogen peroxide or it will KEEP BLEACHING AND EAT YOUR FABRIC – especially wool and silk. It can be painted on fabric with a brush, sprayed with spray bottle, or even used in an immersion bath. Breakdown artists use bleach regularly because it can break down color in the most stubborn fabrics. See some beautiful breakdown work by Jack Taggart in Figure 6.3 that includes the use of bleach in creating Tom Hanks' costume in *Finch*.

Dilute bleach with water to weaken. To test strength of bleach you want to use, try full-strength bleach first, then water it down to decrease strength. **Remember, it will only stop lifting color or "bleaching" when it is neutralized.** 1 tablespoon of chlorine bleach in 1 gallon of water will lighten a pound of fabric. It will be up to you to discern the correct ratio of bleach to water. Do samples! This color remover can be used cold but please use adequate ventilation, a cartridge respirator with P100 acid gas cartridges, and skin protection!!!

Figure 6.3 Breakdown work on a synthetic suit created for Tom Hanks in *Finch*. The beautiful fading was done by breakdown artist, Jack Taggart, using bleach in concentrated amounts then the piece was set out in the sun to lighten. Top left is original suit next to a faded version. Bottom left are Jack's samples. Far right is the completed look. As you can see hardly any of the original color is left.

Photos courtesy of Jack Taggart.

Table 6.2 Important Notes on Color Removers.

	Notes	Hazard Category (1 is most hazardous)
Bleach (Milton UK)	Sodium hypochlorite. The only thing more dangerous than this in the color-removing world is powdered bleach.	**Category 1.** Serious eye damage or corrosion, serious skin damage or corrosion.
Dylon's SOS Color Remover	Benzothiazoline. Breaks fugitive dye bonds.	UK Rating system, causes skin irritation.
Hydro (Sodium Dithionite UK)	Sodium hydrosulfite. Releases gases and compounds that create environmental threat in wastewater.	Category 2, eye, lung, and skin irritant.
OxiClean	Hydrogen peroxide and soda ash (sodium carbonate).	Category 2A

	Notes	Hazard Category (1 is most hazardous)
Rit Color Remover	Sodium hydrosulfite and soda ash, other alkaline additives, and chelation agent to remove heavy metals from solution.	Category 2–4. Causes severe skin irritation; harmful if swallowed.
Rit Fast Fade	Most up-to-date SDS from 1999. Basically a concoction of powdered bleach.	Rating system was different then; causes lung, skin, and eye irritation.
Rit Whitewash	Sodium hydrosulfite and soda ash, other alkaline additives, and chelation agent to remove heavy metals from solution. Only difference between this and Rit Color remover is the presence of chlorine.	Category 2–4. Causes severe skin irritation; harmful if swallowed.
Rit Whitener and Brightener	Basically, a surfactant or super heavy-duty detergent. Contains ethyl alcohol.	Category 2B-3 safety hazard. Causes skin irritation or lung irritation.
Thiourea Dioxide (Thiox)	Thiourea Dioxide. Biodegrades upon heating; safe in wastewater.	Category 2–3, lung and skin irritant.

THIOUREA DIOXIDE (THIOX)

If you haven't picked up what I've been laying down, let me spell it out to you: Thiox is the safest, easiest to use, least toxic for the environment, most affordable, has a better shelf life, and most thoroughly effective color remover. Bleach and Rit Color Remover have their uses but thiox is my go-to color remover.

This product can remove color in most fibers that use fiber-reactive, acid, most union, and direct dyes. It will not remove hydrophobic dyes like disperse and vat dyes. Actually, if you missed the chapter on fiber-specific dyes, it is used in conjunction with vat dyes to reduce the bath before vat dyes deposit color.

Figure 6.4 Artist and amazing dyer Elin Noble's swatches showing discharge results in different time increments.

TIPS ON USING THIOUREA DIOXIDE

1. When using with **silk or wool**, create a neutralizing bath to soak fabric in after the color removal process. For a pound of fabric add 3 cups of vinegar to a bath of water and let soak for 10 minutes.
2. For **silk** do not let thiox bath heat over 185 degrees F.
3. When thiox bath begins to slow down in discharge speed, recharge with more thiox (add another tablespoon to bath, stir, test. Bath can be recharged a few times.
4. When discharge printing, if paste is not lifting enough, add more Thiox to the mixture.

When you are wondering what colors your dyed fabrics will be when you discharge them for different amounts of times or at different strengths of discharge baths, you can discharge samples like in Figure 6.3 to see exactly what will happen. This is especially fantastic when you are working with a palette that you will be discharging – so you can see if all of the discharge colors play well with the original colors. Remember turquoise and yellow will not discharge well.

CREATE A DISCHARGE BATH

To remove overall color you will create a discharge bath using Thiox. The only difference between discharging protein and cellulose fibers is that you add 1 extra tablespoon of soda ash for cellulose and must neutralize silk and wool after discharging. For both fibers, the bath must be almost at boiling* to discharge dye; the longer you leave your piece in the bath, the lighter it will go.

*For silk, do not have bath higher than 175° F – this means you may need to leave silk in longer with a slightly stronger solution.

Supplies
- 2 1/2 tsp Thiourea Dioxide
- 2 1/2 gallons of water
- 2 tbl soda ash for cellulose, 1 tbl for silk or wool
- Pot large enough for your fabric to swish in
- Long-handled spoon for mixing and fishing out pieces
- Stovetop burner (or vat)
- Towel to lay mixing tools on
- ***If discharging silk or wool, 3 cups of vinegar**

Figure 6.5 A piece of blue cotton fabric discharged and overdyed using the arashi method around a huge nylon rope by yours truly, in Elin Noble's workshop "Subtractions and Additions", Pacific Northwest Art School, 2021.

HOW TO USE THIOUREA DIOXIDE IN A DISCHARGE BATH (FOR 1 LB FABRIC)*5

1. **Gear up!** Gloves, apron, acid gas respirator, close-toed shoes.
2. **Set up: Make the discharge bath:** Heat 2 1/2 gallons of water in a metal pot to 175–180°F (79–82°C).
3. Once water is at proper temperature add:
   - **2 1/2 tsp (10 gm) Thiox**
   - **2 tbl (20 gm) soda ash (1 tbl for silk and wool)**
4. Stir bath and **add pre-wetted fiber**. Keep stirring if you want even results. If doing resist and you really aren't interested in "even", you can leave the bath alone removing the cloth when you have removed enough color.
5. **Rinse** in several baths of warm water. The fabric is ready to be overdyed if you are happy with the amount of color removal. If you want to remove more color, after rinsing, add back to the discharge bath. See tips on "Using Thiox", about recharging bath. If you are finished dyeing, rise with warm water and synthrapol at this point.
6. **If dyeing silk or wool**, neutralize fabric by soaking in a bath of 3 cups of vinegar and 1 gallon of water for 10 minutes.

CREATE DISCHARGE PRINT PASTE!

To remove color in areas using stencils, silkscreens, or to hand paint or spray it on, you will want to create a **discharge print paste**. You can add dye to the paste and if it's a color that is difficult to remove (ahem, Mr. Turquoise), your discharge will remove dye and deposit dye simultaneously!

Usually we make our own pastes in the dye world because we can control the thickness of the paste, color, and texture. But! There are many suppliers that make premixed print paste like PRO Chem's Print Paste Mix SH. Each supplier has their own directions for these products but basically the process is similar except with print paste you have to mix it up and leave it OVERNIGHT. When you make your own, the longest you wait is 15 minutes. Now we are getting into the good–fast–cheap triangle again!

Figure 6.6 A piece by fabulous textile artist Kerr Grobowski using discharge paste mixed with turquoise dye as the final layer of this piece.
Photo courtesy of Kerr Grobowski.

Mixing sodium alginate by hand can be a challenge. Many people who use print paste on a regular basis use a blender specially assigned to **dye products only and not food.** This can speed up the process and make your paste smoother.

Supplies
- 3/4ths cup (188ml) 110–120°F (44–50°C) water
- 1/2 tsp (3.5 gm) Metaphos
- 1/4th tsp (1gm) Thiourea dioxide
- 2 tsp (3 gm) Sodium Alginate
- 1/2 tsp (1.5 gm) Soda Ash
- Towel to lay mixing tools on

***HOW TO** CREATE A DISCHARGE PRINT PASTE AND USE IT TOO!*
1. **Add ingredients** in following order to 3/4ths cup (188ml) 110–120°F (44–50°C) water. Stir until dissolved.
    - 1/2 tsp (3.5 gm) Metaphos
    - 1/4th tsp (1gm) Thiourea Dioxide
    - 1/2 tsp (1.5 gm) Soda Ash
2. Once dissolved **slowly add 2 tsp sodium alginate, while stirring rapidly.** A small whisk or spatula works well for this.
3. Let mixture stand to thicken 10–15 minutes.
4. Apply discharge paste to fabric. **Do not allow paste to fully dry on fabric!** Thiox needs a damp environment to lift color. A great option is to batch your print in black plastic and set it in the sun for an hour. Check back to see if your print has lifted, if not, leave it to batch discharge longer. If you have no sun or place to batch lift your discharge, you can steam your piece for 20–30 minutes (for instructions on how to steam your fabric see Chapter 8: Painting and Printing With Dye).
5. **If discharge printing on silk**, add to neutralizing bath (1 cup vinegar to 1 gallon water) for 10 minutes.
6. **Rinse** well in hot water with 1/2 tsp detergent.

RIT COLOR REMOVER (SODIUM HYDROSULFITE)
Readily available at many a supermarket or crafty store near you, this product is straightforward to use. Although not the safest or environmentally friendly product, it can be useful. Because it is sulfur based, it releases some stinky there's-a-hot-spring-nearby rotten-egg smells, so get ready. Don't get me started about the Rit website photo of someone color removing with their bare hands! Please wear gloves and a half-face respirator when using this product.

Supplies
- Rit color remover
- Pot large enough to swish fabric in
- Towel to set wet spoons on

HOW TO USE RIT COLOR REMOVER

(1 lb of fabric)

1. Fill a pot with water and heat to almost boiling ~200°F (93.3°C), basically when water simmers.
2. Add 2 tbl Rit Color Remover and stir to dissolve.
3. Keep pot simmering.
4. Add pre-wetted fabric to the bath.
5. Stir for even discharge; item should lift in 10–20 minutes.
6. Rinse with warm water first then cool water, until water runs clear.
7. Wash in 1/2 tsp industrial detergent (can even be in the washing machine).

DECOLOURANT

deColourant is a paste made by Jacquard that is a premixed discharge paste. It also comes in a mist, if lighter results are desired. These pastes can be made from scratch but you would have to buy the chemicals and put yourself at higher risk, so I have included this safer, premixed product! This product uses different chemicals than Thiox, so make sure to know the risks before you use it (see Table 6.2).

Where areas of paste are thicker, you will find a greater amount of color will discharge. I always find the results of doing discharge printing to be fascinating. You never know what colors will lift and which will stay! I love discharging black because of the dramatic results; black can discharge to red, green yellow – it's anyone's guess. Elin Noble told a story of some fabric she bought from a retailer. It was black fabric – she informed us that fabrics that get screwed up in the printing process get overdyed black and sold as black fabric . . . so she discharged the fabric and out emerged a print! So fascinating! Often discharged pieces are used for utilitarian reasons – to create a light background on a dark foreground and then to get painted into. More drama!

Figure 6.7 A sample for Cousin Topsy (Meryl Streep's) character in *Mary Poppins Returns*. Discharged and overdyed piece of velvet fabric. Face on left, back on right. You can see the discharge went all the way through some of the fabric.
Photo courtesy of Beth Herd.

Supplies

- Jacquard deColourant
- A board to pin your fabric to
- Fabric that you **know** will discharge (Dharma Trading sells loads of fabrics that they guarantee will discharge – but make sure it says that for sure)
- Applicator (depending on how you will apply the paste): a brush? Sponge?
- Stencil? Stamp? Freehand?

Figure 6.8 deColourant paste on the left and deColourant mist with sample on the right. There is not over-dye or paint present. The discharge was much lighter with the mist and a little more uneven. Note on the paste sample the edges are lighter – this is where the pate was thicker.

HOW TO USE DECOLOURANT TO DISCHARGE PRINTS

1. Pin fabric down to a surface with some give (see Chapter 8 on printing with dye).
2. Line up stencil, screen or get out your brush and pin that down too (stencil).
3. Using a sponge, squeegee, or paint brush, apply a thin layer of deColourant to the fabric. Make sure the entire area you want to discharge is covered in paste.
4. Allow paste to dry completely on the fabric but **wash stencils or silkscreens immediately.**
5. While wearing a respirator fitted with acid gas cartridges, use a hot steam iron to heat the dry paste in circular motions. You can create a variation in color by leaving the iron on one area longer than another. If you would like a more uniform discharge, use a press cloth. The process will take more time but your results will be even.

THE BOTTOM LINE

Choose the appropriate color remover for the fiber content and dye type you are using. This doesn't mean not to experiment with removers that aren't intended for those fibers or dyes, but try to choose corresponding removers first. Discharge dyeing is one of my favorite dye techniques and can yield incredible results. Just take care to use appropriate ventilation and personal protection.

NOTES

1. www.clorox.com/learn/how-to-neutralize-bleach-with-hydrogen-peroxide/.
2. Yantai Dastek Chemical Corporation. "Thiourea Dioxide Versus Sodium Hydrosulfite." 2019. http://dasteck.com/News/99.html.
3. Sodium Hydrosulfite/Color Remover/IDYE Color Remover Safety Data Sheet; CHM1025, CHM1300, CHM2300, JID1400, Chem Tel, Inc./Dharma Trading; Petaluma, CA; 03/26/2018.
4. Gun, Guanlei. "Why People Choose Thiourea Dioxide (TDO) to Replace Sodium Hydrosulfite in Textile and Paper Industry." *LinkedIn Post*, 2017. www.linkedin.com/pulse/why-people-choose-thiourea-dioxidetdo-replace-sodium-hydrosulfite.
5. ProChemical and Dye. "Thiox." 2002. www.prochemicalanddye.net.

7

BEAUTY IS ONLY SKIN DEEP

CHANGING THE COLOR OF LEATHER!

Dyeing leather has come a long way from the days of our ancient ancestors. Instead of dyeing large pieces of leather into a general color range using ammonia from urine and dyes derived from plants, we create and match precise colors using advanced chemistry and chemical processes.

We use dye and paint, chemically formulated to bond with leather on large and small portions, alike. As you can see in Figure 7.1, the artisan used a mixture of paint and dyes to achieve depth and aging. Most artisans use a mixture of these products in combination with old-school texture and color changing techniques that don't require a chemical bond – like burning leather and burnishing leather.

Leather tanning dates back thousands of years and became a necessity when animal hides became too stiff in cold weather or rotted in hot weather. Ancient people developed a tanning process that essentially processed raw animal hides into skins of usable leather. The three most popular hides are from cattle, sheep, and pigs but also include buffalo, elk, deer, and many more exotic sources. Currently there are about 60 tanneries in the US but not all of them do the full tanning process. There used to be hundreds more but many tanneries have shut down due to environmental regulations, an increase in synthetic leather, and an increase in imported leather. There are countless accounts about

Figure 7.1 A leather sample hand painted with Angelus leather paint by paint and dye expert Jeff Fender for Victoria's Secret runway show.

DOI: 10.4324/9781351130677-8

by-products from the tanning process entering local water supplies and massive environmental cleanups ensuing.

There are some techniques I will introduce in this chapter that are more toxic than others. I will recommend the lowest-toxicity products first, but sometimes, to get the job done, you have to reach for some harsh chemicals. I just try to limit the use of those and make my go-to's the lower-tox products.

DYEING WHOLE HIDES

At some point, a designer will want to build an army out of the same-color leather – and it will be a strange dystopian time-not-in-time designer–color. This will require dyeing several animal skins the exact same color. Trust me, I speak from experience. I had to dye 9–11 (I can't remember how many) elk hides the same green–blue–grey for Anna Oliver's design for *Cyrano de Bergerac* at the Old Globe (Figure 7.2).

Figure 7.2 Dyed blue elk uniform jackets hanging in stock. Even though they were all dyed the same color in the same dye and processes, they are from different individual animals that have slight variations in hide thicknesses, etc., so they are slightly different colors. This variation can be seen in the jacket at bottom left very well. Old Globe Theater's Cyrano, 2009. Costume Designer Anna Oliver, draper Wendy Miller.

The skin had to stay supple and the color could not rub off (or crock) on their white shirts that were worn under the military costumes. Oh, and did I mention they all had to match? You know, like uniforms do? I had always just dyed smaller pieces of leather with acid dyes and some vinegar to lower the pH – which I tried with my initial samples on these skins. The samples were uneven in color and the leather lost much of it's suppleness. Also, it did not pass a **crock test** (where the color doesn't rub off on a damp white cloth while applying pressure). I enlisted the help of Chemtan, a company that deals specifically with the leather tanning industry, stateside and overseas. Over many hours of phone conversations, they helped me understand the multistep process to successfully reproduce the same color and texture on the hides I had to dye; in the next section is the detailed process.

VAT DYEING LEATHER THE SUREFIRE WAY

First – there are some major components you must have to vat dye hides. To dye entire hides, you must have a vessel large enough to accommodate at least one full hide covered in water, a few chemical components to keep the leather soft and to set the dye, a pH meter is super helpful, and a frame slightly larger than the skin to stretch it out on after dyeing. I used all Chemtan products, which can be found at most taxidermy suppliers. You can also call Chemtan and ask what taxidermists close to you carry their products. They will also send samples.

Table 7.1 Leather Dye and Additive Amounts Based on Weight of Leather.

Pounds of Leather	Water (500% wt)	Detergent (.75% wt)	Leveling agent (1% wt)	Dye (5%)	Fat Liquor (6 %)
1	0.57 gal	1.20 oz	1.60 oz	0.80 oz	0.96 oz
2	1.14 gal	2.40 oz	3.20 oz	1.60 oz	1.92 oz
3	1.70 gal	3.60 oz	4.80 oz	2.40 oz	2.88 oz
4	2.27 gal	4.80 oz	6.40 oz	3.20 oz	3.84 oz
5	2.84 gal	6.00 oz	8.00 oz	4.00 oz	4.80 oz
6	3.41 gal	7.20 oz	9.60 oz	4.80 oz	5.76 oz
7	3.98 gal	8.40 oz	11.20 oz	5.60 oz	6.72 oz
8	4.55 gal	9.60 oz	12.80 oz	6.40 oz	7.68 oz
9	5.11 gal	10.80 oz	14.40 oz	7.20 oz	8.64 oz
10	5.68 gal	12.00 oz	16.00 oz	8.00 oz	9.60 oz

Supplies:
- Nonionic surfactant like synthrapol or laundry detergent
- Chemtan T-13 Levelling Agent
- Chemtan Acid Dyes (other acid dyes may work too but sample first!)
- Fat liquor
- Glacial acetic acid (food grade)
- Dye Vat
- Leather needles

- Stretching Frame – a frame slightly larger than the hide you are dyeing.
- Strong waxed thread
- A stick to agitate the leather
- Optional: pH meter, thermometer

HOW TO VAT DYE LEATHER

1. **Gear Up!** Long heat-safe gloves (I like the ones that go up to your armpits – photo in Chapter 1, Figure 1.7), a half-face respirator with P100 cartridges, a dust filter mask (for pasting out dye), and apron.
2. **Weigh your hide or hides**. All of your measurements of water, dyes, and auxiliary chemicals *are based on the weight of your hides*. Because this is a long and tricky process using chemical additives and liquors, I recommend weighing everything first and starting there. Each hide will weigh in a little differently, so make sure not to create one formula for all of your hides if you are dyeing them separately. You can dye your hides together but make sure you add all of the hide weights together and calculate your water, dyes, and additives based on that total weight.
3. **Add water to vat**. Fill your dye vessel with the appropriate amount of water (using the following equation) and heat it up to 68°–77° F (20–25°C).
   Formula to calculate amount of water needed:
   500% * total weight of leather = Gallons Water
   Example: If we had 10 lbs of hides: 5.0 * 10 lbs = 50 lbs of water.
   Then you have to convert that water to gallons **(water = 8.8 lbs per gallon)**.
   So, 50lbs H_2O ÷ 8.8lbs/gal = 5.7 gallons H_2O.
4. **Add the detergent (or nonionic surfactant)** to the bath. This should be about .75% of hide weight (or literally a capful of detergent).
5. **Add the leveling agent.**
   Add 1% of total weight of hides.
   Our example: 10 lbs * .01 = 0.1 lbs
6. **Wet out your hides.** Add hides to the vat. Allow the hides to soak in the water a minimum of three hours.
7. **Weigh out dye and paste it out.**
   Use 5% dye to hide ratio; a medium saturation of color.

   Our example: 0.05 * 10 lbs = 0.5 lbs or 8 oz. I convert to ounces (1 lb =16 oz) to be able to measure dye with a scale.

   Moving the hides to the side, add the pasted-out dye to the dye bath. (If you're curious about pasting out dye, refer to pasting out dye in Chapter 3. The dye is water soluble so it will dissolve in the solution quickly. In a half hour to 45 minutes or, as Lucas from ChemTan, says, "However long your shoulders hold out", check the color penetration by cutting a small swatch and blow drying it. You don't want a low-water immersion pattern, right? So, keep the leather gently moving. Swish . . . swish . . . swish. Think of it as a meditation. At this point you can add more dye to deepen or tone the color.

8. **Add Fat Liquor.**
   Use 6–10% fat liquor based on hide weight.
   Our example using 6%: 0.06 * 10 lbs= 0.6 lbs or 9.6 oz.

Dilute fat liquor to water in a 1:5 ratio; then, throw it straight into the bath. No need to remove leather. Leave the leather in your bath for a minimum of 2 hours. Feel the skin before and after this step to decide if more time is necessary. After 2 hours, look at your bath – does it look milky or greasy? If so, more time is needed to absorb the fat liquor.

9. **Add the glacial acetic acid** in increments.
   For each increment, use 1% acid based on hide weight. Then add acid in a 10:1 (10 water to 1 acid) ratio to water before adding to bath.
   Our example: 0.01 * 10 lbs= 0.1 lbs or 1.6 oz. Add 1.6 oz to 16 oz of water.

10. ***IMPORTANT: Always add acid to water!* Not the reverse – this will cause a violent reaction.** Add glacial acetic acid in steps so the acid does not damage the leather and so push the color too dark. Add acid in 1% or 10:1 ratio (10 parts water to 1 part acid) increments and leave it the solution for 20 minutes after adding each new amount. **Check the color of your hide after adding first amount of acid –** you still have an opportunity to change color, add dye, and to tone color at this point. Using a pH meter, remove a cup of the bath and let it cool below 100° F. Measure the pH of the water in the cup and continue adding acid until you hit the sweet spot of **2.8–3.2**. It is very important to get within this pH range as the acid will change the charge of the solution to bond the dye with the leather.

11. **Rinse in a Fresh Bath of Water.** Using room temperature water, rinse skins in a bath. Agitate gently and remove skins from bath.

12. **Toggle Dry*.** Leather likes to contract after getting wet and can result in major goods shrinkage. To avoid this, you must stretch the leather when it's wet! Using a wooden or PVC frame, waxed (or just thick) thread, and your leather needle, stretch leather by sewing through the edges and around the edge of the frame (see Figure 7.3) until the leather is stretched evenly over the frame. It may help to pin the leather to the frame in a few places that won't be used in creating your garment. **PIN HOLES are forever!** They will not heal – so choose where you pin, carefully. Make sure your sewing is *in opposite sections* – you can divide it into four or more areas. This will help so you can gradually tighten subsequent areas you sew. Your hide should be stretched but be careful of ripping the hide but pulling too tight!! It doesn't need to double as a trampoline – it just needs to be stretched some so it doesn't shrink too much as it dries. Allow hide to dry completely before releasing from frame.

*If you are dyeing garment-weight leather, you can most likely hang it on the line to dry but it will definitely contract a bit. The clothes pin marks will also be permanent so just pin the very edges or dry flat, face side up, on a large surface.

Problem solving: **If your piece is too dark** . . . you can raise the pH of the solution by adding 0.5 to 1.0% baking soda (based on weight of hides – sense a theme here??!). This will drive the dye from the surface into the hide resulting in lightening the surface color. After leaving the hide in this bath for at least 30 to 60 minutes, cut a small piece off the hide and blow dry to check the color. If it's still not light enough check the pH (to see if it is still very low = acidic) and add more baking soda (same increment as previously) and let soak for 30–60 more minutes. Lucas Paddock

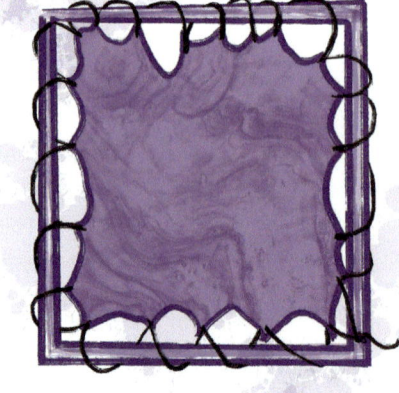

Figure 7.3 Toggle dry your leather on a frame! Make sure that it is stretched tight.

from Chemtan recommends that his technicians check again after 30 minutes and if the skin is not light enough still, leave the skins in the bath for another 30 minutes.

DYEING LEATHER WITH LEATHER DYE OR LEATHER PAINT

Painting leather is a fairly regular task for a painter/dyer. The most important part of the painting process is preparation and finishing of the leather. I have not included an exhaustive list of dyes and paints for leather but included my "most-wanted" frequently used products. The products vary in chemical composition and fall into three categories: oil, alcohol, and water based. The main difference between leather dye and leather paint is that paint sits on the surface of the leather while dye penetrates the leather. There are a range of pros and cons with each type of product. Please see table 7.2 for a comparison of brands, pros and cons.

Figure 7.4 Wool daubers can absorb an immense amount of liquid and are perfect for dyeing leather.

To apply these dyes, you can use a variety of applicators such as a dobber, brush, or rags to name a few. Each applicator will create a different texture depending on the desired end result. Usually the most desirable applicator is one that can be loaded up with a lot of dye. This helps to minimize streaking, especially on natural unfinished leathers. Play around with a few different applicators and techniques to find your dream texture.

PREPARATION!

Preparation is 75% of the work. If you prep the leather well, it will absorb and bond with whatever you decide to put on the surface. Deciding how to prep the surface of leather depends on the leathers' finish and type of leather you are working with. Leather that comes unfinished, like vegetable tanned leathers for example, absorb dyes and paints readily without any stripping. As a matter of fact, the surface preparation you may want to use on unfinished leathers is more like an additive that allows the paint to flow evenly over the leather surface. See Figure 7.6 for a comparison of veg-tanned leather prepared with water vs baby oil using paint and dye.

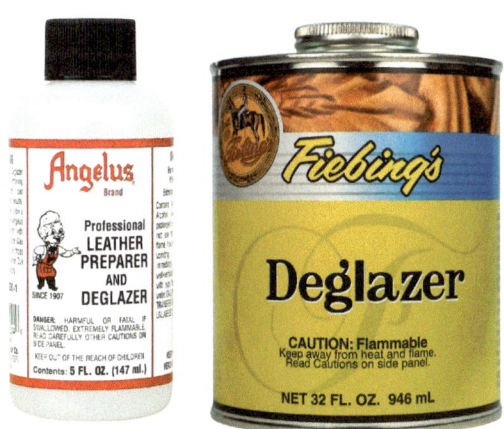

Figure 7.5 Commercial deglazers. These require a respirator to use!

The quickest way I know to prep leather for paint or dye is starting with the least toxic materials first and work my way up to higher-tox products if necessary. Much in the same way a nurse wipes your skin to clean it of oils, bacteria, and whatever else with an alcohol prep pad, I like to use 70% isopropyl alcohol on an old t-shirt or other soft rag and evenly wipe the surface of the leather. Why not use 99% isopropyl, you ask? Using 70% is a great place to start. It is less aggressive than 99% and will not totally dry out your leather if the finish is easy to break through. If your leather has a shiny finish, you will want to use enough alcohol to make the finish slightly dull. In essence you are stripping the finish from the leather, so the pores will be open and ready to accept new color. Some commercially finished leathers can be very stubborn and even if you use something harsher like 99% isopropyl or denatured alcohol, it can be difficult to break through the finish. Angelus and Fiebings make a great leather stripper called "Leather Preparer and Deglazer". These products use acetone and ethyl alcohol (see note on using acetone) so use proper protection advised by the SDS. Funny thing, if you use proper protection advised by the SDS for these products, you will look like you are in the movie *Outbreak* in a full-on hazmat suit! This is why I use these products SPARINGLY, if at all. Also, a 1 liter bottle of rubbing alcohol is around $1.50 while these deglazers are $10 or more.

If you want to remove old paint from leather all together (for example on shoes) you can use acetone but it will really dry out the leather so be prepared to add leather conditioner like Lexol, Leather Rescue, Leather Honey, etc., after you repaint or dye the leather. Remember to do samples first! Leather is expensive!

Another way to prep finished leather (and great in a pinch) is to use very fine-grit sandpaper, 600 or to give the leather a light sanding. I emphasize the word **light**! You will NOT want to do this if you require a very reflective glossy surface as it will dull the surface without the use of a gloss top coat.

USES FOR OLD PANTY-HOSE AND GROSS UNDERSHIRTS!

Can I tell you how many uses I have for old pantyhose and used up undershirts!? I use panty hose to strain dye after I mix it up and as I pour it into my main dyeing vessel whether that is a dye vat, washing machine, or larger pot! Using tights can be a challenge in this application because they are more tightly woven and strain out too many particles that will actually dissolve in your hot water! BUT! If you find you are getting **fugitive dye** specks all over your samples, *do* strain with a more tightly woven hose! I also use pantyhose to create sausages to insert in shoes when I paint them to keep the paint off of the insides. They squish down to go in any shoe but puff back up to put tension against the edges of the shoe – so when you saw that squirrel when you were painting and your brush went astray, the paint gets on the sausage, not the lining of the shoe! See the part of this chapter all about painting shoes on how to make them!

Old undershirts are THE BEST RAGS ever. They are soft, absorbent (because they've been washed 300 times), and generally do not leave lint on your projects. I use them for

Figure 7.6 Panty-hose stretched over a strainer to catch undissolved dye.

applying paint, leather dye, glue, or anything else where I will have to throw away the rag after using. The rags that I use for polishing shoes I just keep in the shoe polish area with the corresponding shoe wax color. I use them to polish metal, apply metal rouge, and to handle a hot piece of metal. I also use the shirt rags as paint applicators when I want to add paint to something without seeing brush strokes and conversely I use them to blot paint off of surfaces where I am brushing on thick paint. Old undershirts are also GREAT to use to create a color sample ring for knit fabrics. We often have to dye knit to match performers' skin colors and it is so fantastic (and FREE) to have a knit skin tone ring to match skin tones! I have used them as knit paint samples for airbrushing and to demonstrate specific dye pattern designs to directors and choreographers when I am designing a show! I'm sure you can come up with 10 more uses!!!

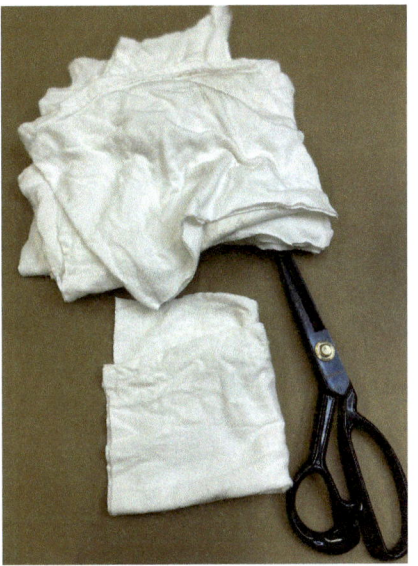

Figure 7.7 I use cut-up shirts for everything. They are not as bulky as towels and it makes me feel good about using these nasty undershirts one more time before sending them to the trash.

Table 7.2 Leather Paint and Dye Comparison.

Product Name	Type of Dye/ Paint	Good Qualities	The Downside	Safety Info
Angelus	Leather Dye (alcohol-based)	Offers many colors. Is pigment rich so it can be thinned with alcohol and remain saturated.	Not sold or shipped to California, less available colors (22 vs 26) than Fiebings.	Hazard category 1–4, causes cancer, toxic to aquatic life.
Angelus	Leather Paint (water-based)	Offers a rainbow of colors, metallics, and pearlescent finishes, water-based, no ventilation required.	Can thicken over time and needs to be thinned, white dries out quickly.	No measurable hazards.
Fiebings	Pro Dye (alcohol-based dye with added oil dye)	Great range of colors, has an added oil dye so colors are richer, doesn't dry leather as much as regular leather dye.	Dries out leather, must condition leather before application, takes longer to dry, fume hood required.	Hazard category 1–4, causes cancer, toxic to aquatic life.

Product Name	Type of Dye/ Paint	Good Qualities	The Downside	Safety Info
Fiebings	Leather Dye (alcohol-based)	Great range of colors, less expensive than ProDye.	Dries out leather, must condition leather before application, leaves residue of powdered pigment, fume hood required.	Hazard category 1–4, causes cancer, toxic to aquatic life.
Fiebings	Leather Dye (water-based)	Beautiful array of colors, water-based, a dye that can be shipped to California.	Streaky, leather is stiffer than using ProDye, colors aren't as saturated as alcohol-based dyes.	NO hazard categories (at least in the 2008 SDS)
Fiebings	Acrylic Leather Dye (alcohol based)	Thin, so applies evenly, saturated colors.	Limited palette of colors, fume hood required.	Not classified as hazardous.
Fiebings	Acrylic Dye (water-based)	Can be used on finished leather; opaque, water-based.	Twice the price of Angelus leather paint, limited color gamut. No glitter, neon, or pearlescent offerings.	Hazard category 2B – eye irritation, otherwise pretty safe.
Eco-Flo Cova Color	Leather Paint (water-based)	Low voc, thin and transparent, can be mixed easily, can be used to tone or tint leather, nice alternative to toxic dyes.	For use on veg-tan leather, acts almost like a dye so doesn't work well on finished leather.	No measurable hazards.
Sharpie Markers	Permanent Markers	Available in an array of color and tip sizes, offer metallics, and white. Cheap! Available many stores.	Can appear less saturated than using paint.	Nonhazardous substance.
Meltonian Nu-Life Shoe Spray	Leather Spray Paint	Available in most shoe repair stores, fast and easy to use.	Super toxic, must wear ventilator even outside, finished item often looks plastic-y.	Hazard category 1–4. Causes cancer, birth defects, toxic.

A NOTE ON ACETONE

Figure 7.8 Acetone.

According to the SDS for Acetone, it is a CNS depressant (or central nervous system depressant). This means if you expose yourself in areas with little ventilation or you use the product without the proper protection you can poison yourself. The CNS is responsible for involuntary (breathing, heart beating) and voluntary (walking, blinking) bodily processes. Believe me, you don't want this to become a long-term poisoning by exposing yourself repeatedly and becoming a vegetable.

The SDS also advises to use Viton rubber or PVA gloves. Nitrile gloves (my favorite) completely disintegrate when using acetone. If you plan on stripping leather shoes or other painted leather with acetone, have some PVA gloves on hand.

CHOOSE YOUR OWN ADVENTURE: DYE OR PAINT?

Leather Dye

If you would like to add a transparent layer of color to your freshly stripped leather, you can use a leather dye like Angelus or Fiebings. There are several different types and colors of dye and some are actually an opaque paint. They offer a stunning array of colors; check out Figure 7.8, the Fiebings leather dyes and paints color chart. Check out fiebings.com to view this chart in larger detail.

There are three conditions you will need to meet to totally change the color of a finished hide with painted dye: it must start in a light color (or you have to make it light in color first), you must be able to strip the finish at least partially, and you must have a finish coat of some sort to seal the leather. **Leather dye is transparent so any color under your dyed layer will show through.** This is a wonderful thing to create depth and to tone leather away from or into another color. Let's say the designer wants to tone some of the red out of a brown leather jacket but wants all

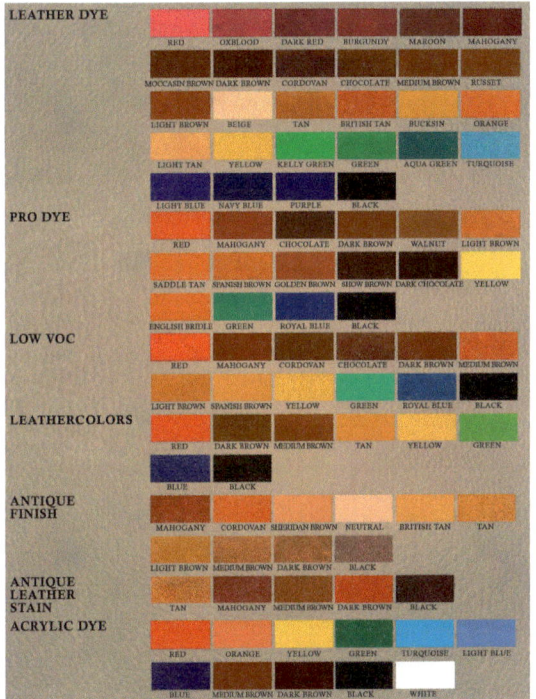

Figure 7.9 The array of Fiebings leather dyes and paints.
Photo courtesy of Fiebings.

of the original distressing to show through. You can find a green leather dye and dilute it with denatured alcohol (illegal in California by the way – in that case use 99% isopropyl), *first trying samples* on the inside of the jacket. For this type of application, I would use an old t-shirt rag or larger sponge and quickly wipe your mixture over the jacket. MAKE SURE to write down what ratios you used of leather dye and solvent (the alcohol), so you can mix up more dye when you run out!!! Add this ratio to the label of your container before you put it back in the flammable's cabinet just in case OSHA decides to stop by!

Begin by shaking the leather dye bottle vigorously. It likes to separate when sitting on the shelf. Using your applicator of choice, make even and nearly overlapping swipes over the leather, edge to edge if possible. If you need a larger applicator, use a whole sponge. If you are mixing dye and solvent, I like to have a package of 1, 2, 4 oz salsa cups on hand with lids – these can be found at most restaurant supply stores much cheaper than Amazon. These are great for mixing different samples – and keeping for touch-ups. For long-term storage a glass container will be best as the salsa cups can let minute amounts of air into the container and dry out the dye.

> ### WHAT DO I DO WITH ALL OF MY LEFTOVER LEATHER DYE?
>
> There are a few options here depending on the scale of the organization you work for. You can often dispose of chemicals in a designated place on the property of your workplace. If you are working for a small community theater or you are creating a cosplay for yourself, you can set the containers outside in a place to dry out. Because these dyes are alcohol-based, they dry out pretty quickly. Make sure that your containers are in a place where they will not get blown over or discovered by anyone who might be curious about your drying containers. Once the dye has dried and the container is completely dry, you legally can throw the containers in the trash.

Leather Paint
I like to use Angelus acrylic paint. It has good coverage and is readily available. After prepping your leather accordingly, find a very soft brush to apply your paint. Add your paint to a palette or dish and pick it up like you are painting with regular acrylic paints. I personally like to brush on some paint; then, with a crumpled t-shirt scrap, I tamp the area lightly to remove some paint. I do this over and over again – it creates a realistic coating that doesn't look plastic and does not peel, crack, or rub off! Finish the leather with a finishing product of your choice – please see finishing section following "leather paint".

Fiebings and Angelus offer an acrylic leather paint that works wonderfully if the leather is prepared and finished correctly! Another brand – a product by Tandy Leather, Eco Flo Cova Color – seems to be the only brand that offers specifically low-voc and water-based leather products, offering a range of opaque and transparent products. According to Hallie Dufresne from Rethreaded,

Eco-Flo Water stains are water-based and transparent, but layered in several coats (3 to 5) create really rich colors. We use it regularly in my shop. I have fund that the easiest application method for working on pieces larger than my hand are round art sponges with a soft t-shirt rag at the ready to buff up excess dye.

In my opinion, these are great if you desire a transparent and painterly look (Figure 7.9) but not great for full coverage as the opacity is not as high as Angelus and it requires more coats.

The exciting thing about Angelus paints (I know I sound like their biggest fan right now . . .) is that they also offer glitter coats that bond to leather and are flexible! They also offer pearlescent and metallic colors as well as neon. In my example I decided to do a drastically different color and go from dark blue to red to illustrate how you can choose to change leather to whatever color you want – you just have to use the right products.

Supplies:
- Rags
- Leather paint
- Isopropyl alcohol or deglaze
- Soft brush or applicator of your choice

Figure 7.10 Shoes painted with leather paint for the film *Scorpion King* to keep the sand out of background performers' sandals.

HOW TO PAINT LEATHER

1. **Gear up!** Gloves and apron! Lay down newspaper or brown paper on workspace.
2. **Prepare leather and shake up your paint!** To prep your leather follow steps in the previous "Preparation" section. Prepare your paint by shaking the leather paint bottle, vigorously. It likes to separate when sitting on the shelf. You can water down acrylic paint if you want a small amount of the original color to show through. Do not water the paint down more than 30% though, as you will decrease the paints' bond with the leather.
3. **Paint and blot.** Like leather dye, using your applicator of choice, make almost overlapping swipes over the leather, edge to edge if possible. Quickly, using your wadded up t-shirt rag, blot the leather paint where lines occurred from painting.
4. **Let your paint dry.** If you skip this step, your next layer of paint will remove your first layer of paint. I know watching paint dry is not exciting, but trust me, it's worthwhile!
5. **Apply a second coat.** Paint and blot a second coat. Once this layer dries if it is not opaque enough add another coat and keep going until you have reached the desired coverage.
6. **Finish coat/top coat.** Using the product of your choice (see

Figure 7.11 Cova color by Eco-Flo was used on this veg-tanned leather mask after assembly. You can see the mid-tones of the leather showing through the paint. Choosing this product for an antique rubbed look worked out!

upcoming section on finishing) and waiting until your leather is completely dry, apply finish coat and let it dry. You'll be good to go!

FINISHING

There are many finishing products out there. A very simple, cheap, and available product is neutral shoe polish. A professional dyer and educator, Teri Tevares, taught me this trick of using shoe polish to finish leather dye or paint – and it TOTALLY works! It also makes your new color look shiny and restores your leather to a factory-finished look. If you're interested in learning more about using shoe polish, I demonstrate how to use it as a finisher in the following "Hand Painting Shoes" section. If you desire a matte or super gloss finish or you just want a brush-on product, Fiebings, Angelus, and ChemTan all make brush-on products. ChemTan makes my favorite dull/gloss products, but you must buy it in large quantities; although they will send samples if you decide you want to try it before you make the investment. It is also thin enough to spray through a pre-val, but then you're back to requiring a half-face respirator and a ventilated space.

Figure 7.12 Topcoats come in many finishes. Angelus, Fiebings, and EcoFlo are some of the manufacturers of leather-specific top coats. Neutral shoe polish is a very inexpensive way to top-coat acrylic paint and you can buff to a high-shine if you want that look!

TRANSFORMING SHOES WITH LEATHER PAINT

This is one of the most frequently requested shoe alterations in theatre. I have met many a jaded costume designer who will refuse to allow crafters to paint a pair of shoes with acrylic leather paint because someone in their past, we'll call her Ms. Spackle, had spackled acrylic paint over pair of shoes for a previous design and they looked terrible – or using shoe spray is just how they do it in New York. Well, with this technique, you will be able to convince even your most stubborn

Figure 7.13 Angelus Glitterettes are a line of glitter coat paints formulated specifically for leather! Bring on those ruby slippers!!!

designer that using acrylic paint to change the color of shoes is a beautiful, longer lasting, and healthier solution. This technique will minimize personal exposure to the high levels of toxic chemicals when using shoe spray.

SHOE SAUSAGES – THEY'RE VEGAN!

I create soft "sausages" to stuff inside shoes when I paint them so I don't get paint on the interior of the shoe. Even though Patty LaPone is a pretty cool person, she would not be happy if she was handed her $500 dance shoes with paint all over the lining!

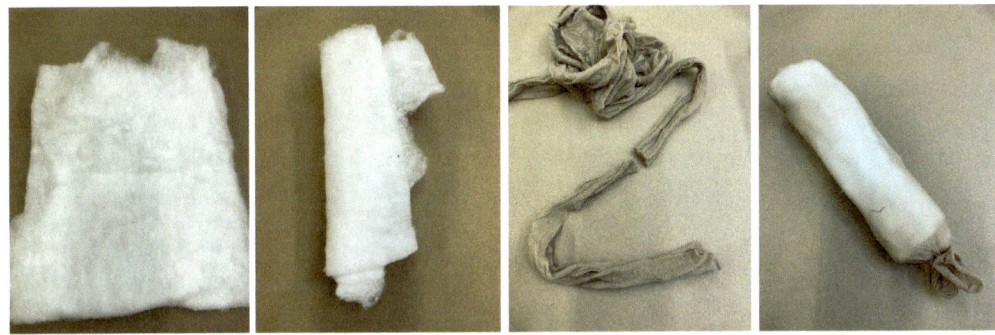

Figure 7.14 Create your own shoe sausages! Roll batting (left 2 images) and stuff into the end of a pantyhose leg. Tie it off and you're ready jam it in that shoe and do some speed painting.

HAND PAINTING SHOES

Figure 7.15 Before (left) and after (right) painting a pair of vintage shoes. Not only do they actually look like they are made of leather now, they look like they came from the store that way.

Supplies:
- Acetone (if they have been painted before)
- 99% Isopropyl Alcohol
- Rags (I like old shirt rags)
- A soft paint brush
- Acrylic Leather Paint
- Painter's tape
- Shoe sausage or something to stuff in shoe
- Optional: Edgecote or a matching sole color

HOW TO HAND PAINT SHOES WITH ACRYLIC LEATHER PAINT

1. **Gear up!** Gloves (NOT NITRILE if using acetone), a well-ventilated area, apron, respirator if using acetone.

2. **Masking.** You know how with painting anything with your house, prep is at least half the work? It's the same here. Start by taping off your shoes' sole by using your fingernail to get the tape around the edge between the shoe upper and the sole. Tape the inside of the heel. Tape the buckle and any other hardware you need to mask off. Don't forget to remove laces and/or add tape to the back of an ankle strap! Stuff your shoe with your sausage – you're masked! See top of Figure 7.17 for an example of a masked shoe.
3. **Stripping.** If your shoes are like the ones I used in my demo photos – which Ms. Spackle got her hands on using acrylic leather paint – using acetone to prep the shoes works well. Make sure you are in a very well-ventilated area when using acetone. Similar to when you remove paint from your nails, soak a small part of your shirt–rag with acetone and wipe the surface of the shoe. Don't get too aggressive and try to take all the paint off; just try remove most of a layer. It will open the grain of the leather to accept the paint more readily and will keep your new paint job from cracking.

    If your shoes are new and are made of factory tanned leather never painted by Ms. Spackle, you are safe to use 70% or 99% isopropyl alcohol (whichever works to knock the finish off and open the grain) wiped over the surface with a rag.

4. **Painting!** The time has come to paint! Make sure to shake your acrylic paint very well; sometimes chunks settle in the bottom. Some people even strain it I don't usually go to that trouble but if I find a chunk I definitely remove it from my palette.

    Mix: With the brush you will be using to paint the shoes, mix up your color and make sure that you have created enough mixed paint to provide coverage for both shoes and a little extra for touchups for the dressers on your show. Make sure to start with your LIGHT color first and slowly add in drops of the darker color – this way you will avoid wasting a lot of paint. Trust me, I have wasted my share of paint this way!

 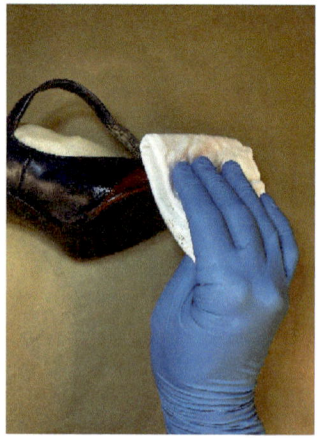 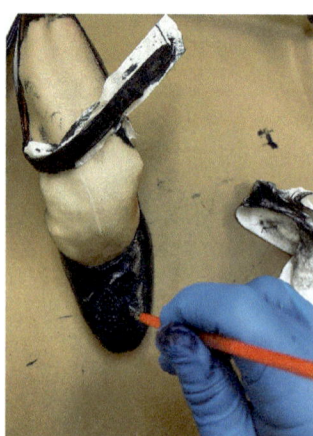

Figure 7.16 Masking and stuffing a shoe so no paint transfers to the inside of Broadway Betty's shoes are the touch of a professional (left). Blotting your first coat of paint removes excess lines or thick areas of paint and makes the paint look natural (middle). Add more paint after your first coat dries.

Paint: Using your soft brush, choose an area of the shoe to paint. I like to paint a shoe in thirds: front, instep, and outstep. This way, your paint doesn't dry before you get back to it to blot it. Start painting in your chosen area and taking a folded or wadded up shirt rag, blot your paint lightly. I use a very light tapping motion and make sure that all of the paint lines are gone.

Then I move onto another third of the shoe. Once you have covered your entire shoe, let it dry and then repeat. Do as many layers as you have to, to get the coverage you need. Make sure to check that you're getting your paint into all of the small holes and in the cracks and crevices.

Show the dressers the blotting technique as well, and you won't end up with big chunky shiny gross areas. I prefer small salsa cups for this purpose – you can even throw a piece of masking tape on the top with the actor/character name to hand off to wardrobe.

5. **Edgecote.** If you don't have Edgecote, that's OK! You can use flat black acrylic leather paint. Just make sure to blot your streaks the same way you did with the upper of the shoe. That's exactly what I did in Figure 7.17.

6. **Seal/Finish**. To finish your shoes after letting them dry for at least an hour and even longer with humid conditions, take cake shoe polish and apply it liberally with a rag. I like to use the soft T-shirt again because it doesn't leave streaks or Harry bits on my shoes. Don't freak out when your shoe looks dull at first. Let the polish set up for about 5 to 10 minutes, then you can take a brush to it with back-and-forth motions; shine that puppy! I used black polish to antique the example shoe but usually I use neutral polish. Typically, I use neutral cake shoe polish because it's clear, cheap, and lets the color come through. In my example (Figure 7.18) I used black shoe polish to antique the navy color of this vintage shoe a little bit more. Make sure you hit the entire shoe and the strap. Don't worry about the soles. The black polish works really well because it sticks in all of the crevices and makes the shoes look antique.

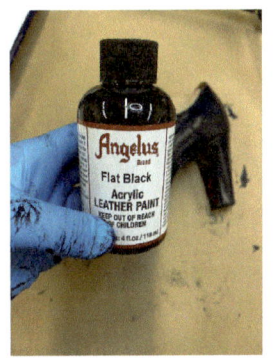 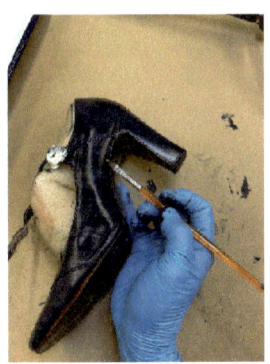

Figure 7.17 If you don't have edgecote, just use black (or matching color) to paint the sole, inside heel, and edge of sole.

LEATHER MARKERS

Leather markers are a great way to add detail to a leather piece. There are a few brands out there formulated just for leather but are really intended to be touch-up markers for leather goods like bags, shoes, and upholstery so they are available in a limited color gamut. Sharpies are the basic go-to as they are permanent, come in a large variety of colors, include metallics and white options, and an array of tip sizes. Another great option is the fillable marker by Angelus. They come in three tip sizes and you can put premixed colors,

Figure 7.18 Finish paint with shoe polish and buff to desired finish with a shoe brush!

Figure 7.19 Angelus fillable markers.

metallics, whatever you like in these markers. They also sell a thinning agent called 2-Thin that thins the paint without weakening the bond to leather. That product can also be used when painting with an airbrush with leather paint. Another type of marker people like to use are comic markers. These are also alcohol-based and come in many colors and tip sizes.

PAINTING WITH LEATHER SPRAY PAINT

This is my **least** favorite way to paint leather. Leather spray is made by several companies, the most common brand being Meltonian Nu-Life Shoe Spray. It comes in small or large spray paint cans. It is a quick and dirty way to change or touch up the color leather. It requires excellent ventilation, a P100 half-face respirator (even when outside), and gloves. The end product is often plastic-y looking and might work for the 5th ensemble guy to the right tapping in the back-back row. *Check out Table 7.2 for health info on this stuff, it's nasty!

HOW TO PAINT SHOES WITH LEATHER SPRAY PAINT

1. **Prepare Leather.** Prepare leather by hitting it with alcohol or stripping the color all together with acetone.
2. **Mask Areas You Don't Want to Paint.** Tape off the shoe soles and insert a rag or batting sausage to ensure spray doesn't go inside of the shoe.
3. **Spray First Coat.** Spray a light mist of shoe spray over the shoe. Make sure to turn the shoe upside down so you get into the arch area. Let dry, depending on how humid your location is, between 15–45 minutes. See box on how to use aerosol paints.
4. **Paint Second Coat.** Spray another light coat. If you have full coverage (check when it's dry) then stop. If you see what painters call "holidays" – empty spots with little paint, then add a third coat.

> ### A NOTE ON PAINTING WITH AEROSOLS . . .
>
> You will want to use light coats of whatever you are misting onto your leather surfaces. If you fail to do this, the leather will look very plastic, the paint may not bond well with the surface, and heavy spraying can leave three-dimensional paint drips.
>
> Spray from side to side. Start misting your paint from left to right, then right to left. Imagine you are spraying your paint and letting it fall onto your surface. You will be more successful with several passes like this rather than hosing the surface directly in one spot with paint. To remove paint, go back to the prepping with the acetone process.

5. **Finish.** You can choose any of the techniques in the "finishing" step of painting and dyeing leather. The most common way to finish leather painted this way is to use neutral polish from the can on a soft rag. Apply polish on rag and rub lightly all over. Wait until it dries (15–30 minutes) then polish the shoe or surface with a shoe brush in a side-to-side motion.

PAINTING AND DYEING UNFINISHED AND VEGETABLE-TANNED (VEG-TAN) LEATHER

You can prep veg-tan in a few ways: using water to wipe off any of the residue that's left on the tanning process or using some sort of oil. You could even do both but I think when you see the results of water vs oil prep it will be clear which one works more effectively!

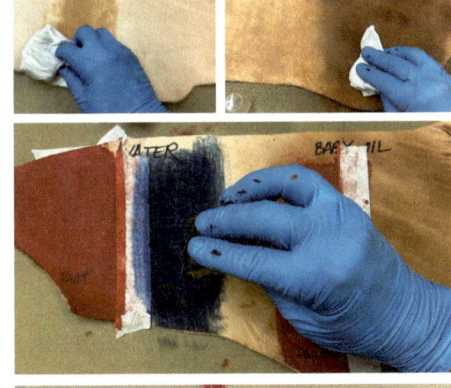

HOW TO PAINT VEG-TANNED LEATHER

1. **Prep leather.** Use either water or oil and wipe or spritz area of leather to be painted. In Figure 7.6, I used a mister to mist baby oil on the right of my sample and water on the left side.
2. **Paint.** In nearly overlapping passes, add paint or dye to your surface. With paint, use the blotting technique I talked about in the painting shoe section to get rid of any paint ridges. I used a 1" wide brush for the paint (angelus leather paint) and a chunk of sponge to wipe on the dye. Let it dry! Apply second coat if needed.

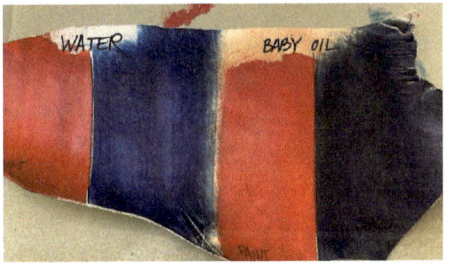

Figure 7.20 A comparison: prepping veg-tanned leather with water vs. baby oil. Top left: applying water with rag, right: baby oil. Middle: applying leather dye with sponge on side prepped with water. Bottom: the dried red paint and blue dye. Note that the water-prepped area is streaky while the area prepped with baby oil is a solid smooth color and darker too.

3. **Finish with your finisher of choice.** Make sure to finish your leather or do a crock test if you don't want to finish it – to see if any of the dye rubs off. If it does, add a finisher.

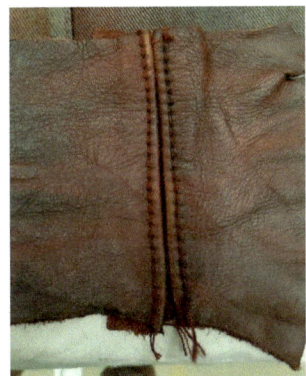

Figure 7.21 Leather and other samples for Chris Pratt's infamous trench coat in *Guardians of the Galaxy*, toned with transparent colors to allow original materials color to show through. Samples and photos by Jack Taggart, a master breakdown artist.

TONING LEATHER

Toning leather is really adding a glaze of color to tone out specific colors or to add highlight and shadow. The principles of watercolor or dip dyeing apply here in the way that toning requires the use of a transparent medium so the original color shows through the final coat. This will create rich realistic textures that designers love. Like toning any other object, using the complement or split complement to the color you want to be done with is key. If you want to add highlight and shadow you can use paint or dye, depending on the finish of the leather. If you want to add a quick shadow for example to a finished breast plate, using transparent leather paint watered down with solvent will give you a nice effect. You can even use watered down acrylic leather paint (as long as it's transparent). Leather dye can be used on unfinished leather for toning, but will need to be "watered" down (with solvent like denatured alcohol – now illegal to sell in California) a great deal to successfully tone your leather. As you may have gathered at this point, I choose the water-based version so I don't have to expose myself to the nasty fumes from solvents. Fiebings has a water-based dye called "Leathercolors" that could be used to tone finished leather. I would most definitely add a finish coat with that product.

Figure 7.22 Leather boots broken down by Jack Taggart with a wood burning tool for *Gray Man*.
Photo courtesy of Jack Taggart.

BURNING LEATHER

Another way to create depth in leather is to burn it. That's right – literally BURN it. People use embossing tools, wood burners, soldering irons, hot metal, whatever burns the leather surface. This is a great technique for aging shoes! Burn the areas that need to look more worn or burnished! See Figure 7.22 for an example of this technique.

BURNISHING LEATHER

Burnishing leather essentially polishing leather. You can burnish the edges of thick leather with a Dremel tool using a custom-made bit or just buy one from Amazon (see Figure 7.23). Wood is preferable because it smooths the edges of leather without burning or ripping the leather like metal or sandpaper could. This is a wonderful and professional finish for the edges of leather soles or armor. To take it up a notch, you can use edge enamel to really create a glossy shine to your finished edges.

Figure 7.23 Gold-foiled leather that has been tooled for *Exodus*, 2014. Fox Studios.

FOILING LEATHER

This process is virtually identical to foiling any other surface. Add glue to areas you want to apply foil, let glue dry, and add foil. Rub foil gently after it is dried to really work it into the leather. If a solid metal surface is required, after your first coat of foil is dry, add more glue and foil to areas where cracks occur. You can also create depth by choosing a base color that your foil metal color would patina to, to show through the cracks of the foil. After burnishing with a soft brush, you can seal the surface all at once. If you want texture with your foil, you can glue items like rope, findings, or even create designs on the leather with a texture medium, then foil over the top. For in-depth process steps and photos, see the Foiling section in Chapter 16.

COLOR REMOVING LEATHER

Did you know you can color remove leather too? There are great directions for resist dyeing leather in Kim Erwin's book *Surface Design for Fabric*. I have never needed to tie-dye leather, but if you do, her instructions include shibori resist and using a chemical resist.

LASER CUT AND SILK SCREEN

This beautiful costume from *X-Men Apocalypse* was made by laser cutting gold leather and overlaying it over screen printed leather to give the garment dimension. Many hours of labor in this costume, and apparently it is quite heavy!!

Figure 7.24 Robe from *X-Men Apocalypse*. Close up of leather screen print (top right) and laser-cut gold leather (bottom). Fox Studios.

THE BOTTOM LINE

Whatever way you choose to change the color of leather, remember to seal, topcoat, or add moisture back into your leather in some way. After all, it is skin, and skin will crack and degrade if not properly moisturized or sealed. Many products intended for leather are very harmful to breathe or absorb through your skin, so please protect yourself!

8

THE THREE S'S
SILKSCREENS, STENCILS, AND STAMPS

To create prints, there are a variety of techniques that can be used; which one you choose will depend on your desired destination. I will discuss many ways to create prints in this chapter including silkscreens, stencils, and stamps – but know that these are only *some* of the ways these techniques can be used; I hope you take this information as a place to start and use it as a springboard, pioneering your own amazing processes using these techniques as a foundation.

Figure 8.1 An example of beautiful use of stencils by artisan Chris Carpenter for Katerina in *Taming of the Shrew*, Oregon Shakespeare Festival, 2014. Costume designer Meg Neville. Actors: Ted Deasy and Nell Geislinger in stenciled costumes on right.
Photo courtesy of Jenny Graham.

DOI: 10.4324/9781351130677-9

SILKSCREENS

There are SO many ways to print with silkscreens that it is almost overwhelming! The most common commercial use of silkscreens employs photo emulsion and drawing fluid to create an image that can be printed on almost anything. However, there are a multitude of techniques that use silkscreens to print images that do not use emulsion or drawing fluid that I will also cover in this chapter.

SILKSCREENS, A BRIEF HAIR-STORY . . .

Silkscreens evolved from stencil art originating ancient China and Japan, from a screen made of a wooden frame strung with a mesh of human hair that kept stencils in place so the artists could repeat crisp intricate designs on paper and fabric. Later, silk filaments replaced the hair mesh and as textile production and the art form evolved, silk fabric stretched on a wooden frame became the go-to material to create prints in 17th century Europe. Modern silkscreens are most commonly made from nylon and polyester but screens made of silk are also still available.

MODERN SCREEN MATERIALS

Modern silkscreen material is called **screen-printing mesh**. It is most commonly made of woven polyester or nylon monofilament in different mesh counts from 10–500 mesh US and 4–200T UK (see table 8.1 for equivalents between US vs UK mesh sizes). **Mesh count** of screen-printing mesh refers to how many threads cross per square inch; the measuring unit is mesh/inch, which tells the density between two adjacent yarns. The second number refers to the thread diameter. Catspitproductions.com has a great example of how to break down silkscreen mesh sizes; please see box for their example to understand the system used in the printing industry. Basically, the smaller the screen number, the larger the holes in the screen. If you are doing a fully black print design with no

Table 8.1 US vs UK Screen Mesh Size. Divide US size by 2.5 to get UK size

US Mesh	UK 'T' Mesh
80	32T
110	43T
140	55T
156	62T
200	77T
230	90T
325	120T

WHAT DO ALL THE NUMBERS MEAN??? EXCERPT FROM CATSPIT PRODUCTIONS SITE (CATSPITPRODUCTIONS.COM)

Example: Screen Size = 355–34Y PW a.k.a. 355/34

The number **355** represents the mesh count of 355 threads per inch. The number after the dash, in this case **34**, refers to the thread diameter. The thread diameter, mesh count, and solid content of the ink will determine the amount of ink that passes through the mesh. The letter **Y** tells us if the mesh is yellow or **W** for white. Those are the two most common colors of mesh. The letters **PW** refers to the weave type of the mesh. **PW** stands for plain weave and **TW** stands for twill weave.

greyscale, you can use a lower mesh like 150 mesh screen. If you want to print grey-scale with emulsion you should use a much higher mesh like a 280 to a 330 mesh. Speedball makes pre-made commercial silkscreen that can be found at hobby and art stores and comes in 110 (most commonly found), 155, 230, and 305 mesh sizes in a variety of frame sizes.

You can create custom screen sizes by buying a frame and adding your own screen to it. This can be created in a number of ways including using a window screen kit from your local hardware store! You can use screen printing mesh or voile, a fabric often used for sheer curtains. Heck, you can even use old sheer curtains – just BEWARE! The mesh in sheer curtains is very open and you will push a lot of ink or dye through your screen when using it, which will not be useful for fine details in a process like photo printing.

Figure 8.2 (Left) Textile artist Kerr Grabowski's homemade silkscreens, made from window screen kits and silk screen fabric (and sometimes sheer curtains!); (right) speedball pre-made screen.

FRAME ALTERNATIVES

You do not need a frame to print with screen printing mesh; rather, this fabric can be stretched and pinned to a table right on top of fabric. It can be useful to draw smoothly on, not getting caught on your drawing instrument like a rougher fabric might, or to hold down a stencil to block out parts of the screened area. It is not only a placeholder for your print design, it is also a tool to employ other techniques like drawing, painting, stenciling, and more!

SQUEEGEES

Squeegees come in many widths, blade sizes, and hardness. When printing or **pulling** a screen, if your squeegee is smaller than your print area, there may be a visible streak in the places in which you overlap with your squeegee on your final print. If you want to avoid this, choose a squeegee that is at least 2" wider than your project. Commercial screen printers use squeegees with an aluminum or wood handle and a rubber blade that comes in different hardnesses. They recommend that you use a harder durometer blade for finer prints. I tend to favor a thin hard blade made of plastic with no real handle, as I feel I can control the medium better on the screen. Kerr Grabowski recommends using Bondo spreaders as they are cheap and have a nice sharp edge. You can get a three pack like the ones in Figure 8.3 for $1.99. When squeegee edges get worn out, they should be tossed as you will not yield sharp prints with a chewed-up squeegee.

Figure 8.3 SQUEEEEGEEEEEEES! Top left: yellow Bondo spreaders; bottom left: speedball thin rubber squeegee; right: a variety of squeegees used by textile artist Doshi.

PHOTO EMULSION SILKSCREEN PROCESS

If you would like to create a detailed print of an image or text, photo emulsion is going to be the ideal product for your project. Even though this magical process provides an excellent replication of your intricate design, it is not a straightforward process for the beginner. Unless you know your controls like temperature, wattage of the exposure light, the distance from your light to your surface, and your transparent weighting device, you will have to do tests. Overexposure can lead to poor **washout**, meaning the design you have burned into your emulsion became overexposed and will not wash out, making your screen useless. Underexposure can cause all or most of the emulsion to wash out also rendering the screen useless. Mistakes are inevitable BUT don't worry – it's not the end of the road. You can **reclaim** your screen using screen reclaimer.

Photo emulsion comes in **pre-sensitized** and **diazo** (a.k.a. unmixed emulsion and sensitizer). The main difference is that premixed comes with the sensitizer already mixed in while diazo does not. The pre-sensitized emulsion creates shorter and more sensitive exposures but is more expensive and has to be ordered online unless you have a local silkscreen supply. The diazo must have the powdered sensitizer mixed with water and added to the emulsion to become active. I have mainly used diazo in my theatre work and will use it in this book to demonstrate how to use photo emulsion because it is cheaper and can be found in art supply and craft stores. It is always nice to have a local option to buy more chemicals when dealing with this stuff if you need more. There are many pros and cons of both emulsion types, but basically, the diazo is harder to screw up and it works well with textile inks and dyes. If you want to start your own screening business, look into pre-sensitized emulsions and other types depending on the mediums you want to use based on the fabric content you would like to screen on.

CREATING YOUR PRINT FILM POSITIVE

If this is your first time creating a photo screen or if you do not know the mesh count of your screen, I would advise choosing a fully black image. It is possible to realize grey-scale imagery with photo emulsion but you need a much higher screen mesh of around 300 and above. You will create your print film positive by printing your design on acetate film intended for your printer – depending on whether it is an inkjet or laser printer. Speedball says you can use white paper or a print film positive but you need to wet the page with water or oil and increase exposure times. I have not tried this but it could be good in a pinch?

If your image is many colors, like Figure 8.4, it must be re-rendered into black and white to ensure a good print. The **film positive** is just that – a positive image of your print, NOT a photo negative. You can see how I decided to create a mockup for a 1-color print in Figure 8.4 (middle) to ensure I had black in all the right places. Also, to see what the final print will look like! This could be a two-screen print where perhaps the soccer ball and "Wolves" logo were on one screen and the wolves on the other. This would allow me to print in two colors. I would use **registration marks**, or small crosses in the corners surrounding the image, to match up multiple screens so the images align. This is how all commercial t-shirts are printed, using multiple screens and ink colors.

Figure 8.4 Left: original image; middle: mock-up for print; right: film positive.

ALWAYS DO TESTS! THE STEP WEDGE TEST AND STEP WEDGE EXPOSURE CALCULATOR

An exposure timing test can be done quite easily and save you many tears. There are a few ways you can do this . . . a step wedge test and a step wedge exposure calculator.

The Step Wedge Test: is free but time consuming. This is an emulsion printing test that you can do with any photo emulsion to see what conditions will be best for your screen. You can download it for free from anthemprinting.com (Figure 8.5 top). Print this chart out on acetate and follow the instructions at the top of the test. Basically, as you expose your screen, you uncover row by row starting at the top for the same time increment. This allows you to discover the correct time that is required to expose your screen. Don't worry – you haven't wasted a

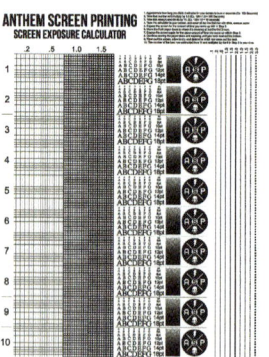
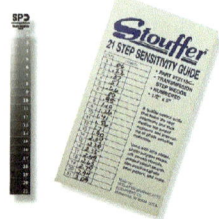

Figure 8.5 Top: step wedge test; bottom: step wedge calculator.

screen, you can use screen reclaimer to wash out the emulsion and start over. Some even say that you can use bleach to remove emulsion if you are short on reclaimer. Remember – you will need more emulsion when you figure out your calculations, which will cost money. So, unless you have a photo emulsion fountain in your dye room, you may want to check out option 2.

A Step Wedge Exposure Calculator: requires a one-time purchase but is fast (the good–fast–cheap model is in play here!). This is a strip (Figure 8.5 bottom) that you add to an area of your screen *in addition to your film positive you want to print!* If you guess the correct amount of time the first time, you're done but most people do a few time tests by exposing the wedge calculator different time increments to see what is the actual time is required. When you wash out your screen, if it is unsuccessful, you will be able to see what the exact correct exposure time is for the next time you use your setup. What's the point? I have under- or overexposed screens many times because I have worked in a variety of shops with different exposure units, with different emulsions, screens, and humidity conditions. This means I have to either waste a lot of emulsion by coating many screens for the ready if my first doesn't expose properly and take the additional time to coat and dry more screens as needed, waste money and time in general, or just do a step wedge test!

HOW TO USE: AFTER EXPOSURE . . .

1. If step 7 or lower (1–6) washes out: you are UNDER exposed. To figure out how much additional time is needed for exposure, multiply your original exposure time by 2.82 to move three steps higher.
2. If step 8 or higher (9–21) does NOT wash out: it is OVER exposed. To figure out how much time to decrease, multiply your original time by .50 (50%) to move 2 steps lower.
3. If step 7 does NOT wash out and 9 does: congrats – you've have the perfect time!

Figure 8.6 Three-step calculator tests.

In my case (Figure 8.6) I did three time tests: 10, 15, and 20 minutes at Jacquard's recommended distance (24″). I was glad to have the step calculator test because Jacquard doesn't supply a time recommendation for a 250W photo flood. The 10 minute test washed out up to 7, from 8–21. This was the most successful test so I used these results and exposed my film for 10 minutes.

USING PHOTO EMULSION

Key terms:
>   **Print side:** the flat side of the screen.
>   **Ink side:** the concave side of the screen that you will add ink to.

Supplies:
- Diazo Photo Emulsion Kit (with sensitizer)
- A blank/reclaimed silk screen *or two for a test*
- Plastic packing tape
- Optional: Duct tape for inner corners of screen
- Squeegee (Figure 8.3)
- Spoon to deliver emulsion to screen
- Exposure lamp. A 250W Photo Flood bulb in a shop light works well
- Flat surface in a room *that can remain dark for at least 6 hours* to dry and expose screen on
- Acetate for inkjet or laser printer
- Newspaper or craft paper for under screen to protect table
- Something to prop screen up off the floor so it can dry flat (ANYTHING will do as long as it doesn't touch the emulsion on the screen)
- **Optional:** scoop coater (see Figure 8.11)
- **Optional:** 2" thick piece of foam cut to size to match the inside of the ink side of the fame.
- **Optional:** Emulsion Remover to reclaim screen

Figure 8.7 The print side is the front of the screen while the ink side is back.

Figure 8.8 The diazo kit (right) includes emulsion, sensitizer, and screen reclaimer! The jacquard emulsion and Ecotex remover (left) are on the left.

HOW TO BURN A SILKSCREEN IMAGE WITH PHOTO EMULSION

1. **Gear up –** gloves, apron, hand towel nearby!
2. **Set up!**
   - Tape your screen. First, add duct tape (if you have some – otherwise use packing tape) to the

TAPING A SCREEN

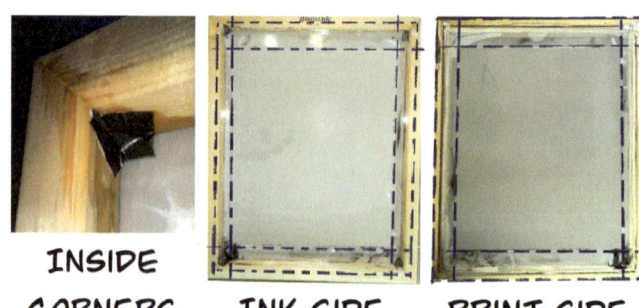

Figure 8.9 Taping a screen.

corners to ensure ink/paint doesn't get stuck in the corners. Second, add packing tape to the ink side of the screen covering your corner tape. Flip the screen and add tape to the print side, matching the tape depth into the printable area on the ink side. Make sure to cover the channels and outer edge of the screen so tape doesn't come off. The tape should go about 1–1.5" onto the screen from the frame. Third, flip your frame to the print side and match the packing tape lines that are on the ink side of the screen.

3. **Coat your screen:**
   - **Mix** water into your sensitizer and shake well. Mix this with your spoon into your emulsion until it is all a blue–green color.
   - **Add emulsion:** With the screen at an angle, add a thick bead of emulsion to the *print side* of the screen. With your squeegee at a 45° angle, pull the emulsion down the screen in strips as wide as the squeegee. It's nice to have a squeegee the same width as your screen, but it's not a must. Continue pulling emulsion down the screen until the print side is coated. Flip the screen and repeat this process to make sure this side is coated as well.

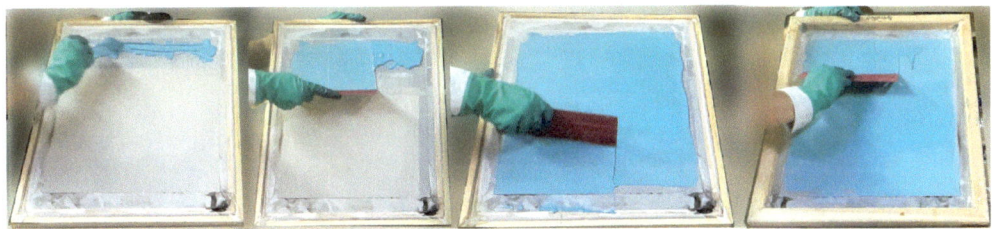

Figure 8.10 Coating your screen can be achieved using your squeegee and pouring emulsion to the top of your screen. Let gravity help you by applying at a 45° angle.

- **If using a scoop coater** (Figure 8.11), add emulsion about halfway up the well, and tilt it gently towards the print side of the screen (at an angle or leaning against the wall), spilling emulsion on the screen and pulling at the same time. Do this to both sides of the screen firmly and slowly. Again it is ideal but not totally required to have a scoop coater the same size as your screen.

Figure 8.11 Using a scoop coater is a surefire way to get an even distribution of emulsion on the screen.

Figure 8.12 Prop screen up on whatever you have. I used a few pieces of wood, being careful **not** to touch the screen surface.

4. **Dry the screen:** Prop up your screen on blocks *print side down* so the emulsion pulls completely through the mesh. Dry your screen for several hours in a **darkish place**. With this emulsion it doesn't have to be full dark but the darker the better. You can even place the screen in a box with a towel over it but it will not dry as quickly. Ideal amount of time is overnight but it can be done in as little as a few hours with a fan. *If doing the photo test, coat one screen for your test and another for the real thing. **You can leave your coated screen unexposed for 1–2 weeks!** Once your screen is **completely dry** you are ready to create prints!

5. **Store –** Screw on emulsion cap tightly and store in a dark dry place. Make sure it is out of UV light. Shelf life is about 3 months (or longer if stored in the refrigerator – but don't let it freeze!).

WHERE TO START WITH THE TIMING ESTIMATE???

You have to start with a time estimate whether or not you are doing a step wedge test or calculator. Speedball has a good guide to start your guesstimate (table 8.2) **if you are using Speedball**. These times are using a 250 watt photo flood bulb in a metal-clip floodlight or a 30 watt UV LED flood light. If you are like me and your dye shop had Jacquard-brand diazo on the shelf, follow their times and distances (Table 8.3). **Note how very different the times are! It is important to always follow the brand's specific instructions.**

Table 8.2 Exposure Times for Speedball Diazo Photo Emulsion.

Frame Size	Lamp Height	Exposure Time
8x10 inches	16 inches	7 minutes
10x14 inches	16 inches	8 minutes
12x18 inches	18 inches	10 minutes
16x20 inches	20 inches	2 minutes
any	Sunlight	45 Seconds

Table 8.3 Exposure Times for Jaquard Photo Emulsion.

Light Source	Distance From Screen	Exposure Time
250 watt photo flood	24"/60.96 cm	9–15 minutes
200 watt incandescent	24"/60.96 cm	22–25 minutes
150 watt incandescent	24"/60.96 cm	30–33 minutes
100 watt indoor flood	18"/45.72 cm	50–55 minutes
60 watt indoor fluorescent	18"/45.72 cm	45–48 minutes
Sunlight	–	10–30 seconds

The clip light and bulb setup can get extremely hot and cause fires if left unattended. The LED light seems like a safer option (especially if you are working with students) that you can also use to test UV makeup and paint as well. A three-fer!

Figure 8.13 A clip floodlight (right) and 30W UV Led lamp.

6. **Set Up 2.0! Exposing Your Image!** Once your screen is dry you are ready to expose it!
    - Set up your exposure light at the appropriate distance listed in the emulsion instructions.
    - Estimate time needed for exposure. See table 8.2 for times based on screen size.
    - If doing a step wedge test or using the calculator, have one of those ready.
    - Some people like to add a piece of foam to the work surface that is covered with dark fabric to minimize light bounce. Lay your screen print side down on top of your foam and/or work surface.
    - Add your **print film** to the center of the screen on the ink side so you have space on either side. **Remember!!! If you lay your film on the print side of the screen for exposure, it will end up mirroring the image.** This really isn't a problem unless you are printing text or numbers – **they will be backwards**. If you are using the wedge step strip, lay it on a part of the screen that you can easily block later with tape and print your design.
    - Add a piece of plexiglass or glass over your film to hold it in place during exposure. It must fit inside the ink side.
    - In a fully dark room, turn on your lamp for the designated time on the chart. The screen will turn from green to a dark blue as it is exposed. **Do not move, bump, or touch your screen at this time – you can ruin your print.**

Figure 8.14 Exposure unit using a flood lamp with photo flood bulb.

7. **Time to wash your screen.** It's the moment of truth! At the end of your estimated time, turn the exposure lamp off and the work lights on. Time to wash your screen . . . soak it with water at *low pressure* for a bit to soften the emulsion and let it soak in for a few minutes. After that, turn your sprayer to a higher-pressure setting and focus on cleaning out the print areas. You can get gradually more aggressive with the sprayer but take it in steps so you don't wash out the exposed emulsion too. You can use a soft toothbrush to work on areas, but most likely if your screen doesn't wash out, it means you have over exposed it. Never scrub with a stiff brush unless reclaiming your screen. You will destroy your print.

8. **Check exposure.** Now that you have a clean print surface, check your wedge step test area to see if your exposure time matches the tests' time. If you are truly underexposed, your emulsion around the print would have washed out. You can expose your image again, but it may be blurry. I would reclaim the screen and expose it again at the specified time from your test.

9. **Reclaim?** To reclaim the screen, use Speedball's Emulsion Remover/Screen Reclaimer (or whatever emulsion remover works with the emulsion you choose) by soaking both sides of the screen with remover, letting that sit for a few minutes, spraying with a kitchen or hose sprayer and then gently scrubbing the rest of the emulsion (Figure 8.15). Your screen will be transparent if all emulsion is washed out. There may be some residual dye left on the screen fabric – that's totally normal.

Figure 8.15 Reclaiming a screen! Spray reclaimer/remover on both sides of screen; emulsion running (left of middle); sprayed with water (right middle); now screen should be transparent (right).

PRINTING!

Now that you've created your screen, you are ready to print!

Supplies:
- Spatula or spoon
- Printing medium: ink, paint, or print paste
- Padded surface
- Your finished screen
- Squeegee

HOW TO PRINT USING YOUR SILK SCREEN

1. **Gear up**! Gloves, apron, hand towel nearby!
2. **Set up!**
- **Set up a print area:** Create a firm but lightly padded surface on which you can pull your screen. You want this surface to have a little bit of give but not too much. This can be a table that you cover in tightly pinned muslin or knit fabric but if you don't have a whole table that you can commit to printing, you can create a portable option. I really like using soundboard from home improvement stores because it can be covered with a few layers of muslin and can be pinned into to secure your work. Also, it can be ironed on, which keeps your ironing board clean, and will not melt like insulation foam does. **Do not use a towel as your surface –** the terry cloth texture will not allow all of the medium to pull through the screen and will leave towel texture!
3. Place your screen face-down on your printing surface, **ink side up**.
4. Drop a bead of paint, ink, or print paste across the top of the screen. A small rubber spatula works really well!
5. While adding pressure to the screen (or enlisting a friend to help) use a squeegee of your choice to pull the medium you are using firmly at a consistent speed to the bottom well of the screen. Scoop excess material out of this well with your spatula. If you are finished, wipe your excess material back into the container if it has not been contaminated by other colors. You can also redeposit the medium at the top and pull the screen a second time. **Once you lift your screen it will be difficult to match it up with your print and pull it again!** So, if you think enough ink/paint/dye did not transfer, then just pull you screen twice. When pulling screens using print paste on deconstructed screen designs, you

can often pull three or four times (more on this in the deconstructed printing section). The speed, pressure, and angle of your squeegee will all affect the quality of your print. Experiment first!
6. Lift your screen from the bottom and rock it towards the top of the screen. Lift it off of your fabric in a vertical motion so you do not transfer any residual ink to your print!
7. Wash your screen with cold–lukewarm water. You can lightly rub it with a sponge or soft brush. Just don't scrub too hard as this will destroy your image.

Figure 8.16 Add paint to area above image (left), using squeegee at 45° angle pull paint over burned area (middle), lift at a 45° angle first sloooowly (top right), finished print (bottom right).

DRAWING FLUID AND SCREEN FILLER SILKSCREEN PROCESS

This is a very straightforward process in which you can make a permanent screen by hand drawing or tracing a design directly onto your screen with **drawing fluid** and then blocking out the surrounding holes in the screen with **screen filler**. Using this technique to create a hand drawn design will allow you to print your design an exponential amount of times with crisper edges than you would achieve with a stencil.

Supplies:
- Speedball drawing fluid
- Speedball screen filler
- Paintbrush
- Pencil
- Blank/clean silkscreen
- Squeegee
- Spoon/spatula
- **Optional:** Speed Clean (to reclaim screen)

Figure 8.17 Jacquard drawing fluid (left) and Speedball screen filler (right).

HOW TO CREATE A SCREEN WITH DRAWING FLUID AND SCREEN FILLER

1. **Gear up** – gloves, apron, hand towel nearby!
2. **Set up!**

- Draw or print your design on a piece of paper for easy transfer
- Place drawing on a surface then place the screen ink side up on top of the drawing
- Trace image with a pencil onto your screen
- Open your screen filler and decant a half ounce or so into a small container (if you're not sharing this with anyone you can dip your brush right into the bottle)

3. Using your paintbrush, **begin to fill in your design** that you wish to print. It is ideal to avoid puddling so try to wipe some material off of your brush after dipping it in the drawing fluid.
4. **Allow your drawing fluid to dry completely.** This may take a few hours depending on temperature and humidity.
5. **Stir** your screen filler in its bottle, making sure to stir the solids from the bottom into the filler mixture.
6. Add a bead of screen filler to the print side of your screen (or whatever side you drew on with the drawing fluid) and with a **single pull** coat the screen as much as possible. If you pull the filler through the screen too many times it may dissolve the drawing fluid.

Figure 8.18 Left: image drawn on screen; right: filling in image with drawing fluid. Leaving some negative spaces for paint to come through.

Figure 8.19 Adding screen filler to the bottom gutter (left), pulling filler across scree (middle), done (right)!

7. **Let your screen dry completely.**
8. **Wash out** the drawing fluid on the print and ink sides of the screen using cold or lukewarm water. Hold your screen to the light to make sure all the fluid has washed out.

Figure 8.20 Dried screen (left), spraying out screen (middle left), using a tooth brush to remove stubborn spots where drawing fluid was thicker (middle right), finished print (right) little chickie!

9. Let the screen dry again and you are ready to print!
10. To reclaim a screen, use Speed Clean by Speedball (designed for removing screen filler) by soaking both sides of the screen and gently scrubbing then spraying out the screen filler.

> ## USING OLD SCREEN FILLER . . .
>
> Did you take out your screen filler and realize you did not buy it six months ago, actually it was 4 years ago . . .? It is separated and chunky and you're not sure how to recoup? You blend the screen filler in a dye blender to cut up all of the chunks to small sizes. Strain the product through cheesecloth (disposable) to strain out any remaining chunks. Most likely, this will be your last use with this particular batch if you planned on putting it on the shelf for another 4 years!

THE SCREEN FILLER ONLY SILKSCREEN PROCESS

This process varies from the previous process in that we do not start with a positive image rather, we start and ends with a negative image. The process is much the same except we are painting with the screen filler and leaving an image uncoated on the screen. This is a very fast process because we are only waiting for one material to dry.

Supplies:
- Speedball screen filler
- Paintbrush
- Pencil
- Blank/clean silkscreen

HOW TO **CREATE A SCREEN WITH SCREEN FILLER ONLY**
1. **Gear up** – gloves, apron, hand towel nearby!
2. **Set up!**
   - Draw or print your design on a piece of paper for easy transfer
   - Place drawing on a surface then place the screen ink side up on top of the drawing
   - Trace image with a pencil onto your screen
   - **Stir** your screen filler in its bottle, making sure to stir the solids from the bottom into the filler mixture.
3. Using your paintbrush, begin to fill in your design **around** where you wish to print.
4. Let the screen dry and you are ready to print!
5. To reclaim a screen, use Speed Clean by Speedball by soaking both sides of the screen and gently scrubbing then spraying out the screen filler.

CREATING A SILKSCREEN PRINT RUBBING WITH WAX

Using wax on a silkscreen to create a print resist is a fantastic alternative to using photo emulsion and drawing fluid. I LOVE this process. It is so fast and so easy to create a screen design *and* fast and easy to remove too! How can this be possible? I'm here to let you know! The only thing that is not fast and easy about this process is that you have to create the wax crayons for rubbing to ensure that you have a good resist on your screen that doesn't flake off (like soy wax has a tendency to do) but that you also can remove the wax easily. You can create a large batch that will keep you going for a while.

**The screens you use for this purpose shall forever be dedicated to this or processes other than photo emulsion and drawing fluid/screen filler. The residual wax may resist these products causing them to fail.

Supplies:
- *To make the crayon*
  - Beeswax
  - Canning/paraffin wax
  - Metal pot
  - Tin can
  - Heat source to heat up wax
  - Silicone (large 1 1/2–2" rectangle or square) ice cube tray
- *To create the rubbing*
  - Clean silk screen
  - Something with texture to rub a design from
  - Printing surface
  - Your freshly made wax crayon!

Figure 8.21 I used wax to create this screen and pulled discharge paste through the screen. A wax-rubbed screen can be used to print many times!

HOW TO MAKE CLEAR WAX CRAYONS FOR RUBBING

1. Create a double boiler by using a tin can and metal pot. Fill the pan halfway with water then set your metal container in the center of the water. This is where you will be melting your wax.
2. Using 4 parts canning wax and 1 part beeswax, melt as much wax as you wish to create the crayons by cutting the wax into smaller chunks and adding it to the tin can. Use a chopstick, or something firm that you don't mind having wax on forever, to stir your wax. Add chunks slowly and stir until melted.
3. When all the wax is melted, decant wax into a silicone ice tray about 3/4ths' high. The best ice tray will have a 1–2" x 1–2" square size. Walmart and Target have loads of these.
4. Let the wax cool. These don't need to be frozen; they will harden on their own when left out to cool.

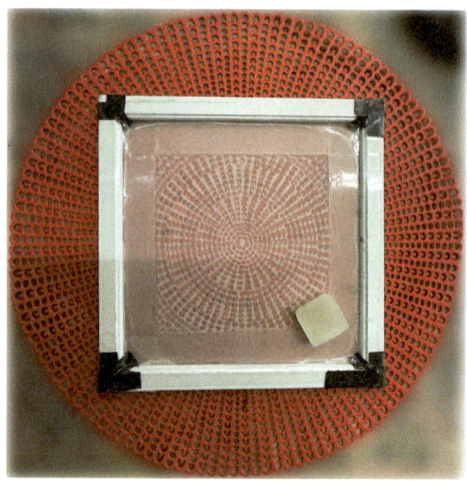

Figure 8.22 Wax and the placemat I used to get the groovy texture.

HOW TO CREATE A SILKSCREEN PRINT BY RUBBING WITH WAX

1. **Gear up** – gloves are optional – if you don't like touching wax, wear them.
2. On your printing area/surface place the items you would like to take a rubbing from (see "How to Print Using a Silk Screen" section on creating a printing area).

3. Place your screen ink side up, on top of the items you wish to take a rubbing from. Using your crayon press firmly rubbing from top to bottom until your print has transferred to your screen. You are done! Now you can use this screen to print textures until you remove the wax! TIP! Try using positive stencils to block areas of the wax design (Figure 8.23)

Removing wax: Place newsprint/newspaper under the print side and on top of the ink side of your waxed screen. With an iron that fits inside the ink side of the screen (travel irons are great for this – you can pick them up at garage sales/thrift stores) iron on top of the newspaper until you start to see the wax bleeding through. If the paper is saturated with wax, add a fresh paper to both sides of the screen and continue ironing until all of the wax is out.

CREATING A WAX SCREEN PRINT: PAINTING WITH WAX

Using wax on a silkscreen to create a print resist is a fantastic alternative to using photo emulsion and drawing fluid. This process lends itself to a more organic and fluid style of drawing that can be difficult to achieve with the chemical processes. Another upside is that you can easily remove the wax by ironing it out of your screen to start over with a blank slate. If you have any experience in batik, the setup is similar except for this process we combine two types of wax to paint a design on the screen. I think it could even be possible to get a batik look using this technique if you iced the wax after application. ****The screens you use for this purpose shall forever be dedicated to this or processes other than photo emulsion and drawing fluid/screen filler.** The residual wax may resist these products causing them to fail.

Figure 8.23 Left: melting was in electric skillet; middle left: wax I dripped and painted on screen; right middle: a print using only the screen; right: a chickie stencil used in the center of the screen. Weird sample? Yes. Cool technique? Definitely.

Supplies:
- Electric griddle dedicated to wax
- Beeswax: 1 part
- Canning wax/paraffin: 4 parts
- Brushes or tjanting tools
- Baking soda
- A clean or reclaimed screen

HOW TO CREATE A WAX SCREEN PRINT PAINTING WITH WAX
1. **Gear up –** gloves, apron, baking soda in case of fire (this is what will extinguish a wax fire).
2. **Set up!**
    - Plug in your electric griddle and set to medium heat. You will eventually discover the sweet spot on the thermostat; make sure to mark this for future projects!

- At a ratio of 1:4 beeswax to canning wax, cut up chunks of both of these and begin to melt in your griddle.
3. Using a tjanting tool or brush, dip into the hot wax and begin adding motifs to your screen!
4. Let your screen cool so the wax is no longer soft.
5. Print!

Removing wax: Place newsprint/newspaper under the print side and on top of the ink side of your waxed screen. With an iron that fits inside the ink side of the screen (travel irons are great for this – you can pick them up at garage sales/thrift stores) iron on top of the newspaper until you start to see the wax bleeding through. If the paper is saturated with wax, add a fresh paper to both sides of the screen and continue ironing until all of the wax is out.

STENCILS

Stencils can be created a number of ways. The method you choose depends on several factors including: the intricacy of the design, desired placement of motif, medium application techniques, and technology access. This is another one of those good–fast–cheap triangle situations where you choose to create a stencil because it is cheap but it may not be as crisp (not as good) as a photo emotion silkscreen would be or it might take longer (not so fast) to go back in and fill in areas where you created bridges (more on bridges in the next section).

There are three ways to make stencils: hand cutting, laser cutting, and using a Cricut cutter. Hand cutting stencils are the go-to method and provide immediate results compared to using photo emulsion or screen filler. For extremely intricate designs that may be larger in scale, laser cutting will be the tool of choice. In this section I will cover a few different materials I've used to cut stencils by hand and pros and cons of those materials. I will also discuss using a laser cutter to create elaborate stencil designs.

HAND-CUT STENCILS

Hand-cut stencils require some planning, a sharp knife, and a steady hand. This is an extremely quick way to make reusable stencils that can be washed. There are two different materials I like to use, acetate and clear contact paper, and the choice depends on how I will be using the finished stencil. When I choose contact paper it is usually because my finished stencil will be used to create motifs on a three-dimensional surface like a bodice or built costume. Contact paper is very flexible and contours nicely but the flexibility of contact paper is not always a desirable quality as the stencil can stretch overtime and become misshapen, especially if you are using a reposition-able quilt spray to adhere your stencil. Acetate stencils are thinner and more transparent than contact paper stencils which make them ideal for stenciling under silk screens but since they are not as flexible, this makes

Figure 8.24 A four-part stencil of a self-portrait created by Edward Snow. They had to do many tests to ensure the stencils matched up correctly. Note the corner-shaped registration marks in the corners; they used these to line up the 4 layers accurately.

it difficult to wrap the stencil around a three-dimensional surface like a costume that is already built. Even though these materials have differing qualities, the process of tracing, cutting a design, and repair is the same!

Supplies:
- X-Acto knife (I like the number 12 scalpel blade with the X-Acto handle)
- Clear contact paper or acetate
- Fine-point Sharpie in dark color
- Cutting mat
- Clear tape for repairs
- Insert roll of clear contact paper and acetate book (Kerr)

HOW TO HAND CUT STENCILS

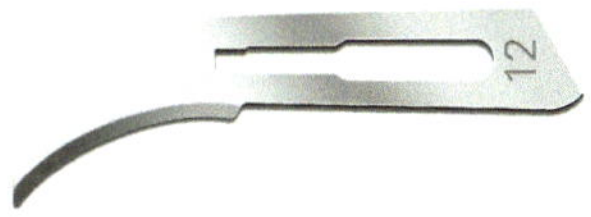

1. **Choose a design.** Print your image on computer paper and draw where your bridges are going to be placed. If you need to add registration marks (see creating registration marks) you can add those later.
2. **Trace your design on stencil material.** Your stencil material will be transparent and you can trace your image and bridges with a permanent marker onto your stencil medium. If you decide NOT to transfer the image onto your medium and would rather have a stencil with no markings on it, you can tape your image to the back of your stencil and cut directly onto of your image. This will destroy your original image, FYI, so have a backup.
   - **If using contact paper:** you can use one side of contact paper but you will not be able to trace a design through unless you adhere it to the back of your contact paper. I was taught by my grad school technical mentor, Teri Tavares, to put two pieces together back to back. That way your material is thicker, won't stretch as much, is transparent, and cuts easily.

Figure 8.25 Number 12 scalpel blades work great for cutting stencils and they fit in standard blade handles!

The Bridges of Madison County are what I always refer to when getting ready to create bridges in my stencils. **Bridges** in a stencil refer to sections that connect two parts of your design so one part of your design stays in position in relation to another part. If you think of making a stencil of the letter "O", the stencil would have the cut out part of the O but also require the letter's center, in order to tell it is the letter O and not a circle. The bridges in your stencil would hold the center of the letter away from the cut edges of the O in a uniform pattern. It would be up to you to choose whether the bridges are part of your stencil design or whether they are completely utilitarian, in which case you will go back in later with the paint you are using to stencil and fill in the bridges. **If you cut away material and need a bridge or to repair an area – JUST USE SCOTCH TAPE!!! It's clear and can peel off for repositioning.** See the illustration in Figure 8.26 for a visual example!

Figure 8.26 Bridges created then filled.

USING THE WHOLE CHICKEN . . .

Traditional stencils usually consist of cutting out a design from the center of a stencil medium leaving a space to push pigment through; this is called a **negative stencil**. The cut out piece is called the **positive stencil** and can be used just as much as the negative piece. Old cave paintings of hands with pigment blown over them to reveal the hand shape is an example of a very old stencil! See Figure 8.27 to see the difference between using these stencil types. The stencil design is cut on the black line, leaving positive and negative stencils. I placed each of these under a silk screen to block out different areas so my discharge paste would not transfer.

Figure 8.27 Stencil design (left), using positive stencil (middle), using negative stencil (right).

WHICH CAME FIRST, THE CHICKEN OR THE PRINT?

When you silkscreen over an acetate stencil, the remainder of the paint or print paste will be left on the part of the stencil touching the print side of the screen. This residual paint can be used and will be in the form of the blocked out print from the screen that was previously used. In Figure 8.28, you can see the positive stencil on the left was placed under a silkscreen with the radiating motif to block out a Lil' Chickie shape in the center of the piece. The middle image is of the residual dye left on the stencil and the stencil has been flipped over and pressed onto fabric to print. On the right, a screen made from print paste (see Chapter 9) was pulled over the stencil and the stencil served two purposes: to block out a Lil' Chicke shape and to transfer the residual dye from the previous screen pull.

Figure 8.28 Using a stencil to create a print!

3. **Add space around:** Depending on how large your design is, add at least 4 inches to every side so that when you use your stencil you have an apron around it to keep your paint from landing on unintended areas! You can always tape more material to the edges later if you have already traced your image or if you need more protection.
4. **Find a fresh sharp blade and cut!** Some people get wigged out when I hand them a scalpel blade because they are afraid they're going to cut themselves. The real danger of cutting yourself when working with sharp blades is when they begin to dull. It takes more pressure and you can slip more easily using a dull blade. Take my advice and start with a fresh sharp blade. I prefer the curved number 12 scalpel which can be purchased at McMaster Carr in bulk and fit in a normal X-Acto knife handle. Some people like the swivel-y X-Acto knife for cutting stencils, but I have not mastered the art of using those.
5. **Paint!** Use whatever medium you choose and paint away. Some people like sea sponges, stencil brushes, or even laying a silkscreen down onto of your stencil to create new designs.
6. Wash. **Make sure to wash your stencils immediately after using so dye and paint do not transfer to other projects (unless you want it to . . . more on that later).**

CREATING STENCILS WITH A LASER CUTTER (OR CRICUT)

To create intricate designs and not kill your hands, a laser cutter or Cricut cutter is a fantastic option. I will discuss mostly laser cutters, but the process for the Cricut is the same, except the Cricut uses blades to cut material while lasers cutters use lasers. Another reason you might use a cutting machine is to cut difficult material that is thicker than a piece of acetate. You may want a stencil that is strong and can be used multiple times and hence may want to choose a sturdier material. Cutting heavy material by hand could cause much pain and cramping (carpal tunnel anyone??) and therefore using a laser cutter is an excellent alternative! Since the software is continually changing but the basics remain the same, I will cover the process that can be used to work with a large laser cutter or a Glowforge cutter that can be used at home.

The materials you choose should be transparent so you can check placement when adding your stencil to a costume. The materials should also be washable so you can use it multiple times. Another consideration in choosing material could be how flexible the material is. Do you need this design to wrap around a costume that is already built in order to apply your stencils? In this case you would want to choose a material that is durable but thin so it remains flexible. Many plastic supply companies offer a variety of transparent materials and will send you samples to play with. **Materials that are plastic will smell extra "death-y",** as my colleague Roger Hanna says, if your ventilation system is not actively sucking the exhaust from the machine. Also, if you are using any materials made with wood or paper, STAY PUT. Don't go to Trader Joe's while your laser cutter is working away on that dense cardboard material; you just might come back to a building in ashes. Also, look at your laser cutter manual for materials that are NOT recommended for use on your machine – some plastics might melt into your machine when cut, causing your warranty to be void and many tears.

Figure 8.29 Stencil design in Procreate (left), stencil laser cut in 1/64th" plastic (middle), the product of airbrushing through the stencil on fabric (right). Stencil design, cutting, and sample created by costume designer of *Sins For Juana*, Purdue 2017, Stephanie Nguyen.

Supplies
- Stencil materials: acetate or thicker plastic (transparent material)
- A design that can be vectorized
- Access to a computer
- A laser cutter

HOW TO CREATE A STENCIL USING A LASER CUTTER
1. **Gear up!** No actual safety gear is required! Yay!
2. **Create your design!** You can use whatever drawing program you choose to either draw or import your image. My favorite is Procreate. I create a drawing in procreate that is in **black and white**, which will make it easier to vectorize and save my file as a PDF or PNG.
3. **Vectorize your design.** In order to communicate with the laser cutter you need to speak its language. Your drawing is in pixels but computers don't speak pixels, they speak vector points, which are based on mathematical formulas. Using a vector program like Adobe Illustrator, Autocad, Inkscape, or Vectornator, import your black and white image and give it vector points. I really like Vectornator because it's a free program and the interface is very similar to Procreate; it can also be used on an iPad, which makes drawing and file transfer extra nice. Once your file is vectorized, save as a PDF, PNG, or SVF file.
4. **Import file.** Import your vector file to the software used by your particular laser cutter. Each cutter has specific software that is used to communicate with the machine. In many of these programs you can continue to do small edits and assign areas to be engraved or cut. For this application you will be choosing all solid black lines because we are cutting out a stencil.
5. **Do tests, then cut!** Don't put all your eggs in one basket by trying to cut only one material for your purpose. You must test materials if you have not used them before in the machine. Maybe your particular plastic melts under the laser? Maybe it shrinks back in an unpleasant way? Do samples. You know this.

STAMPS

Stamps are a fun way to create a design in wood, linoleum, or rubber. The technique I will cover involves a linoleum cutter and linoleum and/or rubber blocks. This is a versatile way to create prints on fabrics, and if you create multiple stamps that work together in a collection, you can create custom fabric! There are other ways to create stamps – really, anything can be a stamp! Someone once made a stamp for a fabric I designed that consisted on neoprene shapes glued on to a piece of wood! Imagination is your only limit here! Some people glue flocking to the surface of completed stamps to hold more dye to the surface. In this example we do not use flocking, but please experiment with that product if you are finding your block is not holding enough paint or dye to create a clear print.

Figure 8.30 Indian wood printing blocks used to stamp patterns in fabric in the back of a store in Santa Fe, NM.

You must be careful cutting linoleum because it takes much hand control and focused strength. I'm not sure how well my hands would take it now if I were to cut a stamp from linoleum, so for that reason, I would probably choose rubber made for stamps that resembles a giant white eraser. It is much easier to cut but a bit more difficult to realize the traditional block cut background texture if that is your desire. Linoleum blocks can be scored and broken but the cleanest solution to cutting them would be to use a band saw. Rubber blocks can be cut with a knife. Printing should be performed on a surface that has a little give, is very flat, and can be pinned into.

Supplies
- Linoleum block or rubber block for creating stamps
- Linoleum cutter
- Pencil to draw design on block
- Print surface
- Optional: brayer

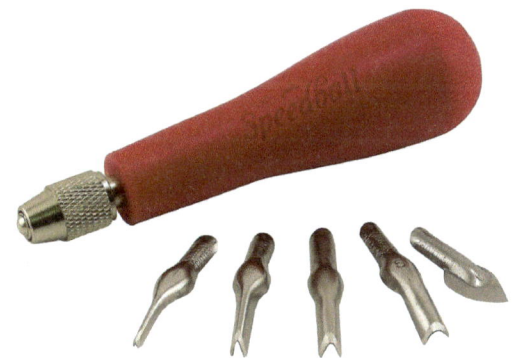

Figure 8.31 Linoleum cutter.

HOW TO CREATE A LINOLEUM OR RUBBER STAMP

1. **Gear up!** No actual safety gear is required, but if you have compromised wrists or tendons, wear a wrist brace!
2. **Transfer your design!** With a pencil, draw the positive design. Remember that a stamp is a positive design with the background and insides of lines removed to highlight the lines of the image. Consider this when designing your stamp.
3. **Sample different blades.** On a scrap or area that you may be cutting away later, sample the different blades at different depths to explore options for your design. **Once you cut, you cannot "undo".**
4. **Carve design.** Carefully carve your design into your block.
5. **Test more!** Using a brayer, roll it in your paint or print paste and gently roll it on your stamp. Press stamp into fabric on your print pad. Do you love it? Do you need to carve out certain areas more? Try a couple colors before you decide you are finished! **If you choose not to waste fabric, test your stamp on paper.**

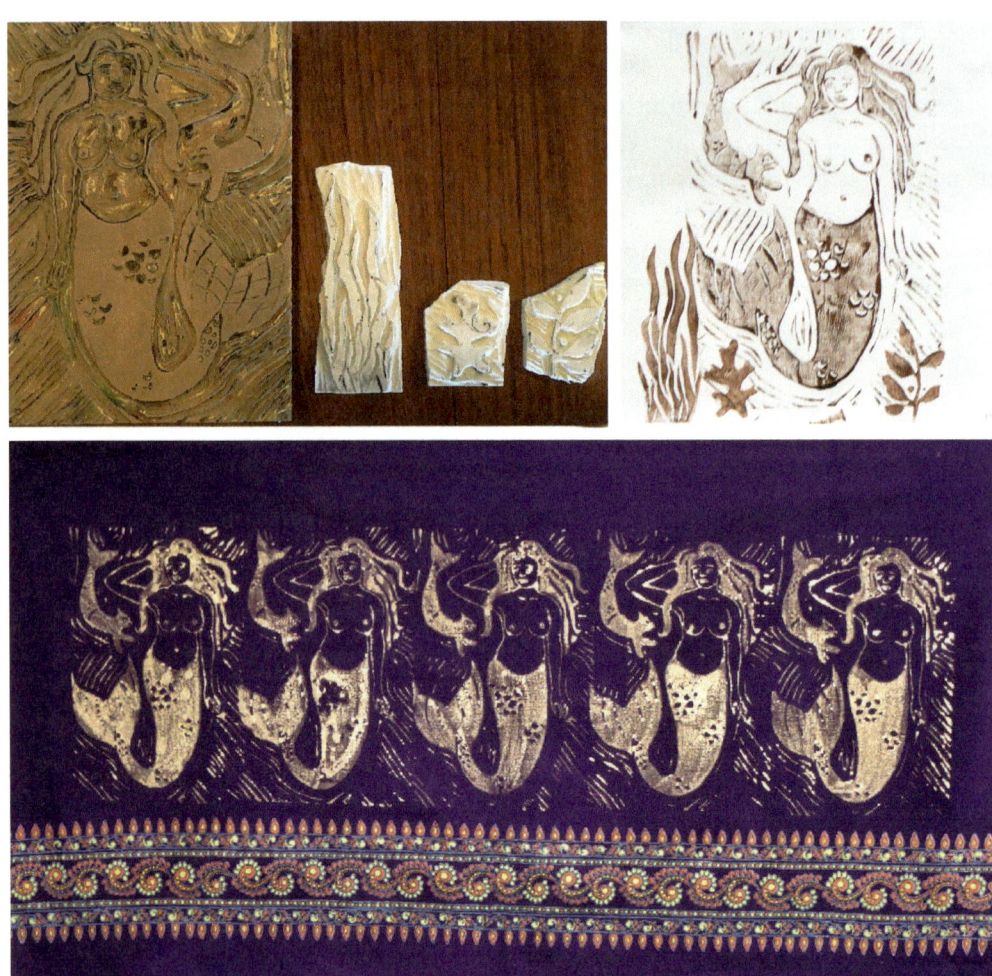

Figure 8.32 Top: linoleum block; middle top: rubber blocks; right top: print with all three together. Bottom: stamp used on embroidered fabric. Design and prints by Kat Rogel.

THE BOTTOM LINE

There are so many choices when it comes to making prints. It comes down to the amount of detail required, how many prints you need to make, how curved the print surface is, the required repeat, and the paint materials you have on hand among other things. Always do tests and be patient – the processes used to create the screen, stencil, or stamp take an investment of time, but when they are complete, printing goes pretty fast!

9

STROKE COUTURE
PRINTING AND PAINTING WITH DYE

Printing and painting with dye is a beautiful way to customize fabric while retaining the material's original hand. Don't get me wrong – textile paints definitely have their place, but, in comparison to using dyes, it can leave fabric stiff and unnatural looking like something is left on the surface of fabric rather than becoming *a part* of the fabric. This chapter's placement, smack in the middle of the book, is because Chapters 1–8 are the necessary foundations required to print and paint with dye, including understanding safety and tools, swatching, additives, fibers and dyes, and printing techniques. When these skills and knowledge coalesce, you are ready to start painting with dye!

In this chapter you will find customizable printing mixtures and process using acid dyes, fiber-reactive dyes, and thiourea dioxide. You will also be able to reference processes on painting with acid and fiber-reactive dyes, and ombré dyeing with dye and color remover. There are more processes that can be used with dye that will be detailed in Chapter 10 as well, as they apply primarily to paint. Most of these processes are adapted from PRO Chemical and Dye's instructions mixed with personal experience, other professional opinions and mixtures from Kerr Grabowski and Elin Noble, tips and techniques from entertainment dyer Jeff Fender, and long chats with Dharma Trading's Elizabeth Holdmann.

Figure 9.1 Hand painted dress from *Lestat*, designed by Susan Hilferty, executed beautifully by Hochi Asiatico.

Photo courtesy of Hochi Asiatico.

DOI: 10.4324/9781351130677-10

PRINTING WITH DYE

CREATING PRINT PASTE

This is the foundation for printing with dye whether it is fiber reactive, acid dye, or even thiourea dioxide. It relies on **sodium alginate** (a.k.a. gum thickener), which is derived from seaweed, to thicken the mixture and create the medium or vehicle for dye. Print paste loves cellulose fibers and it washes out very well; it takes a little more effort to wash out of silk. Dharma sells Sodium Alginate LV (low viscosity) specifically for achieving fine lines on silk and washing out well, but many dyers report sodium alginate curdling when coming in contact with acids needed to bond dye to silk or wool. In some cases when you are tinting your print paste, silk dye may have acids added to the dye, so, even if you are not adding acids and get curdling, this may be the curdling culprit. In the case of protein fibers and print paste, experiment with acid dye and sodium alginate before committing; using guar gum may be a friendlier thickener for use with acids.

Generally, dyers like to control their mixtures because print paste viscosity needs vary by project. However, if creating print paste from scratch is overwhelming to you, ProChemical and Dye sells a pre-made powder that has Urea, Metaphos, and Thick SH (ProChem's brand of sodium alginate) that you just add water to. I have to give a shout-out to Kerr Grabowski who helped me understand all of these textile printing processes on a deeper level, provided loads of opportunities for visual examples for this chapter, and a lot of laughs!

A note before we begin: Kerr includes more metaphos in her print paste recipe than ProChem or Dharma because, as she says, "if you have hard water, it makes it difficult to remove print paste". By adding more metaphos, she ensures her print paste washes out easily. This mixture is for a 1-quart amount and if you omit soda ash or ammonium sulfate and keep refrigerated, it will last for 6 months! You can see why we want to mix it in bulk.

Supplies:
- Synthrapol
- Soda Ash and/or Baking Soda or Ammonium Sulfate (silk only) depending on setting technique you choose (Table 9.2). **If you want to paste to last up to 6 months, then add the sodas or ammonium sulfate to the mixture created right before printing.**
- 1 Cup Urea
- Sodium Alginate: PROChem's Thick SH or Dharma's Sodium Alginate Thickened HV (2–6 tbl) more or less depending on desired thickness
- Container with lid to store print paste
- Optional: blender not used for food
- Optional: 4 tsp Metaphos for hard water
- Optional: Ludigol for leveling

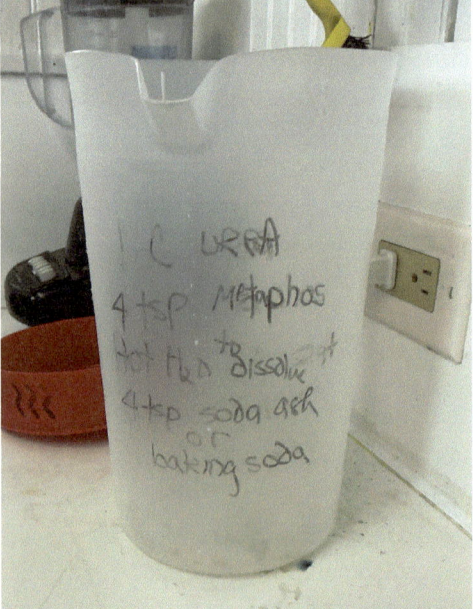

Figure 9.2 Textile artist Kerr Grabowski is an expert in using print paste and uses it regularly to create her art. Therefore, she has written her recipe on the side of the pitcher she uses to mix the ingredients up in! Love it!

HOW TO CREATE PRINT PASTE

1. **Gear up!** Gloves, apron, mask for mixing Urea.
2. **Mix urea water.**
   - 1 quart warm–hot water (don't go above 120°F; Urea will release ammonia at this temperature)
   - 1 c Urea
   - Soda ash/baking soda/aluminum sulfate amounts from table 9.1. Standard protocol is 1 tsp soda ash for 1 cup print paste. **Kerr uses soda ash in all of her print paste because she dyes both cotton and silk, regularly.** You can leave the soda ash out and steam silk or wool and then do an acid soak at the end in 1 cup vinegar to 1 gallon of water per pound of fabric.
   - Optional: 4 tsp Metaphos (for hard water)
3. **Add sodium alginate thickener.**
   - If you have a blender, add all of this to it. Alternatively, you can use a whisk, stirring vigorously. I have had students shake it up in a sealed jar like mixing the flour and milk for Thanksgiving gravy like my grandma.
   - I will use the three bears as an analogy for print paste body.
   - Baby bear: to freehand paint with, use **2 tbl**.
   - Mama bear: to create print paste and draw designs on screens for deconstructed printing, **4 1/2 tbl.**
   - Papa bear: to pull paste through a silkscreen that has a body similar to screen ink, use **6 tbl.**
   - Sprinkle desired amount into your quart of Urea water and mix vigorously (or turn the blender on). Allow paste to sit for at least an hour or two. Overnight is optimal. Stir before using.

Figure 9.3 A good mama-bear consistency for deconstructed printing.

PRINT PASTE USING FIBER-REACTIVE DYES

This paste can be used on cellulose fibers like cotton and rayon but also on silk! There are three ways to set fiber-reactive dyes on cellulose and two on silk, so please read through them in table 9.1 to decide whether you want to do a soda soak in advance (before step 2) or if you would like to add fixative to your dye–paint. At the crafty tie-dye center, they did the soda soak method #1 and handed you a wet T-shirt to tie dye. The method you choose will depend on if you want to set the dye with a bullet steamer, a dryer, or time, which isn't always on our side!

Table 9.1 Techniques to Set Directly Applied Fiber-reactive Dyes.

	#1 Presoak Fabric	#2 Add Mixed Alkalis to Paint	#3 Add Baking Soda to Paint	#4 SILK ONLY Add Fixative to Paint
Time Required	5–30 hours depending if you choose to dry fabrics after soda soak and the depth of color desired.	24–25 hours.	1.5–2 hours.	15 minutes–24 hours.
Fixative	9 tbl (80 gm) Soda Ash	1 tbl (9 gm) Soda Ash per cup of dye–paint	1 tsp (4 gm) Baking Soda	1 tsp (6 gm) Ammonium Sulfate
Water	1 gallon 110°F (43°C)	_____	_____	
Directions	Soak in soda ash bath 10–15 minutes, swishing intermittently. Wring out fabric but **do not rinse**. Let dry or apply to wet fabric.	Mix baking soda and soda ash together. Right before you are ready to paint, add 1 tsp to 1 cup of dye–paint. Mix well. Paint!	When ready to paint, add 1 tsp of baking soda to 1 cup of dye–paint. Mix well. Paint! Not good for silk.	When ready to paint, add 1 tsp ammonium sulfate to 1 cup dye–paint. Mix well. Paint!
Setting	Let dye set by covering piece with plastic for a minimum of **4 hours**. If dyeing dark colors or turquoise, let sit for **24 hours**. Room temp must be 70°F (22 °C) or higher.	Let dye set by covering piece with plastic for a minimum of **24 hours**. Room temp must be 70°F (22 °C) or higher.	Air dry fabric then either steam **15 minutes** in bullet steamer or dry in dryer on hottest setting for **45 minutes**. Room temp for air dry must be 70°F (22 °C) or higher.	Cover with plastic for **24 hours** OR steam set for **15 minutes**.
How Long Does Dye–paint Mixture Last?	1 week	4 hours	2 days	4 days

Supplies:
- Fiber-reactive Dye
- Synthrapol
- **Soda Ash and/or Baking Soda or Ammonium Sulfate (silk only) depending on setting technique, you choose, if you have not added it to your print paste.
- 1/4th cup Urea Water (9 tbl Urea to 1 qt warm water)
- Print paste
- Lots of containers to keep mixes in!

Table 9.2 Fiber-reactive Dye Quantities (From ProChemical and Dye)

	Pale	Medium	Dark	Black
Dye Powder	1/2 tsp (1 gm)	2 tsp (5 gm)	4 tsp (10 gm)	8 tsp (20 gm)

HOW TO MAKE PRINT PASTE WITH FIBER-REACTIVE DYES ON COTTON, RAYON, AND SILK

1. **Gear up!** Gloves, apron, mask for mixing dye (then you can remove it).
2. ***Scour fabric** as usual (1/2 tsp Synthrapol and ½ tsp soda ash). *** If you are doing a soda soak, do it after this step.**
3. **Mix dye with Urea water.** Paste out selected amount of dye from table 9.2 into the least amount of Urea water possible. Add this to 1 cup of print paste.
4. ***Add fixative.** *If you did NOT do the soda soak method, this is where you add alkali mix or baking soda to your print paste (exact amounts and procedure found in table 9.1).
5. **Print!!!** Using your knowledge of silkscreens, stencils, and stamps or even hand painting – get busy making art!
6. **Cure.** This is also where you steam set or cover and stow for several hours. See directions on different setting methods in table 9.1.
7. **Rinse fabric.** Wash in basins of room temperature water several times until the "slimy" feeling is gone and keep the fabric moving so it does not back stain on itself. The slimy feeling is the soda ash. Now to take care of any fugitive dye, create a very hot wash (at least 140°F or 60°C or more – close to boiling is best) with a 1/2 tsp Synthrapol per pound of fabric and add your fabric swishing and soaking for at least 15 minutes. Dark colors or black may require two hot rinses. If you have a tank-less water heater, you can dial it up and throw your fabric in the washing machine! I prefer to do almost boiling washes – it really ensures color will not come out in subsequent washes!

You can also use fiber-reactive dyes in print paste to paint wool. Just follow the instructions in the following section on direct painting with dye, called "Painting Wool with Fiber-reactive Dyes", but where you add the rest of the cup of Urea water to the dye paste, add print paste!

Figure 9.4 Chickie is baaaaack! Print at top is clear print paste pulled through a deconstructed print and bottom three used different fiber-reactive dye colors in print paste to color the background.

PRINT PASTE USING ACID DYES

This is the best way to paint and print silk and wool and will yield the most brilliant results! Instead of adding soda ash to your print paste, you will add ammonium sulfate and dye with the paste to create a protein friendly mixture! Ammonium sulfate is pH neutral in its powdered form, so you can use it with print paste and not expect curdling like with other acids. When this mixture curdles, is can make creating smooth print paste very difficult. Citric acid can be used as well, but it will make the dye strike faster and potentially not yield dark values like ammonium sulfate. Please **experiment first!** You may want to use guar gum instead since it does not react with acid the same way.

Supplies:
- WashFast Acid Dye
- Synthrapol
- 70% Rubbing Alcohol for wool
- Ammonium Sulfate
- PRO Dye Activator or Soda Ash
- Print paste
- Optional: Metaphos for hard water

Table 9.3 Acid Dye Quantities for Painting or Printing with Dye (From ProChemical and Dye).

	Pale	Medium	Dark	Black
Dye Powder	2 tsp (1 gm)	13 tsp (3 gm)	22 tsp (6 gm)	6 tsp (15 gm)

HOW TO CREATE PRINT PASTE FOR SILK AND WOOL WITH ACID DYE
1. **Gear up!** Gloves, dust particle mask, apron.
2. **Scour fabric.** The usual drill here. If washing habotai or China silk, scour as we normally do, in hot water with 1/2 tsp Synthrapol and 1/2 tsp soda ash. For all other silk, especially with floats, do not include soda ask as it can roughen the surface texture. Do not do this for wool. It will felt! Substitute 1 tbl 70% rubbing alcohol in a gallon of water to break surface tension of wool!
3. **Paste out dye and additives.**
   - Measure the dye powder amount depending on your desired value, according to table 9.3, and dissolve the dye powder with 1/4th cup (60 ml) of boiling water.
   - Add 1 level tsp (7 gm) metaphos and set aside until cool.
   - Add 3 tsp (1.25 ml) of Synthrapol to the dissolved dye.
   - Then add 12 tsp (9.5 gm) of ammonium sulfate and stir thoroughly.
4. **Add print paste.** Add 1 cup of print paste to dye mixture.
5. **Paint!** It's your moment! Be free!
6. **Steam set the dye.** This can be done in a bullet steamer or in a homemade bullet steamer. See the box on "How to Make Your Own Bullet Steamer!" Allow to totally dry and steam for 30 minutes for pale shades and 60 for dark shades.
7. **Rinse fabric.** Wait for the piece to cool after steaming before throwing it in a rinse bath. It wants to be washed in room temp water gently. You will want to change the rinse water until it is mostly clear.

PRINT PASTE USING THIOUREA DIOXIDE

This process is basically creating your own discharge paste, but if you read the chart in Chapter 6 about different color removers, this one does not cause birth defects, yay! You will be creating a print paste of Thiox that you can use as is or add dye to. The possibilities are endless! If you would like to deposit dye and remove all other color, choose dyes that do not remove easily like yellow or turquoise.

Supplies:
- Print Paste
- Thiourea Dioxide
- Soda Ash

Figure 9.5 I know you're sick of chickie but this print was done with a wax rubbing, and pulling a screen over a positive stencil using only discharge paste and then batch drying. I went in with a hot iron after batching and brightened some areas.

HOW TO CREATE DISCHARGE PRINT PASTE

1. **Gear up!** Gloves, acid gas respirator, apron.
2. **Scour fabric.** The usual drill here. Wash in hot water with 1/2 tsp Synthrapol and 1/2 tsp soda ash. Do not do this for wool. It will felt!
3. **Measure Thiourea Dioxide and Soda Ash.** This will be a 1:2 ratio (1/4th tsp thiox to 1/2 tsp Soda Ash) **but use a 1:1 ratio (1/2 tsp thiox to 1/2 tsp Soda Ash) if batch drying and not steaming.**
4. **Add print paste.** Add Thiox and Soda Ash to 1 cup of print paste and blend in blender. If you do not have a dye blender, paste out the soda ash and thiox in a little water then add to print paste. This should be the "mama-bear" print paste. If you don't know what I'm talking about, go back to the beginning of the chapter and read "How to Make Print Paste". Play with this amount based on your opinion of how this first batch turned out.
5. **Apply print paste to your piece.** You can use a silkscreen, stencil, or paint or stamp this paste right on your piece!
6. **Set the dye.** You can decide to batch dry or steam set these pieces. Pieces MUST be damp to activate Thiox. DO NOT wait for these pieces to dry before steam setting!

> ### WHAT IS BATCHING??? A SOLAR STEAMER!
>
> Another technique that was unfamiliar to me until JUST this year . . . this is a very cheap if not free and passive way to use the sun to help set your dyes. It goes like this . . . you wrap your damp finished item in black plastic. Fold it into a package and set it near a sunny window or outside for the day. You can even set this package in the back window of your car! Open 24 hours later and voila! The dye is set and you can open your little present and rinse it out!

DECONSTRUCTED PRINTING USING PRINT PASTE (KERR GRABOWSKI METHOD)

Here's where the magic really begins, folx. This process was completely new to me THIS YEAR. I think it could be of interest to the entertainment dyer community as an easy way to create prints with depth and interest that are permanent and do not change the hand of fabric. Yes, it will be for that special project that you get to work on for a week, which I know is out of the ordinary for our field – but nonetheless it will happen and you will have this technique in your back pocket! This process entails creating a super dye-saturated print paste, adding it to a silk screen, then after drying, pulling clear or lightly tinted print paste through the screen, transferring the edges of the pigmented screen resist to the print pulled through the screen. The process of using screen with print paste in this manner is called **deconstructed printing or breakdown printing** because every time you use one of these screens to print, it degrades a bit and changes. Like all screen printing, you can use stencils in combination with these prints and OH! The results! Kerr, my deconstructed printing guru, likes to use the dye suited to the fabric. So, if it is silk or wool, use acid; if cotton or rayon, use fiber-reactive dyes. If you plan on using your design on silk and cotton, not to worry – you can use fiber-reactive dye and steam set both in a steamer or batch dry for 24 hours. See box on "What Is Batch Drying?" for information on that process.

Figure 9.6 Using black print paste with a syringe application (left). Finger-painting to make some dots and allowed to dry (middle). Adding a stencil, used in a print a moment before with dye still wet on the stencil, then placing screen on top to screen plum and blue dye (right).

Figure 9.7 Steamed, washed, and ironed "Big Chikie in Jail" on charmeuse.

Supplies:
- Print Paste
- Fiber-reactive Dye
- Soda Ash or Ammonium Sulfate
- A blank silk screen
- Squeegee – the thin Bondo squeegees are Kerr's fave

Table 9.4 Fiber-reactive Dye Quantities for 1 Cup of Deconstructed Mix (Kerr Grawbowski)

	Pale	Medium	Dark/Black
Dye Powder	4 tsp	10 tsp	6 Tbl

 ***HOW TO* DO DECONSTRUCTED PRINTING USING PRINT PASTE**

1. **Gear up!** Gloves, dust particle mask, apron.
2. **Scour fabric.** The usual drill here. Wash in hot water with 1/2 tsp Synthrapol and 1/2 tsp soda ash. Do not do this for wool. It will felt!
3. **Paste out dye.** Measure the dye powder amount depending on your desired value, according to table 9.4 and dissolve the dye powder with 1/4th cup (60 ml) of warm urea water. If all you do is silk, you can use acid dyes with the amounts of ammonium sulfate from Table 9.1. If you want to use your screen for both silk and cotton for example, stick to fiber reactive. Acid dyes don't work so great on cellulose, but we can sure as heck fix fiber-reactive dyes to protein!

4. **Add print paste.** Add 1 cup of print paste to dye mixture. This should be the "mama-bear" print paste. If you don't know what I'm talking about, go back to the beginning of the chapter and read "How to Make Print Paste". Play with this amount based on your opinion of how this first batch turned out.
5. **Apply print paste to your screen.** Using a syringe, paint brush, dribbling out of a container, a 2"x4", heck I don't care what device you use to create your design . . . just create a cool design. A really cool way to create an organic design is to place a ton of weird but hard and slightly 3-dimensional objects under your screen, and pull over the objects like you are pulling a silkscreen print. When you do this and see shiny areas, those are the ones that will dry and create a print. SO AWESOME!!! See Figure 9.8 for images of a print I made from leaves from Kerr's yard.

Figure 9.8 Left: Creating a deconstructed print with organic and inorganic materials! Top: Arranging materials to create design; top middle: pulled print paste with tobacco-colored dye through screen; bottom middle: pulling materials off screen *carefully* so it can fully cure; bottom: drying screen.

Figure 9.9 (Right) Having fun and making a mess in Kerr's studio. Pulling print paste tinted with a bit of yellow through the screen. You can see in the piece near the bottom of the picture that the tobacco color of the print and the yellow of the screened print paste have mixed to create a nifty gold color. The tobacco color of the print transferred to the edges of the print. So cool.

Printing and Painting With Dye

157

She sent me home with some car gaskets and other neat things to play with for more deconstructed printing – if I could only finish this book so I could play with them!

6. **Set the dye.** You can decide to batch dry or steam set these pieces. Steam setting can be done in a bullet steamer or in a homemade bullet steamer. See the box on "How to Make Your Own Bullet Steamer!" Allow pieces to totally dry and steam silk for 30 minutes for pale shades and 60 for dark shades, and cotton/rayon for 60 minutes for all shades.

PAINTING WITH DYE: DIRECT APPLICATION

Painting with dye allows dyers to create endless possibilities and an organic painterly look while maintaining the fabric's original hand. I separated this area into two sections: Fiber-reactive dyes and acid dyes to paint fabrics. Since fiber-reactive dyes bond most readily with cellulose and acid dyes with protein fibers, I would choose those matches first when exploring painting fabric.

PAINTING WITH FIBER-REACTIVE DYES

PAINTING COTTON, RAYON, AND SILK WITH FIBER-REACTIVE DYES

Using fiber-reactive dyes on cellulose is the most popular technique for tie-dye and dyeing all cottons, rayons, linen, jute, etc. Of course as you well know, it is because of the amazing bond between this type of dye and cellulose fiber! An application of dye directly on the fabric and not soaking it in an immersion bath is called "**direct application**". Those little squeezy bottles filled with dye that you used at the craft center to dye your rubber-banded-to-death garment is this exact process; you were directly applying dye to the fiber!

There are three ways to set fiber-reactive dyes on cellulose and two on silk, so please read through them in table 9.1 to decide whether you want to do a soda soak in advance (before step 2) or if you would like to add fixative to your dye-paint. At the craft center, they did the soda soak method #1 and handed you a wet T-shirt to dye. The one you choose will depend on if you want to set the dye with a bullet steamer, a dryer, or time, which isn't always on our side!

> ## HOW TO MAKE YOUR OWN BULLET STEAMER!
>
> Did you know you can save like $1800 and build your own steamer?! You can! Here's your shopping list: a 5 foot length of metal ducting to fit inside a large pot – it is sold in 4"–12" diameters, portable burner, large metal pot, a round steamer basket or wire cooling rack (my instant has a perfect one!) that fits in the pot. You can forgo the ducting and just get a pot with a large diameter (12"–15" or greater like a big canning pot).
>
> ## HOW DO I USE IT??
>
> If using only acid dyes in direct application, dry your fabric first. Print paste must, however, stay damp to activate. Lay your dyed piece flat on fabric or material that will allow steam to reach the dyed fabric like craft paper, muslin, thin polyester, newsprint (you get the idea). Make sure you have enough material to roll your fabric in so it doesn't not touch itself

and transfer dye. Gently and loosely roll fabric into a tube and fold back in the ends. You can lay several, smaller pieces on the same sheet and make a larger roll; you just don't want the roll or any fabric to touch the sides of the steamer – water will condense and dye can run. Tape this closed at the end so it doesn't unwrap. Add another piece of paper around that roll to ensure condensation doesn't get inside. Alternatively, you can roll your piece up and then roll it again across the width to create a cinnamon roll shape (see Figure 9.10). You can stack these packages on top of each other but you will ensure no dye transfers to other pieces if you steam one piece at a time.

Figure 9.10 Homemade bullet steamer using no ducting but larger pot, and cinnamon-rolling.

Figure 9.11 Homemade bullet steamer using ducting and tube rolling.

Supplies:
- Fiber-reactive Dye
- Synthrapol
- Soda Ash and/or Baking Soda or Ammonium Sulfate (silk only) depending on setting technique you choose

- Urea Water (9 tbl Urea to 1 qt warm water)
- Optional: Metaphos for hard water
- Optional: Ludigol for leveling

Table 9.5 Fiber-reactive Dye Quantities for Direct Application (From ProChemical and Dye)

	Pale	Medium	Dark	Black
Dye Powder	1/2 tsp (1 gm)	2 tsp (5 gm)	4 tsp (10 gm)	8 tsp (20 gm)

HOW TO PAINT WITH FIBER-REACTIVE DYES ON COTTON AND RAYON (WITH HELP FROM PROCHEMICAL AND DYE)

1. **Gear up!** Gloves, apron, mask for mixing dye (then you can remove it).
2. *****Scour fabric** as usual (1.2 tsp Synthrapol and 1/2tsp soda ash). *** If you are doing a soda soak, do it after this step.**
3. **Mix metaphos into Urea water.** Add 1 tsp to 1 cup Urea water for a 1 cup mixture. You can also add 1 tsp ludigol if you are having leveling problems.
4. **Mix dye with Urea water.** Paste out selected amount of dye from table 9.5 into 1/4th c Urea water. When your paste is lump free add 3/4ths c Urea water to create your concentrate.
5. *****Add fixative and cure.** *If you did NOT do the soda soak method, this is where you add alkali mix or baking soda. This is also where you stem set or cover and stow for several hours.
6. **Paint!!!** With your chosen applicator apply your dye–paint to your fabric!
7. **Rinse fabric.** Wash in basins room temperature water several times until the "slimy" feeling is gone. This is you washing out the soda ash. Now to take care of any fugitive dye, create a very hot wash (at least 140°F or 60°C or more) with a 1/2 tsp Synthrapol per pound of fabric and add your fabric swishing and soaking for at least 15 minutes. Dark colors or black may require two hot rinses. If you have a tank-less water heater, you can dial it up and throw your fabric in the washing machine! I prefer to do almost boiling washes – it really ensures color will not come out in the wash!

> ### AND THE BEET GOES ON . . . MICROWAVE VS STEAM SETTING
>
> Vicki Jensen from ProChemical and Dye puts it best when describing the difference between setting dye in the microwave and in a steamer. Paraphrasing what she said: "Do you want a radish or a beet? In the microwave you get a radish: the dye only penetrates the surface not all of the fabric. When you steam set you get a beet; dye has had the time to fully saturate the fabric, yielding better color and depth".

Figure 9.12 Radishes (top), beets (bottom).

PAINTING WOOL WITH FIBER-REACTIVE DYES

This is a process that can be used if you want to use fiber-reactive dyes on wool. There are specific items you must use in this process like sodium bisulfite to fix fiber-reactive dyes to protein fibers. My recommendation would be to use acid dyes when dyeing protein fibers but not everyone has the set up for those dyes, so this would be an option if you needed to dye these fibers but could not use a stovetop pot or bullet steamer.

Supplies:
- Fiber-reactive Dye
- 70% Rubbing Alcohol
- Wool dye assistant SBS (from ProChemical and Dye)
- Citric Acid Crystals OR Vinegar
- Urea
- Clear household ammonia (non-sudsy)
- White distilled vinegar

Table 9.6 Acid Soak Solution Quantities (From ProChemical and Dye).

Method #1 – Citric Acid Crystals	Method #2 – White Distilled Vinegar
1 gallon (4 liters) 95°F (35°C) water	2 quarts (2 liters) 95°F (35°C) water
11 tbl (193 gm) Citric Acid Crystals	2 quarts (2 liters) white distilled vinegar
2 tsp (10 ml) Synthrapol	2 tsp (10 ml) Synthrapol

Table 9.7 Fiber-reactive Dye Quantities (From ProChemical and Dye).

	Pale	Medium	Dark	Black
Dye Powder	1/2 tsp (1 gm)	2 tsp (5 gm)	4 tsp (10 gm)	8 tsp (20 gm)

HOW TO PAINT WITH FIBER-REACTIVE DYES ON WOOL[1]

1. **Gear up!** Gloves, apron, dust particle mask for mixing powder, respirator with acid cartridges for ammonia soak.
2. **Wet out fabric.** Using a few gallons of water and 1 tbl 70% Rubbing Alcohol, soak and gently swish from time to time for 30 minutes. Squeeze out excess water.
3. **Acid soak.** Make Acid Soak Solution from table 9.6. Add ingredients into water and stir thoroughly. Soak wool for 10–15 minutes. Gently wring fabric and throw out soak solution.
4. **Dissolve dye.** Using 1/4th cup Urea water and 1/2 tsp wool dye assistant SBS (ProChemical and Dye product), paste out dye quantity based on desired shade. Add 3/4ths cup Urea water and stir thoroughly.
5. **Paint!** With a brush, sponge, syringe, or the tool of your choice apply dye mixture to wool. The dye will be good for 3–4 days; then you should pitch it.
6. **Fix the dye.** Batch set the dye by wrapping the wool in black plastic and letting it set for 24 hours OR steam set for 15 minutes.
7. **Remove fugitive dye.** Release any fugitive dyes on the outer surface by soaking in ammonia soak by mixing 2 tbl with 1 gallon of room temperature water. Swish fabric 3–5 minutes. Some color will come out – don't worry!

8. **Neutralize.** Mix 4 tbl vinegar in 1 gallon of room temperature water and add fabric. Swish fabric in this final rinse. Squeeze out water and air dry.

PAINTING WITH ACID DYES

PAINTING SILK AND WOOL WITH ACID DYES

This process is very similar to creating direct dye–paint for cotton except the amounts of dye vary a bit, and the additive that we used for silk with fiber-reactive dyes, ammonium sulfate, is used in this process exclusively.

Supplies:
- Acid Dye
- Synthrapol
- Ammonium Sulfate
- Soda Ash

Table 9.8 Acid Dye Quantities for Painting or Printing With Dye (From ProChemical and Dye).

	Pale	Medium	Dark	Black
Dye Powder	2 tsp (1 gm)	13 tsp (3 gm)	22 tsp (6 gm)	6 tsp (15 gm)

HOW TO PAINT SILK AND WOOL WITH ACID DYE[2]

1. **Gear up!** Gloves, dust particle mask, apron.
2. **Scour fabric.** The usual drill here. If washing silk, scour as we normally do, in hot water with 1/2 tsp Synthrapol (NO soda ash). This will felt wool; try 1 tbl rubbing alcohol in a few gallons of water instead.
3. **Paste out dye.** Measure the dye powder amount depending on your desired value, according to table 9.8 and dissolve the dye powder with 2 cups (125 ml) of boiling water and set aside until cool. This mixture will last up to 6 months before adding Ammonium Sulfate. Add 3 tsp (1.25 ml)

Figure 9.13 Dress painted with acid dye for Rutina Wesley as Viola in *12th Night*, Old Globe Theatre. Costume designer David Reynoso, draper Louise Powers, dyer Erin Carignan.

of Synthrapol to the dissolved dye. Then, when completely cool, add 12 tsp (9.5 gm) of Ammonium Sulfate and stir thoroughly.

4. **Thicken Dye–Paint.** If you do not want to watercolor and would like the paint to sit on the surface of your fabric, I recommend mixing in a few teaspoons of print paste and go from there, playing with different consistencies. For the gown to the right, I did not thicken the dye because the fabric was very light and I wanted to use gravity to help with the running dye. If it had been thickened, it would not have blended so well.
5. **Paint!** It's your moment! Go!
6. **Steam set the dye.** This can be done in a bullet steamer or in a homemade bullet steamer. See the box on "How to Make Your Own Bullet Steamer!" Allow to totally dry and steam for 30 minutes for pale shades and 60 for dark shades.
7. **Rinse fabric.** Wait for the piece to cool after steaming before throwing it in a rinse bath. It wants to be washed in room temp water gently. You will want to change the rinse water until it is mostly clear.

OMBRÉ DYEING

Ombré dyeing is a foundational dyeing technique that artisans are asked to perform often. It is a French word translating as shade, shadow, or ghost in English. Ombré dyeing can be done endless ways with endless mediums. I consider it an art usually performed with dye, dye–paint, or print paste, and therefore the subject landed in this chapter! Aside from dip-dyeing fabric to create an ombré, you can directly apply an ombré pattern with a sponge if your design wants a texture-y looking ombré. You could even silk screen a design in overlapping colors that ombré up a garment. The Viola dress (Figure 9.13) was a sponged and painted ombré, not dip dyed. I had a student who created an ombré by spraying a dress with black Dye-Na-Flow (basically commercially mixed dye–paint) on a polyester prom dress from the bottom up (Figure 9.14).

The most traditional way to ombré dye is to dip dye fabric or a garment to create a color gradient. It is helpful if you have a set up that allows you to hang your garment or fabric above a vat (for acid) or a tub (for fiber reactive) and a pulley that allows you to pull your garment/fabric up and down. The dyer at Eric Winterling's, NY, found that a lift system for hunters works very well for ombré dyeing (see Figure 9.15).

Figure 9.14 Ombré created by spraying Jaquard Dye-Na-Flow directly on the garment. It was sprayed on a saran-wrapped dress form. Designer/artisan August Mayer, for *The Hope Project*, Colorado State University.

To begin ombré dyeing you have to decide what type of ombré you are going to do. For example, do you want the transition from color to color to be smooth and seamless or do you want to see lines between colors? More often than not, designers want smooth seamless ombrés that begin at the hem and either fade into another color and then into the original color of the fabric, or just directly into the original color of the fabric. Either way, it is **super important to decide which color to start with!** See Figure 9.16 for a visual of the following description.

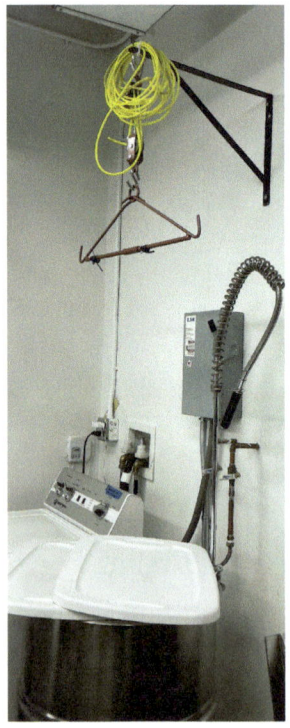

Figure 9.15 A hunters dressing pulley for ombré dyeing in Eric Winterling's dye studio.

Let's say that we have a yellow dress that the designer wants to ombré black to red to yellow, with black starting at the bottom. You will choose to add red first creating an orange color at the top of the red as it layers on top of yellow, next the black will begin. As you can see, this design requires a 3-step process. This will all be done wet or damp depending on how far you would like the dye to travel.

OMBRÉ DYEING ORDER OF OPERATIONS

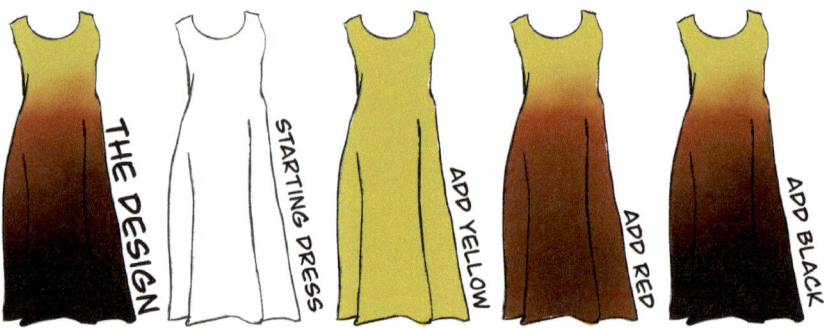

Figure 9.16 The ombré order of operations from a white dress to a finished ombré.

TIPS ON OMBRÉ DYEING

1. **KEEEEEP MOVING!** The first rule of ombré dyeing! This will avoid lines!
2. **Add safety pins** where you would like the colors to stop before starting the process. **This should happen on a finished garment in a fitting.** It can be difficult to keep this in mind when you're in the thick of things.
3. Always **keep it moving.** You will get lines on your fabric the minute you stop moving and splashing dye on your piece.
4. **Keep the rest of the garment wet!** This will also keep the lines from happening but be careful not to dip too far into your bath.

> 5. **Mix fixative in dye first,** not after leveling. We only want to perform this process once for each layer; fix it as you go.
> 6. **You may have to add more dye** if you are trying to get a gradient of one color. The dye will and should exhaust as you dye your piece.
> 7. **Have a spray bottle of water handy.** You can use a spray bottle of water to water down areas that you decided got too much dye. You have to ACT FAST! If you don't spray that line that forms immediately, it may be there for life!
> 8. **Use a spray bottle of dye** to soften borders between colors/gradients.

Supplies:
- Dye
- A pot large enough to allow fabric to move freely
- Something to hang your garment from the ceiling over a pot, tub, or towel.
- Lots of towels
- A pulley rig (this can be a rope pulled through a hanger or carabiner). It is important that you can move your rope freely.
- A few spray bottles that you can add dye to
- Long spoons to splash dye on fabric

HOW TO DIP OMBRÉ

1. **Gear up!** Dust particle mask, gloves, apron.
2. **Set up!** Make sure your pulley is firmly attached to the ceiling or whatever it is hanging from. On a hanger, hang your garment from the pulley and test the action by pulling on the rope and moving the garment up and down a few times over an empty vat. Basically, make sure it works. BTW your garment will be much heavier because it will be wet – so if it fails with dry fabric then butch that pulley up!
3. **Up the amounts of dye you usually use** to 3 or 4 times the amount. Your fabric is moving in and out of this bath and is not saturating immersed the entire time.
4. **Do samples first!** Mix up dye class, based on the fiber you are using (or just use union dye) and do samples on the actual fabric if you have extra. This will help you determine how much dye to use. Trying to fix an ombré dye job can result in some unfortunate lines and messy overlaps, so try to get this right the first time. Go through all the paces. Try splashing or spraying the border lines with the same dye to soften the edges. Then sing "Borderline, feels like I'm going to lose my mind!!!" It will feel that way the first time you do this process.
5. **Mix up a large bucket or vat of dye.**
   - **FOR SILK:** If dyeing silk, use acid dye in a vat of hot water. Follow the steps for acid dyeing (prep, mixing, and amounts). Add acid in the beginning of this process so you don't have to repeat the process and potentially risk creating hard lines. You could technically follow the instructions for painting with acid dyes, but if you were doing a large garment, I would be afraid of dye transfer in the steaming process. With the process outlined previously, no steaming is necessary.
   - **FOR COTTON, RAYON, LINEN:** If dyeing cellulose you can use fiber-reactive dyes to do this process. You can also use union dye. Because time is of the essence in theatre, I have only ombré dyed cotton in union dyes and had pretty good results. Fiber

reactive will of course be brighter in hue, but because fiber-reactive dye takes at least 15–30 minutes to fix to the fabric, if you want an arm workout then go for it!

- **FOR EVERYTHING ELSE:** Use union dyes in a HOT vat. May the Force be with you. This process can be difficult but it's not impossible on synthetics. Maybe you have a blend with a natural fabric? Add the specific additives for that fabric so you can fix some of the dye.

6. **Wet fabric.** You can decide to wet your whole garment or just part of a garment. This is where your sample will help you. I like to wet the area I definitely know I want dye then spritz above that with water in a spray bottle. If you dip to a point that leaves a line, the dye will migrate up to that line and stop, creating pool chemical strip look or a harsh line. Most dyers are NOT going for that look but if you are, now you know how!

7. **Start moving!** Put your fabric on a hanger that is attached that to the pulley over your vat of dye and start dipping. Have dye in a spray bottle handy or a long metal spoon to splash the border line. IT'S ALL AOBUT THE BORDER LINE. Keep moving so the dye doesn't settle in a line and keep softening it with more dye of the same color. You did this with your sample, right? Do what worked then! You can use water in a spray bottle to also soften the borderline but is has to be done immediately.

8. **Move on to next color or add dye.** When you are happy with your first color, dump your bath and mix up the next color. Third verse, same as the first – start moving, spraying, and gently splashing.

Figure 9.17 Three gowns for Juana, Xochitl, and the Viceriene from *The Sins of Sor Juana*, Purdue Theatre. Draper Rose Kaczmarowski. The dress on the left has been ombré dyed in both directions using purple and blue. The dress on the left has been color removed (this is really evident in the embroidery found in the yellow portion of the dress). Note how the sleeves are ombréd in the same pattern but on different areas of the dress; this is specifically why Stephanie chose to dye the sleeves separately. Juana, Xochitl, and the Viceriene from *The Sins of Sor Juana* costume design, and photo courtesy of Stephanie Nguyen, displayed at Purdue University.

 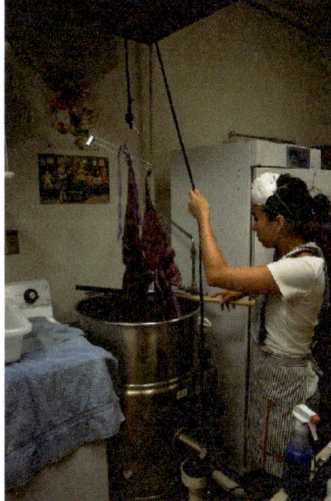 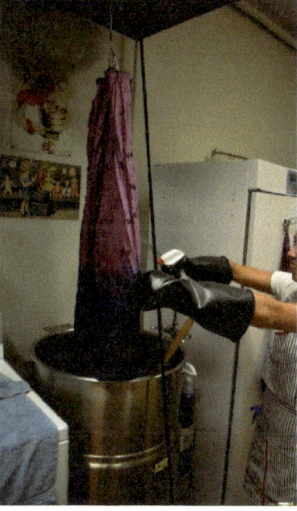

Figure 9.18 Stephanie Nguyen, costume designer and dyer for *The Sins of Sor Juana*, Purdue, utilizes a pulley over a hot dye vat to ombré dye a heavy 17th century gown. Left: her dye sample that began as cream silk; middle: Stephanie dyes the sleeves separately as they would not have the finished look she wanted if she had dyed them on the dress; right: she sprays hot dye on border between the purple and the blue using blue dye.

DID YOU KNOW YOU CAN REVERSE OMBRÉ??

Instead of adding color in a gradient, how about removing it?! Stephanie's design for *The Sins of Sor Juana* was so detailed that she even removed color from the brown embroidery in some cotton she bought, then overdyed it with a golden ombré from the other direction. You can see in her sample to the right the embroidery is darker in the gold portion and cream in the bottom half. To the right is an image of dip dyeing the sleeves and bodice in color remover. The finished garment is shown in Figure 9.19.

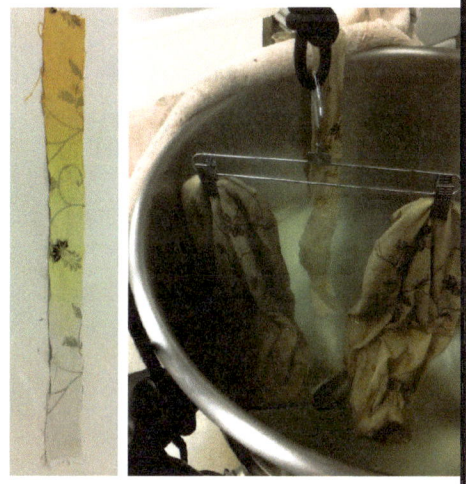

Figure 9.19 Discharge ombré in action.

THE BOTTOM LINE

Hand painting fabric can be frustrating for those who like to control media tightly. It is very akin to the art of watercolor except our paper is often wiggly fabric! Just remember to take a deep breath and do loads of samples so you get the feel of painting with your chosen media on fabric. Creating ombréd fabric can also be a point of frustration. Again, samples will take you time in the beginning but serve you in the long run!!! Happy painting!

NOTES

1 Pro Chemical and Dye. "Direct Application Using PRO MX Reactive Dyes on Cellulose." https://prochemicalanddye.net/downloads/dl/file/id/97/product/0/direct_application_using_pro_mx_directions.pdf.
2 PRO Chemical and Dye. "Direct Application on Wool and Silk Using PRO MX Reactive Dyes on Silk and Wool." https://prochemicalanddye.net/downloads/dl/file/id/98/product/0/direct_application_on_wool_and_silk_using_pro_mx_directions.pdf.

10

ANOTHER DIMENSION
PAINTS, COATINGS, AND OTHER EMBELLISHMENTS

By adding glitz, dimension, or an image that only shows up under black light, we take our art to the next level with paints, mediums, and additives. Much like dyes that are formulated to bond to specific fibers, there are paints intended for use on textiles that remain flexible and bond to a substrate when worn, washed, or dry-cleaned. Every dyer has their favorite brands and types of textile paints and mediums; it is all relative to what corner of the entertainment industry and geographic location they work in. For example, if you are a breakdown artist you probably won't care as much about UV paints and pearlescent extender as someone who works on musicals! However, it's good to have knowledge of it all because you never know when you will need to create that "he-came-out-of-a-freezer-after-170-years" look.

In this chapter I will cover paints, premixed dyes, mediums, bling, foil, coatings, and even processes specific to mediums like marbling! Because of my background in costume crafts there are definitely some crossover materials described in the following pages, as dyer painters often end up in crafts!

TEXTILE PAINT

Textile paints come in every variety of color and opacity. All paints intended for textiles generally work well on leather, paper, wood, and other porous materials like Fosshape and even some thermal plastics (with a sealant). The advantage of using a textile paint over an acrylic paint is that the fabric generally retains the original hand, and with heat setting, you can be assured of the wash fastness of textile paint. With acrylic paint, wash fastness and light fastness can be a crapshoot! Regardless of how I feel about using acrylic paint on fabric, I will talk ad

DOI: 10.4324/9781351130677-11

Figure 10.1 Phenomenal painter–dyer Jeff Fender painted this sample for *The Devil Wears Prada* musical (2022). You can see the finished product in the photo of the completed dress at Eric Winterling's studio.

nauseam about an acrylic artist's color called NovaColor for items that need to be worn but not laundered, like armor for example, later in this chapter.

The most important choice to make when choosing which paint to use is opacity. For breakdown applications and a more painterly watercolor look, using a transparent paint is going to be helpful. To completely block out the fabrics' original color, using an opaque paint is going to be the better choice. Transparent and opaque paints are available in all levels of viscosity from commercial suppliers. Many dyer–painters choose one or two different brands of paints to keep in their stock, depending on which they feel is the most versatile for a wide variety of projects. For example, while Jacquard textile paint isn't necessarily my favorite fabric paint, I always end up ordering it in every shop I'm in because somehow I find its versatility works for me. Many shops use this paint but many others use pigment paints and auxiliaries to allow the artist to absolutely control every element of their paint, more on that product in the next section!

PREMIXED TEXTILE PAINTS

It is good to keep in mind that the majority of textile paints are water-based. This means they can be thinned with water, which is free and nontoxic!!! What many people don't know is that textile paint shouldn't be thinned more than 30% as the binder loses its bonding power at that (or higher) concentration. These paints can be used to silk screen, stencil, sponge, or paint on fabric (often leather and paper too).

Supplies:
- Textile paint
- Water brush-cleaning container
- Enamel or sealed surface paint tray

Figure 10.2 Premixed textile paints by Jaquard. As you can see, our stock is used frequently!

- Paint brush of your choosing (or screen, stencil, stamp, etc.)
- Towel to blot or wipe brush
- Iron or hot dryer to heat set

HOW TO USE PREMIXED TEXTILE PAINTS

1. **Gear up!** Gloves, apron.
2. **Set up.** Fill your brush-cleaning container with water and place on top of your towel. Lay down paper or fabric under your project to protect the surface. Add a tablespoon of paint(s) to your tray.
3. **Paint!** Pick up some paint with your brush, sponge or whatever tool you are using and test the paint on the fabric. I usually like to wipe a little off on my towel first, to work the paint into my brush or sponge.
4. **Let it dry then set.** Let the paint fully dry then heat-set it using a press cloth and the manufacturer's directions. Usually it is a few seconds over each area with a hot iron or a tumble in an industrial dryer. If you have the luxury of having a heat box, follow manufacturer's directions for temperature and time. Do samples first – try to wash them out, this will indicate if your heat setting was appropriate.

CONCENTRATED PIGMENTS

Concentrated pigments are the most versatile textile paint because of the ability to thin, thicken, make transparent, opaque, or even pearl-ize textile paint. Concentrated pigments do not work on their own and require some kind of binder to adhere to fabric. These binders range in viscosity, opacity, and embedded materials – for example, the pearlized binder. Breakdown artists, dyer–painters, and props people utilize concentrated pigments to create custom paint; the film industry has been using these for ages as well as some knowledgeable theatrical technicians. Many large professional shops often stock concentrated pigments and use opaque and transparent binders to create custom hues and values.

Concentrated pigments (CP) can be used in any application imaginable when mixed with the appropriate binder:

- Airbrushing = CP mixed with thin transparent binder
- Silk screening = CP mixed with opaque binder/extender
- Stamping or painting = CP mixed with opaque, transparent, or pearlized binder/extender
- Watercolor look painting = CP mixed with transparent watery binder (ProChem's LoCrock)

A product I am particularly hot for right now is made by ProChemical and Dye and it is a concentrated pigment in liquid form. Use different sorts of extenders and binders to customize this paint. Add bronzing powder to metallicize the paint or use a pearlescent or iridescent medium. They also make thinners and thickeners for this paint – the possibilities are endless. ProChem offers a starter kit of primaries, a binder, and an extender if you want to play with these and spend very little to start out. Dharma Trading used to make this product but no longer offers it because of manufacturing expense. In the UK and Europe, look up London Screen Service for their version of this product.

Supplies:
1. Concentrated pigment
2. Extender/binder (opaque or transparent)
3. Brush-cleaning container
4. Enamel or sealed surface paint tray
5. Paint brush of your choosing (or screen, stencil, stamp, etc.)
6. Towel to blot or wipe brush
7. Iron or hot dryer to heat set

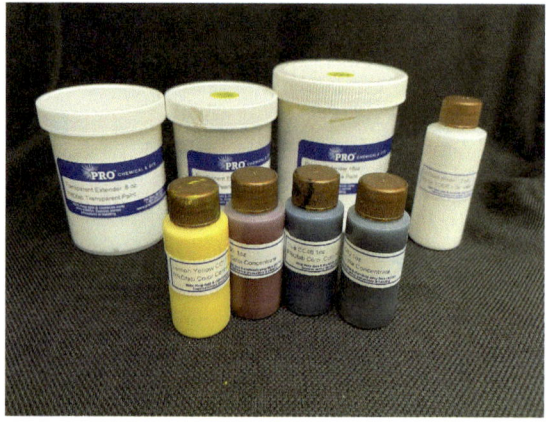

Figure 10.3 ProChemical and Dye's Concentrated Pigment starter kit includes everything you need to get started.

HOW TO USE CONCENTRATED PIGMENTS!

1. **Gear up!** Gloves, apron.
2. **Set up.** Fill your brush-cleaning container with water and place on top of your towel. Lay down paper or fabric under your project to protect the surface. Add a tablespoon of extender of your choice to your tray.
3. Using the tiniest brush or dropper, pick up some pigment and drop it next to your binder. Start by mixing in minuscule amounts – you will be surprised at how far this goes! You need about 4–5 teaspoons of concentrated pigment per cup of extender for medium shades. This is about a 1:3.5 ratio, concentrated pigment to extender.
4. For thin paint add extender and binder that is watered down (follow manufacturer directions).

AIRBRUSH PAINT

Airbrush paint has to meet a few criteria to make it to the top of any artisans list: good coverage, doesn't clog the airbrush, not super toxic (since it becomes particulate matter waiting to be inhaled), and is easy to set.

I'm going to get it out in the open, I love Createx. I have tried to airbrush a variety of thinned paints over the years and once I found Createx, I was in love. I first fell in love with it when I painted white tights with red stripes (yes, like candy canes), for *The Grinch That Stole Christmas*. Usually, I sacrifice something to the dye gods before painting anything on white hoping it won't bleed, but red!? The most unstable color that leaves first?? I masked it off with tape and airbrushed it with a custom color I mixed using Createx and it came out perfectly!

Figure 10.4 Hochi Asiatico's gorgeous airbrushed fabrics tests.
Source: **Photo courtesy of Hochi Asiatico.**

The colors did not migrate when washed either! The body of Createx is just enough that you can achieve really crisp lines when airbrushing. There is a textile fixative you can add for additional insurance, but I hardly ever use it. Maybe I will on the next pair of red and white striped tights, for posterity's sake! Createx is already kind of thin but is easily thinned farther with a little airbrush cleaner and it doesn't break down the binder, meaning the paint stays put! Also, colors are available in opaque and transparent, leaving options to use Createx in a painted or sponged application for breakdown, when a thinner transparent paint is required. It doesn't clog up the airbrush as easily as brands like jacquard (even thinned) do. They also have metallics and neons.

Concentrated pigment colors are also a great contender for the top choice in airbrush paint as you can add an opaque or transparent extender, binder, then thin the whole thing to run smoothly through your airbrush. High flow acrylics can also be used and will perform similarly to Createx, except they are rated as water resistant, which means costumes using this material can get wet and will be fine but they cannot be washed unless you add an additional fixative. Please look up Golden high flow acrylics for more information on this product.

When using a new airbrush, do lots of tests! Test your colors first, as many times, they need thinning. Air brush cleaner, binder, even water can be added to thin these paints. When painting with an airbrush, use sweeping motions and envision you are sprinkling material into the air then letting it fall on the fabric. If you spray too hard for too long in the same place you will get puddles and drips. Test how small or large your spray can be by pushing down and pulling back on the trigger or just moving the airbrush towards and away from your paint surface. **Remember to wear a dust filter mask at the very least!**

See Paint Tools, at the end of this chapter, for a discussion of airbrush and compressor brands, pros and cons, and other tools that can make airbrushing easier!

UV PAINT

It seems like there's been an uptick in desire to coat sets and humans in UV color the last 5 years or so. UV paint on costumes can be very tricky to hide if an "it doesn't exist, until it exists" moment is desired. When I designed *Next to Normal*, there is that scene where the main character has a delusion that her doctor turns into a rock star, and it happens in a moment.

We decided it would be fun to paint a flaming guitar on the back of his jacket so he could turn around and black lights reveal the guitar. We found that even the transparent UV paints (Wildfire UV paint from Rosebrand), when layered the minimum amount to make lights on the grid activate the UV, looked milky under normal stage lights and made the fabric stiff and unnatural. This is not to say it does not work when performers are given UV flashlights or if it is utilized for an installation like Meow Wolf; it is just very difficult for stage if you want to keep the original hand of fabric and create a stunning UV effect.

We came up with an interesting removable technique to use UV makeup on the body and

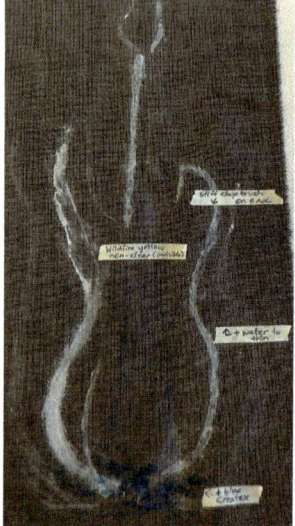

Figure 10.5 Clockwise from top left: Costume rendering for Dr. Fine showing desired flame design; production photo of UV paint on jacket; "invisible" UV fabric paint on sample; "visible" UV fabric paint on sample. From Purdue's production of *Next to Normal*, dir Amy Budd.

costumes that we developed at Colorado State for a scene for *These Seven Sicknesses*. The UV makeup is very bright and much lighter in weight than UV paint. It can also be combined in Vaseline or lotion, and washed out of clothing. We made "mud/blood" out of Kryolan UV makeup and aqua color mixed with a little lotion and baby powder so Electra could bathe in mud that looked like actual mud under stage light and then in a black light scene the whole cemetery and Electra are covered in UV "blood", which all glowed blue. It was great because it washed out of the fabric every night.

Use UV paints the same as you would use textile paints and follow manufacturer directions on heat-setting. Test visibility with inexpensive UV flashlights, in a somewhat dark room, depending on your final show or shoot lighting conditions.

SCREEN PRINTING INKS

Honestly, screen printing inks are thick textile paints with a longer **open time**. Opaque paints are required for silk screening and often have binders that dry out quickly. So, if a screen ink states it has a good open time, that means your paint will last longer and give you a little more working time. Please see Table 10.1 on a comparison of three screen inks adapted from Dharma Trading's website. All of these inks are water-based and therefore they are safer to use than a solvent-based paint.

You do not have to use screen printing inks for silkscreens; I have actually used Jacquard textile paints many times to pull prints. You can also use concentrated pigment paints and opaque binders or a transparent binder depending on what you're going for. The bottom line is that paint with a heavy body will create crisp lines and no bleed at the edges. A bleed can make your precise photo-emulsion screen look muddy and defeat the whole purpose of using photo emulsion in the first place! Please see pulling a print in Chapter 9 for pulling screens with paint and ink.

Table 10.1 Screen Paint Characteristics.

Paint Brand	Name	Advantages	Disadvantages
Speedball	Fabric Screen Printing Inks	• Excellent open time • Excellent washfastness • Soft hand • Iridescent opaque colors – great results on dark fabric • Glow-in-the-dark colors! • Mediums available • Archival quality lightfastness • Clean up with water • Made in USA (if you live in the US)	• Can't use on nylon
Jaquard	Professional Screen Printing Inks	• Designed for all surfaces, does not wrinkle paper • Excellent washfastness • Extended open time, which gives flexibility to add other inks and time to wash screens! • **Works on plastics, vinyl, and other substrates that scare water-based inks!** • Excellent light fastness; archival quality • Clean up with water • Self-fixing (but heat-setting still recommended)	• Stiffer than Versatex, have to buy softening additive to make fabric have better hand
Versatex	Silkscreen paint	• Softest hand of the available silkscreen paint • Heavily pigmented • Large pallet • Transparent colors • Fluorescent colors • Metallic colors • Made in USA (if you live in the US) • Clean up with water • Better performance than comparably priced screen inks • Great texture	• Can dry quicker than other inks • Not so great on paper or nonabsorbent surfaces

PREMIXED DYES/INKS

There are a few premixed dyes out there that are really incredible and easy to use. They were primarily developed to work as silk paint for gutta-resist painters. They are fantastic for this application but also amazing for a variety of uses including breakdown, direct application, using in a spray bottle, as well as many more applications. I love using a sea sponge and sponging on this medium. It is also fabulous if a watercolor look is desired. As we all know, we could premix our own concentrates, but this product is at the other end of the good–fast–cheap continuum. It is not cheap, but good and fast!

Dye-Na-Flow is the Jacquard product that I have used for years and absolutely love. It works on almost all fibers including poly blends. It is actually ink and not dye, as it contains no loose dye but behaves like a dye on fabric. It is very subtle and transparent, which makes it great for breakdown applications. I recently discovered Pro Silk and Fabric Paint, by Pro Chem. This is virtually an identical product to Dye-Na-Flow and is 1/3rd less in cost. They also sell extenders and thickeners that work with this medium. I did a head to head experiment by painting these products onto a cotton t-shirt, and found that they were just as bright after application, washing, and drying. The setting process is identical to textile paint: use a hot iron or industrial dryer.

Figure 10.6 The mottled-watercolor-looking garter, underwear, and gloves were achieved by using a sea sponge and watered-down Dye-Na-Flow. The nipples were created using textile paints, not premixed dye. Ensemble in Anne Hould-Ward's design for *Mahogony*, LA Opera (2007).

MARKERS

Markers are useful tools when trying to hide seam allowance that was just exposed *after* you dyed that garment or to color/patina small areas like under buttons, edges of collars, or to outline a silk screen or other print. There are many uses for markers, but generally, these uses are for small areas. There are SO many brands that I had my research assistant, Lilly Griffin, create a pro–con table of different brands.

Table 10.2 Marker Comparison by Brand.

Product	Pro	Con
Pebeo	• very pigmented/opaque • vibrant	• layering color is difficult
FabricMate	• very pigmented • can layer color	• has a streaky appearance; takes several layers to make solid
TeeJuice	• great pigment and control over line thickness	• mixed reviews on longevity
Shiva	• Works wonderfully on silk • wonderful pigment	• Reviews say that they take a very long time to dry • messy to use • pricey for their overall quality
Fabrico	• Very wide variety of colors and shades • pigment holds up very well	• small amount of reviews say that they don't set well on synthetic fibers
Identipen	• comes highly rated for crispness in color and lines • good for fine-line work	• color running after washing (from reviews)
MARVY	• good pigment level • wonderful layering ability	• expect to use a lot of pressure to get the desired pigment
DecoFabric	• very opaque, the most like paint	• you can't control the opacity as much as other paint pens
Sharpie (Permanent Markers)	• Easy for writing and small details	• runs out of pigment quickly • can't always rely on them being opaque
Deco	• brand offers Opaque, glitter, metallic, and pearl varieties • highly rated for thicker fabrics	• reviews say that they are awful for thinner and silky fabrics and find it hard to get clean and precise lines
Sulky Iron-on Transfer Pens	• really helpful in a lot of multiple transfers • are said to transfer very quickly	• reviews say that they can be quick to dry out and the fine tip doesn't last
Jacquard Auto Fade Pen	• nice lines • good pigment (from reviews)	• reviews say that they aren't always the best at fading successfully • quick to fade, which could be a pro or con for some people
Soft Gutta Pen	• very easy handling, doesn't bleed • very good for people with pain after a duration of squeezing	• challenge to refill

ALL THAT SHIMMERS: BLINGING COSTUMES!

BRONZING POWDERS

If you happen to work in an old theatre, look in the flammables cabinet for the small silver tins marked bronzing powder. They are super-duper toxic and require a respirator, gloves, and goggles, but my lord are they beautiful! There are modern bronzing powders that require dust particle masks but are do not have the metal content the old bronzing powders do. Dharma carries these as well as many art stores. They can be added to transparent mediums or a painted surface that hasn't dried all the way or to a transparent medium like transparent extender on top of a painted surface. When adding to a surface you have to seal it in some way; some use a spray lacquer like shellack or even a watered down flex glue.

EMBOSSING POWDERS

These are similar to bronzing powders and glitter in the way that they are fine powders added to adhesive. There is a kit that emBELLAtex® supplies, which is a one-step process and does not involve heat-setting. Glitter or dry pigments are the colorings that are mixed into emBELLAtex® paste, then applied with a specialty stencil. I have seen some beautiful costumes that were embellished using this product. Sure, one could try to recreate this with mediums, powdered pigments, and glitter, but this company has it already dialed in; so consider this when weighing the good–fast–cheap triangle.

GLITTER

Glitter has come a long way since my kindergarten days. You can buy it in bulk and apply it to any medium it will stick to like flex glue, a gel medium, or a transparent textile extender. You will want to test your particular medium with the actual glitter because some media really deaden the reflective quality of the glitter. For those of you that hate the fact that traditional glitter, which is made of plastic, causes some major long-term pollution, there are new offerings like "bio-glitter" and "eco-glitter" that can be used in paint and makeup applications. They say it is not dangerous if ingested but don't go eating a heaping spoonfull!

If you would like to glitter shoes or fabric, my grad school colleague Megan Edlefsen gave me some tips and instructions that she learned

Figure 10.7 Glittered shoes created by Megan Edlefsen.
Photo courtesy of Megan Edlefsen.

from her shoe glitzing business, DiscoToes. She uses Aileene's Flexible Stretchable Fabric Glue watered down in a ratio of 1–2 parts water to 4 parts glue. Paint mixture on shoe (fabric shoes preferred – less prep and she knows this works on fabric) and sprinkle with glitter. Add a second coat of glue and glitter if needed. When dry, seal with a mixture of 2–3 parts water to 4 parts glue. Dries clear and stretches beautifully. She prefers fine glitter but says chunky will work too. Thanks, Megan!

SOLID GOLD: LEAFING AND FOILING

Adding metallic elements and creating faux metal is an age old trick used since ancient times. Originally, folks added actual gold leaf to glam palaces and religious buildings using actual gold-laden leaf. Modern gold leaf is not made of gold, rather it is made of copper and zinc rolled super thin. It is more delicate than tissue paper and will stick to any remotely humid surface including your hands. Fabric foil is a metallic product usually made of aluminum that is fused to polyester or acetate film and then transferred using heat onto a surface with a print made from glue. The major difference between metal ("gold") leaf and fabric foil is that leaf is used for nonporous hard surfaces and foil is intended to be used for porous flexible materials.

FOILING FABRIC

Foiling is one of the most fun surface modifications I can think of. I am however distracted by shiny objects so . . . This foil, or textile foil as it is called commercially, is made of aluminum and comes in endless color and pattern varieties. Adding foil is similar to leafing (see part of this chapter on gold leafing for more info) as it is a two part process, but foil is transferred using heat and glue versus solely adhering foil to tacky leaf sizing (glue). You can create images using the paste in combination with a printing technique like silkscreens, stencils, or stamps, by hand drawing with the glue, or by using a Cricut cutter. Prints can be made **directly on the fabric or directly on the foil**. Foil adhesive, foil, flocking, and glitter can all be purchased through a screen printing supplier and even found at hobby stores. The more robust adhesive, in my opinion, is the plastisol-based adhesive found at silkscreen supply stores while the brand Decco can be found at JoAnns and Michaels and has a variety of styles of adhesives that they claim work on fabric and paper.

Figure 10.8 shows a hand-printed sample where glue is painted on velvet, foil adhered, left to cool, then peeled away to reveal the foiled image! If you are looking for a crisper image, silk screen the glue on fabric.

Supplies
- Textile foil (heat transfer type)
- Foil adhesive
- Iron (industrial preferred)
- Stencil, screen, stamp, or brush to apply design
- Print surface
- Pins to pin down fabric

HOW TO FOIL FABRIC

1. **Gear up!** Gloves, apron.
2. **Pin down** fabric to your print surface and make sure it fabric is pinned TIGHT. If using a silk screen, use silk pins or other low-profile pins that will not push your screen away from the surface. Put them in at an angle pointing toward the center of the fabric. See pinning fabric for printing box in this chapter.
3. **Transfer glue.** Using foil adhesive, apply the glue like you would a heavy-bodied (or thick) paint. You can screen it on, use a stencil, or just paint directly on to your fabric or foil*. It is rather tacky and can be tricky to use with stencils, so do samples first! * **If adding glue directly to your foil,** make sure your image is a mirror image as you will be flipping it over to transfer your image to fabric.
4. **Let the glue dry** for an hour.
5. Lay down foil, **shiny colored side facing up**, dull side touching your fabric.
6. **Adhere foil.** Lay a piece of craft paper over your object and using an iron set to high, slowly iron in circles, keeping your iron moving for 15–20 seconds over the area. A clam heat press (or transfer iron) is the best way to use this product but not many dye shops have these tools. *You will lower the luster by ironing longer.* Foil can be cut up and pieced together to add multiple foil colors and textures simultaneously. Let foil cool and slowly peel away a corner to reveal your foiled design.

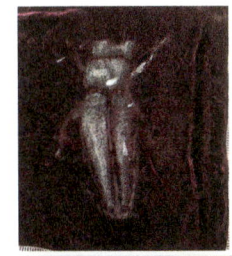

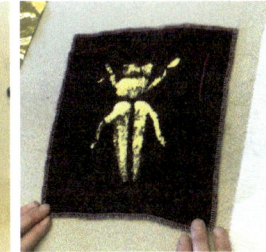

Figure 10.8 Starting at top: a hand-printed sample where glue is painted on velvet, foil adhered, left to cool, then peeled away to reveal the foiled image! If you are looking for a crisper image, silk screen the glue on fabric.

NO-GLUE FOILING?

A little trick Jeff Fender shared was that foil will adhere to plastisol inks! No need for glue! This means you can lay down color via any method (stencil, screen, hand paint) and using a transfer iron, used for t-shirt transfers, lay your foil on dried plastisol ink, let foil cool, then peel away foil! See the beautiful results in Figure 10.9 of Jeff's Cirque du Soleil koi fish sample.

Figure 10.9 Jeff's Cirque koi fish samples using foil on plastisol inks!

Figure 10.10 Leafed headdresses of show girls in musical *Sammy*, costume design by Fabio Toblini, Old Globe Theatre, 2009. Photo courtesy of Charlotte Devaux.

LEAFING SURFACES

I feel that I have spent years of my life leafing. I have always enjoyed it unless it is really hot and I cannot turn on a fan or open a window because the leaf will blow all over the shop! Leaf is often preceded by "gold". But leafing foil comes in many metallic finishes including copper, silver, and bronze. The leaves come in books, between pieces of tissue paper. They are extremely thin and delicate, so take a deep breath before starting your project!

This process is a 3-part process and can be applied to harder yet flexible surfaces like leather, thermal plastics (including variform and Fosshape), foams, trim, and on top of texture mediums. Don't use these on a surface that needs to be washed – use the foil for fabric as outlined previously. These foils need to be burnished to be flat and eliminate lines where they join. Tip: tear leaf and apply torn sections when overlapping. This way you will not see the seams when you are finished!

Supplies:
- Leafing foil
- Leafing glue
- Leafing sealant or acrylic clear coat sealant
- A small soft brush
- Optional: tweezers
- Optional: cheesecloth or soft cloth to push leaf into glue
- Optional: tape for taping off a design, stencil, silkscreen, chip brush to paint directly, etc., for making design

HOW TO METAL-LEAF
1. **Gear up.** Gloves, apron.
2. **Clean and seal the area** to be foiled. If you have a porous substrate, the glue will not sit on the surface and adhere to the foil; you can seal it with the sealant used to finish this process.

3. **Add glue**. Apply a thin coat of foil adhesive to the area you would like to foil. Let it dry until tacky, about 15–30 minutes depending on humidity and temperature.
4. **Apply leaf.** Being careful to place the largest piece of leaf you can on the area that has been sized with glue, pickup your leaf and gently place it onto the adhesive. Using the side of your soft brush, gently press the leaf into the sizing. If you get wrinkles, don't worry, you can burnish them out later (but try to be careful in the first place and not create more work for yourself later!). Don't try to eliminate wrinkles at this point, you will only tear your leaf and make even more work for yourself in the burnishing step. Gently tear excess leaf away and *save for later*.
    - The leaf WILL stick to your fingers, especially if it's hot where you're working. You can use cotton gloves to avoid fingerprints and tearing from sticking to your fingers (I don't use cotton gloves, but if you're looking for a super high-gloss finish, you may want to try this!).
    - To use smaller pieces you can pick leaf up with tweezers or even a soft paint brush and place the pieces where they need to go. Sometimes small pieces are used for patching areas that didn't adhere.
5. **Allow leaf to cure.** Some folks recommend overnight but I think a few hours is fine. This will ensure the leaf has had time to fully adhere and the adhesive has had time to cure.
6. **Burnish!** Here's the fun part, using your soft brush, an old T-shirt scrap, or cheesecloth, gently rub the leafed area in circular movements until all remaining bits of leaf are gone and the piece is to the level of smoothness you'd like. TIP: If you want to dull the shine a bit, keep rubbing with cloth or even try using a stiffer brush to rub the surface. Don't rub too hard, you don't want to tear the leaf.
7. **Seal.** Using sealant that comes with leaf or an acrylic transparent sealant paint on a thin coat with a soft brush. Let this dry for a few hours until cured.

RHINESTONES!!

Rhinestones are named after sparkling quartz pebbles once found on the banks of the Rhine River in Europe.[1] Once these were depleted, they took the form of the synthetic stone that we know and love, today. Rhinestones can add drama and sparkle to costumes. There are a few types of rhinestones: hot-fix, flat-back, and sew-on rhinestone crystals. Which one you choose depends on the substrate you are bedazzling! If your fabric can be very hot, hot fix are the

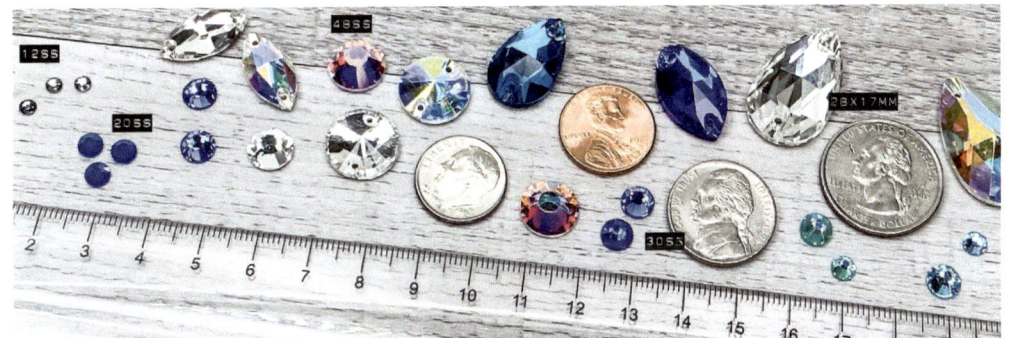

Figure 10.11 There are several types of rhinestones and they are usually measured in millimeters.
Photo credit: **Rhinestones Unlimited, RhinestonesU.com.**

fastest as you can iron on many at a time. If your fabric melts (yes, the glass gets that hot!) you will want to choose glue-on crystals or use a rhinestone mount. If you want giant honking gems that will be super permanent (like for a cruise line costume), the sew-on kind are the best bet. You can buy them online from many stores and can purchase them in bulk by the gross (144). They come in many different sizes using up to three different numbering systems: stone size (ss), Millimeter (mm), or Pearl Plate (pp). Millimeter is the easiest for most to understand because you can look at a ruler and know the size of your stone. Many designers and artisans who use these regularly have a few sizes they love and use; according to Rhinestones Unlimited, the most common sizes sold are 20 ss and 30 ss and folks usually mix them with 12 ss, 16 ss, and an occasional 40 ss. They come in solid colors and 2-color changeable, called AB or aurora borealis.

HOT-FIX CRYSTALS

Sparkle magic is what I like to call these little gems. They are glass rhinestones that have adhesive on the back so when they are heated the adhesive will stick to fabric (or whatever you put it on – like the hot plate edge!). Once the adhesive is "blown" (it puffs up when it's ready to stick) if you do not adhere it immediately, you will not be able to glue this product without using another type of glue. These have a learning curve to use but after a while one can get really fast at applying these. Not all of these

Figure 10.12 Megan Edlefsen's hot-fix crystals on shoes. She gives the excellent tip: "I like to use several sizes of rhinestone so I could really nestle them together . . . usually a combination of 6/8/10 ss".

Source: **Photo courtesy of Megan Edelfsen.**

are made equally; some are high-quality crystals and some are not. The Swarovski variety used to be the gold standard but after their restructuring during COVID, they are no longer selling crystals like they used to and now you have to apply to buy them. There are many other brands that are high quality, meaning they are generally more sparkly and have truer, long-lasting sparkle, and beautiful colors. There are many ways to apply these crystals including a hot plate, iron, or pants press.

Supplies:
- Bent tweezers
- Hotplate
- Hot-fix crystals
- A pencil with eraser

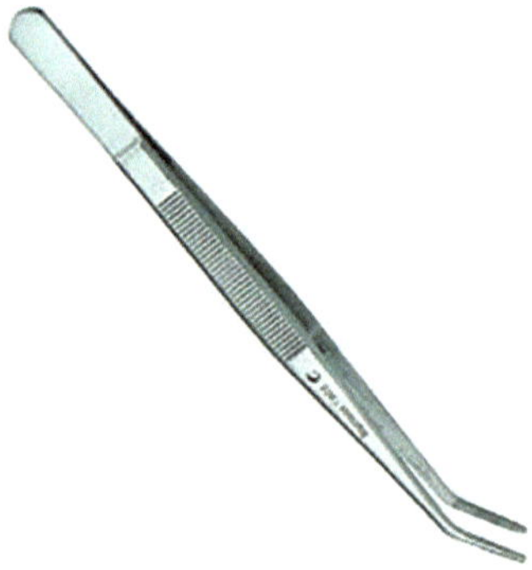

Figure 10.13 The perfect tweezers for applying rhinestones are bent at the end.

HOW TO APPLY CRYSTALS USING A HOT PLATE

1. **Gear up!** Wear an apron and close-toed shoes in case you drop one. These puppies get hot and can burn you! I have scars to prove it!
2. Turn hot plate to medium setting.
3. Place crystals glue side up on the **outer rings** of the hot plate. Wait for the glue to go from a waffle texture to totally clear; sometimes the glue puffs up depending on the brand.
4. Using bent tweezers, pick up the crystal with the tweezer end bending down toward theft plate, and flip tweezers over to place on fabric. Use a pencil with an eraser on the end to push the hot-fix crystal to the fabric.
5. **Did it stick?** Test whether the gem stuck by gently running your finger over it trying (but not trying) to see if the glue will fail.

Figure 10.14 How to use a hotplate to set hot-fix crystals. Pick up the gem, tweezer bend pointing down, then flip over to adhere to fabric.

FLAT-BACK RHINESTONES

Flat-back (not hot-fix) rhinestones can be added to fabric with glue or stone settings; which one you choose depends on how long the garment you are bedazzling will be in use and if the costume will be next to other costumes (like a dance partner for example).

Mounts: If you choose to use mounts, this is a long term solution, since the prongs can snag nearby costumes or other parts of the same costume. It is also very time-consuming using stone mounts as each prong has to be pushed through the fabric and wrapped around the stone. The two most popular styles of stone mounts: Tiffany and ring sets.

Glue: You can easily glue rhinestones on to your garment with glue. I would use Gem-Tac because it is nontoxic, dries clear, and does not stain as badly as other clear fabric adhesives can. Some prefer E-6000 but I would not recommend that unless Gem-Tac isn't working or is not available, because vapors from E-6000 can cause central nervous system damage. Both require ventilation, but E-6000 should be used with a respirator in addition to ventilation. Acrylic glues become brittle at cold temps which lead to acrylic-glued rhinestones to flake off. As always, test first!

To glue flat-back rhinestones to fabric, fist make sure you are gluing on a single layer. The glue can run through the garment and transfer to the other side. For example, if you are rhine stoning fishnets, cut a leg form out of cardboard and glue the stones on both sides of the fishnets independently. Using a very pointy object like a pin, toothpick, dental tool, etc., pick up some glue and add a small dab where you want to place the crystal. Place the crystal on top and use the eraser on an old-timey #2 pencil to gently press the gem onto the glue and into the fabric. This is a time-consuming process but worth it if you cannot use hot-fix gems; it's a great alternative.

SPOTS AND STUDS

These are attached to fabric or leather by a similar system used by the rhinestone mounts. Usually spots are attached to substrates by piercing the surface and folding leg in towards the center of the spot.

SILICONE

Figure 10.15 Installing spots by bending legs.

Many people like to use silicone for a variety of results. For example, silicone can be used to create a wet-shiny gloopy look that will stay shiny but also flexible. Using the appropriate silicone is a must for health and safety. Some amateur dyers reach for the clear silicone caulking from the home-improvement store. While this is a cheap and quick solution, what you may not know is that these silicone caulks contain lead and very high VOCs; they are also not skin safe and can poison your actor. Choose a platinum cure silicone like Smooth-On's 2-part dragon skin. It is a clear silicone that you can thicken or thin, you can use a kicker to

Figure 10.16 Silicone is added to a bra to add some burned flesh and to provide chest coverage for the actress playing Serilia in episode 2 of *Sleepy Hollow*.

make it set faster and there are also options for higher durometers (strength of the silicone when cured). There are some fun techniques using silicone that can add texture to your piece including stretching a stretch fabric, pinning it, and adding circles of silicone. When the fabric dries and is unpinned, it creates a bubble shape in the fabric as the fabric remains stretched where the silicone is applied.

Silicone can be super useful in a variety of permanent applications including but not limited to: creating slime, creating a wet look, tinting silicone to blood colors and applying to fabric creating an eternal freshly seeped blood look, dripped on outerwear to look like rain, embedding fabric into a mold with silicone to create an infinite number of appliances and textures. In Chapter 14, there is a great example of using silicone to create a fresh blood look.

A product called slacker can also be added to matte and soften the silicone into a "fleshier" feel, if shiny isn't what you want. Some effects like burned skin are an excellent application of silicone with slacker and some black pigment. See Figure 10.16's burnt skin bra for an example of burned flesh from the TV show *Sleepy Hollow*. This is where we often dance on the line between SFX makeup and textile manipulation. You can also embed a stretch fabric in to the

back of a mold that you've poured silicone into, creating a long-lasting stretchy base that can be sewn and worn. I won't go too far into this technique as it is really a makeup appliance, but I think it could be useful to some of you. See a biomechanical example for Dr. Doom in *The Fantastic Four* (2015). There is a great book out by Todd Debreceni called *Special Makeup Effects: Making and Applying Prosthetics* if you want to learn more about embedding casting materials in fabrics with cool effects.

Figure 10.17 Silicone embedded in a stretch fabric allows Julian McMahon, playing Dr. Doom in *The Fantastic Four* (2015), to be in a rigid-appearing costume that is actually flexible at the neck.

PUFF PRINT ADDITIVE, PUFF PAINT, AND MORE

If you have ever seen a superhero film, you have seen this technique used. Puff print is a material you can add to screen ink. Once you flash it with heat, the material puffs up. It releases some amazingly toxic gasses in the process and hence has earned the nickname "poison printing". The SDS says that prolonged exposure can cause nervous system damage and when heated, a necessary step, you will be exposed to hydrogen chloride, carbon monoxide and carbon dioxide – so use in a well-ventilated space! It gives a wonderful background texture to fabric that can simulate a futuristic material or mixture of materials. It is often silkscreened on fabric and heated in a conveyer oven (think bagel oven). Fabric is sent out to screen printers like By Design (in Los Angeles) or other companies that are set up to flash heat yardage. You can do this in your studio with a heat gun, just be careful not to burn your fabric and keep the heat gun moving.

Many children of the 80s remember puff paint – it can still be purchased at craft stores in small bottles. These puff up on their own and can be used to create interesting hand beaded looks, when in a pinch. One of the most successful puff paint examples I have seen is the glitter puff paint which is often called glitter glue. Basically, it's the transparent medium embedded with glitter. This can be a great substitute for sewn-on sparkles. I don't have a preferred brand, but I would test several out to see if the paint flattens out or stays puffy.

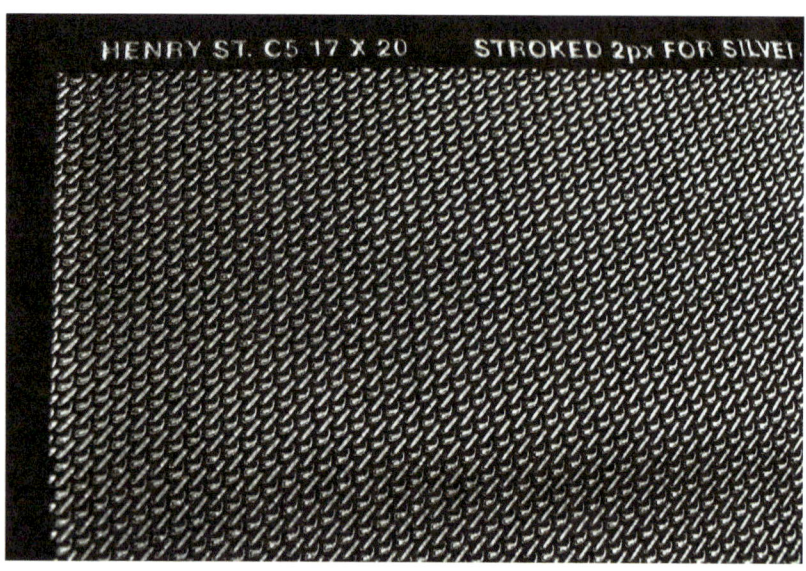

Figure 10.18 Puff printed fabric used for *The Fantastic Four*, labeled Henry Street, the movie's production code/working title.

COATINGS

Coatings can transform a raw material into something otherworldly. They can help the artisan create endless 3-D embellishments that remain somewhat flexible, if desired. Using coatings on costume pieces requires that the material you are coating has some sort of heft. It doesn't need to stand on its own completely but it should be on its way to holding its shape before you start coating. Materials that are conducive to this process include industrial felt, thick felt, felted sweaters, Fosshape, thermal plastic, leather (veg tanned is best because the coatings really bond better), or any thick-ish semi-porous material that can be sewn or glued together to hold a shape, e.g., a corset! If your material is not semi-porous, you can rough it up with sandpaper before coating.

Figure 10.19 Three helmets using coated Fosshape and embedded trim. Costume designer Clancy Steer for *As You Like It*, Old Globe Theatre, 2012.

When I pitched this book to my editor several years ago, I intended to write about sculpt or coat or crystal gel in this part of the book. Since then, the pandemic has changed a few things, making those products unavailable. Artists mediums are pretty good substitutes; my favorites are from a brand called Nova Color. They have some really fantastic textile-friendly mediums that can be sculpted, sanded, tinted, and painted.

I've included Figure 10.19 to illustrate how sculpt or coat in combination with paint and other bits of lace and trim was used. Don't be sad, this can be easily duplicated with texture paste and flex gel mediums or flex bond. The beauty of this example is that it illustrates how you can use certain coatings like flex bond (a.k.a. flex glue) or Nova Gel as a coating and glue, much like flexible decoupage for 3-D elements. The coatings also are a great tool to use to cover joints and joins of thermal plastic, leather, or felt. I have recently tired two new Nova Color products and had great success: 209 Super Gel and 213 Flex Gel. They both hang on to glitter well (minimal flaking) and can be sanded.

My favorite opaque product is Nova Colors' Tintable Texture Paste. I used that product to create the base coats, and 3-D rivets on my *Flexible Iron* corset made from a felted sweater. You can pipe the material on to a substrate with a squeeze bottle or syringe, wait for it to dry then sand the tops, knocking off the tips. It's great because it adheres to itself. This texture paste also comes in black, if you want a super saturated paste. It sticks to fabric, leather, closed-cell foam, felt, and sanded plastic; it is water-based so it can be watered down.

Creating Flexible Metal Using Coatings

So this how-to covers using coatings as a surface layer and to create 3-D shapes. Yes, it borders on a crafts project, but so many projects, especially in theatre, bounce back and forth from crafts to the dye shop. This project came from the desire to teach students how to create armor on an academic budget but also an exploration of sustainable materials that could perform like new pricier materials.

Figure 10.20 *Flexible Iron*, a felted sweater coated and embellished using tint-able texture paste and other mediums, artisan Erin Carignan.

In professional theatre I would be asked at least 2–3 times a year to make a piece of armor, helmet, or other large metallic accessory for stage. I found myself always searching for new materials to make a lighter, more comfortable, and stronger piece that would withhold the use and abuse of multiple performances. I tried numerous materials, at every price point, coupled with coatings/ treatments that were water-based, low-VOC, and as low-tox as possible. I found industrial felt, veg-tanned leather, and thermal plastic were the best foundation materials, coupled with Sculpt or Coat and Roscoe's flex glue to provide best structure and usability with the least toxicity. In my first year in academia, I taught a costume crafts class where we made theatrical armor. At professional Theatre X, I would have ordered some pricey thermal plastic or industrial felt that ranged in price from $125–150/yard but in academia I quickly realized that my budget was not going to accommodate the use of these materials. This and my interest in sustainability led me to create "metal" samples using a felted sweater in place of the other more costly items.

I love this project because it combines time-tested techniques I learned from designers like Lewis Brown with new-school techniques and much less toxic materials. There is no need for a respirator or intense ventilation. I use a combination of coatings like NovaColor Tintable Texture Paste, Roscoe Flex Glue, and acrylic artists color that was UV resistant. I used untraditional costume materials such as a felted sweater, pop-rivets, and metal cable in the piping to create this corset.

Supplies:

- Something to coat; I used a felted sweater reconstructed
- Nova Color Tintable texture paste or comparable (haven't found comparable but maybe you have)
- Nova Super Gel or Flex Bond
- A form to keep material in shape while coating
- Squeeze bottle with fine-tip application
- Fine-grit sand paper (400 and above – do samples to choose best grit)
- A chip brush
- Soft brush for paint
- Acrylic paint in a low lite, midtone, and hi-light
- Optional: bronzing powder, hinges, extra decor

HOW TO CREATE A FLEXIBLE, SAND-ABLE, 3-D SURFACE USING COATINGS

1. **Gear up:** gloves, apron.
2. **Felting**: I chose a lightweight sweater that is 100% wool. After felting, sweaters shrink in length, so, to keep the materials consistent throughout, I cut the arms off and seamed them to the bottom of the sweater. Any other scraps that were trimmed off were saved for other purposes (like aglets). To felt the sweater: wash it on HOT with about a cup of detergent (I use free and clear for actor allergies) in the washer (with a spindle if you can) then dry it on high in a dryer repeatedly until it is felted to desired thickness.
3. **Pad out a dress form** to the desired finished shape. Make a positive mold and add all dimensional elements. I used silk pins so they would be invisible. Layer what you have: towels and batting, wrap with ace bandages, and cover it all in thick plastic wrap (the

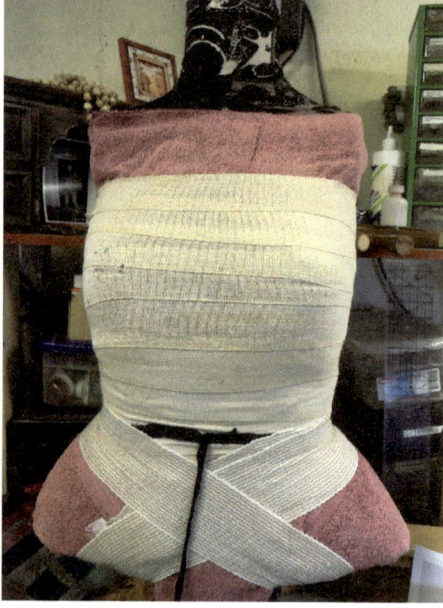

Figure 10.21 Step 3: Create the shape that your piece will take.

best is the stuff used for moving furniture). I defined the waist with elastic to get a "nipped in" look.

4. **Stretch** the felted sweater while it is damp and stretch the sweater over the form and pin it with long ball headed pins (for easier extraction later) so the sweater stays in place as it dries.

5. **Add texture paste:** Using a chip brush to really push the medium into the felt, add texture paste and let it dry. When dry, give it a good sanding to smooth any lines from the application.

6. **Trace design on first layer and cut!** Using a #12 scalpel blade, I cut the drawn shapes out of the sweater. I cut at this point because it is easier to cut – many more layers of paste and glue make cutting a hand-wrenching experience. Cut the shoulders, arms, neckline, and lower perimeter. Do not cut the center, yet!

7. **Add a few more layers** of texture paste. Allow to dry. This will coat the insides of your cutouts.

8. **Add "rivets"** using a fine-tip bottle filled with texture paste; pipe on Hershey-kiss-shaped dabs. Allow to dry and sand the tops off.

9. **Paint!** Paint the corset with a base coat and then add hi-lites and low-lites. I dry-brushed a dark green mixed with black on the textural areas then wiped it away when wet.

10. **Remove from form.** Once the paste is dry cut the front and shoulders open, taking the corset off the form. Trim the inside edges to clean finished lines using craft shears.

11. **Finishing touches:** Using a hand drill, drill holes for the front closures and rivet these on with pop-rivets (because of the rivets' combination of low-profile and high strength). I made piping with metal cable in velvet for edges and glued it on with flex glue.

12. **Do a final coat** with Roscoe Flex Glue, a thick, clear, sand-able flexible medium. This allowed an overall skin to stretch, keeping the foam coat from cracking. You could also use

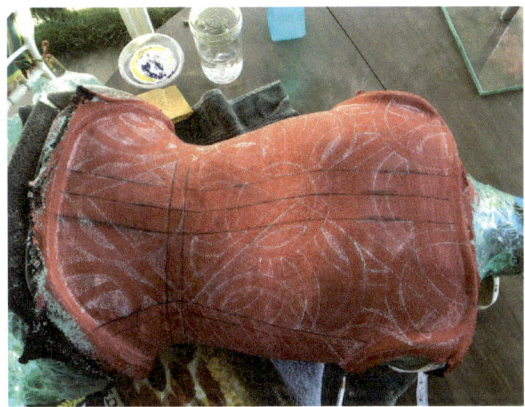
Figure 10.22 Step 6: Trace design on the dried texture paste.

Figure 10.23 Step 11: Add finishing touches – I added cable and glued piping over it, clamping with clothespins to secure.

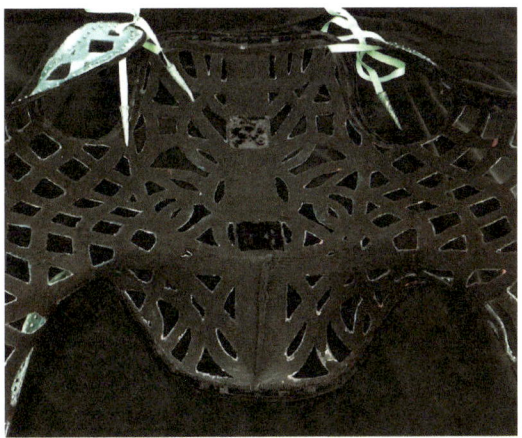
Figure 10.24 The inside remains a soft felted sweater!

Nova Color Super Gel which can be purchased in smaller increments than Flex Glue. For aglets, cut a triangle out of the felted sweater, glue and wrap it around petersham, and then coat it with texture paste and faux rivets. Using the cutouts at the shoulders, feed petersham through to create an adjustable shoulder point.

FEV OR FRENCH ENAMEL VARNISH AND PREMIXED VERSIONS

French enamel varnish is a theatrical concoction, originating in the scenic department, that has been used for generations to add a lovely light patina or stain to any surface. It can be used on wood, leather, a leafed surface, metal, plastic, glass, and more. You can create overall color washes, textured washes, stained glass, and antiqued depth. It can be painted on directly, sprayed with an airbrush, Hudson sprayer, pre-val, sponged, etc. Traditionally it has been made of denatured alcohol, shellack, and tinted with leather dyes. Less people are using this mixture now with the advent of products like Piñata Color Alcohol Inks and the laws changing in some states regarding denatured alcohol. I substitute denatured alcohol with 99% rubbing alcohol as the vehicle. Basically, you need something that will evaporate quickly but also help spread the dye. Not exactly the same, but it gets the job done. The shellac gives the piece luster after the alcohol evaporates and leather dye or pure pigments add color. The color needs to be alcohol soluble to mix with the shellac and alcohol. I'd say, if the artisan understands how to use this product, they should keep it in their back pocket and use it sparingly because of exposure to toxins; we make choices every day and some days they are bleach, others water-based paints, others FEV.

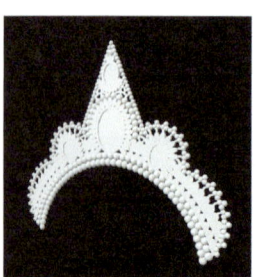

Figure 10.25 Vanessa Lopez, crafts artisan at the Guthrie Theater, 3D printed this crown and then hit it with FEV to give it color and dimension.

There are companies that make ready-made FEV. Flints in the UK sells it in 5L containers, while here in the US, Jacquard sells it in teeny tiny bottles under the label Piñata Color. They even sell extender, which I'm convinced is just denatured alcohol. It really does help change the color of metal though. Time after time I've been given silver rings and asked to make them gold, or gold rings and am asked to make them "less gold". Piñata Color is awesome for this because someone else has already dealt with the exposure of mixing the products, I just have to mix colors and paint it on (in excellent ventilation of course!!!).

I remember in graduate school creating a half-scale samurai costume and of course I chose the one with the wonderful antiqued metal "horns" coming out of the head piece. I used flex glue on the metal to create a rough surface and once it dried, FEV. It looked amazing.

FEV Recipe: 1 part alcohol, 2 parts shellac, 1/4th part dye. Example: 1 tbl alcohol, 2 tbl Shellac, 1 tsp leather dye.

LIVER SULFUR

This product has a similar effect of FEV except that you cannot vary the color but at least you can still order this in California! This is a product that comes in raw chip form (very long shelf life) or premixed in liquid. It will create an antique patina on silver and copper bearing alloys like brass, copper, silver, or bronze. This product requires excellent ventilation and a respirator. The concentrated form is used by creating a solution by dropping a chip of liver sulfur in water, allowing it to dissolve, and then painting with a robber preferably onto the surface of metal. You can control the depth of color of this patina by rinsing it under cold water as soon as it gets to the depth you require. If you want it to go darker, add more liver sulfur. To take the liver sulfur away, steel wool the metal or buff it out with a felt polishing wheel on a rotary tool. See Figure 10.25 for a crown that I took back and forth, from shiny to old and back to shiny with liver sulfur.

 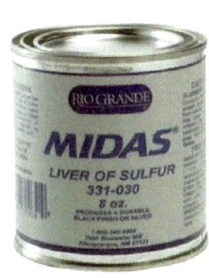 

Figure 10.26 A brass and copper crown I made, patinaed with liver sulfur for one show, buffed bright for another, then patinaed again for a different show! Old Globe Theatre.

MARVELOUS MARBLING!

Marbling is a process of floating paint of the surface of cellulose water, then swirling and stirring the paint to get beautiful effects. Marbling originated in Japan (suminagashi) around the 12th century, spread to Turkey, Persia, and India hundreds of years later (ebru), then a few hundred years later to Europe. In the mid 1850s, two books came out by European authors in England and Germany, simplifying and redefining the marbling process and influencing an increase of marbling in Europe and the US.[2]

Almost anything made of fabric can be marbled – even canvas shoes! This process requires a certain amount of space, time, and patience, but when you get the knack, you can even try some ebru or basically painting on water. If you'd like to take a moment to breathe and enjoy gorgeous art being made, search on YouTube ebru painting. You're welcome.

This is a 2-step process in which you mix up two solutions in advance: a soaking solution so the fabric grabs the paint (the equivalent of a soda ash soak with fiber-reactive dyes) and a cellulose solution to float the paint on. Both need time to work, so it's best to do this the day or several hours *before* you want to actually marble. Also, the container you plan to marble in must be found or created and be able to accommodate the material you are marbling. To create a custom marbling tray a cheap solution is to glue cardboard boxes to the appropriate size and then line it with plastic from the hardware store. The box must have a lip of at least 3" as you will be filling it with 2" of methyl cellulose solution. If you are marbling smaller pieces of fabric or an object, like shoes, I like the disposable aluminum chafing pans from restaurant supply stores as they can be used a few times and then tossed when they get really gross.

In my opinion, this process as applied to costumes is not super applicable to the professional painter–dyer (especially in theatre) as the marbled fabric needs to cure for 7 days before it can be washed. If marbling a pair of shoes or a hat that will never be washed is desired, by all means it could be useful!

Supplies
- Alum
- Methyl Cellulose
- Marbling paint
- Soda Ash
- Household Ammonia (no dyes or perfumes)
- Industrial detergent
- A waterproof container that will hold at least 2" of water and fit your project
- Newspapers cut into 1/4th page sizes (for skimming surface before adding paint)
- Towels/paper towels
- Line to hang marbled pieces to dry
- Teasing comb, pointy stick, or toothpick to create design in paint
- Three buckets for soaking and mixing solutions and rinsing
- Drop cloth and craft paper to keep things clean!
- Optional: distilled water, marbling surfactant (**highly recommended**), white distilled vinegar

HOW TO MARBLE FABRIC! (ADAPTED FROM PROCHEMICAL AND DYE)
1. **Gear up!** Gloves, apron, dust particle mask for mixing solutions.
2. **Set up! A few solutions and things to prepare in advance:**
   1. **Scour fabric** to be marbled (as per usual instructions – hot water, 1/2 tsp Synthrapol or Metapex, a 1/2 tsp soda ash (do not use soda ash on silk).
   2. **Create Alum Soak:**
      - Fill bucket with 1 gallon hot water (120°F/60°C)
      - Add 4 tbl (60g) of Alum; stir until dissolved
      - With GLOVES add scoured fabric and soak 10–15 minutes, stirring intermittently (make sure fabric can move freely)
      - Wring out excess solution into the same bucket
      - DO NOT RINSE!
      - Hang dry – do not put in dryer; use a COOL iron only (no hot irons)
      - Use fabric within 3 weeks or it will disintegrate; alum solution will last up to 3 months or until crystals form at edges of bucket
   3. **Create Methyl Cellulose Solution (Methyl Cel):**
      - Fill bucket with 1 gallon room temperature water (75–95°F/24–35°C)
      - Slowly stir 3 1/2 tbl (25g) of Methyl Cel powder

- Add 2 tsp clear household ammonia and stir (**this is important for proper paint float!** The ammonia is used to dissolve the methyl cel and allow the paint to float.)
- Stir until solution in the bucket appears clear and stir intermittently every 30 minutes
- Solution is ready after 30 minutes.
- *If you have alkaline water add 1 tsp white vinegar

4. **Tear newspaper** into 1/4th page size (create a nice pile of these)
5. **Create or find marbling tray**; lay down drop cloths/newspaper; prepare laundry line.
6. **Fill** rinse bucket with water; add a towel under this bucket.
   3. **Fill marbling tray 2–3" (5–7.5cm) of Methyl Cellulose Solution**
      - Skim the surface of methyl cel with newspaper by laying half the page down on the surface and then dragging it towards you. Squeegee off the excess methyl cel by pulling it gently toward you over the side of the marbling tray; discard paper. This will clear any bubbles or old marbling color. Don't worry about the extra paint at the edges of the tray.
   4. **Prepare marbling paint!**
      - **Shake paint** well before each marbling session
      - **Test color*** by adding paint to methyl cel surface by dropping one drop of color on the methyl cel. It should float and spread out to a few inches. Test each color you plan to use to make sure they play well together. Add marbling surfactant if the paint sinks to the bottom or doesn't spread much larger than the initial drop. *Double check you used the appropriate amount of ammonia! Too little ammonia will also cause your paint to sink!* **It is important that you are using ammonia that has NO additives.**
   5. **Add paint to the methyl cel!** At a distance of 1/2" to ~8", above the surface of methyl cel, place as many drops as you like, covering the surface with whatever colors you choose. You can add color drops inside other color drops.
   6. **Make the pattern!** This is the fun part! Run your stick, pick, or whatever implement you choose through the colors. You will notice that the stick drags the colors into a marbled pattern.
7. **Marble your fabric!** The moment of truth! In one fluid movement, add fabric by holding diagonal corners and dropping the middle to the surface of the methyl cel, first. Then let the edges drop to the surface.

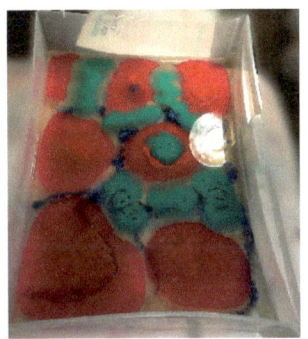

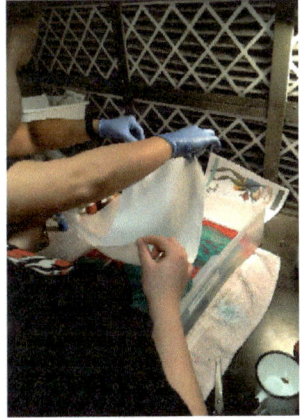
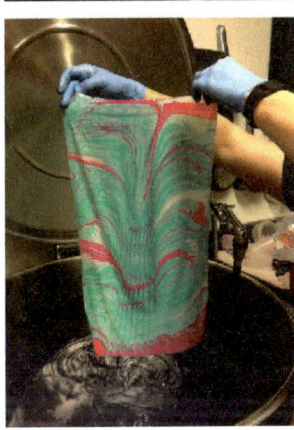

Figure 10.27 (Top) Paint added to surface, (top middle) paint combed into design, (bottom middle) silk is carefully dropped onto surface, (bottom) fabric is rinsed in clean water.

8. **Remove and rinse** fabric in the bucket of water. Several dips in the water may be needed to remove methyl cel. Do not wring your fabric before dipping several times, you may transfer paint to unwanted areas. Squeeze gently and hang to dry. **The paint will come off if you rub it! Dip only!** The paint should cure 7–10 days for optimum adherence but you can also batch cure these in less time in a plastic bag. Batch times will vary depending on where you are geographically.
9. **Clean surface of** methyl cel by skimming with newspaper. You may need to do a few skims to pick up all the paint. As you continue using this bath, you will see color drop to the bottom of the tray – this will not affect your marbling as your item will only pick up what is on the surface.

*Notes: do not use soap for cleanup, use only water and a stiff brush. Methyl cel is totally biodegradable and can be poured down the drain.

If color sinks: add marbling surfactant into the marbling color, 3–4 drops at a time and test. Industrial detergent, rubbing alcohol, or dishwashing soap can also be used as a surfactant but remember **once you add a surfactant to your paint, you cannot remove it!**

Please see Dharma Trading's or ProChemical and Dye's websites for a host of solutions to other marbling issues!

PAINTING TOOLS!

There are a wide variety of paint applicators and tools available to the artist from artists supply stores to home improvement stores. Which tool to choose depends on the job and mediums required. There are many more tools and other useful items for painting costumes than is listed here. You will find that you have your favorites; the following are some of mine. I have also tried to demystify airbrush and compressor options as this is a question that comes up regularly.

AIRBRUSHES

When shopping for an airbrush, you're really shopping for two items: the airbrush and the compressor. Choosing the right airbrush and compressor can be difficult with all of the brands and options available. There are a few things to consider when choosing an airbrush: airbrush paint feed style, bottle/cup types and sizes, adaptors available, ease of cleaning, tip sizes, and how it feels in your hand. Considerations when choosing a compressor are: noise level when running, auto shut off, power output, size, tank/no tank, and pressure regulator and gauge. All of these choices depend on whether you are a novice (or you are working with novices, like students) or a seasoned

> **A MESSAGE ABOUT AIRBRUSH SAFETY:**
>
> Even if you are using a water-based paint, you are forcing **particles into the air** that will ultimately end up in your lungs. Please wear a particulate mask (N95) and work with excellent ventilation. This is just as bad as inhaling dye, especially when using airbrush cleaner – that stuff is toxic.

artisan and what sort of needs you have related to the airbrush. For example if you need to travel with it, you have a high volume of goods to spray, you only use an airbrush once in a while, etc.

AIRBRUSH OPTIONS!

Feed styles are **siphon**, **gravity**, and **side feed**. Gravity feed have the cup that screws on top of the airbrush and hence uses gravity to deliver paint. Siphon feed is situated below the gun and requires more pressure to deliver paint. Side feed is the attempt at a happy medium between the previous two and offer more flexibility with pressure.

Action is another element to consider. A **single action** airbrush allows the user to pull back on the trigger to vary the amount of air used to propel paint. A **double action** airbrush allows the user to press down on the trigger to release air and to pull back to release more paint. Really, the action style you choose depends on the level of user experience. Usually, shops have single action airbrushes for the newbs and the seasoned artisans bring in their personal double action brushes.

Tip sizes commonly range from 0.2 mm–0.7 mm or larger. The smaller the tip, the more detail you can achieve. Be careful when shopping for an airbrush to pay attention to the tip size range. When buying a cheaper airbrush, often called a beginner airbrush, the size ranges from 0.5 mm–1.0 mm. This may be fine for a simple job but if you are shopping for something to do detailed work with, look at another brush.

Airbrushes can be complicated or very simple. You must take an airbrush apart to clean it. Trust me, you can pretend to clean it by running cleaning solvent through, but on your next job when you have a solidified minuscule chunk of acrylic paint stuck inside and you have to fish it out with a microscopic bottle brush, you will wish you had just fully cleaned it the last time you used it. You will pay more for an airbrush that is simple because it is easier to clean!

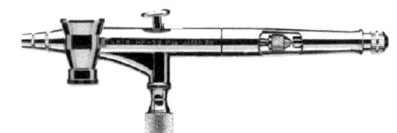

Figure 10.28 Three airbrush feed styles: gravity, siphon, and side siphon.

Table 10.3 Airbrush Elements Pros and Cons.

		Pros	Cons
Feed style:	Gravity = Cup on top	• Less waste • Can use any pressure (detailed work requires low pressure • Easier to clean (less parts) • Less expensive than side feed	• Does not hold as much paint
	Siphon = cup underneath	• Holds a variety of small to large cups and bottles • Large bottles = less refilling paint reservoir • Less expensive than side feed	• Requires higher pressure to operate
	Side Feed = cup on the side	• Holds more volume than gravity • Operates better at lower pressure than siphon	• Difficult to clean • Leaks are common • Most expensive
Action:	Single	• Simple to use • Great for novices	• Trigger only controls air volume • To control paint volume requires adjusting needle depth
	Double	• Trigger controls paint volume and amount of air • More flexibility and control • Better for fine-detail work	• Can be complicated for beginners
Tip sizes	0.2 mm	• Provides very fine detail	• Sprays less paint
	0.5 mm	• Good multiuse size for a variety of applications	• Not great for super detailed or very large work
	0.7 mm	• Can spray more paint	• Creates wider line • Harder to control

Cleaning an airbrush! Lay out a towel, so airbrush parts will not roll off the table! Generally, the process is to run water or cleaning solution through the gun to remove the majority of paint then to take apart the gun and clean the inner and outer parts, leave them to dry, then put the gun back together. As I take the gun apart, I am very careful about how I lay out the parts. Often, I lay them out in the order the gun came apart. Take special care to mind the tiny parts. **If you lose a piece, your airbrush will not function.** I like these cleaning pots that come with an extra container with lid to put small parts in to soak in cleaner. You can spray the cleaning solution through the gun into

Figure 10.29 The airbrush cleaning pot also comes with screw-top container to soak/clean small parts! The set of tiny brushes are intended specifically for cleaning airbrushes.

the bottle (and NOT need a mask!) to clean out the airbrush, then take the gun apart, adding the small pieces to the other container. I also like these multi-size bottle brushes. Just make sure when using the tiniest one to clean the tip, gently, making sure **not push through the tip with any force.** You can misshape the tip and the spray will be wonky, causing you to buy a new tip.

COMPRESSOR OPTIONS!

Choosing a compressor depends on the job size. Do you need to do small detailed work or paint yardage of fabric? Do you need to work consistently for long periods or can you take several breaks? Do you use an airbrush all the time or once in a while?

For example, folks that do makeup with an airbrush choose tank-less compressors (potentially cordless) with auto shutoffs that are also very quiet when they run, since they are in close quarters with actors or bridezillas! They don't need the high-powered compressors that an auto body shop would need because they are not using anywhere near the same volume of paint and the body shop requires longer running time from a compressor to complete the large task of painting a vehicle. To decipher these compressor terms, I've broken down each element that becomes a choice when buying a compressor.

Figure 10.30 Iwata Studio Series suitcase compressor is a popular choice among travelling breakdown artists.

I have a Grex gun and compressor for our makeup area and an older Iwata Eclipse for our dye room. Compressors have really come a long way; comparing the new quiet Grex compressor to the 15-year-old Iwata compressor is night and day as far as noise levels go! The newer Iwata suitcase compressor seems to be a favorite for film dyers because it's powerful, much quieter than my old Iwata, dependable, and has a square shape and therefore is easy to transport and not break.

Auto-off function is when the airbrush is not actively in use or if you're using an air compressor with a tank, the tank is full. This is fantastic for noise levels, as there is not a continuous loud machine running the whole time the compressor is on. This function can reduce noise levels up to 75% and decrease energy use.

Capacity is the amount of air your compressor can hold. The more air it can hold, the longer you can use it before it has to quit and rebuild pressure.

Size is affected by the tank size, power output, and type of compressor. The larger all of these things are, the larger the compressor. Tank-less compressors are the lightest but do not run as long or have as much power. These are good for smaller jobs.

Horsepower is important but for textile airbrushing we really don't need anything above 1/3rd hp. This allows for a maximum PSI (pressure per square inch) of around 85 while 1/6th hp allows for a max of around 60. The higher the horsepower, the higher the max pressure.

Pressure determines the volume of paint that will be able to push through the airbrush. Smaller amounts are fine for detailed projects like our bridezilla artist while larger amounts of pressure are required for Mr. Auto Body.

Pressure gauge and regulators can be very helpful for the beginner as the pressure is maintained by a regulator once it is set where a beginner might not know if their problems are stemming from pressure or paint. The gauge allows the user to dial in the needed pressure based on the job and change the pressure as needed.

Hoses are important too! Choose a compressor with a hose long enough for your purposes. If you have to send your compressor to Never Never Land (the other room) because of noises, think of how long you will need that hose to be to travel from your compressor to your workspace and to allow you to move freely to paint. However, a long hose decreases the PSI while a short hose maintains the PSI.

Fittings for airbrushes and compressors can be tricky as you would think that all pneumatic tools had similar fittings, right? Unfortunately, this isn't true because each brand of airbrush can potentially have proprietary fittings that aren't very universal. The most useful fittings I have found are the quick release fittings to connect the hose and airbrush. There are fittings to change bottle sizes and other elements of old airbrushes to be used with newer compressors.

Options that make life a little easier include weight, airbrush holders, and moisture filters. Lightweight compressors are more expensive but are amazing if you travel for work. Some compressors have airbrush holders on them so you don't have to worry about setting them down and having the gun a paint bottle/cup tip over and make a mess. Think of these as a holster for your airbrush! Moisture filters remove moisture and debris before they travel to your storage tank or through your airbrush thus preserving your tools much longer.

Table 10.4 Compressor Elements Pros and Cons

		Pros	Cons
Auto-off		- Reduces noise by 75% - Creates a calmer atmosphere	- More expensive $$$
Pressure	10 LPM	- Great for detailed work: nails, tattoos - Light - Small	- Not appropriate for larger scale work or use with **textile paints** - Must use thin paints
	20 LPM	- Great midrange for detailed work and larger coverage	- Works for most but not all applications
	30 LPM +	- The largest coverage; used for cars	- Not great for a novice as they can dial up pressure too far
Cordless		- Great where power is an issue	- Has a limited running time before it has to be recharged
Tank Size (capacity)	Small	- Very portable	- Has to shut off and run more frequently to maintain pressure
	Medium	- Can use more than one airbrush at a time - Has more pressure and doesn't have to stop to rebuild pressure as much as small	- Heavier than a small tank - More expensive
	Large	- Doesn't have to run as much to keep up air volume - Can use more than one airbrush at a time	- Less portable; larger in size and heavier - Most expensive

USEFUL HAND TOOLS FOR PAINTING FABRIC
APPLICATORS AND PALETTES

Brushes: There are an unlimited amount of brushes available but the ones worth mentioning here are chip**, acid, chalk, and artists brushes (Figure 10.31)**. **Chip** brushes are one of my faves because they are cheap, can be bought in bulk and trimmed to the desired shape or texture without sacrificing an expensive brush. I have kept some chip brushes that are the perfect texture, for years. **Acid** brushes are similar, as they are cheap and can be bought in bulk. They are the smaller version of a chip brush and are also somewhat disposable. These are great to use with latex or silicone, where the brush must be disposed of after use. **Chalk** brushes are a favorite of many breakdown artists. Paint can be worked into the tightly packed bristles and applied on the fabric in light to heavy amounts, but usually in layers. **Artist's** brushes are handy to have around when a softer bristle is required. I have probably around 100 of these floating around in my life and often buy them at garage sales or in bulk packages.

Figure 10.31 Left: 2", 1" chip brushes, 1/2" acid brush, middle: chalk brushes, right: variety of artists brushes.

Brayer: this can be seen in Figure 10.32 and is used to roll on a light layer of paint or dye to a stamp or other surface. These are also handy when even pressure is required to adhere one item to another.

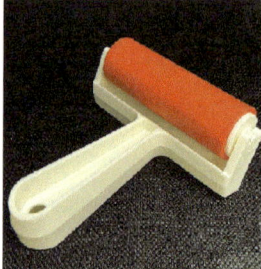 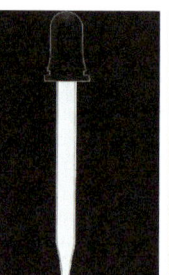 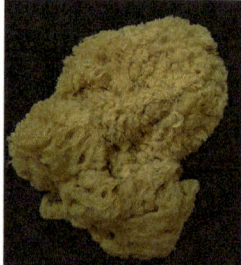

Figure 10.32 Left: brayer, middle: dropper, right: sea sponge.

Droppers: like an eyedropper, these are fabulous for delivering paint or dye to a pallet or other mixing container.

Sea sponge: this is a must-have for stenciling, breakdown, or any sort of watercolor look! Get one of these wet for softer marks or keep it dry for high texture. They can be ripped apart to create smaller sponges as needed.

Squeeze Bottles: there are a variety of styles of squeeze bottles available; which one to choose depends on the job and how much material is in use. For example, if dye concentrates

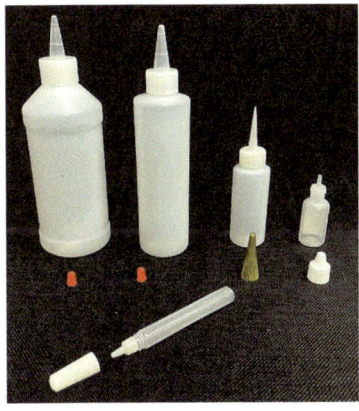 

are mixed up to be squirted on fabric, a large bottle like on the left in Figure 10.33 would be necessary. For smaller applications, the smaller bottles would be more useful. For extremely detailed applications, a **needle bottle** (Figure 10.33) is required. These are so great and come with a variety of needle tip sizes. These can be used with gutta or water-based resist, paint, thickened dye, or coatings. All of these bottles are available from dye suppliers, hardware suppliers like McMaster Carr, and craft stores. **Tip**: some of my favorite bottles are recycled from other products that are used up and then reused for a different application.

Figure 10.33 Left: variety of sizes of squeeze bottles, right: needle bottles for fine detail.

Palettes: again, there are many choices when it comes to palettes and which one to choose depends on the scale and type of application. I use **enamel trays, watercolor pallets, Tupperware lids, cafeteria trays,** or anything else I think will work. Enamel trays are nice because they can be cleaned easily and thicker paints can be easily peeled off. If you are using very liquid pigments a paint palette is required. Salsa cups and lids come in 0.5 oz–4 oz and are fantastic for mixing and storing paint as well.

 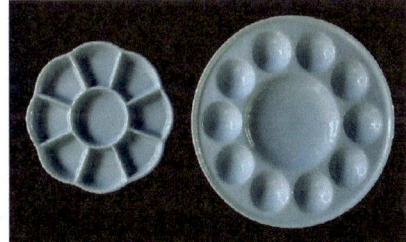

Figure 10.34 Left: two lunch trays – one with divided sections (bottom), right: palettes can have individual wells or be a flat enamel tray – the choice depends on medium viscosity.

  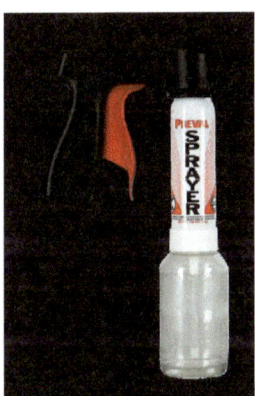

Figure 10.35 Left: squirt bottle and mister, middle: Hudson sprayer, right: pre-val with handle.

SPRAYERS

Hudson Sprayer/Yard Sprayer: this can be seen in Figure 10.35. They are great for spraying large areas with paint or dye and are traditionally used for yard applications such as applying pesticides. These sprayers can be purchased at any home improvement store.

Pre-val with handle: these are sprayers (pictured in Chapter 12 in Figure 12.13) that a bottle of paint can be attached to. There is an optional handle for those who find the spray paint type nozzle troublesome. These are a GREAT alternative to an airbrush if you don't have one. These can be purchased at any home improvement store.

Spray bottle/mister: there will never be enough of these around a dye room! Having a sprayer full of water to dilute a heavy dye or paint application is necessary! These are great for breakdown as well as adding dye or paint in patterns to fabric. A mister can be helpful where you would like a light spray that will not leave droplets on the fabric. They can be purchased at home improvement stores or beauty supply if a mist spray is required.

OTHER HELPFUL ITEMS

Polyethylene plastic sheeting – this is plastic that is available in many thicknesses and is used to cover floors, walls, and tables! It comes in 12' widths and is sold by the foot. This will protect surfaces from liquids, stains, and paint spills. It can also be used to protect dress forms if it is thin enough. Purchase from home improvement stores.

Tape: load of masking tape is also a must have. I like the cream-colored masking tape because it sticks better than the ones intended for interior painting. Also, they come in a variety of widths! There are a variety of brands and sources like home-improvement stores, McMaster–Carr, and craft stores.

THE BOTTOM LINE

There are many products, tools, and techniques for embellishing fabric. Experiment with some of these tools and products to choose your favorites!

NOTES

1. Rhinestones Unlimited. "Why Are Rhinestones Called Rhinestones?" January 16th 2019, https://rhinestonesu.com/blog/why-are-rhinestones-called-rhinestones/.
2. Dharma Trading. "Marbling History and Techniques." www.dharmatrading.com/techniques/marbling/marbling-history.html.

11

RESIST!!!
MAKING MARKS WITH RESIST DYEING

Figure 11.1 Several samples of shibori from textile artist Doshi's stash.

Resist techniques date back thousands of years as they are the simplest way to pattern fabric in dramatic ways. In this chapter we will explore several types of resists, dyeing, and painting – from the Japanese art of shibori, to Indian batik, the French Serti technique, and many other physical resist techniques that come from experimenting with dye and fabric like low water immersion, ice dyeing, and more!!

DOI: 10.4324/9781351130677-12

SHIBORI

Shibori is the ancient art of resist dyeing. The word means to press, wring, or squeeze, which is exactly what we do to cloth with this art form! This particular technique requires loads of experience to fully understand what the finished piece will look like, otherwise it is a total surprise when the dyed shibori package is opened. I always tell my students it's kind of like Christmas, since they are all new to the process.

Figure 11.2 Shibori vs tie-dye.

The major differences between tie-dyeing and shibori is that tie-dyeing uses a broad brush to create motifs by binding large areas of fabric in spiral twists or other patterns, paired with every color in the rainbow to dye, while shibori creates intricate designs and often features a limited palette.

There are six types of shibori that are the most popular: **kanoko, miura, kumo, nui, arashi, and itajime shibori**. Each type of shibori have Western counterparts that are derivatives; I will discuss each of these counterparts with their derivatives. Please note: if you want to do uber-traditional shibori, I am providing very general technique guidance to create patterns, not to create culturally accurate shibori designs. There are many ways to implement these basic categories of shibori and each method has a different name. You will find loads of conflicting information out there on names and origins as the art has evolved through ancient Japanese family lines. To go deeper, I recommend one of the dozens of books on shibori, that can be purchased online or found in your local library!

BINDING MATERIALS

There are many kinds of string, thread, and tape that can be used to bind fabric. Choosing which one depends on the width of the design you're after, how sharp of a resist you want, and whether you are doing multiple small resists in succession or one large resist.

Sinew, cotton string, nylon cord, and **ikat tape** are some common materials used to bind cloth. **Sinew** is an artificial version of animal sinew that is a waxed, flat material that is very

Figure 11.3 Binding materials used for resist: sinew, nylon cord, cotton string, ikat tape, and rubber bands.

strong and thus enables extremely hard pulling and minimal breakage. The bonus is: it sticks to itself!!! It comes in a variety of **tests** (strength and weight) of 15–70 lbs; the smaller the number the smaller the width of sinew. This is great for someone who is regularly doing shibori and doesn't want to tie a million knots. Cotton cord is another popular binding material and is cheap and ubiquitous but will be permeated by dye, potentially allowing some dye to seep into your resist. Nylon cord is great because it will repel most dye and create a good resist as long as you pull tight and knot off correctly. Ikat tape is a flat transparent Japanese product that can be pulled very tightly and stretched, creating a very tight binding; it also repels moisture (since it's plastic). It can be used to thread through a casing in fabric to pull tight and create a resist that way.

KANOKO SHIBORI OR TIE-DYE

This type of shibori inspired western tie-dying and it creates a circular shaped resist pattern. Traditionally this is done with thread or string, but we often use rubber bands to tie or bind sections of cloth to create similar looking resists. You can create some really interesting techniques if you fold the fabric first, then do kanoko shibori! This type of shibori is best to arrange when fabric is damp as the cloth is easier to manipulate and it stays in place as you tie or rubber band it off; lines are sharper if dyed damp as well!

MIURA SHIBORI

This type of shibori creates patterns that look like rippling water. This resist is created by plucking a small piece a fabric with the tip of a curved needle, wrapping damp thread around the plucked peak of fabric and moving on to the next pluck and peak. Traditionally these are not knotted and are held together by tension alone.

KUMO SHIBORI

Kumo shibori is translated as "spider shibori" and is where fingerlike shapes are created by plucking a piece of fabric, straightening the ends and twisting the fabric, then tying the fabric diagonally to the end and crossing over those threads on the way back to where the tying began. These create beautiful spiderweb-looking designs that are similar to kumo shibori but are more intricate.

Figure 11.4 Kanoko shibori tied and final sample.

Figure 11.5 Kumo shibori tied and final sample.

NUI SHIBORI OR STITCHED RESIST

Nui shibori is a resist created by sewing a pattern into fabric and then pulling the thread tight to create the resist. It is extremely time consuming when stitching by hand but yields gorgeous results! You can create different patterns by changing your stitch length, how many layers of fabric are sewn through, or whether the sewing happens on the center of the fabric or edge of a fold. In traditional shibori, each type of nui shibori has a different name; I will not be going through each of them but will review some of the different techniques they entail.

An amazing cheat, taught to me by Elin Noble, is to use a sewing machine to create nui resists. The trick is to use *rayon thread in the bobbin*, which breaks easily, and therefore is easy to remove from fabric after the piece has been dyed. Woot! This also is fantastic because the upper thread, which can be polyester, remains strong and can be pulled tightly to create the resist.

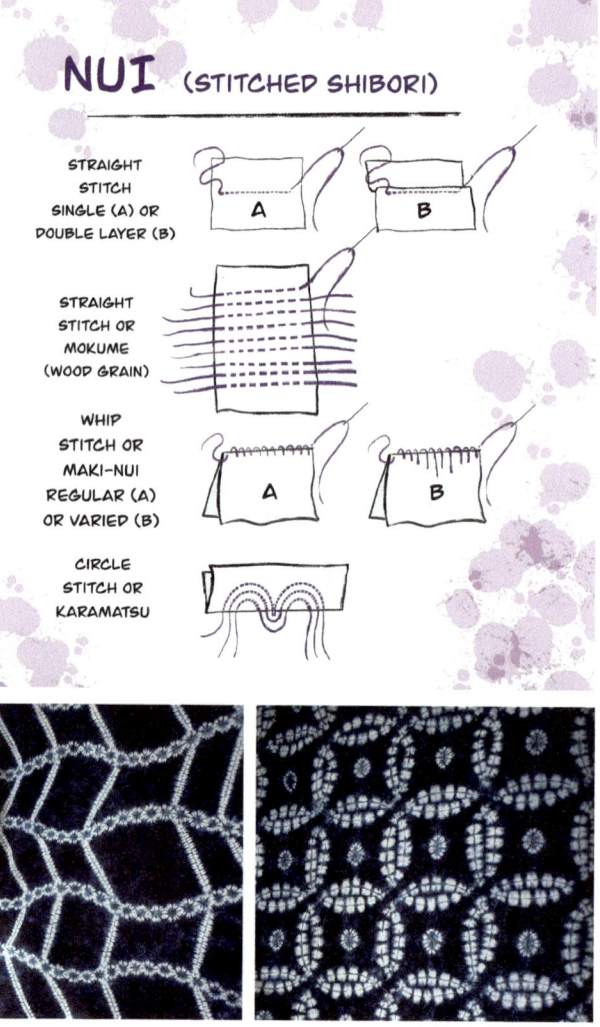

Figure 11.6 There are many ways to create nui or stitched shibori.

Figure 11.7 Two types of arashi shibori in the dyepot: one tied around a rope, the other wrapped and scrunched around a metal tube.

ARASHI SHIBORI OR POLE WRAPPING

This is one of my favorite types of shibori, as the pattern is easy to create, detailed, rhythmic, and organically beautiful! This technique is also called pole wrapping because we are doing just that – wrapping fabric around a pole, tying and bunching it to create the resist. Any size poll can be used; the one you choose will depend on how much fabric you are dying, how much of an ombré is desired, and how small or large the required pattern scale. It should be noted that the fabric on the outside of the pole wrapping will be more saturated with dye or discharge than the inside, which creates a beautiful ombré. The tighter the fabric is wrapped, the more ombré will be present from outside to inside wrapping.

These can be tied off with thread, string, rope, chain, ikat tape, or anything else you can possibly think to use. Choosing a material that will not absorb dye will allow all of the dye to be absorbed by the fabric; this will also alleviate future dye transfer to another project when using the same binding.

One of the coolest ways to do arashi, taught to me by Doshi and Elin Noble, is to use a large rope instead of a pole, to create extremely beautiful patterns. The example uses a 2 inch twisted rope; the most interesting rope to use (in my opinion) is braided 2″ or 3″ rope as it creates an even more intricate pattern. See Figure 6.5 in Chapter 6 for an example of using braided rope, discharge, and overdyeing to create a cool pattern.

The last major variation of this technique is to sew a sleeve by hand or machine basting, then adding fabric to a pole and bunching it down then tying it. This results in the fabric that resides off of the pole to dye a solid color and the fabric on the pole to have the beautiful striations of arashi.

Figure 11.8 Arashi instructions (left), wrapped and tied fabric (center), the result of the wrap-resist used for the fashion show in the film about a woman with black and white hair (right).

ITAJIME SHIBORI OR FOLD AND CLAMP

Itajime shibori is synonymous with "folding and clamping resist" as patterns are created by folding fabric and clamping shapes of wood, plastic, or whatever found objects you have on either side and then dyeing. This process can be extremely fun if you fold, clamp, dye, change your fold and clamp, and then dye or discharge over that.

Figure 11.9 Left: clamped and folded fabric. Right: the results! Both samples from Doshi's shibori workshop (2017).

Figure 11.10 illustration on Itajime (left), Deb Dryden's fold and clamp sample from Elin Noble's workshop "Additions and Subtractions" (right).

MORE SHIBORI-BASED RESIST TECHNIQUES

Unless you are using traditional Japanese techniques, tools, fabrics, and dyes, you are doing nontraditional shibori! There are SO many ways to do resist folding, stitching, bunching, and clamping – really your imagination is the only limit.

If you want to do something super intricate and interesting, try a variety of folds combined with different dye techniques. There is a book of folds that was introduced to me by the shibori artist, Doshi, called *Shadow Folds* by Rustsky and Palmer. Doshi paired these amazing folding techniques with dye and had dazzling results! See Figure 11.11 for her sample!

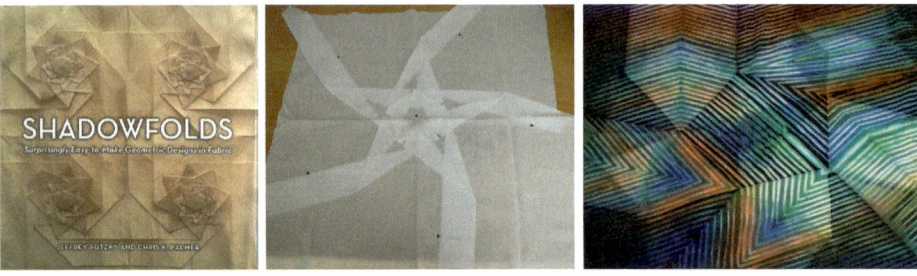

Figure 11.11 Shadow Folds book (left) with sample folded in a pattern from the book (middle), final results (right).

SERTI TECHNIQUE OR RESIST SILK PAINTING

Serti technique (a.k.a.gutta resist) means "fence" or "closing" in French and is used to describe a process where a resist product such as gutta or water-based resist is drawn on to stretched fabric in closed cell shapes, then filled in with silk or fabric dyes or inks. The closed cells, much like stained glass, contain the liquid color. It is a wonderful and useful tool in the dye arsenal if the final design includes detailed hand-drawn imagery or light colors with a dark background.

This technique was developed primarily for silk but is very useful for any fabric. Lightweight fabrics allow the resist to penetrate from front to back so dye cannot flow between cells, and this is why silk, like habotai or china silk, is preferred. This technique can be taken one more step after washing the first layer of resist: add resist over a painted area and then overdye or paint around that color. A disclaimer –

Figure 11.12 Bianca Del Rio in hand-painted dress using the serti technique; by artist Jeff Fender of Jeff Fender Studio. Photo courtesy of Jeff Fender.

silk painters are a large group that love to use these products and techniques. Therefore, there are many ready-made frames and tools; books and websites on this topic are plentiful. In this section I will provide the basic techniques and supplies that can be extrapolated to any level of financial commitment you choose in purchasing your silk painting tools.

TIPS FOR THE SERTI TECHNIQUE:

- Have a sacrifice piece of silk handy to test colors and thicknesses of resist. Don't ruin your whole piece by not testing first!
- Have a damp hand towel nearby to wipe the tip of the gutta bottle to avoid a fat bead of resist when you continue drawing with resist.
- For Pebo (or anything that comes in a metal tube) avoid squeezing the tube too hard when you start a line or it will eternally leak from the pressure of the crimped metal tube and creates lumpy lines.
- For a quick and cheap stretching frame, use the back of a silkscreen frame. As long as the silk doesn't touch the screen, you're good to go!
- Draw your image on the back of the silk to avoid seeing pencil lines on the front. Center image over something white in order to see lines on the back.
- After drying the resist, insure all of your lines are complete and closed. If not, your dye or paint will spread outside the lines.

- Using salt: there are different salts that can be used ranging from coarse to fine table, Himalayan, sea salt, or salt specifically sold to be used with silk painting. I have used all with success depending on the finished look desired. The coarser the salt, the more dramatic the resist. The most important part of using salt is to **add salt when dye is wet and let the dye dry completely.** If you brush off salt before it dries, it can cause streaks across the fabric and the pattern from the salt will not be as dramatic.
- To paint cells evenly, add water first! Like watercolor painting, you may choose to add water to the cell first then drop in your color. This will create a paler version of your color but you will be guaranteed that your color won't puddle or stain in one area.
- If you want hard lines, paint on dry fabric, don't pre-wet!
- To keep colors at the edges of an area that slowly fade into other colors, thicken your dye with sodium alginate (Chapter 9) so it stays put.

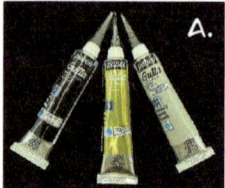

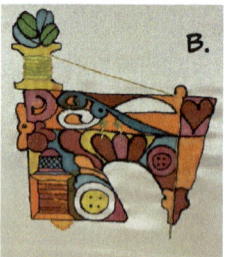

Figure 11.13 Pebo gutta resist comes in colors and is intended to be washed. I had success with the black Pebo resist, but the gold washed out.

Traditional **gutta resist** is a solvent-based product that has been a staple for silk painters for many decades and hence is why we often call the serti technique gutta resist. It is available in many colors including gold and black however, many of the colors are NOT intended to be removed and therefore are not great for use on costumes that must be laundered. The clear gutta resist is intended to be dry-cleaned, that is, if you can find a dry cleaner that will process your goods with gutta on them. I have heard anecdotally that some folks use dry-cleaning fluid to remove gutta themselves, but this seems like a toxic endeavor that might be best left to a dry cleaner. Because of the off-gassing from solvents, application of gutta resist should occur in a well-ventilated room.

There are a few other great products on the market made by Jacquard and Pebo. These products are intended to be washed out but the saturation of most of the products are still nowhere near as strong as that of solvent-based gutta resist. There is one product, however, that the talented entertainment dyer, Jeff Fender, recommends: Resistad. This product comes in a high viscosity and can be thinned with water or dye. There is no curdling like with the sodium alginate-based print paste and acids so it works nicely on silk and wool. The high viscosity means it can be pulled through screens or stencils and will stay put. I have used Jaquard Water-based Resist on silk and lightweight muslin and it works well, although the lines are not as fine as they are on silk. Jeff Fender[1] says that the Jaquard Water-based Resist is like using a tube of toothpaste, as it doesn't flow in fine lines or very smoothly but that Jacquard's Resistad is excellent and he has used it on both cotton and silk.

The following resist instructions are for water-based resist from Jacquard (water-based resist, Resistad) and Pebo. This resist is applied the same way as gutta resist but can be removed with water, so, if you intend to use Gutta, after step 6, take it to the dry cleaner to remove the resist. The user-friendly aspect of a water-based vs. solvent-based products really outweigh the negatives of water-based resist. This product can be tinted with dyes or paints to create colored lines; color concentrates would be best but remember to add a fixative or binder in addition to the concentrate so it doesn't wash out!

Supplies:
- Frame for stretching silk – this can be a wooden square, rectangle, or embroidery hoop!
- Habotai or china silk 10–12 mm
- Jacquard Water-based Resist, Resistad, or Jacquard Resistad
- Ink or dye intended for silk: DuPont's Silk Dyes, Pro Chem Silk and Fabric Paint, Jaquard Dye-Na-Flow, or an acid or fiber-reactive dye concentrate (this will require steaming after it dries)
- Tape, hooks and rubber bands (if fabric is hemmed), or silk pins to secure silk to frame. **Something that will NOT leave large holes in the fabric!**
- Needle bottle (see Chapter 10 for examples)
- Pencil or water marker (DO TEST FIRST!) for transferring or drawing image
- Watercolor brushes that taper; a good one that holds a generous amount of liquid
- Wash water for brushes
- Towels
- Dropper to add silk paint to watercolor palette
- Watercolor palette

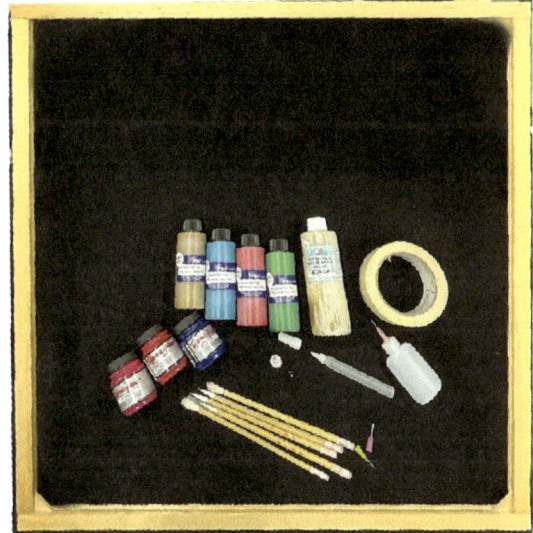

Figure 11.14 Supplies for using the serti technique with water-based resist.

HOW TO PAINT SILK WITH THE SERTI TECHNIQUE

1. **Gear up!** Gloves and apron. If using solvent-based gutta, good ventilation is a must!
2. **Set up!**
   - **Cut silk** to the appropriate size for your frame.
   - **Stretch silk** over the frame by pinning, taping or stretching on hooks side to side then top to bottom. Then secure upper left corner and lower right, upper right then lower left. (Create diagram for this step).
   - **Transfer design** to silk using removable ink or lightly tracing with a pencil. Make **sure to test** that removable ink will come out after applying resist.
   - **Fill palette with paint/dye.** Using a dropper add dye to a palette for painting.
   - **Add resist to needle bottle.** This can be tricky – getting a thick goop into a tiny bottle. A dropper is helpful here. If you decide to add color to the resist, do it before adding resist to the bottle so you can adequately mix the color into the resist.
3. **Draw or trace** your design with your needle bottle.
4. **Let resist fully dry.**
5. **Add color!** Using your brush, pick up some paint–dye from your palette and touch the paint to the cell of your choice. You can add multiple colors on top each other and/or salt to create some beautiful effects.

Figure 11.15 Order of operations to create a silk painting with the serti technique and water-based resist.

6. **Let paint or dye dry**. Set silk colors. If you used acid dye concentrates or other silk paints that must be steamed or heat set, **steam/iron/heat set fabric before washing out resist and dye**, otherwise your color will wash out too. **If you are using gutta resist, stop at this step and proceed to the dry cleaner.**
7. **Gently wash** the fabric by feeling where the clumps of resist are and rub these between your fingers to help the resist release. Do this until you can no longer feel any hard resist and the original had of the fabric remains.

BATIK

Batik is a process originating in Indonesia, and also heavily used in parts of Africa and India, that uses wax to resist patterns on fabric. Often wax is placed on already colored fabric and then cracked and overdyed. The cracks in the wax give batik its characteristic look. Many layers and dye sessions are used to create the most intricate batik patterns. Specialized tools and stamps are used with batik and they are easy to procure. There are several types of wax available to use in this process and each have their own character. See table 11.1 for a comparison of different types of wax for batik.

Something to consider when using this technique on costumes is that *this process can result in changing the hand of the fabric/garment* to a stiffer hand unless you take it to a dry cleaner as your last step. If the dry cleaning is not completed, the wax will never be all the way removed from fabric, adding that stiff hand. To some designers this is desirable!

Specialized tools used in batik are **tjantings** (or an electric tjanting), tjaps, and an electric griddle or double boiler. Tjantings are tools that have wood handles and metal heads with a hole on top to scoop up hot wax and a nozzle on the bottom to draw with the hot wax on fabric. These come in different nozzle size from 1 mm to 2 mm in single and double nozzles. Electric tjantings are available and can simplify the process of drawing on fabric as the tool regulates temperature, which in turn regulates wax flow. Tjaps are Indonesian stamps made of metal specifically to be used with hot wax. The electric griddle or double boiler is used to melt wax. The electric griddle can be bought new or at the thrift store (rather inexpensively) or a double boiler can be made cheaply with an aluminum disposable round tray in a metal pot of water. Either way, pay attention to the maximum temperature of the wax you are using so it doesn't start to smoke, or like paraffin, BURST INTO FLAMES.

Figure 11.16 Jeff Fender's technique of batik – a beautiful mixture of fine-painting and splattering of wax. Notice how wonderful the hand of the silk is even though wax has been used all over the fabric.

Folks use either their own mixtures of wax (i.e., 3 parts canning wax and 1 part beeswax) or wax that is premixed and sold as "batik" wax. Mixing your own wax gives you room to make the wax more or less crackly: using more paraffin makes more crackle. Either way, you should boil your fabric after dyeing, to remove a large part of the wax. Ironing out the rest by sandwiching the wax-laden fabric between newsprint then using a hot iron over the newsprint until wax appears will get most of the rest, even though it will never get all wax out. Most dry cleaners will not clean waxed fabric anymore as the super toxic solvent used to remove wax, perchloroethylene, is being used less frequently by dry cleaners BUT if you have done your due diligence of boiling and ironing, all that should be left will be an oily spot, and this may be acceptable to dry cleaners.

The process using water-based resist for a batik look is virtually the same as the previous Serti technique; the difference is that you add areas of resist in larger and thicker strokes on the fabric which enables cracking when it dries. I will say, it works ok, not great.

Table 11.1 Wax for Batik Pro-Con List.

Name	Pros	Cons
Soy Wax	• No nasty fumes • Comes in flake form; easy to measure and melt • Easy to remove from fabric with hot water • Lower melting point than other waxes	• Doesn't crack as easily unless frozen • Soda ash breaks down this wax • Takes longer to solidify than other waxes • Doesn't penetrate thicker fabric because of lower melting temperature • Difficult to get saturated overdyed colors using an immersion bath • Doesn't resist as much as traditional wax
Paraffin	• Cracks very well • Very cheap • Melts at 125°	• If heated over 240° it will burst into flames • Must be mixed with another wax (bees or sticky) or will flake off fabric if used alone • Must be cut with knife and takes a while to melt • More work to remove from fabric than soy wax
Beeswax	• Can be used to create solid (non-cracked) areas in batik • Can be mixed with paraffin to increase crackle • Smells nice • Melts at 143–149°	• Expensive • Will smoke when too hot • More work to remove from fabric
Sticky Wax	• Can be used to create solid (non-cracked) areas in batik • Can be mixed with paraffin to increase crackle • Cheaper than beeswax with similar qualities • Melts at 140°	• Creates nasty fumes – requires good ventilation • More work to remove from fabric
Liquid Cold Wax	• No melting required • Can use for projects with kids	• Cannot be immersed in water (like other waxes) • Have to apply thickly to get a crackle and often to both sides of the fabric to resist
Batik Wax	• Premixed paraffin and sticky wax, ready to go! • Good crackle • Great for newbies • Convenient • Can be boiled out	• Cannot alter crackle quality • Stinky fumes – requires good ventilation

Supplies*
- Tjanting
- Brushes
- Wax of your choice; use enough to fill your melting container 1"
- Double boiler or electric skillet to heat wax (my fave)
- Fabric ink/paint/dye or fiber-specific dyes for immersion baths (must be cold-water dyes)
- Iron
- Newspaper – like an entire *NY Times* (weekly)
- Pot for boiling out wax
- Something to skim wax off surface like large spoon
- Colored fabric light enough to be overdyed
- Baking soda for wax fires
- Optional: stamps or tjaps for printing

Figure 11.17 All supplies needed to perform the batik process.

*It is important to remember **all tools used for batik will now and forever be tools used with wax (unless using soy wax)** as the wax will never completely remove from tools and brushes.

HOW TO BATIK

1. **Gear up!** Apron, close toed shoes, good ventilation.
2. **Set up!**
   - Cover area you will be batiking in with paper, cardboard, or a drop cloth to avoid spilling wax on surfaces.
   - **Plan your design!** Looking at your fabric, decide how many layers and colors you would like to end with. Always layer from light to dark hues. Do you want to end with a yellow, orange, and red fabric? Start with yellow, add wax, crackle that wax, and add orange. Add more wax over areas that are now orange, crackle, and add red dye. The most intricate designs used many layers of wax and overdyeing.
3. **Turn on skillet or double boiler** and cut up wax to add. Plan on using enough wax to be able to dip your tjanting in the container and be able to fill it – this is about 1" of wax. Remember, when you turn off the skillet/double boiler, your wax will harden and be ready to be melted again for next time.
4. Dip tjanting or stamp in wax, if using a stamp, give it a jiggle to knock off extra drips of wax. Print or draw on fabric. Reload. Repeat!
5. Allow wax to cool, then crackle.
6. Add a layer of color by painting or immersing in dye or fabric ink.
7. When fabric is dry, add another layer of wax over this new color.
8. Crackle and overdye.

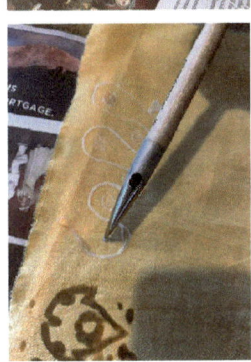

Figure 11.18 Top: dipping Indian wood stamp in wax. Middle: stamping wax on fabric. Bottom: using a tap to create fine lines.

Figure 11.19 Left: fabric sandwiched between newspaper and ironed. Middle: fabric put in boiling water to remove remaining wax. Right: finished!

9. Continue this process for as long as you want to create the design.
10. When all layers are complete and dry, iron slowly between several layers of newsprint, TOP AND BOTTOM. This should set the color on the silk if you are using Dye-Na-Flow or ProChem's Silk and Fabric Color. **Do not iron directly on the batik, you will clog your iron.** If you used acid dye on silk, make sure to steam your piece before boiling off wax.
11. After setting color, add fabric to a pot of boiling water. You will see wax float to the top – skim this off as a skin is created.
12. Remove piece from pot and with an iron, press fabric between two layers of newsprint. As layers begin to get waxy, swap out the paper. Do this until you get most of the wax out.
13. Wash fabric in cold water to remove any residual dye, hang to dry; **DO NOT THROW THIS IN THE DRYER – it will coat your dryer in wax!!**
14. If you choose, ask your dry cleaner to remove the rest of the wax.

ICE DYEING

This technique adds a kaleidoscopic motif to any fabric by using ice and dye powder. The pattern is unique because the dye powder that is added on top of the ice, which melts slowly, allows the dye to slowly deposit and blend with other colors. I often say that the result looks like ice crystals.

This technique is limited to cold-water fiber-reactive dyes and cotton (although one could use union dyes but they would have duller color results). The fabric can be arranged in any resist pattern you desire – really this technique is *how* the dye is applied. So, you could do shibori, tie-dye, fold and clamp, or bunching then ice dye.

GEODE DYEING – A FORM OF ICE DYEING?

Many folks are geode dyeing, which is really doing a tie-dye/Kumo technique but not arranging the pulled up fabric into a perfect circle; rather, the circle is manipulated to be irregular and then tied. This look is really successful when similar hues in varying saturations are used. Once tied and placed on an elevated rack (like a cookie rack), the piece is soaked in soda ash solution, dye is sprinkled on top, and ice is layered over that. As the ice melts, the colors flow into the fabric over a period of hours. Very beautiful organic results!

Stephanie Howerton, owner of The Local Artisan Collective in Ogden, Utah, specializes in geode dyeing. See her geode-dyed pants in Figure 11.20. Instead of using ice to disperse the dye into fabric, she uses a gentle stream of cold water in circular patterns to disperse dye. She says that the process is faster (no waiting for ice to melt) and that she gets very similar results! Thanks, Stephanie!

Figure 11.20 Stephanie's beautiful work on a pair of palazzo pants.

Supplies:
- Ice:
- Amount depends on how many pieces you will dye. For one yard of fabric I would use 1/2 of a 5 pound bag of ice or about 8 cups.
- Size and shape of ice cubes will change the shape of the resist – experiment!
- Metal grate to elevate fabric from bottom of pan
- Pan to catch melted–ice–dye–water
- Cold-water fiber-reactive dye
- Spoons to scoop and sprinkle dye
- Any implements/string/bands to create resist design
- Soda ash soak (2/3rds c soda ash to 1 c warm water – see Chapter 3 for details)

HOW TO *ICE DYE*

1. **Gear up!** Apron, gloves, particle mask.
2. **Set up!**
   - **Soak fabric** or garment in soda ash soak.
   - **Add grate** to bottom of pan.
   - **Arrange fabric** on grate. You will leave your fabric in this position for the entire dye process.
3. **Add ice** on top of fabric. I like to use enough ice to fully cover the fabric. You can even create a layer on top of a layer of ice and dye to blend colors on top of each other slowly.

Figure 11.21 Left: shirt in wrinkled and clipped with clothespins. Middle: ice is layered on garment and dye is sprinkled directly on. Right: finished! By Jan Nimlo.

4. **Add dye powder to ice**. Sprinkle with a spoon. Any colors next to each other will blend at the edges.
5. **Allow ice to melt fully.** I like to leave the ice to melt overnight. This way you are assured all the ice will melt and the dye will bond with the fiber.
6. Rinse fabric in cold water until the slimy soda ash feeling is gone.
7. Add fabric to almost boiling water (simmering) and allow it to cook for a least 10 minutes. This will break any fugitive dye bonds! Rinse one more time in Luke warm water until the water runs clear.

LOW-WATER IMMERSION DYEING

This immersion dyeing technique uses bunching fabric regularly or irregularly in a container that is partially filled with dye. The point of using low-water and not fully immersing fabric is so the fabric slowly sucks up the dye in irregular saturations creating a random and organic result. This is a great way to create background textures in fabric. It also lends itself to breakdown dyeing in adding a grimy overall texture to fabrics before going in and really adding saturated breakdown. This technique is virtually identical to immersion dyeing with fiber reactive dyes except in this process, the fabric is not covered in dye, but filled half way. You can squeeze the fabric to push the dye through it to fully cover

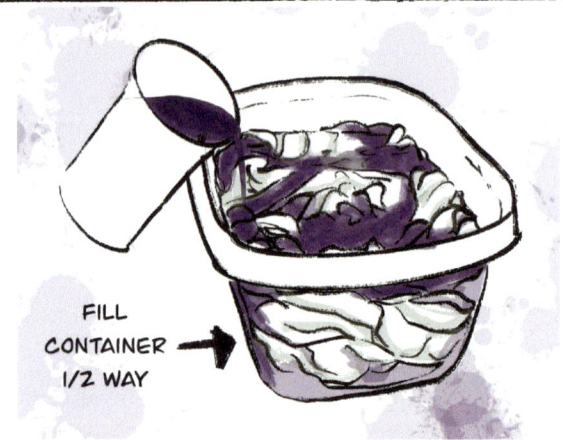

Figure 11.22 To do low-water immersion, add your fabric to container and fill with dye halfway. Leave fabric in pan for at least 2 hours.

Figure 11.23 I used a low-water immersion technique to make the texture on the biketards worn by the dancers in "Flock Behavior". Projections by Doster Chastain, lighting design by Price Johnston, choreography by Susie Garifi. Photo courtesy of Jennifer Clary, Colorado State University.

another color; the immersed areas will be darker still. Fabric stays in the low-immersion bath for several hours. I like to leave my pieces in overnight whenever possible.

THE BOTTOM LINE

Resist dyeing is definitely a crowd favorite. In my opinion it's because no matter how tightly you control your resist techniques there is always a small (or large) amount of surprise and discovery. Those who can nail a technique every time, like seasoned shibori artists or professional dyers with lengthy careers, do so from loads and loads of practice. So, why not start practicing today?

NOTE

1   Jeff Fender's website. www.jefffenderstudio.com.

12

BURNED OUT?
TRY DEVORE!

Devore is a chemical process that dates back to the turn of the 20th century. It was devised in Lyon, France to create a cheaper and quicker way to make a version of lace. The term devore comes from the French word devorér meaning "to devour". This makes complete sense as the chemical process used in this art form literally devours specific fabrics! This type of fabric was all the rage in the 1920s and made a comeback (especially in the 1990s) many times in the years to come.

This process creates a semi-transparent fabric; it is manufactured commercially and can be made by an entertainment or home dyer. The transparency is created by burning cellulose or protein fibers away, leaving the other thread fibers behind (which are very sheer). The most notable fabric

Figure 12.1 Original 1920s vintage multicolored devore velvet flapper piano shawl.
Photo credit: Black Sheep Antiques, Suffolk, UK.

DOI: 10.4324/9781351130677-13

used in this process is silk–velvet and rayon–silk satin. While you can get fine lines and detailed prints in silk–velvet, satin is user-friendly in achieving a clean print with etching paste.

There are many other fabric blends that can be used in conjunction with devore, but testing is always a must, as it can be uncertain if a rayon-poly blend will burn out correctly unless the fabric is specifically known to work for this process. Fabrics sold specifically for devore (so you know from the start the burning process will work and you don't have to do a bunch of samples to find out) can be purchased at Dharma trading and other silk-dye providers.

A standard devore process uses a chemical called sodium bisulfate. It is an acid that, when applied to cellulose fibers, literally burns the fibers away under the right conditions. You can create your own etching paste or you can purchase Fiber Etch from many sources. I choose to just buy Fiber Etch. Mixing up your own etching paste is messy and a bit dangerous; Fiber Etch has it dialed in! I buy mine from Dharma Trading because I like to support a small company but you can get it from many suppliers including the ever-present Amazon. If you would like to burn protein fibers instead of cellulose fibers, there is not a premixed commercial product for that. The directions to create protein etching paste can be found at the end of the chapter.

Figure 12.2 An example of satin devore. "Cornflower blue sunflowers floral hand dyed burnout devore satin" sample from Prism Silk. Using this type of fabric makes it much easier to achieve a clean print with etching paste. Using this type of fabric makes it much easier to achieve a clean print with etching paste.

Photo credit: Prism Silk

DEVORE PROCESS

The time has come – are you excited? I am always excited (and a bit wary) to use this product. Like every other technique in painting and dyeing, tests should always be done first to discover the amount of product used, the hand of the product, and how well it etches your chosen fiber.

This product devours the cellulose fabric from fabric that is a blend of fibers. Many people use silk–velvet for this process. In most cases, the BACK of silk velvet is actually silk and the pile is rayon. You will be applying devore paste to the root or surface of this rayon pile. In this process the rayon is burned away leaving the silk backing to create a pattern.

Figure 12.3 Fiber Etch made by Silk Paint Co.

> # A NOTE ON SAFETY AND THE POSSIBILITY OF RUINING YOUR FABRIC!
>
> This product is a mild acid. It will destroy your clothes over time and even etch your hands! When applying and ironing this product, be in a well-ventilated room and wear an acid gas respirator, gloves, and an apron. Even the etched particles can lodge in the lungs and cause major irritation – so keep that respirator on, or at least wear a dust particle mask when brushing the fibers away. I recommend reading the SDS for this product before using it. **If you leave this acid on your fabric too long, there may be long-term damage.** To ensure this damage doesn't occur, complete your devore process in areas in the same day.

Supplies
- Fiber Etch
- Silk–velvet, or part cellulose part "other" fiber
- Tape or pins
- Smooth surface to tape or pin to and possibly get dirty
- Applicator: brush, sponge, or just use the tip of the Fiber Etch bottle
- Hair dryer (optional)
- Iron

Figure 12.4 A needle board used specifically for ironing velvet.

HOW TO DEVORE

1. **Gear up!** Gloves, apron, close-toed shoes.
2. **Prep fabric.** Make sure to iron your fabric first! You can use a needle board (Figures 12.4–12.5), a steamer, or an iron. You will want a smooth, flat surface to apply your etching paste!
3. **Pin your fabric** to a board covered in muslin or thin fabric that you can stretch very flat. You can use foam from the hardware store or even foam core (in a pinch). The thicker the more stability you will have (Figure 12.6).
4. **Choose a design and placement.** For your first design you can choose to apply the paste by hand or make a small stencil. I recommend using the bottle or a brush to apply the etching gel to experience the burning process. Then you can play around with several advanced ways to apply

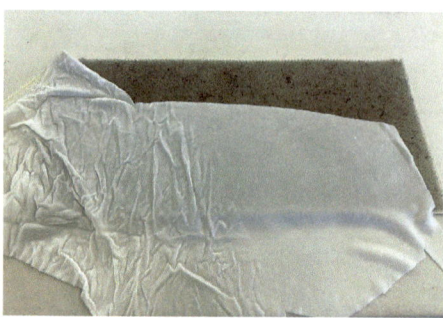

Figure 12.5 Make sure to iron your fabric first! Half is ironed on a needle board.

Figure 12.6 Pin your fabric to a board covered in muslin or thin fabric that you can stretch very flat. You can use foam from the hardware store or even foam core (in a pinch).

designs! Some of these ways are: Stencils, painting by hand, taping sections off, silk screen, stamping, and airbrushing.

5. **Apply Fiber Etch** or DIY paste to fabric! Choose whether you will apply devore paste to the face or the back of your fabric. A trick that I learned is to pin your fabric down face down and apply the paste to the BACK of the fabric. This way you are applying the material to the root of the pile. I would do experiments applying paste both ways.

If you choose to paint on fabric that is pile side up, paint like you are doing a wall stencil with a tightly packed stencil brush and lightly tap the pile fibers, working the paste into the fibers. For a more organic design, you can also use the bottle to directly apply etching paste and free-hand your design onto the fabric. **Make sure you don't cut your etch bottle tip down too far – the paste will come out very quickly and it is difficult to achieve detailed motifs** when the product is flowing too fast from the bottle.

Figure 12.7 Experimenting using a stencil brush and applying Fiber Etch to the back of the velvet.

6. **Let the paste dry.** Be patient, I swear it's worth it. A technique I used as a professional dyer was to let the paste dry almost completely, then let it go for a spin on high in the industrial dryer. It almost always dried and heated the fiber etch to a crispy texture. You can recreate this without an industrial dryer by drying your project with a hair dryer (Figure 12.8). Again, don't burn the fabric!

7. **Burn out**! Using an iron on cotton/high setting and a pressing cloth (or old piece of muslin), give the fabric a good press by making a circular motion with the iron and not stopping on any area. When your paste is activated, it takes on a brownish burnt hue. If you choose not to use a press cloth, make sure to use some iron cleaner when you are finished ironing if using a shared iron. Don't worry about crushing the velvet – you'll see why in the next step.

Figure 12.8 Using a hair dryer to dry etching paste before ironing.

A word of caution- you will most certainly burn the silk backing on your first sample should you choose to apply paste on the back of the fabric. This is something you learn – what temperature your iron should be at and how long you should hold the iron over the fabric.

9. **Flake away the burned material.** Using a fingernail or back of a seam ripper, gently rub the crispy pile or fabric where the burn out paste was applied (Figure 12.10). Is all of the material in your design coming out? This is where you can choose your own adventure and do one of two things: you can wash out your fabric and then dry it in the dryer – this will release random fibers that didn't come out with the rubbing technique OR you can reapply more burn out paste to the areas that did not fully burn the fibers. If the areas that are holding on for dear life are crunchy, you may have enough paste already imbedded in the fibers and you just need another trip to the iron. Usually, a good wash will release the residual fibers.

10. **Press out your fabulous work!** You can use a velvet needle board to press velvet face down. This is the best way to get a smooth pile surface. You can also use a garment steamer and steam your sample or use steam from a domestic iron. The latter of the techniques will take the longest, so be prepared. Really, I wait in front of the dryer and take it out right when the cycle finishes to reduce wrinkles.

Figure 12.9 Etched areas darken after ironing.

Figure 12.10 Begin to flake away burned fibers to expose your design (left). Then wash your fabric to remove the residual fibers (right).]

WAYS TO ACTIVATE YOUR ETCHING PASTE . . .

In the techniques I have outlined in this chapter, I used an iron and a domestic or industrial dryer because those are the most readily available tools to all dyers. However, there are other tools you can use to activate the paste, you just have to have access to them! One of these tools is an oven specifically for dyeing*. You can bake your etching paste around 280° F (140° degrees C) for five minutes or until the fabric turns a burnt brown color in the etched areas. You really have to keep an eye on this fabric so it doesn't start a fire. The other way you can activate the paste is to use a transfer iron used for applying heat transfers to T-shirts (takes me back to my days at Stoopid Clothing working the transfer, iron printing T-shirts all day!). You have to be careful again not to burn your fiber as a transfer iron is just a giant one-sided iron. A drying box like a wig dryer may work but only on the highest setting.

DEVORE PROCESS TO CREATE DETAILED WORK

They say necessity is the mother and of invention; this is true in the circumstance of *Time and the Conways*! I figured out a very cool process working on a design by David Reynoso for *Time and the Conways* (Figures 12.11–12.12). This was a huge process of discovery and the beauty of working in professional theater as a crafts head and dyer is that you have often slower times in your production calendar where you can spend a week experimenting! In this section I will share what I learned trying to recreate David's many geometric designs and fine parallel lines. My best advice is: **have a lot of fabric to fail with**. This is NOT a foolproof process!!!

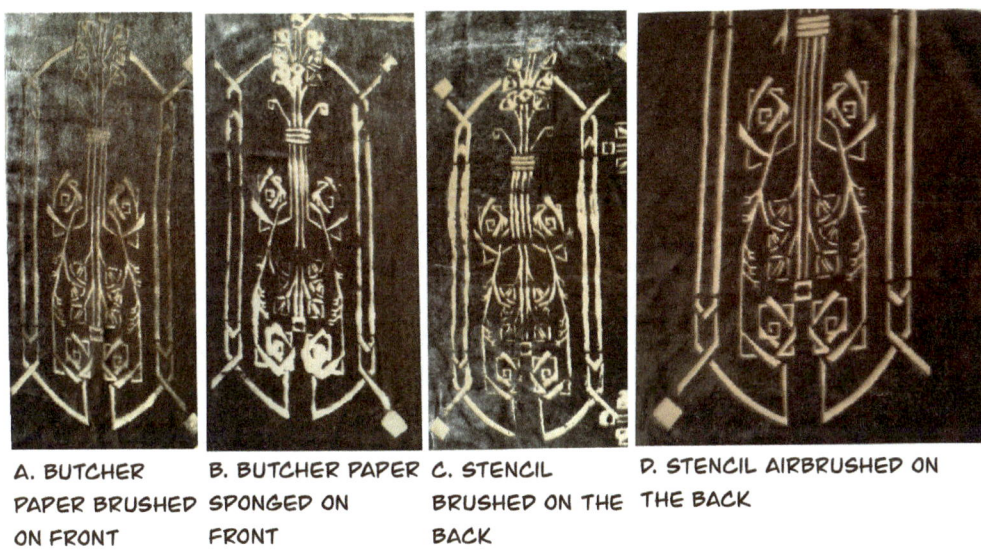

A. BUTCHER PAPER BRUSHED ON FRONT

B. BUTCHER PAPER SPONGED ON FRONT

C. STENCIL BRUSHED ON THE BACK

D. STENCIL AIRBRUSHED ON THE BACK

Figure 12.11 Samples created using different application and masking techniques for Old Globe Theater's *Time and the Conways*.

Materials:
- Fiber Etch
- Silk–velvet (silk back, rayon front)
- Temporary fabric adhesive (a.k.a. repositionable quilt spray or basting spray)
- An airbrush (ideal) or Preval or foam brush
- Tape or pins
- Smooth surface to tape or pin to and possibly get dirty.

HOW TO DO DETAILED FIBER ETCHING

1. **Gear Up!** Gloves, apron, close-toed shoes.
2. **Choose a rayon–silk velvet and a design.** Make sure your design has bridges if necessary (for a review of bridges, see creating a stencil in Chapter 8).
3. **Create a stencil out of contact paper.** (See Chapter 8: Creating a stencil out of contact paper). Make sure your stencil is double sided (two layers of contact paper). It needs to be STRONG for what we are about to put it through. You can also use freezer paper and iron it on but this is a one-use process. Cutting a stencil is A LOT of work – and you cannot reuse freezer paper well (it tears).

Figure 12.12 Temporary fabric spray adhesive. There are many brands! Also called basting spray.

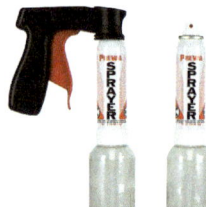

Figure 12.13 Pre-val sprayer found at your local hardware store. Glass bottles are great for cleaning. This is a wonderful alternative for small jobs if you do not have the budget for an airbrush.

4. **Pin or tape your fabric FACE DOWN** to some kind of surface that you can make vertical (if spraying Fiber Etch). Preferably a muslin covered surface, NOT a towel (the terry cloth will get in the way of Fiber Etch getting down into the fibers and encourage the paste to bleed). At this point, you should hold up your design to your fabric and create some registration marks. These are marks that you make at the corners or sides of your stencil, so you have a precise spot to line your stencil up when you are about to "do the thing". This way you know you have placed the stencil exactly in the right place. These especially help for repeated motifs!

5. **Apply temporary fabric spray** to the back of the stencil. Apply 1 time, let it get tacky, then apply a 2nd time. This is the magic step. This will allow you to apply or spray the fiber etch through the stencil, it will not bleed through the lines or areas you don't want to fiber etch to go. It's kind of like using masking fluid for watercolor.

6. **As your stencil back is very tacky with two layers of adhesive, stick it to the back of your fabric (which should be pinned face down at this point).** Make sure to line up your stencil with your registration marks! Remember those? Oh yeah, we thought ahead! Gently pat your stencil down to the fabric. Make sure there are no air bubbles and that the stencil is smooth. Pin the corners of the stencil in place too.

7. **Spray (or brush on) the Fiber Etch in the areas that are cut out of your stencil.** Don't go too heavy, as the fiber etch wants to and will bleed. So, if using a foam brush to do this, try to use even steady strokes saturating but not oversaturating the material.

8. **CAREFULLY unpin the velvet and stencil from your board and hang it up to dry.** You have applied the product lightly so there will not be a risk of running BUT if you leave it on your fabric-covered board to dry, the product may bleed. Make sure you let the medium dry completely. If you don't let it dry completely, the etch can transfer to another area on the fabric and create unintentional burned-out areas.

9. **Step back and look at your piece. Is it exactly how you wanted it? Did it bleed in areas that make you unhappy?** Here we have another chose your own adventure step. If you do not like how your piece turned out and you're like "Dude, I am not made of money, I can't keep sacrificing all of this silk velvet!" then I have some good news for you! You can wash out the Fiber Etch/devore paste and start over!!! The other choice would be to go on to the next step (10).

10. **Iron that puppy!** Many directions including the ones on the fiber edge bottle tell you to use a press cloth when ironing the product. I found that I had the best results when I did not use a press cloth and I use the iron straight on my fabric. You are obviously at a higher risk of burning your fabric so you really have to be careful. I've learned this lesson the hard way!

    You can use a medium–high iron setting (but of course you know the iron temperature is going to be good because you did samples, right?) and slowly iron the back of your piece. You have to be very careful not to burn the silk backing of your fabric. Do you smell something burning? That's your silk. Stop now and turn your iron down.

    Plan on cleaning your iron when finished!! If Fiber Etch is left on your iron it will etch other things that you don't want etched. Trust me, just clean your iron. You can also send your velvet through a very high heat cycle of the dryer. An industrial dryer works best as they get very, very hot. You would want to do this before you iron so the dryer does most of the work for you.

Figure 12.14 Left: Back view of velvet dress. Middle: detail view of devore. Right: Morgan Hallett as Madge Conway in J.B. Priestley's *Time and the Conways*, costume designer David Reynoso, draper Wendy Miller, Old Globe Theatre.
Photo credit: Jim Cox.

11. **You're there! Wash out your fabric and tumble dry! Congrats, you made something really cool!** If you find all of the fibers did not come out in the dryer, you can go back in and touch up the areas you want to burn out with a very fine brush. Go through the entire process again and may god be with you. Sometimes fibers can be stingy! Be diligent! You will succeed!

> A note about applicators and devore . . . Fiber Etch/burnout paste has a hand very similar to watery acrylic paint. If you want to create patchy textures, use a sea sponge, crinkled up paper towel, or whatever you can find to stamp the fiber etch on to your fabric. The only limit to apply this product is your own imagination!
>
> You could (and should!) try some of the other ways of applying this etching paste: stencils, painting by hand, taping sections off, silk screen, and stamping. Try using different applicators like an airbrush, sea sponge, foam brush, paint brush, or a stamp!

OTHER TECHNIQUES USING ETCHING PASTE

There are a few other techniques that are an interesting twist on using etching paste. One of them is to create a reverse appliqué. This technique uses two pieces of fabric with different fiber types, stitched together in patterns, and etching the top layer away to reveal a contrasting fabric underneath. I've detailed how to do this in the next section. The other technique is to create cutwork without cutting. This is achieved by protecting areas with stitching, paint, glue, etc., and burning out specific areas of your fabric. To be honest, I am not sure why you would want to do this – it is much easier to cut things out than use an acid-based product, and safer too, unless you are really terrible with scissors.

REVERSE APPLIQUÉ TECHNIQUE

1. **Choose 2 fabrics.** 1 – the top layer: 100% cellulose fabric. 2 – the bottom layer: anything BUT cellulose. This is a good use for all of those JoAnne's polyester fabrics that are pretty but you can't use.
   - **Choose the areas you want to remove.** Pinning layers together on all sides around the area you are going to etch out, using 100% polyester thread, satin stitch around the areas you want to remove. Apply etching paste with a detail brush to that area.
2. **Let dry.** Use hairdryer, air dry, or industrial dryer.
3. **Iron until etched areas get crispy.**
4. **Flake away burned fabric.** Reveal the magic!

Figure 12.15 Cotton fabric stitched to poly fabric. Etching is the brown and yellow striped flowers on either side of the white flowers.

COOL DYE TECHNIQUES FOR DUAL-FIBER FABRICS!

Another trail on the devore map is to choose two totally different colors for the backing fabric and the pile fabric. Let's say you want to dye the background fabric (that does not burn away), bright red and you want to make the pile fabric that remains a bright blue. You can use fiber-specific dyes and mordants to achieve this! Cool, right?

Figure 12.16 Fabric dyed two colors using specific fiber-reactive dyes. Dye work and photo courtesy of Sylvia Gray Designs.

> 1. **Start by dyeing the brighter color.** I would start by using acid dyes and citric acid crystals to create a hot bath for your background color. Rinse dye completely out. Your rayon or cellulose may be slightly tinted. No worries, your over dyeing is going to be waaaaay more vibrant. For more on fiber-reactive dyein, see Chapter 4: Fiber-specific Dyes.
> 2. **Next, you will soak your fabric in soda ash for 20 minutes or so then over dye your fabric with cold-water fiber-reactive dye.** See the Chapter 3 section on 2% Soda Ash Soak for instructions. You can hand paint this layer with a variety of colors using the same cold-water fiber-reactive dyes to achieve the colorful look of the 1920s shawl in Figure 12.1 at the beginning of this chapter!

DIY DEVORE PASTE

So, I seriously do not have the time to use this product and Fiber Etch is so easy to find and use. BUT for those purists out there, here are some recipes. I would love feedback on how your products turned out! You can add a few drops of food coloring to your paste so you can see it on fabric. Do not use red – it will stain. As always, do a sample first!

DIY CELLULOSE DEVORE PASTE

(1 quart of paste; adapted from ProChemical and Dye)

Supplies:
- Sodium bisulfate
- Synthrapol
- Guar gum
- PRO Dye Activator or Soda Ash
- Glycerin
- Blender, hand mixer, or whisk and a strong arm.

HOW TO MAKE DEVORE PASTE FOR CELLULOSE BURNOUT

1. **Gear up!** Gloves, dust mask, closed-toe shoes, and apron. You do not want sodium bisulfate on your skin!
2. **Prepare fabric.** Make sure your fabric has been scoured and dried, ironed then pinned to a print surface. One that is padded and covered with fabric is ideal (see Chapter 8 to create an economical print surface).
3. **Mix it up.** In bowl measure 1/3rd cup (50 gm) of guar gum. With a blender or mixer (or strong arm and whisk) *gradually* mix in **2 cups (500 ml)** room temperature water (75°F to 95°F; 24°C to 35°C). Leave this paste to thicken at least a few hours or even overnight.
4. **Create the burnout paste.** Mix up this paste right before you are about to use it – it only lasts *3 days*.
   In a bowl add:
   - 3/4ths cup plus 2 tbl 100°F (38°C) water
   - Dissolve 1/2 cup (200gm) sodium bisulfate in water **(ALWAYS add acid to water not the other way around)**
   - 1/3rd cup (80 ml) glycerine
   - Thickener paste from step 2

   Mix up this paste with your mixer until it is totally smooth.

5. **Apply the burnout paste**. You can apply this paste using the same techniques as the ready-made Fiber Etch paste.
6. **Let it dry!** Air dry, use a hair dryer, or a clothes dryer – just make sure the print paste isn't super wet to avoid paste transfer.
7. **Burn out**! Using an iron on cotton/high setting and a pressing cloth (or old piece of muslin), give the fabric a good press by making a circular motion with the iron and not stopping on any area. When your paste is activated, it takes on a brownish burnt hue. If you choose not to use a press cloth, make sure to use some iron cleaner when you are finished ironing if using a shared iron. Don't worry about crushing the velvet – you'll see why in the next step.
8. **Flake away burned/carbonized material GENTLY!** Just like using the premade paste, you can choose a few different ways to wash out the burned fibers: a gentle hand wash, brushing out the fibers using a brush or your hand, or using a teeny vacuum (like the keyboard ones).
9. **Wash fabric.** Send your fabric through a gentle wash cycle on hot (around 110°F or 44°C). Hang dry and iron with a velvet board.

THE BOTTOM LINE

I hope you allow yourself time to play around with the tips, tools, and techniques for applying etching paste. You may be daring enough to even create your own paste! I hope you also play with the exciting process of dyeing the different fibers in the same fabric different colors and even hand paint the rayon face of your fabrics. If you are interested in a book specifically about this process I found Iris Lee's *Fabric Etching* book very informative.[1]

NOTE

1 Iris Lee, *Fabric Etching*. Columbus, OH: Dragon Threads, 2000, 96.

13

IT'S GETTING REAL

PERMANENT AND REMOVABLE AGING, DISTRESSING, BREAKDOWN, AND SPECIAL EFFECTS

Just as costume designers are charged with creating and supporting character through color, silhouette, texture, and overall costume design, the breakdown artist is charged with making aged, distressed, shot-at, jumped-out-a-plane, swam-the-English-channel costume look believable. This is no easy task and this process requires as much skill as creating a beautiful harmonious painting, sculpture, or any other work of fine art.

So, what is this art of aging you ask? What are the materials, tools, techniques used in this art form? Why are there so many names for the same thing!!? Aging? Distressing? Breakdown? Answers to these questions and related skills are detailed in this chapter in the following sections: permanent breakdown, removable breakdown, specific garment breakdown techniques, specialty effects, breakdown dyeing, breakdown mediums, and sources used in aging and breakdown. There are detailed tips, tricks, techniques, and products that should help you travel down the breakdown road with confidence to work on your projects. Remember, that while the steps may seem gratuitous, they are not. Like my mother earned every wrinkle, so our distressed costumes earn the depth and beauty of a proper breakdown technique. Beth Herd leads us into the theatre:

> When an actor walks on stage, before they say a word, the audience has begun to decide who the character is by taking in their appearance and forming subconscious opinions about their race, age, occupation, social class, education, and more. My job as a textile artist varies from aging the costumes so they continue the narrative of the character, to giving the garments dimension so they don't appear flat on stage. If the play calls for a hardworking farmer who has been on the farm all day, he will not appear on stage in brand new overalls.

DOI: 10.4324/9781351130677-14

Rather, he will appear in well-worn work wear that has distressed fiber, dirt, mud, and depending on what kind of farmer, blood.

Beth addresses distressing for film versus stage:

> Film is high definition and is shown on a large screen, so the aging must be subtle and the most realistic. As you move into theatre and opera, the levels of aging required increases as the audience moves further away from the actors and the lighting intensifies. The aging and contrast between highlight and shadow is exaggerated because stage lighting will often kill so much detail and flatten the costumes, so more time and emphasis will be placed on creating contoured costumes for stage. In the workroom this will look odd, but on stage it works. I always recommend going lighter on the breakdown to start. Once you see the costume on stage; how much the lights flatten the costumes or the detail lost, then you will have information to add more breakdown to the costume.

Beth Herd, A-list film breakdown artist, dyer for the Royal Opera House and Santa Fe Opera, has contributed greatly to this chapter, and many of the following techniques, tips, and photos are hers. I will refer to her often in the following pages!

Figure 13.1 Beth Herd.

WHAT ARE THE TERMS?

In US theatre we have traditionally used the term distressing to describe the action of making clothes look like they've been faded from wear or attacked in a zombie apocalypse. In the UK/EU, the term breakdown is used, which has always felt much more accurate to me. Some costume designers like to use all three terms to describe the same thing and others will say "I just want it aged, not distressed." It is important to patiently process and respond to designers with thoughtful questions such as: how long has the character been wearing these clothes and how long have they owned these clothes (**aging**)? Have they been sweating, shot at, run over by a lawnmower (**distressing/breakdown**)? It's important to know things like time period/occupation/age/lifestyle so you can jump off your diving board into the sea of research ahead and recreate accurate aging and distressing. Beth's opinion on the subject:

> I prefer to use the term aging. It better describes the actual process. When the term distressing or breakdown is used, most people think we are trashing the garment (which is not true). The term also takes away the acknowledgement of the skill level that is required to do the job.

FILLING THE VISUAL BANK: RESEARCH

So, how do breakdown artists decide where to put that dirt, sweat, mud, and blood and make it look realistic and not like a bad Halloween costume? I always tell my students to "fill their visual banks", meaning research, research, and more research! Beth agrees on the importance of research:

> To understand how people wear their clothing it is best to look at research pictures of similar people, in a similar time, in the same occupation so you can observe what happens to their clothes in reality. There are several books and web sites that have great research images and examples [see last section of this chapter for sources]. The more references you have to look at, the better you will be able to recreate realistic aging.

Figure 13.2 Randy Wooten, a local working cowboy, poses for me out front of the grocery store. The humans in our everyday lives can often offer wonderful examples of real aging and breakdown.

Another source that I find quite helpful is humans in our world! When I'm out and about I like to take photos of people who have fantastic wear on their clothes. For example, I live in Northern Colorado where cowboys still wrangle cattle and ride horses. One day at the grocery store, this cowboy was checking out in front of me. I mustered up the courage to ask if I could take a photo of him, as it would be useful to me as a costume designer. He kindly indulged me and now I have a great reference photo for realistic distressing for a cowboy! See Figure 13.2 for Randy's photo and notice the grass on his boots, the saddle mud stain on his inner thighs, the smudges of dirt and bits of hay on his hat! He is a great example of a "put together but worn look", like he actually works in his clothes but isn't homeless. This image is useful to me as a costume designer to render a character with actual aging and also to handoff to a breakdown artist when I want this look recreated. It will help the artisan to see the actual wear that happens around the cuffs, knees, pockets, crotch, and headwear.

DON'T PUT THE CART BEFORE THE HORSE!

No matter what the piece is that is getting aged, **it is best if the costume is all put together and complete before the aging process starts.** If you work tirelessly to achieve the perfect dirt patina on the front of a blouse only to have fresh clean sleeves added on later, your work will be doubled as it is VERY hard to match distressing across a garment that has been aged somewhat and has new parts added to it. Also, if your aging has been done and there is a lot more sewing to be done on the garment, the thread cannot alternate matching your distressed areas. In theatre, the actor is usually far enough away that a neutral thread can be chosen and disappear in distressed costumes. In film, this is nonnegotiable. Fresh 1-color stitching will appear, running through your lovely distressing. This will require a touch-up from the dye shop/breakdown artist (which is common but not generally enjoyed or suggested).

BREAKDOWN MADE EASIER: THE WASHER AND DRYER

Using the washer and dryer for breakdown can spare your hands, arms, and back from a great deal of repetitive stress. Entertainment artisans around the world use domestic and industrial washers and dryers to speed up the process of breakdown. Depending on your garment and fiber type, you may or may not be able to use this method. Beth's tip on using the dryer for breakdown: "If you are able to tumble dry the clothing, add cut-up rubber bath mats to the dryer and clothing. This will help beat the clothing and break up the fibers." You can also sand the garments, then wash and dry them again to loosen and fray the fibers further. The dryer will also help to heat-set many breakdown products!

BREAKDOWN WASHING FORMULA: JACK WASH!

The following is a breakdown wash developed by one of the primo breakdown artists in the film industry (and coincidentally a student of Deb Dryden!), Jack Taggart. His co-workers dubbed this recipe "Jack Wash"! Jacks' process work is featured many times in this book!

Figure 13.3 Jack Taggart.

Jack Wash!
- Soda ash
- Lemon juice
- Orange citrus cleaner
- Cheap harsh Mexican soap (Roma)
- Powdered Biz

Jack adds, "The soaps have a lot of enzyme, and the lemon juice mixed with the soda ash react to foam up and scrub the garments. Run in an extended wash, several continuous cycles, rinse and tumble dry with cut up rubber bath mats. It's such a handy tool to break down bulk garments, and makes for a nice in-house 'stonewash' effect you can control. And yep, it even hits the poly blend uniform stock in a nice lived in slightly dated way. A lifesaver for us down and dirty folks".[1]

Beth's advice is to make the washing machine work for you:

> If you are going for a very worn, faded or heavily distressed/broken down look, I would repeat the washing process several times. I would use a strong detergent, Vanish, or Napisan to help break down the fibers, if appropriate for the garment.

You must make sure these detergents are appropriate for the fibers you are distressing. For example, any enzyme-based cleaner like OxiClean (similar to UK's Vanish or Napisan) contains enzymes whose sole purpose is to break down proteins, starch, and grease. This does not fare well for protein fibers as it breaks down silk and wool the same way it would break down a stain. Following is a list of detergents that will help strip the newness out of a garment. I've also included "Jack Wash", which is a brilliant combination of these materials that works wonders on very resilient new clothes to take them down several levels without breaking yourself.

List of Detergents that will knock back the "I just came from the store" look:

Simple green, lemon juice, soda ash, salt, dishwasher powder, dishwasher liquid, vinegar, Synthrapol (dharma, PRO Chem, Jaquard), Metapex (same as Synthrapol but in UK), Vanish *(UK), Napisan (UK) orange cleaner, fast fade(Rit), super cheap powdered laundry detergent, TSP (trisodium phosphate). TSP is known as sugar soap in UK and can add a lot of phosphate to waste water; some artisans swear by it and others say it does nothing.

*Vanish in AU and UK = Napisan. The US version of Vanish = Resolve, only in carpet cleaner format.

These detergents can be used on their own or in combination. *Make sure you are not mixing chemicals that will have bad reactions and cause toxic vapor (i.e., ammonia and bleach).*

PERMANENT BREAKDOWN: THERE'S NO TURNING BACK!

In the following section, Beth shares her order of operations in distressing clothes permanently. Like all breakdown artists, Beth prefers to distress in a series of layers and uses these layers regardless of whether the costume needs light aging or heavy aging. Beth begins this process with the overarching message:

> Whatever the desired outcome, there are several layers/steps to follow to get the correct look. I use these steps for all aging no matter if it is high-definition film or on a proscenium stage. Just because there is only a little aging to do doesn't mean it will take any less time. The lightest aging can sometimes take longer than the muddy bloody soldier. There are many different products and approaches used in aging a garment. Which ones you use depends on a lot of factors. Is the garment rented or bought? What products are available to you in your geographical location? What your set up is like and what equipment do you have?

Another consideration is how much time, money, and labor are available to your project. This is discussed in terms of the good–fast–cheap triangle.

THE GOOD–FAST–CHEAP RULE . . .

Breakdown dyers work in a variety of conditions from a small theatre in Russia that only has old watered-down paint and minimal tools (speaking from experience here) to a huge film studio dye shop where the equipment is world-class and the dye and paint stock boast amazing mediums and new tools. Regardless of conditions, most jobs follow the good–fast–cheap rule: you can only choose two of the conditions, good, fast, or cheap, at a time. If you have expensive mediums, the work may go a bit faster = good and fast, not cheap. If you have watered down dye and a gritty sidewalk to age your costumes, the work will be slower = good and cheap, not fast. If you have all of your costumes run over to the local acid wash to be taken down a few notches it will definitely be fast and good, definitely not cheap!

Figure 13.4 The good–fast–cheap triangle. Pick 2!

Supplies:
- Fine-grit sandpaper
- Strong detergent or combination (from earlier)
- Brushes, sponges, spray bottles
- Towel for dry-brushing
- Paint in hi-light, low-light, and mid-tone colors of garment
- Washing machine

***HOW-TO**: BETH'S PERMANENT BREAKDOWN LASAGNE (IN 7 LAYERS OF MEATY GOODNESS)*

1. **Gear up!** Gloves, mask (if using powders), apron, close-toed shoes.
2. **Set up:**
   - **Add portions of paint** to a tray set up a wash water container.
   - **Choose** brushes or sponges.
   - Put a **folded towel** next to tray (to dab paint on/dry-brush).
   - **Cover your work surface** so it doesn't become permanently distressed.
   - **Decide what detergent** you will use in your wash and how long your cycle will be.
   - **If sanding,** make sure you have a ham or appropriate sanding surface ready.
3. **LAYER 1: Wash, Wrinkle, and Sand**
   - **Wash** the garment if you can; if the garment cannot be washed then wet the garment through and gently spin out excess water in washing machine using a low spin for only a few minutes. If it is a very delicate garment then wrap in a towel before putting in the washing machine or just wring it out with the towel to dry.
   - **Wrinkle:** hang dry with arms/legs tied up and add weights in the pockets and in the bends of elbows and knees. Use wider strips of fabric, muslin, calico. This will help the folds look more natural. A thin strip of fabric or string will leave a crease line and look bad. Weights can be anything; I have used bags of sand, rice, stones, bolts, and washers (see Figure 13.4).
     - You can also steam or iron in wrinkles. The placement of the folds and wrinkles should be where folds naturally occur; be patient and arrange these carefully – if done sloppily, the folds will look wrong and you will have to press them out and start over. Getting this first step set up correctly will help later in the process with placement of shadows and high lights, as the folds will guide you where to put them. Beth likes to use a sleeve board as it allows wrinkles to be set on the surface and *not through* to the other side. Make sure the iron *is the correct setting for the fabric,* and hold the iron a little above the fabric. Let the fabric absorb the heat, and then allow it to cool without undoing the folds. This heating and natural cooling will help the folds/creases set.
   - **Sand!** Once the garment is dry, sand the worn areas on the garment. Use a very fine-grit sandpaper, 600–1200 depending on the fabric. Do not sand at this point for big effect; just break up the fibers. Do not sand the stitching! **Collars, hems, cuffs, knees, pocket edges**, the places that would be worn most. If going for an all-over faded, worn look, gently sand all over. After this step, throw garments in the wash again – this will help breakdown the fibers and give a worn look.
     - *For a light aging:* wash, sand, wash again, then hang dry. This is similar to heavy aging but not repeated as many times.

Figure 13.5 Jacket tied up with strings to add wrinkles with "weights" in pockets. From *Angel Has Fallen*, costume designer Stephanie Collie (not used in film).

Photo Credit: Beth Herd.

- At this point, if you want to add in more wear and tear, then I would use a larger-grit sandpaper and rough up specific areas that continue the narrative of what the character has been through. I would not go all out here. This is just another layer, not the final one.

BETH'S TIPS FOR SANDING!

Always make sure the fabric is flat, with nothing underneath that might cause bumps or lines. Take the time and work in small areas to make sure your fabric is flat and smooth. Some people prefer to work on a dress form, mannequin, or lay the garment on a flat surface; it's all personal preference. I like to work flat but I use a ham to work on curved areas like shoulders, arms, and legs. Always move the seam allowances, and the inside of pockets, out of the way when sanding! If these areas are sanded it will create an outline of these shapes. For sleeves and pant legs I like to use a sleeve board or a custom-made ham, so that the creases and seams from the underside don't affect my sanding on the surface.

You can make your ham using really thick canvas and firm stuffing, like hamster bedding or saw dust. The result is a pillow shaped item in the shape you need. I have one for sleeves and one for legs. I cover my ham with a thin sheet of compressed foam (Figure 13.5), which makes the surface smooth and my life so much easier.

Don't sand stitching! Beth shares, "On one film we had to heavily breakdown some knee boots. There was no time and in the frantic rush to get everything done, someone sanded all over the heck out of the boots, when the actor went to put them on all the stitching came apart and the boots were in pieces."

Figure 13.6 Beth's custom hams created for sleeves, pant legs, and other areas difficult to flatten.

Photo credit: Beth Herd.

4. **LAYER 2: Shadows!**
    - **Spray in the shadows** using colors that would naturally occur in the garment if it was in shadow. NOT just BLACK! Impressionist painters looked at nature to get their shadows and they didn't see black. They saw darker shades/tones of the actual color. Mix colors and use an air brush to spray in the shadows along the sides, under the arms and inside of the legs, and then spray where the more soiled areas would be hems and cuffs. Think back to your character and what their clothing has been through to help determine where these areas might be. If you have a dark-color garment you can skip this step, if the spraying won't show up on the fabric.
    - **When spraying**, start in an inconspicuous area and start the spraying off the garment and end off the garment. That way you are less likely to get a circular, heavy spot. Use a light misting, going over the areas a couple times, you will slowly build up the color. Use a steady sweeping motion and avoid obvious horizontal and vertical lines. DO NOT OUTLINE!!! You want to use a sweeping motion in a diagonal when spraying. DON'T do a concentered spray in one spot to save time, this will look bad. Allowing the mist to fall onto the fabric, slowly build up the layers of spray to get the depth of shading required. Take a step back from the garment so that you can judge if it is at the correct level. Once you think it is at a good level wait for it to dry and then look again to make sure before moving on.
    - ****ALL SPRAYS MUST BE USED IN A SPRAY BOOTH OR OUTSIDE** with correct PPE! Please refer to your SDS or COSHH sheets for the required level of protection needed for each product. Frequently used spray-able products are Dye-Na-Flow, Createx, fiber-specific dye, and acrylic paint. Please see Chapter 10 on airbrushing for paint descriptions and uses.
5. **LAYER 3: Midtones!**
    - **Mix up your colors** to complement the color of the garment. One trick in theatre, when aging a complete outfit, is to bring the colors of other pieces in the outfit into your palette and marry the garments. Example: if you have a red top and brown trousers you could add a bit of brown to your shadow color on the top and in the trousers add a little of the red to the shadow color. This helps marry the two garments together. It is a subtle way of adding and blending in the color.
    - In this layer the technique for applying the paint is called **dry brushing.** This is where you pick up a small amount of paint with the brush, and then remove the excess paint by brushing it off on a towel, leaving a small amount of paint on the brush. Gently brush remaining paint onto the garment. For those of you familiar with applying blush makeup, after you put the blush on the brush you tend to blow off the excess blush before

Figure 13.7 Left: An example of dry brushing. Right: Beth's favorite brushes: chalk brushes.

Photo credit: **Beth Herd.**

gently applying it to the face. This allows you to slowly build up and blend in color – same idea. Repeat this process until the shaded area is built up to the level required. Beth's favorite brushes to use for breakdown are chalk brushes.
- **Add more mid-tones** and shading to the areas the most heavily used by the character (as mentioned previously in the shadows section). See Figure 13.6 for an example of this.

6. **LAYER 4 (If Required): Heavy Distressing/Breakdown**
   - **Using larger-grit sandpaper**, seam ripper, cat's paw (Figure 13.8), or shoe rasps, break down the fibers more (mostly rips and tears, more fraying along the hems and cuffs). When adding holes and rips, you have to think about how the garment is constructed and not damage the integrity of the garment. If you are making holes and rips talk to the costume maker and let them know. After you are done they might want to put in supportive stitches to make sure the hole/rips don't get any bigger. We don't want the garment to fall apart on stage.

Figure 13.8 A cat's paw or rougher.

7. **LAYER 5: Highlight**
   - **Paint highlight areas** to add contour to the garments and show fading and wear. Don't spray in highlights as it is not opaque enough and would take a lot of product and time to get any effect. For highlight colors, use the lighter value of the original fabric hue. Using straight white does not look natural and it can read too cool. Highlight in a warmer tone reads better and looks most natural.
   - Using the dry brushing technique, apply the highlight color to the **collars, shoulders, elbows, tops of winkles, knees, backside of trousers, frayed and torn edges, anywhere the worn places or faded areas would be on the garment.**

> **BETH'S ADVICE ON RIPS AND HOLES . . .**
>
> Look at your research and see where the rips and tears are, how big they are, don't just go to town. This is not a Halloween costume with a jaggedy rough-cut hem – this needs to look real, believable. Cheese graters are *rarely* used. Once the rips and tears are made, it helps to trim back the frayed edges or rub them with fine-grit sandpaper and add dingy color to them, so they don't look brand spanking new. Take a step back and look at the garment, see how it reads before you move on to the next layer.

   - After the layer of highlight is applied, go over it, lightly, with 800–1200 sandpaper again. This helps to blend in all the layers and keep the paint from looking like it is sitting on the surface.

PREFERRED PERMANENT PAINTS AND WHEN TO USE THEM!

Beth prefers different paints for breakdown depending on whether it's for theatre or film and she considers the fabric, the paint it's being applied to, and if the hand of the fabric will be affected. The common paint brands used are Rosco Supersaturated Paint, Acrylic paint, Jacquard fabric paints, Dye-Na-Flow fabric color, or concentrated pigments and binder/extender.

Beth says, "In film in the UK, we mainly use translucent screen printing binder and pigments (concentrated color and extenders in the US) as a subtle way of layering and adding in color. This creates a realistic effect for film close ups. In theatre and opera, we tend towards paint. This is better for creating an effect that will be visible from a distance. When aging for theatre remember to keep the contrast from painted areas to non-painted areas. This will help it read from stage. If you blend too much you will lose the definition and contrast and the garment will read as flat".

She continues with tips on acrylics: "Rosco and acrylic paint are very concentrated in color and can dry out very quickly. When you are working with these paints you can add water to them to help thin them down and keep them from drying out too quickly. The other drawback to acrylic paints is they don't glide across the fabric as well as fabric paint. To remedy this, instead of thinning down with water, I will add binder (screen printing, universal translucent binder) to the paint. I mix a small to medium amount of binder in with the acrylic paint to help thin it out. This allows the paint to glide across the fabric and keeps it from drying out as fast, it also helps the paint stay flexible on the fabric. This also takes the opaque paint and gives it more of a translucent quality. The more translucent you want it, the more binder you add to the mix. The paints are heavy and can affect the drape and hand of the fabric. Adding water or binder to thin down the paints can help a little. Rosco and acrylic paints don't need to be heat set. Once they are dry they are set".

Beth on using concentrated pigments: "When using screen-printing binder and pigment, the pigment is very, very concentrated so you might only need less than half a drop of the color when mixing your colors. Translucent binder is used most in aging. These need to be heat set". See Chapter 10 for more info on concentrated pigments.

BETH'S TIPS ON ADDING COLOR RE: HIGHLIGHT, MID-TONE, AND SHADOW . . .

When aging a costume, I like to break it down into 3 color ranges: highlight, mid tone, and a shadow. We are trying to age and contour the garment bringing out the shape and having these 3 tonal ranges helps to do that. If it is white, cream, or very light color garment than the color of the garment acts as the highlight. So you then paint in a mid-tone and a shadow. For a garment that has mid tone as a base color, a highlight and shadow would be added. Then for a dark garment of black/dark grey/brown, paint in a highlight and mid tone.

When applying color, NEVER START CENTER FRONT! And always test your color first!

8. **LAYER 6: Finishing Layers**
    - In this layer, the finishing touches are added. These can be blood, darker sweat, marks, dust, etc. For specific products and application techniques, see the section in this chapter called: Specialty Effects.

    After these layers are done, take a step back and look at the overall garment. Are there areas that are too dark or need to be darker? Does the highlight and overall effect look believable? Now is the time to adjust anything. Congratulations! The major work of aging a costume is now complete. The next layers are the finishing details, which are very specific to the character and action they have gone through so not necessarily needed on every costume. Specialty layers are addressed in the Specialty Costume Effects section, at the end of this chapter.

REMOVABLE BREAKDOWN: IT'S MONEY IN THE BANK!

There is an entire world of removable breakdown products and techniques; many of them are not traditionally intended for fabrics but remove fabulously. These can be paired with an array of removable bloods, which will be detailed in Chapter 14. I hope you are as excited about these techniques and tips as I am – they can GREATLY increase your budget, as they either dry-clean or wash out of rented garments!!

A tip I picked up along the way about using removable mediums is to put (washable) costumes in a wash with a healthy amount of fabric softener so it creates a "film" on the clothing – it is said to make the removable products wash out easier! Beth learned most of the following removable techniques from working in film where she learned about several quick cheats to age and breakdown costumes on set. This is where she was introduced to oily/greasy rags, color petroleum jelly, Dirty Down sprays, and Kryolan makeup. She recollects,

> In 2017 I was hired to head up a dye/breakdown department for a film. It was military based and 90% rentals. Armed with the knowledge of removable products, I finally had an arsenal of supplies that could be used to get a heavily broken-down look that could be washed out. It worked great!

Beth and I are both excited about these techniques because it's been a struggle to get the level and quality of permanent products with removable products.

Beth uses the same layering method used with permanent breakdown except she doesn't sand, fray fabric, or add holes (can't undo those!!). See table 13.1 for a pro–con list for a variety of removable breakdown products. She adds, "I don't think one of these products is good enough on its own, but when you use them together you get a very good result".

Supplies:
- Fine grit sandpaper
- Strong detergent or combination (from above)
- Brushes, sponges, spray bottles
- Towel for dry-brushing
- Paint in hi-light, low-light, and mid-tone colors of garment
- Washing machine

Table 13.1 Removable Distressing Product Pro–Con List

Product	Pros	Cons	Notes
Dirty Down Sprays	• Great for spraying in shadows. • Fast coverage of large areas. • Quick knocking back of color. • Large can = lots of use. • Good range of usable colors. • Good for use on heavy materials, military uniforms, wool, corduroy.	• Can stain on certain materials, like dress shirts and thinner fabrics. • Need good extraction/ventilation. • Sits on surface of fibers. • If sprayed in a concentrated spot, when washed out can leave a residue mark. • Strong smell. • Can rub off a little. • Can only buy in UK and Europe (for now).	• Wash in cool, lukewarm water with strong detergent. Hot water wash could set color and stain.
Dirty Down Wax Sticks, Shmere	• Commercially available on many websites. • Great for small marks.	• Messy. • Can rub off easily. • Time consuming for large areas.	
Streaks and Tips Color Hair Spray	• Locally sourced (Sally Beauty). • Decent range of colors. • Lowest in the price bracket.	• Need good extraction ventilation. • Sits on surface of fibers. • Blonde has glitter in it. • Small cans so might have to buy a lot. • Can rub off.	• Reds and browns might stain if sprayed in a concentrated area; test first.
Kryolan Color Hair Spray	• Reasonably local (big cities) but will have to be shipped. • Wide range of colors, so can be used for many different applications on costumes, not just breakdown.	• Need good extraction ventilation. • Small can – most costly. • Shipping required if not in large city.	

(Continued)

Table 13.1 (Continued)

Product	Pros	Cons	Notes
Patin-A Paste	• Goes on like paint. • Can work into fibers. • Colors mix like paint. • Good coverage of a larger area. • You can also use Patin-A for highlights. • Colors mix well.	• Short shelf life = 3 months for dark brown and dark grey; white and yellow and clay grey seem to last longer. • Does not dry as quickly as regular paint. • Can rub away (but takes a lot of effort to do so) • Based in Germany so have to pay shipping BUT they are very quick at getting things mailed out • Not as useful for highlights as you need to use a lot of paint to build up the color.	• Only buy what you need – some products dry out quickly! • Has a translucent quality; slowly build up color. • Patin-A paste works in the same way paint does, it is great!
Patina-Creams	• Really nice sweat soil and greasy colors. • Good shelf life. • Good range of premixed colors.	• More pricey than make your own. • Shipping from Germany.	•
Patin-A Dust	• Great range of colors.	• Dust is lung irritant, use proper ventilation. • Messy. • Can rub off easily; needs to be reapplied often.	• Patin-A ivory dust is quite yellow, and the clay brown is very orange.
Schmutz	• Great range of colors.	• Dust is lung irritant, use proper ventilation. • Messy. • Can rub off easily; needs to be reapplied often.	• Fullers earth is cooler color and lightest of all the dusts but has a slight red/pinkish hue to it. • Rotten Stone is quite a dark grey.
Fuller's Earth	• Quick application. • Great "dust" look.	• Messy. • Can rub off easily; needs to be reapplied often.	• Requires hairspray for adhesion.

Table 13.1 (Continued)

Product	Pros	Cons	Notes
Kryolan Aquacolor Makeup	• Quick! • Saturated color. • Can mix colors to get the exact color you want. • More permanent than dust – can rub off but takes effort.	• Chalky finish. • Browns/reds can stain. • Can't apply with lots of water, this might cause it to stain. • Have to be careful, under some lights and angles you can see the brush strokes.	• I dry brush on – only use very little water • Browns are quite red.
Bees Wax	• Great for greasy/oily areas. • It stays flexible when cool and doesn't tend to crack.	• Cannot tumble dry – wax can re-melt and get all over the other garments and inside of the dryer.	• You should only use as little wax as is necessary to get the effect. IT MAY STAIN. USE WITH CAUTION!
Colored Petroleum Jelly	• Make your own cheaper than premixed products. • Mix up own colors by adding dust to petroleum jelly. • Can make color stronger or weaker depending on amount of dust used in mix. • Good for adding color and sweaty look. • Shiny patches.	• Messy to make.	• Have to wear dust mask when working with dust and be in a well-ventilated area.
Oily/ Grease Rags	• Add color and shine to a garment quickly. • This is a very quick way to add grime to collars, cuffs, shirt fronts that are too bright. • Make your own = cheap.	• Less control when applying to fabric.	• When the rag dries out just add more baby oil or glycerin, whichever one you started with. • Must wear dust mask when mixing up dust.

HOW-TO: *BETH'S REMOVABLE BREAKDOWN LASAGNE (IN 7 LAYERS OF MEATY GOODNESS)*

1. **Gear up!** Gloves, mask (if using powders), apron, close-toed shoes.
2. **Set up:**
   - **Add portions of removable paint** to a tray set up a wash water container.
   - **Choose** brushes or sponges.
   - Put a **folded towel** next to tray (to dab paint on/dry-brush).
   - **Cover your work surface** so it doesn't become permanently distressed.
3. **LAYER 1: Wash and Wrinkle**
   - Wash and wrinkle, same as permanent aging but NO SANDING!
   - Start by washing (if you can) hang dry with arms/legs tied up and weights in pockets and in bends of elbows and knees. If you can't wash garments, steam/iron in wrinkles.
4. **LAYER 2: Spray Shadows**
   - Spray in the shadows where the more soiled areas will be: hems and cuffs. Think back to your character and what their clothing has been through to help determine where these areas might be. See tips on spraying shadows in permanent section.
5. **LAYER 3: Paint Shadows**
   - Beth recommends Patin-A paste for painting shadows: "I paint in darker colors, darken specific and more-worn areas with each layer getting a bit more detailed. Great for dry-brushing."
   - You can also use Kryolan Aquacolor for shading. Put a very small amount of water on the pallet, load the brush with makeup, remove excess and apply. You can mix the colors easily. Although when dry it has a chalky appearance so it might not be the best to use for shading, if you don't want a chalky look.

Figure 13.9 Kryolan Aquacolor and Patin-A Paste used in removable breakdown.

6. **LAYER 4: Highlight**
   - Using **Kryolan Aquacolor:** put a very small amount of water on the pallet, load brush with makeup, remove excess from brush and apply. You can mix the colors. DO NOT use a lot of water, only a small amount! If you use a lot of water and apply wet, it might stain. The 4 colors for the best Kyrolan highlights: white, yellow, brown, and green. Be careful, under some lights and angles you can see the brush strokes so, check all angles after applying. To blend away any brush stokes, gently rub the fabric against itself or use a water wipe to blend away.

- Using **PATIN-A:** You can also use Patin-A for highlights but this will take longer as you need to build up the color.
7. **LAYER 5: Grease and Shiny Spots.** This adds an extra layer of depth, where the costume has been worn a long time there might be greasy, oily sweat spots, or stains where the fabric has been rubbed a lot and the fibers pushed down and shiny.
    - You can use Patin-A creams, Schmere wax sticks, custom color petroleum jelly, custom oily/grease rags, baby oil or glycerin. Custom means – make your own. Beth's recipes can be found at the end of this chapter.
    - If you want the costume to have a wet, sweaty look but not have any added color than you can use clear baby oil or glycerin. **Beth's tips on using baby oil:** "I prefer to put the baby oil in a spray bottle and spray it onto the costume where the character would be sweaty. You **MUST BE CAREFUL DOING THIS AS IT WILL MAKE THE FLOOR SLIPPERY!!!!!** It is best to do this outside and not where people will walk."
    - The custom creams, petroleum jelly, and oily rags can be rubbed onto the area for desired sweaty or shiny area. These will come out in the wash! So, you will have to reapply this step after every wash. This is what had to be done for *Carmen* at the Santa Fe Opera. The designer wanted the soldiers to look really sweaty every night but didn't want the sweat painted on. So the actors and costumes were sprayed and dabbed with baby oil and glycerin every night before they went on stage.
8. **LAYER 6: Dust**
    - You don't have to apply this layer. It depends on the character's story. This layer will also *wash out* so **note** that it might have to be reapplied after every wash. Take continuity photos so your look can be repeated – especially for film/TV.

HEALTH WARNING FOR DUST

Any powder – even cosmetic powder – consists of fine dust. When mixing or using powder/dust always check COSHH and SDS sheets first. Always wear a mask, gloves, and eye protection and work in a well-ventilated area. Apply dust to garments only and never apply to a garment when it is on a person. Unless the person is also wearing a mask and eye protection but even then, it should be avoided. Some textile/breakdown artists won't use dust at all. Never apply to the costume when the actor is wearing it.

- **Dust Alternative:** To get a dusty effect, without using dust, use Kryolan Aquacolor make up. The browns are a bit red so mix in green to tone down the red. To use this product, it is best to spray a fine mist of water on the makeup palette, then load the makeup onto the brush, remove the excess on spare cloth, then dry brush on to the areas where it would be dusty. The Kryolan Aquacolor will dry with a dusty/chalk like appearance. When using this method, be very careful and aware that you might be making brush strokes on the fabric. To remedy this once the makeup is dry, rub the edges of the fabric against itself to blend in the edges or brush marks.
9. **LAYER 7: Finishing Layers**
    - In this layer the finishing touches are added, just as in permanent breakdown. These can be blood, darker sweat, marks, dust, etc. There are some products and application techniques in the next section: Specialty Effects.

RECIPES FOR REMOVABLE BREAKDOWN MEDIUMS!!!

These recipes were created by Beth as she learned removable breakdown from working in film and theatre. Use these as a base to create your own custom mixtures. **ALWAYS WEAR A DUST MASK/RESPIRATOR EYE PROTECTION AND WORK IN A WELL VENTILATED AREA**

DUST BAGS
Companies that make colored dust are Patin-A and Schmere. Beth says:

> Patin-A ivory dust is quite yellow, and the clay brown is very orange. Schmere fuller's earth is a warm dust but also has a touch of pink in it. Their Rotten Stone is quite a dark grey. I like to use a mix of both company's dusts to get the right color I want.

Beth makes up custom dust bags, mixing different colors of dust together to get a realistic color; light colors for dust, darker dust colors for dirt. Beth notes:

Figure 13.10 Powder added to pot to be mixed (left), powder in child's sock (right).

> It's also good to layer different colors as this can give more depth. When mixing up custom dust colors it is similar to mixing paint colors. Start with the lightest colors first, then slowly add in the darker colors. If your mix happens to get too dark it will take too much light dust to lighten it back up. If it does get too dark take a small amount of the dark mix, put it in a new container and add in the light to that. You will need to test your dust color as you mix because it is hard to know what color it is until it is applied. To apply the dust: I take my color mixes and then put them in a pounce bag or a child-size sock, knotted at the top. I then tap the bag/sock over the desired area to add dust to it. To get the dust to stick there are a few methods: hair spray, petroleum jelly, glycerin, or baby oil can be used. If I use hair spray, I first spray the hair spray lightly over the areas I want dusty, then add dust, then hair spray. This is repeated until desired look is achieved, remove any excess dust with a brush. If I use baby oil, glycerin, or petroleum jelly, I use them sparingly; only a light layer is required. This process might make the dust appear darker. Test first. If a large quantity of these products are used the dust will end up looking more like mud.

Supplies:
- PATIN-A or Schmere Dust
- Container for mixing
- Children's socks (these are the dust bags)

HOW TO CREATE YOUR OWN DUST BAGS
1. **Gear up:** dust mask, apron, gloves.
2. **Mix up pigment color** you want from Patin-A or Schmere dusts. I tend to mix mine up in a pan. But any large container will do. I usually use a light base as it is easier to make darker then to lighten! Ivory beige Patin-A is very yellow. Fuller's earth schmere is lighter but a bit pink. The red clay color a little goes a long way.
3. **Fill sock with dust.** Once your color is mixed, take a child's sock and put 8–10 heaped table spoons of dust in each sock. I use children's size socks because you do not need that much dust to do the job, they are easier to handle and fill and you don't have to make up as much dust to fill them.
    - **To fill sock:** open sock, with the ankle edge folded over, around edge of cup or container. Scoop in mixed color dust, pack down after each spoonful. I usually only fill up to the heel. Tie off top. You're done!

OILY/GREASY RAGS
Beth uses these for more of a quick fix on films

Supplies:
3. PATIN-A or Schemere Dust
4. Baby oil or glycerin
5. Rags/cut up fabric pieces (at least 8" x 8")
6. Zip loc bags for storage

Figure 13.11 Rags put in oily–dusty mixture.

HOW TO CREATE OILY/GREASY RAGS
1. Mix up pigment color you want from Patin-A or Schmere dusts.
2. Put baby oil or glycerin in container add dust color. The more pigment = the darker shade.
3. Put rags in oil dust mix, wring out excess oil. You can have rags very "wet" with lots of oil or really "dry" very little oil, depends on what you like. If they dry out over time you just add in more baby oil or glycerin, which ever you used in the first place. I keep my oily rags in zip lock bags and then in a plastic box with a lid to prevent any leaks.

(Figure 13.10)

COLORED PETROLEUM JELLY
Supplies:
- PATIN-A or Schmere Dust
- Pan to melt petroleum jelly in (or you can put it in direct sunlight as long as it's hot enough to melt petroleum jelly)
- Petroleum Jelly
- Containers for mixed colors

HOW TO COLORED PETROLEUM JELLY
1. **Gear up:** gloves, dust mask, apron.
2. **Mix up dust color 1st**, can use same colors as dust bags and oily rags.

3. **Melt the petroleum jelly**

   first = easier to mix in dust.
   - Options for warming up melting petroleum jelly are: put in sunlight to warm up, this works great in the summer or warm climates and if you have time to wait.
   - OR put the container in a pan with some water on low heat, heating slowly on stove top effectively creating a double boiler, stirring as you go (I use this method most).
   - OR microwave, but be careful on how long it's in there!!!!!! Heat it little by little, mixing as you go. This method could go wrong very easily and could scold or burn because the microwave doesn't heat evenly.

4. **Add dust:** Once melted and **wearing dust mask,** add in dust. For weak/light color mixture, add in 1 tsp of dust color, for a stronger/darker color add in 4tsp or more for a large container of petroleum jelly.

Figure 13.12 Petroleum jelly melting in pan (left), mixing dust into melted jelly (right).

SPECIALTY COSTUME EFFECTS

GREASE, SWEAT, SHINY SPOTS

When sweat, grease, and shiny spots are added to a distressed garment, it adds an extra layer of depth showing long-term wear on a costume. There are many different products that can be used for this layer. The most wanted areas include around the collar, along the neck, down center front and back, and under the arms or where the fabric has been rubbed a lot and the fibers pushed down and made shiny. Shiny areas could also include the knees and elbows, along the center front edge of the jacket, or along the side brim of a hat.

Grease

Permanent: Grease needs to look a bit shiny and dark in color, usually close to black. Paint, acrylic gloss, and puff binder would all work well.

Removable Grease: Greasy rags, Schmere, Patin-A, or even black tailors wax would all work well for this effect. Always test first!

Shiny Spots

Permanent shiny spots: Beth advises:

> Shiny spots can be made by rubbing bees wax on the area, then setting in with the iron(the iron that is only used for breakdown). This process can be repeated and layered until the desired effect is achieved. Beeswax is best as it stays flexible when cool and doesn't tend to crack."

Beeswax is permanent.

Removable shiny spots: Colored petroleum jelly matched to a darker version of the garment (that would indicate wear in the shiny area) is a great way to add shiny spots.

Sweat
Permanent Sweat:

If painting sweat, it can be applied earlier in the process. Sweat around the collar and under arms can be achieved by dry brushing or spraying in the "wet" color of the fabric. You can figure out what color this is by simply wetting the fabric! Often we use a fabric ink/paint like Dye-Na-Flow or Prochem's Silk and Fabric Paint (permanent), in a color like Ecru or a brownish yellow, watered down and put in a spray bottle and sprayed around the collar and pits. It is helpful to have another squirt bottle of water handy to spray at the costume and water down the mixture if it ends up too dark or yellow.

Removable Sweat: Sweat can be removable as well, using any number of removable products like Patin-A, glycerin, or colored petroleum jelly in the same sweaty areas. Please see the recipes before this section to make temporary products including sweat.

WET LOOK, SLIME, VOMIT
At some point you will be asked to make a garment or accessory look wet, slimy, or barfed on. I have included some permanent and temporary solutions to these challenges but I would caution: when a special element like slime or vomit is **not required to be** edible, I would not recommend using food or anything sweetened if not absolutely necessary because of the fact that food-based products break down quickly and attract insects.

For permanent wet-look effects, Smooth-on's platinum silicones, Dragon Skin and Ecoflex, which I mention in Chapter 14 (to create a permanent wet-look blood), is very useful. It will stay shiny but can be difficult to control; unlike using silicon caulking, it won't kill you because the products are tin-free and skin-safe (safety measures must still be taken). If the product is too thick for drippy rain or vomit, Smooth-On makes a product called Silicone Thinner which cannot be more that 10% of the total volume when mixed into Dragon Skin and it rocks. If the material is too thin, another Smooth-On product called Thivex can be used to thicken Dragon Skin. If the material is too shiny, Slacker (by Smooth-On) can be used. These products can be tinted with SilcPig, Smooth-on's own line of silicone pigments. This product is not cheap but good and fast, yes. I STRONGLY caution you NOT to use silicone from the hardware store. It is full of metals and poisonous VOCs. It is even harder to control and you cannot regulate the viscosity.

Another fantastic product that is discussed in Chapter 10 is Nova Colors' Flexible Gel Medium and Nova Colors' Super Gel. They don't yellow with age, stay fully flexible (although it does stiffen the hand of the fabric a bit), and you can imbed other things like glitter or gems and it will not dull the shine. This is the closest product to crystal gel or sculpt-or-coat that I have found.

Acrylic gloss from Rosco is another product I have used, and it can be seen in the section on aging hats. The important criteria for acrylic medium or gloss is that it is thick enough to not totally soak into felt or fabric. A base coat of a gel medium could be helpful in creating a seal to apply a shiny acrylic gloss over.

Temporary wet looks could include products mentioned previously in the Breakdown–Greasy–Shiny section, like baby oil, glycerin, Vaseline, or washable glue! In this section we add in methyl cellulose as a base for slimy effects.

Wet Look
Permanent wet look: To know what color to choose to make a garment appear wet, wet the garment, then you will see exactly what color you must use to achieve believability. Dye matched to this color can be used to achieve this effect, but if it's shiny just-came-in from-the-rain wet and needs to stay that way, a silicone, nova gel, or any of the other products mentioned previously should work.

Removable wet look: Again, wet the fabric to see the color it turns when wet. Really wet. Then you may want to tint, with aqua color or food coloring gels, water or glycerin to this color if the fabric is not very absorbent to finer mists from spray.

Slime
Permanent Slime: Slime is another request for those working on supernatural film and TV (think *Ghostbusters*). All of these wet-look techniques use the same products, the artist just needs to vary the additives. For example, for slime, the artist will need to make sure the slime is the correct viscosity and color, matching the slime that is being used on set if there is slime landing on the actors. To create slime with Smooth-on's platinum silicones like Dragon Skin or Ecoflex, thicken with Thivex, thin with Silicone thinner.

Removable Slime: A great product for temporary slime is methyl cellulose (methyl cel). If used on the body and costumes, this should be a food-grade methyl cel, not sold through dye distributors but sold through food sources with the intended use to thicken food. This is the same product used to float marbleizing paints and it can be tinted, depending on whether or not it must be edible, with food coloring or aqua color makeup.

Vomit
Permanent Vomit: For vomit, the silicones mentioned above can be a great product, adding chunks of foam that are painted different colors and are different sizes, to a potentially thicker mixture (thickened with Thivex). The silicone can be tinted whatever background color is desired and the shininess can be controlled with Slacker.

Removable Vomit: Like slime, this recipe can also use methyl cel to thicken and a variety of items can color this mixture depending on desired base color and whether it needs to be edible. The edible chocolate syrups and food coloring, or non-edible aqua color or Patin-A temporary paints would work here. Real food can be used and depending on whether we see the person vomit or not – matching the liquid coming from the mouth. Consideration of what the person was likely to eat would be important here, but really some ground up cornflakes or other edible substance that would become mushy but hold some sort of shape, would be ideal.

Mud
There are many different ways to make mud and it all depends on the texture, color, and whether you want the mud to be removable or permanent. We strongly recommend researching the color that the mud would be where your play/film is set! For example, Alabama mud is very different than Scottish mud! In my early days as a painter/dyer I was chastised by a

British costume designer for creating a very red iron-rich Southern California mud stating "that's not pale English mud at all!" Considering I have an undergraduate degree in geology, I should have known that – but often we paint what we know!

Beth has included several mud mixtures and urges you to play around with quantities and discover the perfect mud mixture for yourself! She cautions "when applying mud to always be very careful not to leave any hand or finger prints!"

Permanent Mud: Using Paint

Paint can be used as a mud effect. Mix the desired color you need and apply it to the garment. If you want texture, add in saw dust or hamster/rabbit wood pulp bedding.

For wet mud add in acrylic gloss medium with the paint or apply the gloss medium once the paint is dry.

Permanent Mud: 3D Mud

This is a mixture of white plaster, PVA glue (white glue similar to elmer's), water, and paint. You will mix up your plaster and water to get a medium consistency, not too runny or too thick and then add in PVA (approx. 10% of the mixture). Add paint to the mixture to make a base mud color. The PVA will help the plaster stay flexible and stick to the fabric. You will have to be able to test this mixture to get it right. Plan for this in timing and fabric. Once your mix is ready, apply it to the garment where you want the mud to be. Let it dry completely. Once dry, flex the fabric and get some of the mix to break off, this will help in the realistic look. Now, if all of the mix crumbles off there wasn't enough PVA, if none or very little of the mix crumbles off then there was too much PVA. This is why this must be tested! Once the loose mix has come off then use an air brush/Pre-val or dry brush in more mud colors. This helps blend the mud mix into the fabric. Remember adding a couple different colors will add to the depth and real look of the mud. If you want to keep the wet look, paint a gloss medium over the top.

Removable/Permanent Mud: HBO Series Mud

This mud uses clay-based kitty litter. Add in water slowly to make a thicker consistency glob. Take a bit of this mix and test the color on scrap fabric similar to the color of the garment. The dried mix might be the correct color or you might want to mix in paint to get the color (if you use permanent paint, this will make the mud permanent!!!). Once the tests are done and you have the correct color, take a scoop of the mixture, make a ball in your hand and then rub it onto the garment where the mud would be.

Removable Mud: Real Mud

Dig up some dirt/mud from outside. You will need to do a test swatch to see if the mud stains. Add water and isopropyl alcohol. This will kill most bacteria and keep the mud from going moldy. DO NOT USE ON ACTORS SKIN!!!! It still might have microorganisms that could get into the skin.

Removable/Permanent Mud: Patin-A

Patin-A makes a removable mud, PATIN-MUD. It is water soluble and there are 6 colors that can be mixed or layered to create the right color. It is applied with a damp sponge and can wash out. Do a test first as a stain remover might need to be added for product to fully wash out. This is also skin safe!

Tar/Oil

Permanent Tar/Oil: For oil marks on a mechanic's overalls, Beth has used black tailors wax; rubbing the wax on the surface of the costume then using an iron, which is for breakdown only, she melts the wax into the fabric. She applies this several times until she had built up the coverage and shine she wanted. An alternative option for tar or oil could be to use black acrylic paint and a gloss medium. Either paint on the black first and then apply the gloss medium or mix in the gloss medium to the paint and apply. Another product, UltraTar, is made specifically for a tar/waste oil effect. It is also permanent.

Removable tar/oil: Beth has had to do grease, tar, and oil many times. She tells a story about another breakdown artist:

> one of the things you will get to do as a breakdown artist is come up with solutions to things on the fly. Jack Taggart, Head Ager Dyer on Dunkirk, had to do just that. When the tar they were given was staining the inside of the vintage rescue boats, He quickly came up with a solution that looked real and washed out. He used a mixture of hair gel, pomade hair wax, black pigment and baby soap. This mixture was very successful.

Marks

Permanent Marks: Beth recommends to be very specific when making marks on costumes:

> Marks are very specific to the character and their job or story. It can be paint spatter, grass stains, dirt marks, oil stains, etc. Refer back to your research of where these marks occur and what they look like. These marks can be made with paint, color wax sticks, or dust pounced over a greasy area makes a nice dirty removable mark. There are so many possibilities of different marks, you will have to try different things and see what works best.

Removable Marks: For dark dirt marks Beth uses a variety of products. One technique is to make up a dark dirt mark oily/grease rag, then dust the area with the mark color, then go over the top again with rag. This will make a very quick dirty mark. Beth also uses wax sticks such as: Schmere, Patin-A, and Dirty Down. These come in many different colors and are great for making detailed marks, but not so good for covering large areas.

Mold

Permanent mold: A technique Beth has used to achieve a moldy look is adding puff binder to paint:

> Gently apply a very small amount of puff binder to the fabric in little dots to where the mold needs to be. Using a hair dryer, heat the binder until it puffs up. Be very careful not to overheat and burn the surrounding material. Using acrylic paint, paint the puff binder and surrounding areas to look like mold.

Removable mold: Dirty Down Sprays have a mold color spray (UK), Beth would use this only as a base color and then paint more detail into the fabric.

Rust

Beth worked on an opera where the designer wanted there to be rust marks on the costume: "I used two different techniques to achieve the look. I found lots of research images of rust to see all the different colors and marks rust can make on fabric."

Permanent Rust: Texture Using Screens

Beth describes this process using concentrated fabric pigments, binder or extender, and silk screens:

> Using binder and pigment, mix up 3 different rust colors. Printing in layers, screen the three colors through silk screens that feature a textured image. Tape out sections on the screens to produce a more interesting images. While the first pull is still wet, move the screen only slightly and go over the same spot again in a different rust color to add depth; let the color bleed a little to get a more realistic look. The color can also be screened on and then spritzed with water so the binder bleeds, which softens the edges and dilutes the color in some places.

Permanent Rust: Objects to Create Patterns

This technique uses rusty found objects to transfer the rust onto fabric.

Supplies:

- Vinegar
- Tap water
- Rusty metal objects in a variety of sizes
- Basin/tub large enough to contain a small bath and fabric
- Spray bottle

Figure 13.13 (Top) Textured silk screen for rust effect. (Middle) Image of print on skirt fabric, with rust color binders. (Bottom) Sample using actual rust. For *Susanna* at Royal Opera House, costume designer Grace Smart.

HOW TO ADD PERMANENT RUST TO FABRIC

1. **Gear up!** Gloves, apron, decent ventilation.
2. **Set up:** add 1:1 mixture of vinegar and water to a basin, creating enough mixture to fully saturate fabric. Add fabric to soak for a half hour.
3. **Choose rusty objects** and place them on the vinegar soaked fabric (you can also wrap your fabric around the object(s).
4. **Seal in plastic to retain moisture.** You can use press and seal to keep objects flat inside and create a plastic pocket or a use a plastic Ziplock. Put this in a WARM place as rust will oxidize faster in a warm environment. Check the fabric regularly; if it is beginning to dry, spritz it with more vinegar.
5. **Leave the object** in fabric for a minimum of 24 hours.
6. **Rinse fabric.**

7. **When pressing**, make sure to use pressing cloths on both sides so rust isn't transferred to the ironing board!

Temporary Rust: Dirty Down SFX makes a rust effect paint for plastic, metals and nonporous/absorbent surfaces. This would be a good option for costume props. Additionally, Dirty Down spray has a rust color for fabrics too.

Salt Stains

Permanent Salt Stains: Using white Dye-Na-Flow, paint a concentrated line where you want the salt stain, then spritz with fresh water to blend down the color to create a defused line. Beth's experience with permanent salt stains:

> I had an accident with white Dye-Na-Flow once, where a jar was dropped and splashed on my trousers. I quickly tried to wash it out in the sink but it left a white line along the edge of paint spot. I realized, this might be a way to permanently add a salt line.

Temporary Salt Stains: Beth on removable salt stains:

> In an opera, the designer wanted the hems of trousers to look like they had waded through salt water. To achieve this effect, I dissolved salt in warm water and dipped the hems of the trousers into the solution. I then sprayed fresh water along the edge of the hem. This pushed the salt to the top edge of the water line and when dry created a white line. The more salt in the solution the stronger the white line will be. I dipped the hems a couple times and repeated the process to make it look like the character had walked through salty water several times and had built up the salt line.

Snow

Permanent Snow Using Puff Binder: Beth outlines using puff binder to create a snow look, discovered while working at the Royal Opera Hose, UK:

> Using a small amount of puff binder, dry brush lightly the wool hairs on the jacket. With a heat gun or hair drier used the hot air to puff the paint. You must be very careful with this one. Too much paint and it completely covers the area and doesn't look like snow. Also, make sure the heat gun doesn't get too close to the paint or jacket as this will scorch the material. As always, test an area and never start center front. The natural color of the binder worked for our snow. Pigment can be added if you need a different color or paint can be sprayed over the top if you need to add color or shading.

Permanent Snow With Help from Friends in Props – Plastic Flakes: A chunky and less subtle snow effect can be achieved with help from props; the material they often use to create snow resembles shredded plastic flakes. Mix the flakes with clear acrylic medium and then dab onto costumes; it really stays put! You can buy similar artificial snow flakes online. Other available products that are permanent: UltraIce – a clear Ice effect, Frost effect – frost SFX Spray, and Patin-A make a film snow, Patin-Snow. This can make a light dusting of snow to snow–slush/ice effects.

Removable Ice/Snow: Removable options are: Kryolan's Ice Effect kit (Figure 13.15) using different sized ice particles stuck to a washable sticky material called Gaffquat (most likely not cost effective but can be adhered to skin as well) and Dirty-Down Spray – Frost and Snow. The latter is UK based and may not be able to ship to US.

Burnt Clothing

Whether it's a light singe or gone through an explosion, in film this one seems to come up a lot. Beth likes to use actual flame and burn/melt the pieces of clothing, but this method is more of an art piece than can actually be used on stage. She says:

Figure 13.14 (A). Snow effect puff paint close up (B). Snow effect puff paint jacket. From *Il Trovatore*, Royal Opera House 2016. Costume Designer Meentje Nielsen.

> If you use real flame to burn and scorch your fabric it is very hard to control, you could burn the whole thing (and natural fibers burn rapidly); if it's synthetic or a blend of fibers you can get scorch marks and melting but it weakens the fibers and the garment could fall apart. I had a one-off piece that needed to look like it went through an explosion, so I was able to use real flame. To get the look right I had to get research images, but here again be very careful what

Figure 13.15 Kryolan Ice Effect can go on costumes (washable) and on skin. Kryolan.com

search words you use as there are very graphic images that can come up. I like to stick to burnt fashion pieces. This search gives you some real images of burnt fabrics but not the graphic pictures. Here is where artistic license helps. Remember the audience has come to escape from reality- they just need to believe the garment was burnt; they do not have to be confronted with an ultra-realistic image.

Permanent Burn/Scorch Using Real Flame and Paint

Beth's tips on creating a burned look: Start by using real flame – a blow torch works well, hovering over the fabric to singe and melt the fabric. Depending on the blend of fabric in your "burnt" garment, you

Figure 13.16 (A). Shirt burned with actual flame. (B). Ecru Dye-Na-Flow added (C). Added brown and pewter Dye-Na-Flow and soot. From *Commuter*, costume designer Betsy Faith Heimann.

Photo Credit: **Beth Herd.**

may get some interesting colors and textures but they most likely will not be enough to read as an explosion/large fire/etc. Try airbrushing ecru, pewter, and brown Dye-Na-Flow (or ProChem's Silk and Fabric Paint) in and around the burn areas (Figure 13.16 A, B) slowly building up layers of color to imitate burned fabric. To finish, dry brush on black, very lightly, for soot (Figure 13.15 C). When using black paint or powder, a little goes a very long way; it can obliterate all that you have done, so less is more.

Permanent Burn/Scorch Using Paint and Acrylic Sealant

Beth recounts when she had to make a burn effect without using real flame:

> Another time I needed to have the clothing look burnt and singed but could not use actual flame as we didn't want the integrity of the fabric compromised. To start, I dry brushed and airbrushed burnt colors onto the garment, in the areas I wanted the burn to be. Then to make the fabric look melted I used a translucent acrylic based sealant (NOT SILICONE). With acrylic based sealant you can add in acrylic paint or inks to add color. It is also less likely to go cloudy when it gets wet, always test first. I mixed up a burnt color and mixed in the sealant. I then applied small amounts of this to the costumes and while using a hair dryer on the sealant to help it dry faster, I squeezed the material and worked the sealant into the fabric. The finished effect was the look of melted fabric without actually melting the garment. The clear and translucent acrylic sealants are found in your home improvement stores, in the caulking and sealant aisle.

Another technique, when no torch, holes, or large-scale physical breakdown is permitted, can be used to airbrush paint in layers to build up a scorched or burned look, like Jack Taggart has done on Tom Cruise's Maverick costume (Figure 13.18).

> Dry brushing would only sit on the surface. {I built} up successive layers of airbrushed color, starting with flat white base so the later colors actually read on the black fabrics. Several scorch tones applied in order, a bit of punched up hit marks and highlights by hand, and a spare touch of gloss black puff paint for melted singed effects. Bits of texture paint here and there.[2]

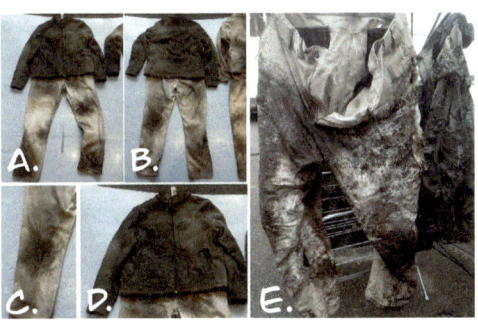

Figure 13.17 (A) Front view of burned outfit. (B) Back view. (C) Close up. (D) Close up of trouser leg. (E) Same costume actually burned with fire. For *Angel Has Fallen*, costume designer Stephanie Collie.

Photo Credit: Beth Herd.

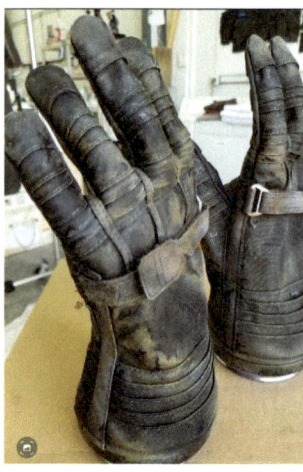  

Figure 13.18 Jack Taggart's work on *Maverick*, jacket and gloves worn by Tom Cruise.
Photo courtesy of Jack Taggart.

Blood

Adding blood should happen last. There are several removable products available commercially as well as bloods you can mix up yourself. For blood techniques and products including permanent shiny/fresh blood, blood drops and running blood, products available commercially as well as bloods you can mix up yourself, and since there is SO much other territory to cover about blood, it has its own chapter, Chapter 14.

BREAKDOWN DYEING

Sometimes, an overall base color, texture, fading, or patch dyeing is required to age costumes. Here are a few techniques using dye (and color remover).

FADING

A fairly common technique used in aging is fading. For an all over fade – the washing machine can be used at the hottest temperature the fabric can handle, adding in a strong detergent from the section "Breakdown made Easier" or the Jack Wash recipe. This might take several washes and an extended wash cycle is best. This can also be done with a large pot on a burner or dye vat, getting the water very hot (keeping the fiber content in mind), and adding the detergent(s) and letting the garment soak, stirring often. If you want a patchy fade don't stir that much and let it sit, but always keep an eye on it – you don't want it to go too far. If you want to just fade the neck and shoulders you will need a large pot on the stove top and only let the part you want to fade in the water. Be careful to keep the garment moving so you don't get a straight hard line across it. This is like a reverse ombré but instead of adding color you are trying to remove only a little bit of it. Not all garments will fade back. Where you don't have access to a stove or hot plate, Beth has used a large bucket and really hot water out of the tap or kettle with Milton sterilizing fluid. This is normally used in the UK for sterilizing baby bottles. It does work as a gentle fading agent, also.

From Rachel Pollock, I learned that some folks use Woolite heated up to almost a boil to lightly fade costumes (I have not tested this; if you decide to try this, wear a respirator in a well-ventilated space). Rit Fast Fade also works well, but is basically powdered bleach so use a respirator in a very well-ventilated room. There are many other color removing techniques that can be successfully used to fade costumes; see Chapter 6 on Removing Color. Note, in that chapter, there is a wonderful example of Jack Taggart's fade and breakdown on Tom Hank's orange suit, using bleach in concentrated amounts and then set directly in the sun. Beautiful results!

OVERDYEING

Sometimes we are given garments that are just a bit too bright and they need to be knocked back. For example a bright yellow shirt needs to look "not brand new". A fast way to fix that is to overdye the shirt in a very light version of the complementary color, so with the yellow shirt, use a very weak purple dye. We are not trying to change the color, only take back the newness. So, always start with a very weak dye solution and build up from there. Usually, union dyes are used for this purpose. See Chapter 5 on "tech" formulas using union dyes. Overdyeing can also happen in patterns to add texture. Please see Chapter 11 on Low Water Immersion for a wonderful technique to add texture to a fabric background.

Potassium Permanganate, a.k.a. the Purple Stuff

A product that is used often in film to tech white fabrics is called potassium permanganate. It creates a purple solution and if often referred to as "the purple stuff". Wear an acid/gas half face respirator, goggles, and elbow length gloves when using this product, as it is category 1 and 2 in the SDS health section. This product is also used in tiny amounts to treat eczema as it is an astringent; the amounts required to tech fabric is greater, so, don't let the medical uses fool you into not using PPE. This product is also damaging to aquatic life and wastewater so this is a huge no–no for use in areas with septic systems that do not perform secondary waste treatments. See SDS for Potassium Permanganate in the SDS Appendices in supplemental materials on the Focal Press website.

SHADE/SHADOW DYEING

You can use dyeing to add shading in your garments. This is a nice way to emphasize the fading you might have done on the shoulders or this can be a good way to put color back into the garment if too much came out when you were trying to overall fade the garment. To shade the garment, the dye color should be a slightly darker version of the garment color. If you are adding color back in, then mix up a dye similar to the original color. To add in shading on a garment top, wet and spin out excess water, then fold the garment in half vertically, lining up the side seems. I then gently lower the sides into the dye. Moving the garment in an up and down motion, in and out of the dye, trying to create an ombré effect along the sides. I then will do the same along the hem. Being careful not to create any obvious lines but to gently blend the shading along the sides and hem. This can also be done with pants/trousers and shorts. You will need to line up the inseams of each leg and then keeping the inseams at the same level, fold the legs in so that you can hold it and fit it in the pot. Gently ombré the inseams until you have reached the color you want. Then repeat this process with the out seams. Once the inseam and out seam have been dyed I usually will also dip the hem of the legs in too. Just lightly for a few inches to give a bit of weight to the bottom edge. In the photos in Figure 13.19 Beth notes:

> I have not wet the garment through I have dipped a dry garment in water just to show how when you fold the garment the areas that would dye. The harsh line is not what you want to achieve. I only did it this way to show where you want to dye. Also keep in mind the garment will be going on around a body so dye your areas with that in mind.

SWEAT PATCH DYEING

This is where you use dyeing to add in sweat stains. Make up a dye color similar to what the actual fabric color would be when it is wet, and then very carefully lower the neck line into the dye where you want the sweat stains to be. Once the color is reached rinse and spin the garment, then dip the under arm area in the same dye to get sweat stains there.

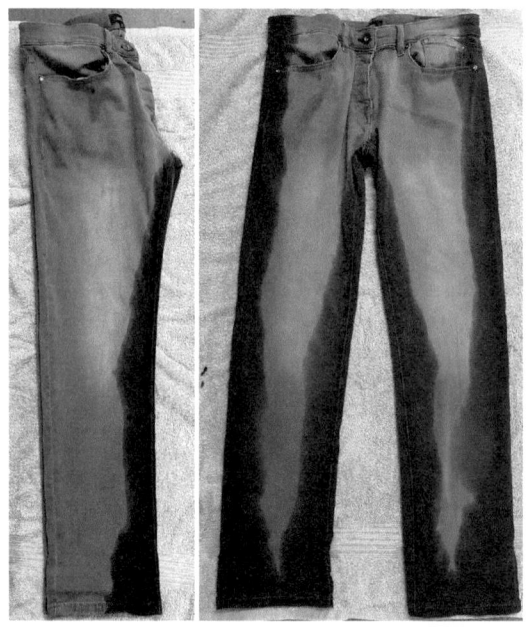

Figure 13.19 Shadow dyeing example.
Photo credit: Beth Herd.

AGING SPECIFIC COSTUME PIECES

AGING SHOES

Now that you have painstakingly broken down that costume in multiple layers, it is time to distress the shoes to match!

Beth wants us to be aware of what we are signing on for, distressing shoes:

> Like clothing, aging shoes can also range from very light to heavily broken-down. There are a few things to remember when aging shoes: they must still be able to support the actor's foot and, whatever you do, do not make them uncomfortable for the actor to wear!

Supplies
- Shoe stretcher spray or rubbing alcohol
- Wood burner
- Fine-grit sandpaper
- Leather paint or acrylic paint

HOW TO AGE SHOES

1. **Gear up!** Gloves, apron, depending on products used: a respirator.
2. **Add folds and creases** that would naturally occur when worn.
    - Beth also recommends using leather stretcher spray if the shoes are made of leather, "This softens the leather, doing this will help save your hands from getting tired. Then, work the material with your hands: folding, twisting, and imitating the action that would happen when wearing. Be careful <u>not to crush the heel</u>, you don't want this to hurt the wearer."
    - A hack we used at the Old Globe Theatre for many years: isopropyl alcohol in a mister bottle, spraying from the inside. With this technique you will have to put some of the moisture back into the shoe eventually with leather conditioner or saddle soap. We used this technique to stretch shoes too.
3. **Remove the laces.** Do not age the shoes with the laces still on the shoe.
    - Distressing laces should not be done with abrasives. This will shred the laces and potentially make them impossible for the actor to wear. When you remove the laces, you will see where you need to sand for highlights and potentially shadow for lowlights. If you want your distressing to be removable, you can do some highlights in the "peaks" where the laces create bumps when they are tightened, and do shadows in the "valleys" where the laces live in the ruts on the shoes. You can distress laces by adding some pigment to one hand and drawing the laces through that hand; this gives an uneven soil to the laces.
4. **Rough up the shoe.**
    - Beth likes to go over the high areas with a fine grit sand paper. You want to gently ruff up the area without leaving scratch lines. I use 1200 grit sandpaper very lightly on leather but 800–600 grit paper on other materials. You will need to test which will work best first. This will help imitate worn areas. Look at your research most of the worn areas are on the big toe, folds across the top of the foot, inside of the ankle and heels. She also sands over the high points of the folds as it will produce a highlight.
5. **Add shadows and dirt, then highlight.**
    - Add in shadows and dirt with paint by dry brushing on a shadow color in the folds, along the arch and other areas where the shoe might pick up dirt. Working in small areas, add in the shadow then with a clean cloth wipe off the surface. I do this several times trying to build up the color in the creases where it would naturally occur. After the shadow, add the highlights. This is where I sanded previously. I take a lighter color of the shoe and dry brush a light amount on the tops of the creases and worn areas.
    - Jack Taggart uses a soldering iron to add realistic shadows and aging to leather shoes (not black). This is a very realistic look on film but care has to be taken not to burn the shoe! See Figure 13.20 to see his work on Ryan Gosling's shoes for *The Grey Man* (2022).

Figure 13.20 Jack Taggart's work on shoes for *The Grey Man* (2022).
Source: **Photo courtesy of Jack Taggart.**

*Don't forget the soles of the shoes, any edge stitching along the soles, and laces. These areas need to be knocked back too but do not sand the stitching.

KNOCKING BACK LIGHT-COLORED SOLES

Many breakdown notes for shoes are that the soles are too bright and need to be knocked back. There are a few options for this, most of them permanent.

USING SPRAYABLE DYE OR INK

Mask off the upper part of the shoe, so that only the sole will be painted. For rubber-soled shoes like Converse, using Dye-Na-Flow or other fabric ink, and an airbrush or Preval, you can lightly spray some color on the sole to help knock it back. Be careful not to dilute these products more than 20% as they may not stick to the shoe. Ecru Dye-Na-Flow works nicely but can be a bit yellow so you might need to mix a less-yellow color. Another spray is Nu-Life (formerly Magix) shoe spray. This is VERY toxic and requires a respirator and proper ventilation. Beth likes that they have many different colors and to use a light spray of of Nu-life on the sole. She goes on to suggest "if you don't have any sprays then you can dry brush very lightly a light acrylic mix. This is more difficult to get an even cover on the sole and could scratch off".

USING DYE

Figure 13.21 Hot dye and vinegar sprayed directly on leather shoe to knock back white color. From *Clybourne Park*, costume designer Erin Carignan.

Another popular technique is to over dye the shoe all together! A popular shoe has been and will always be the tennis shoe. These always need to be knocked back because of the glaring white sole. I often dip these in a hot (not boiling) bath of ecru. If you have white leather like in Figure 13.21, you can spray ecru dye mixed with vinegar straight onto the shoes. This will also create a dingy, worn look. Some further breakdown may be needed. For this show, they only had to be "not so bright".

Hot dye and vinegar sprayed directly on leather shoe to knock back white color. From *Clybourne Park*, costume designer Erin Carignan.

Aging Hats

I have to say, I watched every season of *Little House on the Prairie,* and, not until I started in breakdown did I notice what awesome distressing was done on the hats! Hats are VERY similar to breaking down costumes so I won't bore you with every step. I *do* want you

Figure 13.22 Hat distressed by Erin Carignan for *The Whipping Man* for Charlie Robinson as Simon at the Old Globe Theatre, costume designer Denitsa Blitznakova.

to keep in mind: the head sweats. The sweat will look like a lighter version of your hat when it is wet. Generally, like costumes, there will be a highlight, mid-tone, and shadow around and under the band of the hat. There will also be dirt and grime on the brim of the hat where it is taken off or tipped in hello (if doing a cowboy film/play). Also, men put on blocked hats, like cowboy hats and fedoras, holding the front crown of their hats – so keep this in mind if you need a heavily distressed hat.

Another common hat request is to make it look wet. Please see Wet Effects in "Specialty Costume Effects" section.

THE BOTTOM LINE

Wow! We made it through a very distressing chapter! This chapter has the content of a book itself – and these techniques are invaluable and are usually only passed down from one breakdown artist to another. I hope that Beth and I ingrained in you several points: always do a test sample, never start center front, build up a beautiful breakdown in carefully considered layers, always follow safety protocols to protect your beautiful self, and experiment!!! The more time you put into the first few steps will set up how successful your final look will be. As in tailoring, if you skimp on the foundation your final piece will never look as good. You need to do all the steps and build the foundation to have realistically aged costumes.

So, now that you have the information, what are you going to do with it? Have FUN, you get to make art in a really strange and messy way!

NOTES

1   Taggart, Jack. Breakdown Artists/Ager Dyers Worldwide Networking, November 8th, 2022 https://www.facebook.com/groups/1112065622259460/permalink/2332837010182309.
2   Taggart, Jack. Facebook post on personal page, July 9th, 2022 https://www.facebook.com/groups/1112065622259460/permalink/2622823647850309.

14

ARTERIAL MOTIVES

PERMANENT AND REMOVABLE BLOOD FOR COSTUMES

As a painter–dyer you will be asked to create blood effects more than a few dozen times. Visual research paired with answers from the artistic team, combined with knowledge of products, the nature of blood, and how to apply blood, all contribute to a realistic effect. In the following chapter are detailed techniques and products that professionals use. This is not an exhaustive list of bloody techniques, but it will give you a great start. For a deep dive into blood effects for props and makeup folks, please see another punny author's fantastic source on stage blood: *Bloody Brilliant: How to Develop, Execute, and Clean Up Blood Effects for Live Performance* by Jennifer McClure.

Jack Taggart discusses blood as he recounts working with one of his filmmaking idols, Quentin Tarantino:[1]

> The infamous hat plucked from the dead man and worn by our hero in the first scene in *Django Unchained*. When you are working with Quentin Tarantino, better be prepared to keep adding more blood and gore on the day. Hell, the man will usually step in and sling the blood

Figure 14.1 Jack Taggart's blood work on *Django Unchained*.

Source: Photo courtesy of Jack Taggart.

DOI: 10.4324/9781351130677-15

with you right before shooting the scene, with Jaime right there. The man loves his blood like no other working director. He's Picasso with stage blood. Favorite brand KNB Effects (Greg Nicotero's studio of WALKING DEAD fame) and they have THE BEST line I've ever worked with. Every shade, every hue and consistency. It doesn't run pink in water and it washes out quite well. Big fan. And I gotta say, slinging blood on set toe to toe with one of my filmmaking idols . . . a HUGE high point in my life. When he and Christoph labeled me "the Dirt Magician", well, it don't get much better than that.

See Figure 14.1 for a close up of the *Django Unchained* hat in Jack's process.

All of the things Jack mentions about blood turning pink when wet, the consistency, hue, etc., are very important when choosing a blood; that choice will depend on location of the wound, when the injury occurred . . . See Figure 14.2 for a list of questions you should ask the creative team when tasked with adding blood to costumes. Even though the blood he mentions is not sold on the public market, I offer discussion on some other brands that work pretty well.

QUESTIONS TO ASK ABOUT BLOOD...

- WHAT IS THE SOURCE OF THE BLOOD?
- WHAT CREATED THE WOUND AND WHAT KIND OF FORCE WAS USED?
- WHEN DID THE WOUND OCCUR: IT JUST HAPPENED, YESTERDAY, LAST WEEK?
- DOES THE BLOOD NEED TO BE PERMANENT OR REMOVABLE?
- WILL THE PERFORMER BE GETTING WET?
- DOES THE CLOTHING NEED TO BE LAUNDERED EVERY NIGHT?
- WILL I NEED TO DO MULTIPLES?
- DOES THE BLOOD EFFECT NEED TO LOOK REALISTIC OR DOES IT WANT TO BE EXAGGERATED?
- WILL THE PERFORMER BE USING BLOOD ON THEIR SKIN THAT SHOULD MATCH BLOOD ON THE COSTUME?

Figure 14.2 Consider these questions when you are asked to design or execute a blood effect.

When you have answers to these questions, then your research can begin! Do not look at other artists' versions of these bloody wounds or splatters – you may be re-creating something that looks very fake. A really great website for real gore (warning: this can get pretty gross) is Sciencephoto.com; there are many others but this one is nice because you can search by keyword.

Through your research, you will find that blood varies in color from bright red to dark red, depending on the age of blood and where it is bleeding from body! Blood that is coming directly from the heart (**arterial blood**) will be bright red as it is freshly oxygenated, while blood from your hands and feet (**veinous blood**) might be a bit darker since oxygen becomes depleted from blood the farther it gets from the heart, and as this happens blood becomes darker red/purple. The darkest blood is dried blood and usually found at the edge of a pool of blood, where the

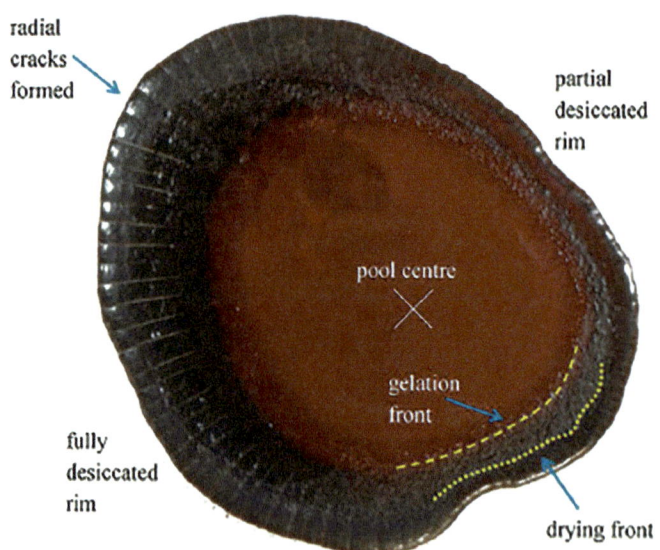

Figure 14.3 Close-up view of a drying pool, with several defined properties of the pool. The yellow dashed and dotted lines represent the gelation and drying front, respectively.

Photo Courtesy of *Forensic Science International*.

blood would dry first. See Figure 14.3 to see a close up of a pool of blood as it dries! You can clearly see that the edges are darker, the gelation front is a mid-tone, and the brightest blood is in the center of the pool. As blood ages and dries a fabric, it gets darker and can even turn into grey/yellow tones. This all depends on the specific fabrics, age of blood, amount of blood, etc. Another great image, found in an article in *Forensic International*,[2] analyzes blood pools as they dry over time. This is excellent research for a project that includes several stages of blood (Figure 14.4).

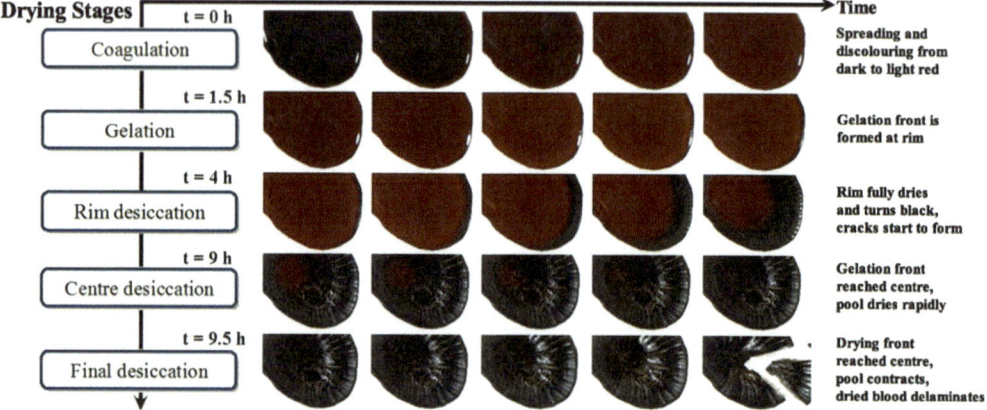

Figure 14.4 Drying stages of blood and how they change in appearance.

Photo Courtesy of *Forensic Science International*.

Beth Herd feels strongly about researching the conditions concerning blood on costumes:

> You need lots of information to be able to make a blood effect believable. Start by reading through the script and find any details or references about the blood or wound you can, ask the designer/director about the action and placement of the blood or

wound and then carefully look for research images. When doing a search for blood effects on the internet choose your search words carefully, there are very graphic images that can come up. I like watching crime scene dramas because they actually give you a lot of forensic information about wounds and blood that aren't too graphic.

Whatever the blood you are using, whether it be from a commercial source or homemade, do MANY tests and wait until they dry to fully understand the blood's properties. For example, if the blood you've sampled turns pinky purple as it dries, which looks super fake, then you will want to tweak your color mixture or choose a different commercial product.

PERMANENT BLOOD

There are many ways and products to create permanent blood. Some techniques are better for stage or film, just make sure to work with the makeup department if your blood is to match makeup blood.

For permanent blood Beth prefers

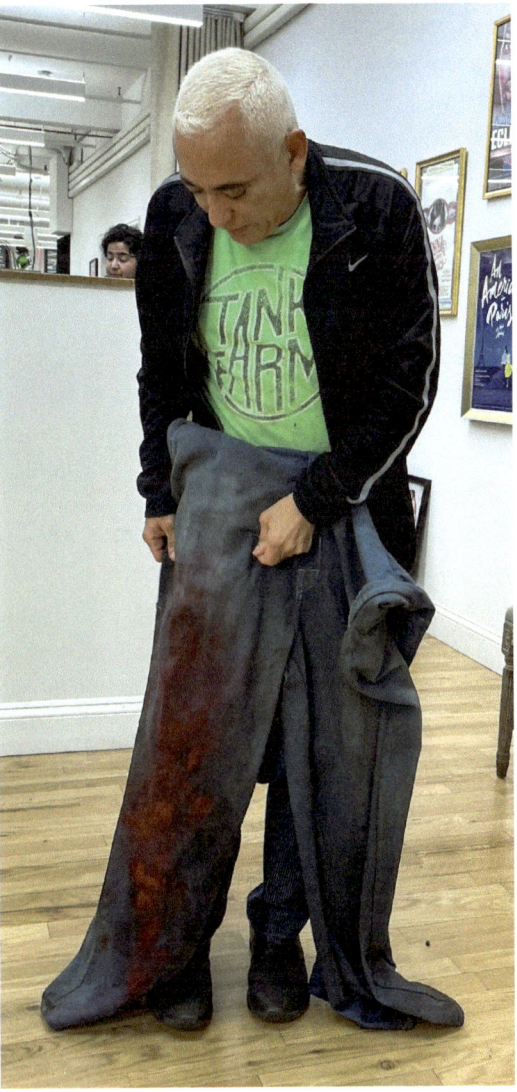

acrylic paint mixed to the correct color for the action and story. Then, once dry and if the action calls for fresh blood, I paint a layer of gloss medium on top to create a shiny wet look. Always test first as acrylic dries darker. For runny blood look, try Dye-Na-Flow.

Blood should always be transparent to look like real blood, even if it is dry.

An interesting thing to think about when applying blood came up in conversation with painter–dyer extraordinaire Hochi Asiatico, when he showed me the garment he was currently working on for a Broadway show. He said that in the fitting, the actor told him that the script says the wound was supposed to be near the front of the leg but that he would be sitting in a sideways position respective to the audience, and therefore they would only see the side of his leg. Hochi chose to move the darker, more concentrated areas of blood over to the side of the leg closest to the audience so the effect would be more potent. See Figure 14.5 for Hochi and the blood effect in progress. This is evidence that effects don't always make sense out of context!

Figure 14.5 Hochi Asiatico holds up costume with blood effect placed where it will be the most potent for the audience, not where it makes the most sense related to the wound.

WET, SHINY BLOOD

A costume designer and technician, Stephanie Nguyen, created a beautiful wet blood look for *Vietgone* at East-West Players (Figure 14.4) using the Smooth-on product, Dragon Skin. She said there were audible gasps in the audience when the blood-soaked shirt was revealed!

Dragon Skin comes in different hardnesses, opacities, and working times and Smooth-On sells a lot of companion products to change the quality of the silicone. It is a platinum silicone, which means it is skin safe and will not poison your performer. The pros of this product: has a high shine wet look, is dry cleanable, machine washable, once it's set it won't bleed, and has the weight of blood-soaked fabric. The cons of Dragon Skin include that it will keep the shape of whatever form you paint it on, can become tacky if it's not mixed properly, it's expensive, fabric does not retain original hand, if it dries with wrinkles or folds in the fabric they will become permanent,

Figure 14.6 Tong's nightmare scene in East-West Player's *Vietgone*. Costume designer Stephanie Nguyen.
Photo courtesy of Christina Jun.

and it has a long setting time. The silicone can be tinted with Silc-pig, Smooth-On's silicone tint. A little of this product goes a long way and is mixed to part A of the silicone before mixed with part B; see colors to create blood look in Figure 14.2: blue, red, brown, and blood red. Always use disposable brushes or tongue depressors when using this product!

BLOOD DROPS

To create blood drops on a garment like someone has been hit in the nose and their bloody nose dripped down to their shirt, I find using an eye-dropper (looks like a tiny turkey baster) with a very watery dye–paint, like Dye-Na-Flow or ProChem's Silk and Fabric Paint, works wonders. I have even put on a shirt and dropped the blood from the general area of my nose to create this effect. Whatever the effect, examine your research and look where the blood is concentrated, where it is wiped on the costume, and where the drops or flow of blood appears.

BLOOD SPLATTER

Splatter fairly common blood effect. It is important to think about what direction the blood is supposed to appear to have splattered from before you begin splattering. Blood spatters in many sizes but usually there are areas of larger splatter, medium, and fine splatter. Fabric paint, Dye-Na-Flow or ProChem's Silk and Fabric Paint can be used with this technique as well as any of the removable bloods, as long as they are of the correct consistency. Splattering can be achieved by loading up a dense stiff brush with blood mixture and, while holding the brush in one hand, bluntly tap that hand with the other. This can also be done by tapping your brush with a stick or another brush. This will create less directional blood splatter that looks more realistic. No matter how hard you try, with this technique there are always some tails to the splatter, which indicate direction. For finer spatter, use a smaller brush like a toothbrush. To create large drops of splatter, combine this technique with blood drops, previously.

REMOVABLE BLOOD

The best commercial removable bloods are Fleet Street, Gravity and Momentum's Blood Jam, Pigs Might Fly South, and Kryolan. Whatever the blood used, it is advised to have a bucket with warm water and detergent ready to plunge the bloody garment in, right after the performer removes the costume. This will ensure the best chance of blood removal. All bloods, even ones advertised as removable, should be tested on a small area of the costume to make sure it washes out. We (Beth and I) did a sampling of several commercial and DIY bloods for our workshop at USITT; see Figure 14.8 for before and after pics as evidence of what washed out the best! We found that the detergent based homemade bloods washed out the best right next to Blood Jam. See Table 14.1 to see how commercial and DIY bloods compare! Many of the recipes for blood can be found after the comparison chart.

Removable bloods have a limited number of bases: corn syrup, Hershey's chocolate and strawberry syrup, dish soap, laundry detergent, baby shampoo, and methyl cellulose. Often, cornstarch, tahini, peanut butter or other thickening agents are added to these bases to thicken the viscosity. To color these bases, the options are GEL food coloring, Kryolan Aqua color, or tempura paints. Kryolan reds can stain, so make sure that you test first.

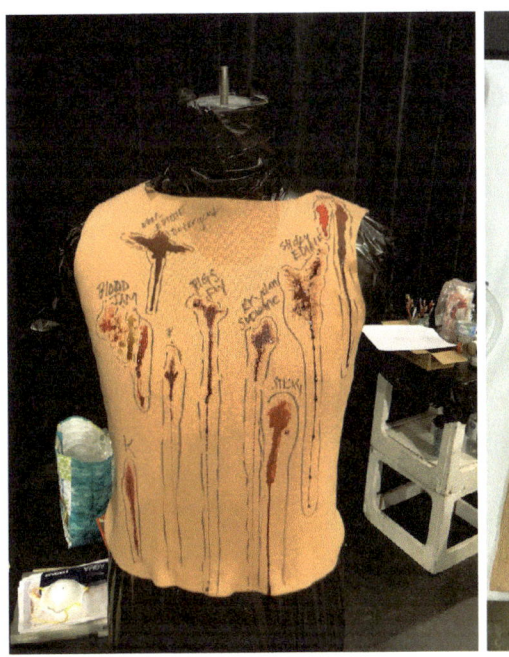

Figure 14.7 Removable blood test on silk shell before and after washing (blood sat for an hour). Products used left to right: Blood Jam, Kryolan HD Blood (below Blood Jam), Detergent Blood Recipe (Bev Boyd), Pigs Might Fly South, Kryolan Supreme Dark, Sticky Blood Recipe Non-edible (Bev Boyd), Sticky Blood Edible (Bev Boyd), Dish Soap Base Blood lighter, Dish Soap Base Blood darker. Non-edible detergent and Kryolan Extreme Dark were the only ones not to wash out.

Beth's hilarious bloody story:

> One of my favorite blood stories is when I was working on a historic battle film. It was the epic battle day, grey and rainy. All the soldiers lined up and then charged into the battle lead by a Lord on a white horse. Special effects were chucking mud and blood at the actors as they were battling. The director called cut and re set, the actors lined back up, then action. They all charged into battle again lead by the Lord on a **pink** horse. Special effects got the cheapest blood they could find (as they do) and it turned pink in the rain. It also stained all the costumes which were light natural colors to pink, and it was not removable!! We did find that when we soaked the pink stained garments in fabric softener it helped to remove the stains. For some of the costumes we had to paint over the pink stains and send them back to the actors that way. I'm not sure how long the poor horse stayed pink.

Figure 14.8 (Left) Hand-painted tunic before washing with Pigs Might Fly South removable blood. (Right) Washed! Voila! For *Outlaw King*. Costume designer Jane Pretrie.

Source: Photo Courtesy of Beth Herd.

Table 14.1 Commercial and DIY blood products and notes.

Product	• Products Offered	• Notes
Fleet Street Bloodworks (US)	• Two color options: fresh and dark.	• It doesn't turn pink in the rain. • **EDIBLE.**
Blood Jam by Gravity and Momentum (US)	• Blood Jam, Blood Juice, and Blood Syrup. • Two color options: bright red and dark red.	• Washes out really well. • Product has relatively short shelf life of 6 months (G&M recommends using within 60 days). • **EDIBLE.**
Pigs Might Fly South (UK)	• Two colors: fresh and dark.	• Goes a little orange when watered down. • Washes out great! • **EDIBLE.**

Product	Products Offered	Notes
Kryolan Blood (US and UK)	• Blood Paste, Drying Blood, F/X Blood, HD Blood, Show Blood, Simulated Blood, Special Blood, Supreme Blood External, Supreme Blood Internal. • See a fabulous chart from Kryolan Australia's website: • Search for "Kryolan AU Fake blood"	• Will wash out but it goes pink when it gets wet. • Looks very realistic and works well on camera. • Many different products offered. • Some products are food-grade (edible). • Not used much in film (exterior shots) just in case of rain. • **Some are EDIBLE, some non-edible. See Kryolan's website.**
Detergent Blood Recipe (Bev Boyd)		• Thicker and more opaque blood. Creates nice drops and drips. • Has a shelf life of 6 months. • The red food coloring seems to want to stain the fabric so it's best to test on your fabric first! • Alter detergent used for specific fiber content. • **Non-EDIBLE.**
Sticky Blood Edible (Bev Boyd)		• Will stain your garment. • This blood is good for any need that involved thick blood that stays in place. It is very sticky because of the corn syrup and needs hot water to wash out. Has a shelf life of 6 months. • **EDIBLE.**
Sticky Blood Recipe Non-edible (Bev Boyd		• Will NOT stain your garment. **Add detergent to the "Sticky Blood" recipe.** • This blood is good for any need that involves thick blood that stays in place. It is very sticky because of the corn syrup and needs hot water to wash out. Has a shelf life of 6 months. • **Non-EDIBLE.**
Dish Soap Base Blood (Bev Boyd)		• This blood is a sticky blood that can be used on costume and washes out with warm or hot water within 3 days on the costume. • **Non-EDIBLE.**

BLOOD RECIPES: MAKE YOUR OWN BLOOD!!!
Many of these recipes come from the veteran head of wardrobe of the Old Globe Theater in San Diego, Beverly Boyd, who spent many hours of her life creating, tweaking, and washing out these blood recipes. There are a few additional recipes from McClure's *Bloody Brilliant*[3] as well!

SOAPY BLOOD RECIPE BY BEVERLY BOYD
This type of blood **is not edible,** squirt bottle ready, and washes out of clothing fairly well. This is most likely due to the presence of liquid detergent. This blood is thick and creates nice drops and drips. Has a shelf life of 6 months. The red food coloring has the capacity to stain fabric, so test first!

Stir each of the ingredients together until well blended.

Supplies
- 1/3rd cup of liquid detergent (or "4 second pour" as Bev puts it)
- 5 tablespoons corn starch
- Just under 1 tbl red food coloring gel
- Just under 1 tsp caramel food coloring gel
- 3 drops blue food coloring gel
- Measuring cups, measuring spoons, gloves, apron

ARTERIAL BLOOD RECIPE BY BEVERLY BOYD
This **edible** blood replicates arterial blood: blood that is squirting directly out of an artery. It is water based so it flows well. It can be put into a spray bottle, blood pouch, and the mouth. This washes well **if** laundered in hot water the same evening *after* a cold-water hand wash with Shout, of the blood stains. Would not be good on dyed fabric. Has a shelf life of 6 months to 1 year.

Mix all ingredients into a bowl and whisk together till fully dissolved.

Supplies:
- 3 cups of water
- 2 teaspoons of red food coloring gel
- 1/2 teaspoon brown food coloring gel
- 2 drops blue food coloring gel
- Measuring cups, measuring spoons, gloves, apron

STICKY BLOOD RECIPE BY BEVERLY BOYD
As the title states, this blood is sticky! It is **edible** blood that will stick to the actors face/skin but harder to wash out of fabric potentially staining your garment. This would be a good candidate for a pre-wash of fabric softener to create a light barrier between blood and costume. This blood is great when an edible blood is required that doesn't run too much. Has a shelf life of 6 months.

Stir together until blended.

Supplies:
- 1 Cup Karo Syrup (Light corn Syrup)
- 1/2 Teaspoon red food coloring gel
- 1/2 teaspoon caramel food coloring gel
- Three drops of blue food coloring gel
- Measuring cups, measuring spoons, gloves, apron

DISH SOAP BASE BLOOD BY BEVERLY BOYD
This **non-edible** blood is a sticky blood that can be used on costumes and washes out with warm or hot water within 3 days of first contact with the costume. Has a shelf life of 3 months.

Stir together until color is even.

Supplies:
- 2/3rds cups Corn Syrup (Karo)
- 1/3rd cup Chocolate Syrup
- 1/3rd cup clear dish soap (Joy or store brand)
- 3 to 5 drops of red food coloring
- 1 to 2 drops of blue food coloring for desired color
- Measuring cups, measuring spoons, gloves, apron

CORN STARCH BLOOD – THIN BY BEVERLY BOYD
This is an **edible,** non-sticky, no-soap blood that has a nice rich color. This is Bev's go-to as it washes out of fabrics very well.

- 2 cups cold water
- 3 tbl cornstarch
- 1/2 tsp red food coloring gel
- 1/4th tsp + dribble caramel food coloring gel
- 4 drops blue food coloring gel
- Measuring cups, measuring spoons, gloves, apron
- Food-safe pan (if going on skin)
- Burner

Mix water and cornstarch together in a food-safe pot over medium heat. Cook 2 minutes and stir. Add food coloring, stirring until desired consistency is reached. Use less water for a thicker blood mixture that clings well to skin.

THE BEST BLOOD RECIPE EVER BY MICHELLE MOODY FROM BLOODY BRILLIANT[4]
For this **edible** recipe McClure writes,

> It is recommended to use Hershey's® brand chocolate syrup or any other high-quality syrup, as cheaper versions are not as thick. If you only have access to or a budget for a generic brand, you may need to add more corn starch to thicken the recipe. The same is true for using Coffee Mate® brand creamer – generic brands did not wash out as

well. This recipe was developed to wash out of a lightweight white fabric. Michelle says she read that Coffee Mate® helped remove tough stains and thought to try it in her blood recipe that was staining fabric in tests, and it did the trick.

Supplies:
- 16 oz dark corn syrup
- 250 ml chocolate syrup
- 1 C warm water
- 1 tbl (heaping) corn starch
- 1 tbl (heaping) Coffee Mate®
- 3 drops yellow food coloring
- Add red food coloring to make it look natural

McClure adds mixing instructions:

> Heat the corn syrup and the chocolate syrup in a pot on low. Dissolve the corn starch and Coffee Mate® in the water and mix it into the syrup. After this, add the food coloring. Let this all warm for about 15 more minutes, mixing and squishing the Coffee Mate® blobs with a fork every 5 minutes.

> Press a sieve on the top of the blood to help blend the unmixed chunks of Coffee Mate. Pour into storage containers and let cool to room temperature before closing the container Once cool, this can be stored in a refrigerator for up to two weeks. Makes approx. 4 cups.

> If you want it to be extra thick, triple the amount of dry goods.

METHYL CELLULOSE BASE RECIPE FROM MCCLURE'S BLOODY BRILLIANT[5]

Also from *Bloody Brilliant*, this **non-edible** recipe uses Methyl cellulose as its thickener:

> This thick, clear base can be used with any colorant. It is especially economical for large quantities of blood. It needs to rest overnight to fully gel, so this is not a good option for a recipe that is needed quickly.

Supplies:
- 3 qt near-boiling water
- 1 qt cold water
- 1 C methyl cellulose
- 2-3 additional quarts hot water

McClure's mixing instructions and options for coloring:

> Add 3 qt near-boiling water into heat-resistant mixing container Slowly add 1 C methyl cellulose to near boiling water until fully dissolved. Once dissolved, add 1 qt cold water Continue to stir mixture occasionally as it cools to avoid separation. Allow mixture to sit overnight while refrigerated to fully gel. Add additional hot water to achieve ideal

blood thickness. Coloring options: Tempera paint – approx. 1 tbsp per quart, to desired color [or] Beet root powder – approx. 2 tbsp per quart, to desired color.

CLEANING COSTUMES

To ensure that blood washes out of costumes there are many factors including tests, time, barriers, and detergents. Tests must be done allowing blood to stay on fabric for some time; in *Bloody Brilliant*, McClure comments on testing wash-out over a period of time:

> Some effects happen at the very end of the show and can be immediately cleaned up, and costumes can be laundered as soon as they are taken off. Others take place in the first act and the actor wears that costume for another two to three hours before it can make its way to the wardrobe supervisory. A blood recipe or product might wash out beautifully if only on fabric for five minutes but irreparably stain if hours pass before it is cleaned up. Use the amount of time you determine for you production as the minimum. Amount of time the blood is left before cleaning during testing.

Sometimes adding a barrier like fabric softener to a wash before adding blood may help as it can create a film on the clothing. This will depend on your actor, as some have allergies to strong detergents like fabric softener. Choosing specific detergents that will work with specific fiber content will also help the cause depending on actor allergies. For a presentation on laundering stage blood from a variety of fabrics, please see the *Out Damn Spot!* USITT presentation by Holly Poe Durbin and Jessica Mueller.[6]

THE BOTTOM LINE

Remember to take all of the facts and requirements into account before reaching for that bottle of blood or box of blood-making supplies! Does it need to be edible, washable, permanent, always shiny?? Then start with samples as usual! Take note when blood supplies stain your hands. This means the blood will most likely stain costumes too. And don't forget to have a bloody good time.

NOTES

1. Taggart, Jack. "Breakdown Artists/Ager Dyers Worldwide Networking Group." *Facebook*, February 13th, 2021. www.facebook.com/groups/1112065622259460/user/545347613.
2. Nick Laan, Fiona Smith, Celine Nicloux and David Brutin. "Morphology of Drying Blood Pools." *Forensic Science International*, vol. 267, 2016, pp. 104–109. https://www.sciencedirect.com/science/article/pii/S0379073816303358.
3. McClure, Jennifer. *Bloody Brilliant: How to Develop, Execute, and Clean Up Blood Effects for Live Performance*. New York, NY: Routledge, 2022.
4. McClure, Jennifer. *Bloody Brilliant: How to Develop, Execute, and Clean Up Blood Effects for Live Performance*. New York, NY: Routledge, 2022.
5. McClure, Jennifer. *Bloody Brilliant: How to Develop, Execute, and Clean Up Blood Effects for Live Performance*. New York, NY: Routledge, 2022.
6. Mueller, Jessica and Holly Poe Durbin. "Out Damn Spot." PDF Presentation, 2010. https://pomo2k.files.wordpress.com/2010/03/out-damn-spot-powerpoint.pdf.

GLOSSARY

Acid brush: disposable brush used first by the plumbing industry to apply acid flux to pipes.

Additives: chemicals that can change the chemical structure of a bath, thus facilitating many processes including but not limited to bonding dye to fiber, softening water, lowering pH, etc.

Additive color: how color is visually perceived when colors are mixed.

Analogous color: colors next to each other on the color wheel. Examples: green, blue–green, yellow–green.

Ammonium Sulfate: Used mainly as an additive to acid dye baths to slow the strike time of dye.

Arashi shibori: pole-wrapping fabric and binding and scrunching fabric. Also known as broom stick resist.

Arterial blood: blood that is freshly oxygenated as it is coming directly from the heart and will be bright red in color.

Auxiliaries: Dyeing auxiliaries includes dye-fixing agents (like Retayne), cationizing agents, dispersing and leveling agents, etc. Interchangeable with additives.

Burn Test: a test used to burn fabric and identify the fiber content.

Aqueous solution: dye bath or liquid solution.

Cats Paw: roughing tool with many sharp needles attached to a replaceable pad at the end. Used to tear and shred fabric and leather.

Batching: to wrap dyed materials in plastic and allow to cure either in or out of the sun, from several hours to a day. I prefer to use black plastic as it creates a hotter environment.

Batik: process using wax to create resist that is then crackled and overdyed. Has characteristic crackling in variety of colors throughout.

Binder: compound that binds pigment and other items to fabric.

Brayer: small hand roller used to apply ink or paint thinly to a surface.

Bullet steamer: a tool used to steam set fabric after it is dyed.

Burnishing: polishing leather with sandpaper or a rotary tool to give it a high shine and sealed finish. This technique can age leather as well.

Carrier: chemical component that carries the dye into the fiber by changing the physical properties of the fiber.

Calsolene Oil: This product can be added to a dye bath or pre-soak/scour to break the surface tension of water even more than an industrial detergent.

Chalk brush: a brush, typically round, that can hold a lot of paint, used in the home-improvement industry for chalk paints. Breakdown artists love these; they create strokes of a very painterly hand.

Chip brush: somewhat disposable brushes that were originally used to sweep away wood chips from machinery. These are great for applying material when a smooth finish isn't required.

Chromophore: the color part of the molecule that is removed or becomes invisible from discharge process.

Citric acid crystals: powdered substance that lowers the pH of a dye bath. Used in acid dyeing. Mid-level acidity.

Color: any color visible to the human eye.

Color fastness: a textile's resistance to fading or running; this is a property of the dye itself and is affected by the processing techniques.

Color primaries: the principal hues used to mix colors into a variety of color.

Complementary colors: colors found directly opposite on the color wheel from each other.

Concentrated pigments: pigments that bond with fabric when mixed with a binder or extender. Very little pigment is required for saturated color.
Cool colors: colors that evoke cool temperatures: blue, green, and purple.
Compressor: device used to power air tools, like an airbrush.
Crock test: a test performed by wiping a wet cotton rag on leather (or fabric) to see if any dye rubs off; tests whether all dye is bonded with material.
Deconstructed printing: a printing process using dye-saturated print paste to create the design on a silk screen. The design breaks down with every pull of the silk screen.
Devore: the process used to create a motif by burning a specific fiber from a fabric blend.
Diazo emulsion: a chemical compound that, when mixed with sensitizer, decomposes when exposed to light. Un-sensitized photo emulsion.
Direct application: the process of adding dye directly to the substrate without immersing fabric in an immersion bath (immersion dyeing).
Discharging: removing dye from fabric.
Discharge print paste: paste created by mixing sodium alginate thickener and a color remover like Thiox.
Drawing fluid: the substance that temporarily fills the pores of a silkscreen to resist a design area to pull screen filler over. Later is washed out to reveal design.
Dropper: a tool that can pick up small increments of paint/dye and drop them accurately in the desired location.
Dry brushing: technique where paint is added to a brush, then some is removed on a towel, creating a look made by a "dry" brush. Adds light amounts of paint to fabric.
Dye classes: groups of dyes based on what fibers will bond with specific dyes and/or how the dyes or applied.
Dye concentrate: this is a concentrate made with dye powder and urea water that can be diluted for immersion dyeing or used as is for direct application.
Edgecote: paint specifically created to coat the edge and bottom of leather soles.
Exhausting agent: usually salt, facilitates the movement of dye molecules to the fiber, which "exhausts" dye from the dyebath.
FEV: French enamel varnish; used to patina surfaces.
Film positive: acetate print or drawing used to create print using photo emulsion. Synonymous with print film.
Fixative: chemical that fixes dye to fiber; is introduced usually after the dyeing process to ensure dyes with poor wash fastness remain intact in the fiber.
Fugitive dye: dye that has not bonded with material; rubs off easily in a crock test.
Generic name: the name given to a product usually related to the product's chemical origin.
Glacial acetic acid (food grade): a very concentrated acetic acid with very little liquid (especially compared to vinegar) at a whopping 99.7% acetic acid. It gets the name glacial because it becomes ice when cooled to 61.7°F/16.5°C.
Glauber's salt: a type of salt that some like to use when dyeing silk, nylon, or wool and using fiber-reactive turquoise; the claim is that it can yield brighter colors!
Gutta resist: solvent-based material used to create lines in serti technique.
Hudson sprayer: large-scale sprayer traditionally used for yard applications; can be used to cover more area with paint and dye.
Hue: colors perceived by the human eye that can only be created by red, yellow, and blue lights.
Hydro phobic: water-hating.
Ikat tape: tape used for resist that is non-adhesive.

Incident light: light that falls on a subject.
Ink side: the side of a silkscreen that ink is applied to. The "back" of the screen.
***Itajime shibori*:** folding and clamping fabric.
***Kanoko shibori*:** synonymous with western tie-dye. Creates circular shape.
***Kumo shibori*:** spider *shibori*; creates web-looking circle.
Leveling: evenness in color.
Leveling agent: substance that helps the dye penetrate evenly into leather or fabric.
Ludigol: keeps the dyes from reducing as they normally do when mixed with water, hence creating more vibrant colors.
Mesh count: The tightness of the weave of a screen. Higher = better print resolution.
Metamerism: the ability for the human eye to perceive a variety of mixtures of colored light as the same color.
Metaphos: additive used to soften water.
Milsoft: an industrial fabric softener that can help if your dye process has left your fabric rough or stiff.
Monochromatic color: same color of varying chroma and value.
Mordant: chemicals that create a bond between dye and fiber; typically used with natural dyes.
***Muira shibori*:** looped binding; looks like water.
Needle board: a tool that is fashioned with needles sticking up to nestle into any kind of pile fabric and allow the fabric to be ironed.
Negative stencil: a stencil made by removing material to create a design.
Non-iodized salt: usually used as an exhausting agent in dyeing. It has an electrostatic charge that pushes dye through the water on to the fabric but at low pH can actually hold dye off of the fiber.
***Nui shibori*:** stitched *shibori*.
Ombré: a gradient of hues or a gradient of shades of one hue.
Open time: the time paint will dry out.
Overdyeing: when an entire garment or fabric is dyed a solid color or continuous texture.
OSHA: Occupational Health and Safety Administration. A federal entity that sets standards for SDS sheets and other workplace conditions.
Permanent breakdown: breakdown materials and techniques that cannot be reversed, hence permanent.
Positive stencil: a stencil made by cutting a shape out of stencil material to block areas in that stencil's shape.
Pre-sensitized emulsion: photo emulsion that has sensitizer added already. This is what the pros use.
Pre-Val sprayer: an aerosol sprayer that siphons from a glass jar; any thinned material will flow through this tool to create a spray painted or airbrushed look.
Print film: the acetate your design is printed or drawn on to create the design to be burned. Synonymous with film positive.
Print paste: a paste consisting of a mixture that includes sodium alginate thickener. This paste is the vehicle for dye to stay where it is placed, allowing fine detailed lines and longer cure times.
Print side: the side of a silkscreen that is in contact with and faces the fabric. The "front" of a screen.
Pulling a screen: the process of printing a silkscreened image.
Puff binder: a compound that will bind pigment to fabric and, when heated, will puff up.

Reclaim: to use reclaimant to remove emulsion from a silkscreen.
Reducing Agent: a chemical used to make specific dye pigments ready to bond with specific fibers. Often this is hydrosulfite and thirourea dioxide.
Registration marks: marks that allow one to match up a stencil, screen, or stamp to ensure proper spacing and placement.
Removable breakdown: breakdown materials and techniques that can be washed or dry-cleaned out.
Retayne: fixative that helps positively charged dye molecules to improve adherence to fabric.
Scouring: using an industrial detergent in conjunction with soda ash to wash out any remaining oils, gums, sericin in fibers.
Safety data sheet: these sheets provide basic health and safety information about products handled in the workplace. Formerly known as MSDS (material safety data sheet).
Saturation or chroma: the intensity level of a hue. Bright to dull.
Screen filler: a substance that blocks all pores in a silkscreen.
Screen printing mesh: the "silk" fabric portion of a silkscreen. It can be made of polyester or silk and comes in a variety of mesh sizes and weaves.
Secondary colors: colors created by mixing two primary hues.
Serti technique: means "to close fence"; technique to create fine lines in fenced areas and add dye to areas.
Shades: any hue that black is added to.
Shibori: Japanese art of resist by squeezing, folding, or clamping material and overdyeing.
Sinew: string that mimics animal sinew and sticks to itself. Great for *shibori* using wrapping.
Soda ash: a chemical that causes a molecular reaction to take place between fabric and dye. Also known as sodium carbonate. Also used to scour fabric before dyeing.
Sodium alginate: thickener used to create print paste made from seaweed.
Sodium hydrosulphite ("hydro"): this additive is used to reduce vat dyes, removes color from fabric, and helps whiten antique textiles as it is not as aggressive as bleach. It is the main reducing agent for indigo dye, a type of vat dye. The main component in Rit and Jaquard Color Remover.
Split complementary: a hue plus two hues on either side of the complementary color.
Stencil bridges: areas added to a stencil design to allow the center portions of designs to remain intact and not fall out like a doughnut hole.
Strike: the moment the dye takes to the fiber. Dyes have different strike times; red strikes first.
Substantivity: the chemical bond that forms between fiber and dye. The higher the substantivity, the stronger the bond.
Subtractive color: how light is perceived when reflected off of a surface; how the surface absorbs color affects which colors we perceive.
Surfactants: wetting agents in the form of industrial detergents, which break the surface tension of water.
Teching: to dye garment in a weak dye bath in order to make a color less vibrant or to look dirty or used.
Tertiary colors: colors created by mixing all three primary hues; often an earthy palette.
Test: weight of string.
Thiourea dioxide ("Thiox"): a reducing agent that lifts specific types of dye. Must be used hot. Released an acid gas as it decomposes – wear a respirator!
Tints: any hue that white is added to.
Tjanting: tool used to create fine lines in batik process.
Toggle dry: a technique used to stretch leather over a frame to prevent shrinkage.

Tone: any hue that grey is added to.

Toning: to dye using complements and other colors to slightly change the color of fabric.

Trade name: the brand name of a product.

Urea: a synthetic nitrogen compound that increases the solubility of dye. It makes dye think it is in more water than it really is, so this is great for mixing up concentrated solutions.

Value or lightness: darkness or lightness of color.

Vectorize: the process of turning a pixel-based drawing into a vector-based drawing.

Veinous blood: blood from your hands and feet has less oxygen and is darker in color.

Vent box: usually portable but sometimes built into a wall, these boxes have one open end and a back wall or ceiling that houses a vacuum to suck the air through filters and either expel filtered air into the room or outside.

Vent booth: similar in design to a vent box but larger; one can completely stand inside a vent booth.

Vinegar: very little acid at 4–10% and a lot of water; used to lower the pH of a dyebath.

Warm colors: colors that evoke warm temperatures or temperatures of heat: orange, red, yellow.

Water-based resist: water-based resist used in serti technique.

Washfast: the dye stays in the fabric and does not wash out. This happens when a chemical bond of dye and fiber cannot be broken. Poor wash fastness means dye washes out of fabric and fabric eventually fades.

Washout: in terms of good or poor, how well the design burned into an emulsion-coated screen washes out. Poor washout is a result of the screen being overexposed, hence blocking screen fibers; good washout occurs at the proper exposure to light, leaves the intended print area open on the screen.

Water insoluble: will not dissolve in water.

Water-soluble: able to be dissolved in water.

APPENDIX 1: BIBLIOGRAPHIC REFERENCE

A bibliographic list of useful dye books! There are many more, but these are the ones I have personally used.

BATIK
- Fraser-Lu, Sylvia. *Indonesian Batik: Processes, Patterns & Places*. Oxford University Press, 1986.
- Krevitsky, Nik. *Batik Art and Craft*. New York, NY: Reinhold Publishing Corporation, 1964.
- Meilach, Dona Z. *Contemporary Batik and Tie-Dye; Methods, Inspiration, Dyes*. New York, NY: Crown Publishers, 1973.
- Samuel, Evelyn. *Introducing Batik*. London: Batsford; New York, NY: Watson-Guptill, 1968.

BREAKDOWN IMAGE SOURCES
- Barrett, Sue and Katy Rutherford. *Worn Volume 1*. London: The Vintage Showroom, 2015.
- Beardsley, John, William Arnett, Paul Arnett and Jane Livingston. *The Quilts of Gee's Bend*. Atlanta, GA and Houston: Tinwood Books in Association with the Museum of Fine Arts, 2002.
- Brodie, Mike. *Mike Brodie: Tones of Dirt and Bone*. Santa Fe, NM: Twin Palms Publishers, 2014.
- Brodie, Mike and Jack Woody. *Mike Brodie: A Period of Juvenile Prosperity*. Santa Fe, NM: Twin Palms Publishers, 2015.
- Gunn, Douglass, Roy Luckett and Josh Sims. *Vintage Menswear, a Collection from the Vintage Showroom*. London: Laurance King, 2012.
- Penn, Irving, Virginia A. Heckert et al. *Small Trades*. Los Angeles, CA: J. Paul Getty Museum, 2009.

DIGITAL PRINTING
- Cotterill, Wendy. *Inkjet Printing on Fabric: Direct Techniques*. London: Bloomsbury, 2015.

DYE-ADJACENT BOOKS: BLOOD AND SAFETY
- McClure, Jennifer. *Bloody Brilliant: How to Develop, Execute, and Clean Up Blood Effects for Live Performance*. New York, NY: Routledge, 2022.
- Rossol, Mona. *The Artist's Complete Health and Safety Guide*. New York, NY: Allworth Press, 2001.

DYE ARTISANS
- Westphal, Katherine. *The Surface Designer's Art: Contemporary Fabric Printers, Painters, and Dyers*. Asheville, NC: Lark Books, 1993.

DYE INFORMATION (INCLUDING CHEMISTRY)
- Ingamells, Wilfred and Society of Dyers and Colourists. *Colour for Textiles: A User's Handbook*. Bradford: Society of Dyers and Colourists, 1993.
- Kay-Williams, Susan. *The Story of Colour in Textiles*. London: A&C Black, 2013.

FABRIC ETCHING/DEVORE
- Lee, Iris. *Fabric Etching: Creating Surface Texture & Design Using Fiber Etch.* Columbus, OH: Dragon Threads, 2000.

FABRIC PRINTS
- Meller, Susan et al. *Textile Designs: 200 Years of Patterns for Printed Fabrics Arranged by Motif, Colour, Period and Design.* London: Thames & Hudson, 1991.
- Picton, John and Barbican Art Gallery. *The Art of African Textiles: Technology, Tradition and Lurex.* London: Barbican Art Gallery in Association with Lund Humphries, 1999.
- Sarabhai, Mrinalini, and Bank Duta Jakarta. *Patolas and Resist-Dyed Fabrics of India.* Jakarta, Indonesia: Mapin Publishing, 1988.

MULTI-TOPIC DYE BOOKS
- Brackmann, Holly. *The Surface Designer's Handbook: Dyeing, Printing, Painting, and Creating Resists on Fabric.* Loveland, CO: Interweave Press, 2006.
- Dryden, Deborah. *Fabric Painting and Dyeing for the Theatre.* Portsmouth, NH: Heinemann, 1993.
- Irwin, Kimberly. *Surface Design for Fabric.* New York, NY: Bloomsbury Publishing, 2015.
- Johansen, Linda. *Foolproof Fabric Dyeing.* Concord, CA: C&T Publishing, 2020.
- Knutson, Linda. *Synthetic Dyes for Natural Fibers.* Loveland, CO: Interweave Press, 1986.
- Laury, Jean Ray. *Imagery on Fabric: A Complete Surface Design Handbook.* Lafayette, CA: C&T Publishing, 1997.
- Maile, Anne. *Tie and Dye; as a Present-Day Craft.* New York, NY: Taplinger Publishing Co., 1969.
- Noble, Elin. *Dyes & Paints: A Hands-on Guide to Coloring Fabric.* East Freetown, MA: Elin Noble, 2003.
- Wells, Kate. *Fabric Dyeing and Printing.* Loveland, CO: Interweave Press, 1997.

MARBLING
- Cohen, Daniel et al. *Marbling on Fabric.* Loveland, CO: Interweave Press, 1990.
- Maurer-Mathison, Diane V. (Diane Vogel). *The Ultimate Marbling Handbook: A Guide to Basic and Advanced Techniques for Marbling Paper and Fabric.* New York, NY: Watson-Guptill Publications, 1999.

NATURAL DYES
- Booth, Abigail. *The Wild Dyer.* Tunbridge, Kent: Search Press, 2017.
- Dean, Jenny. *Wild Color: The Complete Guide to Making and Using Natural Dyes.* New York, NY: Watson-Guptill Publications, 1999.
- Luhanko, Douglas and Kerstin Neumüller. *Indigo: Cultivate, Dye, Create.* Tunbridge, Kent: Search Press, 2018.
- Pate, Maggie. *Natural Colors Cookbook.* Tunbridge, Kent: Search Press, 2018.

PRINTING AND PAINTING WITH DYE
- Corwin, Lena. *Printing by Hand: A Modern Guide to Printing with Handmade Stamps, Stencils, and Silk Screens.* New York, NY: Stewart, Tabori & Chang, 2008.
- Johnston, Ann. *Color by Design: Paint and Print with Dye.* Lake Oswego, OR: Ann Johnston, 1997.

- Johnston, Ann. *Color by Accident: Low Water Immersion Dyeing.* Lake Oswego, OR: Ann Johnston, 2001.
- Newman, Michelle and Margaret Allyson. *Handpainting Fabric: Easy, Elegant Techniques.* New York, NY: Watson-Guptill, 2003.
- Peverill, Sue. *The Fabric Decorator.* Boston: Little, Brown and Co., 1988.
- Tuckman, Diane. *The Complete Book of Silk Painting.* Cincinnati, OH: North Light Books, 1992.
- Tuckman, Diane and Jan Janas. *Creative Silk Painting.* Cincinnati, OH: North Light Books, 1995.

RESIST DYEING
- Bowen, Marjorie. *Designing with Dye Resists, Batik and Tie-and-Dye.* London: Stephen Hope Books, 1974.

SHIBORI
- Callendar, Jane. *Stitched Shibori: Technique, Innovation, Pattern, Design.* Tunbridge Wells, Kent: Search Press, 2017.
- Hemmings, Jessica. "Shibori on Knits: A Single-Minded Exploration." *Fiberarts*, vol. 30, no. 4, 2004, pp. 18–20.
- Hirai, Noriko and Genshō Sasakura. *Tsutsugaki: Ai No Ka = Tsutsugaki Textiles of Japan: Traditional Freehand Paste Resist Indigo Dyeing Technique of Auspicious Motifs.* Kyōto: ShikōSha; 京都：紫紅社, 1987.
- Muerdter, Catharine. "Woven Shibori." *Shuttle, Spindle & Dyepot*, vol. 31, no. 1, 1999, pp. 32–36.
- Murashima, Kumiko. *Katazome: Japanese Paste-Resist Dyeing for Contemporary Use.* Asheville, NC: Lark Books, 1993.
- Southam, Mandy. *Shibori Designs & Techniques.* Tunbridge Wells, Kent: Search Press, 2008.
- Wada, Yoshiko Iwamoto et al. *Shibori: The Inventive Art of Japanese Shaped Resist Dyeing: Tradition, Techniques, Innovation.* Tokyo and New York, NY: Distributed in the U.S. by Kodansha International/USA Ltd., Through Harper & Row, 1983.

APPENDIX 2: CLEANING UP: STAIN REMOVAL

A common query for dyers concerns stain removal. Following is a limited list of the most frequent stains and their cleaners. Please **test** in an inconspicuous area before going whole-hog with these products.

Blood	- Always use cold water (hot will set stain) - Oxygen bleach and water directly on stain - Spit of person who bled - Hydrogen peroxide (caution: can remove color of garment) - Kiss-Off
Chocolate	- Saturate in heavy-duty detergent 15 minutes, then launder - Carbona Pro-care
Coffee	- Run hot water through the stain, then vinegar and water; rub off with detergent - Kiss-Off - Fels-Naptha Bar Soap
Deodorant	- Soak in a cup of vinegar and water for 1 hour then launder - Fels-Naptha Bar Soap
Fruit	- Dishwashing detergent or synthrapol then vinegar and enzyme cleaner
Grass	- Using a toothbrush, rub heavy-duty detergent into the fabric, leave 15 minutes and wash - Soak in oxygen bleach - Kiss-Off - Fels-Naptha Bar Soap
Grease/oil	- Fels-Naptha Bar Soap - 1:1 Vinegar and water, then soak area with detergent. Don't launder until stain is gone - Drip blue dish soap (Dawn) onto stain and rub into spot, leave for at least 2 hours, then launder - Soak up grease with baking soda, baby powder, or cornstarch, then wash with detergent - 3:1 Hydrogen peroxide and dish washing soap (be careful; can remove color)
Lipstick	- Mineral oil, then 1:2 ratio of ammonia and water. - Carbona Pro-care - Vinegar and liquid dish soap - Kiss-Off - Fels-Naptha Bar Soap

Pen	• Rubbing alcohol • Toothpaste
Sharpie	• Rubbing alcohol • Vinegar
Sweat	• Vinegar • Fels-Naptha Bar Soap
Urine	• Vinegar and detergent soak overnight.
Wine	• Mix hydrogen peroxide and blue dish soap (Dawn) • Carbona Pro-care • Wine away (Amazon) • Fels-Naptha Bar Soap
Wax/gum	• Freeze item, flake off wax/gum • Iron out remaining wax onto newspaper

NOTES ABOUT SELECTED CLEANERS

- **Carbona Stain Devils:** A variety of stain-specific cleaners. They each target a different group of stain types like grass, dirt, and makeup or chocolate, ketchup, and mustard. There are 9 total. Beware, the fumes are strong – use with good ventilation or break out your respirator.
- **Enzyme cleaners:** These contain a range of enzymes to break down fats, grass, grease, smells, etc. *Brands*: Presto! Laundry Detergent, Arm & Hammer BioEnzyme Power, Rockin' Green, Carbona Pro-Care (there are many more!!).
- **Fels-Naptha:** *Does NOT contain Naptha!!* This is a soap your grandmother's grandmother used. Originating in 1893, it is one of the best 99-cent laundry soaps and works fantastically on stubborn stains. We used this to get makeup out of chiffon nightly. This is also grated and included in homemade laundry soaps. Has some reactivity with peroxides, so beware of using with oxygen bleaches/cleaners.
- **Heavy-duty Detergents:** These contain enzymes, surfactants, and stain removers. *Brands:* Tide, Persil ProClean.
- **Oxygen Bleach Brands:** These are sold as color safe bleaches. *Do not use on silk or wool – they will damage fibers! Brands*: OxiClean, Country Save Bleach, Purex 2 Color Safe Bleach, Seventh Generation Chlorine free Bleach, Amway Legacy, of Clean All Fabric Bleach, OXO Brite, Nellies All-Natural Oxygen Brightener.

APPENDIX 3: SWATCH SHEETS

As an intro to what this is: "Dyers take notes a variety of ways. I've included 5 different swatch sheet templates that are on the Focal Press website, ready to be printed out!"

APPENDIX 3.1 THE OREGON SHAKESPEARE SWATCH SHEET
Production/Garment

Original Swatch (to be dyed)	Color Desired	Final Swatch
Dye(s) Used	Formula, Temperature, Weight of Fabric, Notes	

Original Swatch (to be dyed)	Color Desired	Final Swatch
Dye(s) Used	Formula, Temperature, Weight of Fabric, Notes	

APPENDIX 3.2 MULTIPLE SWATCHES ON 1 FABRIC
Production/Garment

Original Swatch (to be dyed)	Color Desired	Final Swatch
Swatch	Dye(s) Used	Formula, Temperature, Weight of Fabric, Notes
Swatch	Dye(s) Used	Formula, Temperature, Notes

APPENDIX 3.3 SWATCH SHEET WITH DETAILS

Production:	Original Swatch:
Role:	Weight of Fabric:
Swatch #1: (dyed swatch here)	Formula:
Time In:	Water Temp/pH:
Time Out:	Notes:
Swatch #2: (dyed swatch here)	Formula:
Time In:	Water Temp/pH:
Time Out:	Notes:
Swatch #3: (dyed swatch here)	Formula:
Time In:	Water Temp/pH:
Time Out:	Notes:

APPENDIX 3.4 THE DEBI J./WINTERLING'S SWATCH SHEET

Date IN:	DUE:
Show/Client:	Actor/Character:
Sketch #:	Garment:
Pieces:	Yards/Lbs:
Final use/next process (circle one): Trim Swatch Lab Dip Dark Color Mottle Dye Ombré Dye Discharge Paint Print Distress	
Formula Notes:	

Original	Standard	Final
Date IN:	DUE:	
Show/Client:	Actor/Character:	
Sketch #:	Garment:	
Pieces:	Yards/Lbs:	
Final use/next process (circle one): Trim Swatch Lab Dip Dark Color Mottle Dye Ombré Dye Discharge Paint Print Distress		
Formula Notes:		

Original	Standard	Final

APPENDIX 3.5 THE ASHLEY SWATCH SHEET (JEFFFENDERSTUDIO.COM)

Show:	REC:	DUE:
ITEM:	**QTY:**	**FIBER:**

Add notes to blank area below on pre-wash, process, water temp, and swatches to this page. Split page as necessary. Ashley Truj of Jeff Fender Studio uses this system in a small binder.

INDEX

Page locators in **bold** indicate a table
Page locators in *italics* indicate a figure

acetone 11–12, 36, 112, 115, 119–120, 122
acid brush 202
acid dye 132; anionic 57; baths 43; cationic 58; classes 58–59; concentrates 59, 61; immersion dyeing 60, 62; leather 35, 43; painting 162; pH **57**; print paste 154; process 51, 55, **56**; silk/wool painting 162–163; tips on use 60
acids 43–44, 58, 70, 150, 154, 212
additive color 26–27
additives: bonding 45, 55; ratios **74**, **76**, 154; safety 42, 58, 77, **100**, 195; stabilizing **7**; variables, tracking 49, 52–53
aging: fading 260; hats 264; process 233–234, 237, 242; shoes 262–264
airbrush paint 172–173
airbrushes 196–197, **198**, 199
Aljo (dye brand) 29, **56**, **62**, 70–72, 74
ammonium sulfate 43–44, 59, 150, 154, 157, 162–163
analogous color 30–31
apron 11
aqueous solution 55
arashi shibori 209
arterial blood 373
artificial flowers 93
auxiliaries *14*, 42, 55, 86, 170

basic dye 76
batching 155
batik 214–215, **216**, 217–218
beet vs radish 160
binder 170–173, 175, 213, 242, 251
black (colorant) 27–30
black light 169, 174–175
bleach: chlorine-based 34, 96–98; cleaning with *85*, 86; color remover *95*, 96; hydrogen peroxide-based 97; never stops bleaching 96; sulfur-based 97
blood: costume cleaning 277; creating 266–269; drops/splatter 270; permanent 269; products **272–273**; recipes 274–276; removable 271–272; removing 97; wet/shiny 270
brayer 147, 202
breakdown 233–234, 236; good-fast-cheap rule 237; permanent 237–243; removable 243, **244–246**, 247; removable, mediums 249; sanding 239

breakdown artist 28, 46, 79, 95, 98, 169, 171, 202, 233–237, 248, 255, 265
breakdown dyeing: fading 260; overdyeing 261
bronzing powders 172, 179
brushes 202
Buddhist monk 35
bullet steamer 22, 151, 154, 158, *159*
burn test 36–38
burnishing 106, 124–125, 183
bussing tubs 20
buttons 92–93

Calsolene oil 44, **68**
Carpenter, Chris 25, *58*, *126*
carrier 35, 42, 52, **56**, 70–73
CAS Number (Chemical Abstract Service) 9
catspitproductions 127
cellulose fibers 33, 75, 101, 150, 223
chalk brush 202, *240*, 241
chemical: disposal *5*, **9**, 17; exposure 3, 15, 54, 59–60, 119; reaction **8**, 46, 55, 59, 66, 96, 110, 237; vapors *5*, **8**, 13, 15, 23, 97, 124, 185, **216**
chemical names 9
chip brush 182, 190–191, 202
chromophore 96
citric acid crystals 43, 57–58, 60–61, 72–73, 83, **161**, 231
clean up *4–5*, **8**, **176**
Clorox bleach 96
closed-toe shoes 11, 231
clothesline 22
CMY/CMYK color systems 27, *28*
coatings 189–191
color: additive 26–27; complementary 28, 30; cool 29; fastness 36; mixing 25–27, 31, *64*; names 39; perception 25; primaries 25–26; saturation 30, 52, 83, 109, 212, 229–220; secondary 28–29, 70; subtractive 25–27; tension 24; tertiary 28–29; theory 1, 25–27, 31; values 30; variations 29; vibrant 44, 59, 65, 79, **178**, 231
color remover: sodium hydrosulfite (Rit) 96–97, **99–100**, 103; turquoise, fuchsia, yellow 64; use of 15, 95 *see also* bleach
color wheel *27*, *28*, 30–31
colorfast 55
communication 9, 25, 146

compressor 199–200, **201**
concentrated pigment 171–173, 175, 242
contrast 24, 229, 234, 242
conversion chart 51
costume: design 22, *165*, *182*, 233; designer 24–25, 118, 233–235, 254, 264, 270
cotton: etching 225, 230; fiber-reactive dyes 153, 160, 166; gloves 183; string 206
Createx 172–173, 240
crock test 108, 123
crystals, hot fix 184–185 *see also* citric acid

deColourant 98, 104–105
deconstructed printing 155–157
Devarux, Charlotte 25
devore: detailed fiber etching 227–229; DIY paste 231–232; etching 223, 229; etching paste activation 226; process 223–226; safety protocol 224
Dharma Acid Dye 44, 58, **62**
Dharma Textile Detergent 36, 40
Dharma Trading 59, 65, 72, 149, 172, 175, 196, 223
diazo emulsion 129, 132, 134
dimension 125, 169, *192*, 233
direct application 42, 46, 58, 66, 158, 177
direct dyes 54, **56**, 75, 162; additives **76**; process 76
discharge: agent 46, 102, 105; bath 101–102; print paste 102–103, 155; speed 101
discharging 95, 101, 104
disperse dyes 70–72
disposal *5*, **9**, 17
distressing 233–234, **244**, 262–263, 265
Dragon Skin 252–253, 270
drawing fluid 127, 137–141
dropper 172, 202, *202*, 213, 270
dry brushing 238, 240–241, 243, 252, 259, 263
Dryden, Deborah 24, 236
drying cabinet 21
dual-fiber fabric dyeing 230–231
Dufresne, Hallie 87–88, 91, 116
dust bags 249–250
dye: classes 25, 42, 54, **56**, 76–77; concentrates 42, 59, 61, 66–67; cooking 3, 10, 17, 62, 81, 220, 275; house 28, 79; pasting out 42, 62, 162; reducer 13; storage 14; swatches 49, 53; tools 18, 21
dye powder: airborne 3, 15, *48* 83–84; colors 65; exposure 4, 15, *48*, 59–60, 80; mixing 42, 59, **68**, **74**, **76**, 153, 154, **156**, 157; sustainably sourced **56**; water-soluble 10

dye room: accessories 21–22; chemicals 9; dryers 21; dye storage 14; dye vats 16–18; safety *5–6*, 6–7, **7–9**, 10, 22; safety items 11–13; setup 3, 14; sinks/tubs/washers 20; thermometers 19; ventilation 15
dye vat: steam-jacketed 17–18; stove-top pot/kettle 17–18
dyebath: acids 43–44; drain 17; fiber-reactive 69; pH levels 46, **57**, 58; process 55, 83–84
dyeing leather: additives **108**; leather dye/paint 111–112, **113–114**; tanning 106; vat dyeing 108–110; whole hides 107
Dylon **56**, 71, 80, **99**

Edgecote 119, 121
elastic 92
embossing powders 179
emotion 24, 142
etching paste 223, 226, 229
exhausting agent 45, 66
eyewash station *19*, 22

fabric: distributors 19, 27, *32*; drying 41; preparation 36; swatch 47, 52; type 24, 33–34, 36; wetting out 40
Facebook 87
feathers 57, 79, 91–92
felt hoods 93
Fender, Jeff *106*, 149, *170*, 181, *211*, *212*, *215*
FEV *see* French enamel varnish
fiber reactive dye: cotton/rayon 160; direct application painting 158; dye bath from concentrates 68; powder dye 68–69; troubleshooting *69*; wool painting 161
fibers: cellulose 33, 75, 101, 151, 223; identifying 33, 36; synthetic 35, 41, 70–71, **178**
film positive 130–131
final rinse 39–40, **56**, 162
first aid kit 22
fixative 66, 151, **152**, 158, 173, 213
flesh tone 79, 89
foiling fabric 180–190
French enamel varnish 15, *192*–193
French Serti technique 2, 205 *see also* serti technique
fugitive dye 38, 49, **99**, 112, 161, 220

generic name 9
geode dyeing 229
glacial acetic acid 43, 58, 108, 110
Glauber's salt 45, 60–62, 66–68

glitter 179–180, 187, 189, 252
glitz 169, 180
gloves: butyl 12; cotton 183; latex 12, 59, 66, 72; nitrile *11*, 12, 115; thermal 12
goggles *5*, 13, 40, 74, 96, 179, 261
gold leaf/foil 180
grease **246**, 248, 251, 255, **286**
grey 25, 87–88, 107, 128, 242, **245**
Grey Man 263
Grobowski, Kerr *102*, *128*, 129, 149–151, 156–157
gutta resist 177, 212, 214

hair: animal 57; burning 13; dryer 224–225, 232, 255, 259; dyeing 93
Hanna, Roger 145
Hanson, Becky 87, 91
hazardous substance *5*, *7*, **7–8**, 9, 42, 70, **114**
heat press 181
Herd, Beth 28, *79*, 87–88, 91, 233–234, 268
Holcomb, Debi Jolly 86, 91
Hudson sprayer 192, *203*, 204
hue: color perception 29; custom 166, 171, 217, 229; pale **56**, 83–84; principle/primary 28; shades 30–31
hydrophobic/water-hating 70

ice dyeing 218–229
ikat tape 206–207, 209
immersion dyeing: acid dye concentrates 60–61; acid dye powder 61–62; color intensity **67**; fiber reactive dye bath 67; low-water 220
incident light 26
industrial dryer 21, 41, 171, 177, 225–226
ink side 131–132, 135–136, 138–139, 141–142
iron: color removal 98; drying with 49, *50*, *155*; first! 224; heat set 171–172; hot steam 105, 214, 226; transfer 181; wax removal 141–142, 215
isocyanates 9
itajime shibori (fold and clamp) 206, 210

Jacquard Synthrapol 40
Jacquard (dye brand) **56**, 62, 70–71, **72**, **82**, **134**, **176**, 212–213
Jensen, Vicki 160

kanoko shibori (tie-dye) 207
kettles 17
Kraft, Bridget 87–89
Kresto Kolor 13
kumo shibori 207, *208*, 229

labels 4, 6
lace 91, 93–94, 189, 222 *see also* wig lace
lanaset dye/premetallized dye **57**, 59
leafing/metal leafing 182–183
leather: burning 106, 124; color removing 125; dye 106, 111, **113–114**, 115–118, *123*, 124, 192; finishing 118, 125; foiling 124; markers 121; paint 116–117; spray paint 122; toning 124; veg-tan/unfinished 123
leveling (evenness) **57**, 58, 160
leveling acid dye **57**, 58–59
leveling agent 2, *108*, 109, 150, 160
linen 33, 66, 75, 158, 166
Little Mermaid 90
liver sulfur 193
LM ring 90
Ludigol 44, 150, 160

mannequin 22, 239
marbling 193–196
markers 177, **178**
masks 10, 12 *see also* respirator
master dyer 22, 28
material safety data sheets 1, 5, 7–8
McClure, Jennifer 266, 274–277
measuring tools 21, 48, 51
mesh count 127, 130
metal ramp 18
metallics **113–114**, 117, 121–122, 172–173, **176**, **178**, 180, 182, 189
metamerism 25
Metapex 36–38, 237
metaphos 45, 72, 75, 103, 150–151, 154, 160
Milsoft 45
miura shibori 207
mixing: area 15; box 14–15, 47, 80; color 25–27, 31, *64*; dye 10, 15, 25, 42, 66, 153, 160
monochromatic color 30
mordant 32, 42, 55, 77, 230
mordants 32, 42, 55, 77, 230
motifs 2, 25, 142, 143, 206, 218, 225, 228
mud 253–254
Mueller, Jessica 277
Munsell 31
mystery fibers 36, 54, 78

natural dyes **56**, 76–77
needle board 224, 226
needle bottle 203, 213
negative stencil 143
neon **113**, 117, 173

Nguyen, Stephanie *167*, 270
Noble, Elin 13, 15, 55, 66–67, 73, 84, 96, 104, 149, 208–209
notations 48
nui shibori 206, 208, 248
nylon: cord 206–207; dyeing 84; pantyhose 61–62, 67; synthetic fiber 35–36, **56**

Occupational Safety and Health Administration 9, 116
oily/greasy rags 250
Old globe Theater 25, *29*, *107*, *227*, 274
Ombre dyeing 163–167
open time 175, **176**
Orvus paste soap 38
OSHA *see* Occupational Safety and Health Administration
overdyeing 79, 209, 217, 261
OWG (on weight of goods) 86

paddle 18
painter-dyer: blood-effects 266, 269; professional *170*, 194; safety 3
painting: acid dyes 162; aerosol 122; direct application 158; fiber-reactive dyes 158, 161; horizonal 21; leather 122–123; shoes 119; tools 196, 202, 211; with wax 141
palette dyer 86–87
palettes 101, 202–203, 206, 213
Pantone 30, 89
pantyhose 42, 61–62, 72, 81, 83–84, 86, 112, *119*
pearlescent **113–114**, 117, 169, 172
permanent breakdown 233, 237–238, 243, 248
personal safety 10
petroleum jelly, colored 243, **246**, 250–251
photo emulsion: bleed 173; exposure times 134; key terms 131; silkscreen process 129, 132; step wedge test 130–131, 134; supplies 132
polyester: disperse dyeing 70–72; dyeing **56**; working with 35–36
positive stencil 141, 143, *155*
pots 17–18
pre-mixed dyes/inks 56, 93–94, 102, 121, 170–171, 177, 192
pre-sensitized emulsion 129
pre-val sprayer *228*
print: film 130, 135; greyscale 128, 130
print paste: acid dyes 154; creating 150–151; deconstructed printing 155, 157; discharge 102–103, 155; fiber-reactive dyes 151, 153; thiourea dioxide 155

print side 131, *132*, 132–133, 135, 138, 141, 144
prints 126; discharge 105; finger 21, 254; vinyl 95
PROChem 4, 40, **56**, **61**, 65, 70–71, **72**, 98, 150, 172
Prop 66 (California) 5
protein fibers 34–35, 38, 43, **57**, 92, 150, 158, 161, 222–223, 236
puff binder 251, 255, 257
puff print/puff paint 187, *188*, 258–259
pulling a screen 128, *155*

rainbow 24–26, **113**, 206
ratio 51–52, 58, 87, **97**, 98
rayon 33, 41, **56–57**, 75, 151, 153, 158, 160, 166
reclaim 129, 135, *136*, 138–139
reducing agent 46, 73, 75
Reduran 5, 13
registration marks 130, *142*, 143, 228
removable breakdown 233, 243, 247, 249
resist techniques 2, **56**, 205, 210
respirator: acid gas 96, 102, 155, 224; disposable 4, 12; half-face 46, 72, 74, 103, 109, 118, 122, 261
Retayne 45, 75–76
reverse appliqué technique 230
Reynoso, David *162*, 227, *229*
rhinestones 183–184
Rit (dye brand) 14, 29, **56**, 70–71, *78*, 80, 91
Rit color remover 9, *96*, 97–98, **100**, 103–104
Rit DyeMore 70–71, **72**, 92
Rossol, Mona 6
Royal Shakespeare 28

safety: closed-toe shoes 11, 231; eye wash station *19*, 22; first aid kit 22; products 10
Safety Data Sheets *6*, 7, **7–9**
safety guidelines 4
safety products 10
salt, non-iodized 45, 66, 67–68, 82–82, 85
saturation (chroma) 30, 52, 83, *84*, 109, 212, 229–220
scouring 36–38, 69, 97
screen filler 137, 139
screen printing ink 175, **176**
screen printing mesh 127–128
screen reclaimer 129, 131, *132*, 135, *136*
SDS. *see* Safety Data Sheets
secondary color 28
serti technique 211, 213, 215
shade/shadow dyeing 261–262

shades 30
sheeting 204
shibori: binding materials 206; resist dyeing techniques 206, 210
shiny spots 251, 252
shoe: aging 124, 262; painting 94, 112, 118–119; sausages 119
silhouette 24, 233
silicone: elastic 92; ice tray 140; uses 184–187
silk painting: acid dye 162; serti/resist technique 211–212
silkscreen: burn with photo emulsion 132–133, 135; drawing fluid/screen filter 137–138; hot wax rub 139–142; photo emulsion 129; printing 136; screen filler 139; timing estimates **134**
sinew 206–207
sink (dye room) 14, 19
skin tone 25; matching *79*, 89–90, *90*, 91, 113 *see also* flesh tone
Smokey the Bear 23
soda ash (recipe) 46
sodium alginate 103, 150–151, 212
sodium hydrosulphite/hydrosulfite (hydro) 46, 73–74, 97–98, **99**, 103, 105
special effects 251–252; blood 260; burnt clothing 258–259, *260*; marks 255; mold 255; rust 256; salt stains 257; snow 257
split complements 28, 124
sprayers 204
squeegees 128–129
stamps: designing with 147–148; linoleum/rubber 147–148
steamer (bullet) 22, 158
stencils: bridge 142–143; creating 142; design 144–145; hand-cut 142–143; laser cut/Cricut 145–146
step wedge test 130–131
stove-top pot/kettle 17
strike 43–44, 64, 84, 94, 154
substantivity 55, 64
subtractive color 25–27
super-milling/milling acid dye 43, 58–59
surfactants 36
swatch card *50*
swatching 32, 47–49
sweat 28, 234, 243, **245**, 251–252
sweat patch dyeing 262
synthetic fabric 70
Synthrapol 36, 38–39

TA-OSH Nhudes swatch ring 89–90
Taggert, Jack 98, *99*, 236, 255, 259, 261, 263, 266
tar/oil 255
teching 20, 87–89, 94
Tempest (Shakespeare) 24, 77
tertiary colors 28–29
test (string weight) 206–207
test fabrics 52, 86
textile paint 169–171
thermometer 19
thiourea dioxide (thiox) 2, 97, 100–102, 149–150, 155
three-dimensional 142–143, 157
tint 28, 30
tjanting tool 141–142, 217
toggle dry 110
tone 25, 28, 30, 79
toning: leather 124; process 87; skin tones 91
Toth, Virginia 27
trade name **7**, 9

undershirts 112–113
union dyes **56**; concentrates 80–81; defined 78–79; immersion dyeing 82–83; machine dyeing 85–86; mixing 87; nylon 84; odd items 91–94; tips 80; wool/silk 83–84
urea 46–47
UV (ultra-violet) paint 174–175

value (lightness) 30, **66**
variables, logging/tracking 47, 52–53, 57
vat dyeing: gloves 12; leather 107
vat dyes: large 55; pasting out 42; process 73–75; reducing 46; safety 74; tips 75
vectorize 146
veinous blood 268
vent box/vent booth 15
vent hood 10, 15, 47, 67
ventilation 15
vibrancy 24, 64, 87
vinegar 43–44, 57–58, 75, 85, 92, 96, 108
viscosity 8, 150, 170–171, *203*, 212, 252
VOCs *see* volatile organic compounds
volatile organic compounds 13

warm colors 29
washer/dryer 20
washfast 55, 58, **61**, 154
washout 57, 129

waste/wastewater *5*, 97–98, **99–100**, 198, 237, 261
water insoluble 70
water-based resist 203, 212–213, *214*, 215
water-soluble 10, 109, 254
wax: crayons 140; heated *5*; painting 141–142; removing 141–142; silkscreen 139–140
Weeden, Derek 24
weight of goods 38
Westland, Steven 25–27
wet effects 252–253

wig lace 89, 91, 94
WOG. *see* weight of goods
wool: acid dyes 58, 60, 162; bleaching 96, 98, 101; discharge bath 101–102; drying 41; dyeing 45–46, **56–57**; fiber-reactive dyes 66, 161; print paste 150–151, 153–154; protein fiber 34; scouring 36–38; union dyes 83–84

Year Without A Santa Claus 29

zippers 94